MACMILLAN AND CO., Limited
LONDON · BOMBAY · CALCUTTA
MELBOURNE

THE MACMILLAN COMPANY
NEW YORK · BOSTON · CHICAGO
DALLAS · SAN FRANCISCO

THE MACMILLAN CO. OF CANADA, Ltd.
TORONTO

HUMANISM

BY THE SAME AUTHOR

RIDDLES OF THE SPHINX
A STUDY IN THE PHILOSOPHY OF HUMANISM
NEW AND REVISED EDITION
LONDON: MACMILLAN AND CO., Ltd. 1910.

"AXIOMS AS POSTULATES"
IN
PERSONAL IDEALISM
Edited by HENRY STURT
LONDON: MACMILLAN AND CO., Ltd. 1902.

STUDIES IN HUMANISM
SECOND EDITION
LONDON: MACMILLAN AND CO., Ltd. 1912.

FORMAL LOGIC
A SCIENTIFIC AND SOCIAL PROBLEM
MACMILLAN AND CO., Ltd. 1912.

PLATO OR PROTAGORAS?
BEING A CRITICAL EXAMINATION OF THE 'PROTAGORAS' SPEECH IN THE *THEÆTETUS*, WITH SOME REMARKS UPON ERROR.
OXFORD: B. H. BLACKWELL.
LONDON: SIMPKIN, MARSHALL & CO. 1908. 1s. net.

HUMANISM

PHILOSOPHICAL ESSAYS

BY

F. C. S. SCHILLER, M.A., D.Sc.

FELLOW AND SENIOR TUTOR OF CORPUS CHRISTI COLLEGE, OXFORD

SECOND EDITION, ENLARGED

MACMILLAN AND CO., LIMITED
ST. MARTIN'S STREET, LONDON
1912

COPYRIGHT

First Edition, 1903
Second Edition, 1912

TO MY DEAR FRIEND

THE HUMANEST OF PHILOSOPHERS

WILLIAM JAMES

WITHOUT WHOSE EXAMPLE

AND UNFAILING ENCOURAGEMENT

THIS BOOK WOULD NEVER HAVE BEEN WRITTEN

PREFACE TO THE SECOND EDITION

THAT a new edition of *Humanism* has not appeared simultaneously with that of *Studies in Humanism* is due to the facts that both volumes could not be passed through the press together, and that *Humanism* needed rather more revision. I have also taken the opportunity of enlarging it by the addition of four papers published between 1907-9, which seemed congruous with its subject. They have been inserted after Essay XII in order to produce a minimum of dislocation in the old order.

The only other point to which attention need be drawn in this Preface is that its forerunner in the first edition has not been found to prophesy falsely. The prediction that Protagoras would be found on re-examination to hold his own against Plato (p. xxi of this edition) has been fulfilled in Essays II and XIII-XV of *Studies in Humanism*, the pamphlet on *Plato or Protagoras?* and articles in *Mind* Nos. 68 and 78. The prediction (p. x, p. xiv *f.* of this edition) that Pragmatism would be found to be primarily a criticism of the traditional Logic and the promise of a reformed Logic, has been to some extent fulfilled in my *Formal Logic* (1912), though a complete systematic exposition of the Logic of Real Knowing has not yet appeared, and meantime the two *Humanism* volumes together with *Axioms as Postulates* must be regarded as containing aspirations towards it.

Lastly, it may be noted that the choice of the word

'Humanism' as expressive of what is the most distinctive novelty in the Pragmatic Movement has been vindicated not only by the copious misunderstandings to which the obscurity and clumsiness of the word have exposed 'Pragmatism,' and by the confirmation of the ancient Humanism of Protagoras, but also, quite specifically, by the criticisms of *Formal Logic*. It has there been shown, by a systematic examination of the traditional 'Logic,' that at *no* point do its doctrines escape from the fatal dilemma 'either verbalism or psychology,' until it is confessed that its fundamental presupposition is to abstract from meaning altogether. It follows that it is in fact impossible to abstract from the human aspect of knowing, and to dehumanize Logic. *Expellas hominem logica, tamen usque recurret.* The effort to do so only ends by making Logic meaningless and worthless, and further refutes itself by rendering the traditional Logic, *even formally*, self-contradictory, because after all it is not openly admitted to be, what in fact it is, viz., in the strictest sense, *nonsense*.

OXFORD, *June* 1912.

PREFACE TO THE FIRST EDITION

I

THE appearance of this volume demands more than the usual amount of apology. For the philosophic public, which makes up for the scantiness of its numbers by the severity of its criticism, might justly have expected me to follow up the apparently novel and disputable position I had taken up in my contribution to *Personal Idealism* with a systematic treatise on the logic of 'Pragmatism.' And no doubt if it had rested with me to transform wishes into thoughts and thoughts into deeds without restrictions of time and space, I should willingly have expanded my sketch in *Axioms as Postulates* into a full account of the beneficent simplification of the whole theory of knowledge which must needs result from the adoption of the principles I had ventured to enunciate. But the work of a college tutor lends itself more easily to the conception than to the composition of a systematic treatise, and so for the present the philosophic public will have to wait.

The general public, on the other hand, it seemed more feasible to please by an altogether smaller and more practicable undertaking, viz., by republishing from various technical journals, where conceivably the philosophic public had already read them, the essays which compose the bulk of this volume. I have, however, taken the opportunity to add several new essays, partly because they happened to be available, partly because they seemed to be needed to complete the doctrine of the rest. And the old material also has been thoroughly revised and considerably augmented. So that I am not without hopes that the collection, though discontinuous in form, will be found to be coherent in substance, and to present successive aspects of a fairly systematic body of doctrine. To me at least it has seemed that, when thus taken collectively, these essays not only reinforced my previous contentions, but even supplied the ground for a further advance of the greatest importance.

It is clear to all who have kept in touch with the pulse of thought that we are on the brink of great events in those intellectual altitudes which a time-honoured satire has described as the *intelligible* world. The ancient shibboleths encounter open yawns and unconcealed derision. The rattling of dry bones can no longer fascinate respect nor plunge a self-suggested horde of fakirs in hypnotic stupor. The agnostic maunderings of impotent despair are flung aside with a contemptuous smile by the young, the strong, the virile. And there is growing up a reasonable faith that even the highest peaks of speculation may prove accessible to properly-equipped explorers, while what seemed so unapproachable was nothing but a cloud-land of confused imaginings. Among the more marked symptoms that the times are growing more propitious to new philosophic enterprise, I would instance the conspicuous success of Mr. Balfour's *Foundations of Belief*; the magnificent series of William James's popular works, *The Will to Believe, Human Immortality*, and *The Varieties of Religious Experience*; James Ward's important Gifford Lectures on *Naturalism and Agnosticism*; the emergence from Oxford, where the idealist enthusiasm of thirty years ago long seemed to have fossilized into sterile logic-chopping or to have dissolved into Bradleian scepticism, of so audacious a manifesto as *Personal Idealism*; and most recently, but not

PREFACE

least full of future promise, the work of the energetic Chicago School headed by Professor Dewey.[1] It seemed therefore not impolitic, and even imperative, to keep up the agitation for a more hopeful and *humaner* view of metaphysics, and at the same time to herald the coming of what will doubtless be an epochmaking work, viz. William James's promised *Metaphysics*.

II

The origin of great truths, as of great men, is usually obscure, and by the time that the world has become cognizant of them and interested in their pedigree, they have usually grown old. It is not surprising therefore that the central thought of our present Pragmatism, to wit the purposiveness of our thought and the teleological character of its methods, should have been clearly stated by Professor James so long ago as 1879.[2] Similarly I was surprised to find that I had all along been a pragmatist myself without knowing it, and that little but the name was lacking to my own advocacy of an essentially cognate position in 1892.[3]

But Pragmatism is no longer unobserved; it has by this time reached the 'Strike, but hear me!' stage, and as the misconceptions due to sheer unfamiliarity are refuted or abandoned, it will rapidly enter on the era of profitable employment. It was this latter probability which formed one of my chief motives for publishing

---

[1] They have published a number of articles in the *Decennial Publications* of the University; their *Studies in Logical Theory* are announced, but have not yet reached me. Though proceeding from a different camp, the works of Dr. J. E. MacTaggart and Prof. G. H. Howison should also be alluded to as adding to the salutary ferment. For while ostensibly (and indeed ostentatiously) employing the methods of the old *a priori* dogmatism they have managed to reverse its chief conclusions, in a charming but somewhat perplexing way. I have on purpose confined this enumeration to the English-speaking world; but in France and even in Germany somewhat similar movements are becoming visible.

[2] In his 'Sentiment of Rationality' in *Mind*, O.S. No. 15.

[3] In *Reality and 'Idealism*.' Cp. pp. 119-121.

these essays. The practical advantages of the pragmatist method are so signal, the field to be covered is so immense, and the reforms to be effected are so sweeping, that I would fain hasten the acceptance of so salutary a philosophy, even at the risk of prematurely flinging these informal essays, as forlorn hopes, against the strongholds of inveterate prejudice. It is in the hope therefore that I may encourage others to co-operate and to cultivate a soil which promises such rich returns of novel truth, that I will indicate a number of important problems which seem to me urgently to demand treatment by pragmatic methods.

I will put first *a reform of Logic*. Logic hitherto has attempted to be a pseudo-science of a non-existent and impossible process called *pure thought*. Or at least we have been ordered in its name to expunge from our thinking every trace of feeling, interest, desire, and emotion, as the most pernicious sources of error.

It has not been thought worthy of consideration that these influences are the sources equally of all truth and all-pervasive in our thinking. The result has been that logic has been rendered nothing but a systematic misrepresentation of our actual thinking. It has been made abstract and wantonly difficult, an inexhaustible source of mental bewilderment, but impotent to train the mind and to trace its actual workings, by being assiduously kept apart from the psychology of concrete thinking. Yet a reverent study of our minds' actual procedures might have been a most precious aid to the self-knowledge of the intellect. To justify in full these strictures (from which a few only of modern logicians, notably Professors Sigwart and Wundt, and Mr. Alfred Sidgwick,[1] can be more or less exempted) would be a long and arduous

---

[1] Whose writings, by reason perhaps of the ease of their style, have not received from the experts the attention they deserve.

undertaking. Fortunately, however, a single illustration may suffice to indicate the sort of difference Pragmatism would introduce into the traditional maltreatment.

Let us consider a couple of actual, and probably familiar, modes of reasoning. (1) *The world is so bad that there must be a better;* (2) *the world is so bad that there cannot be a better.* It will probably be admitted that both of these are common forms of argumentation, and that neither is devoid of logical force, even though in neither case does it reach 'demonstration.' And yet the two reasonings flatly contradict each other. Now my suggestion is that this contradiction is not verbal, but deep-rooted in the conflicting versions of the nature of thought which they severally exemplify. The second argument alone it would seem could claim to be strictly 'logical.' For it alone seems to conform to the canons of the logical tradition which conceives reasoning as the product of a 'pure' thought untainted by volition. And as in our theoretical reflections we can all disregard the psychological conditions of actual thinking to the extent of selecting examples in which we are interested merely as examples, we can all appreciate its abstract cogency. In arguing from a known to an unknown part of the universe, it is 'logical' to be guided by the indications given by the former. If the known is a 'fair sample' of the whole, how can the conclusion be otherwise than sound? At all events how can the given nature of the known form a logical ground for inferring in the unknown a complete reversal of its characteristics?

Yet this is precisely what the first argument called for. Must not this be called the illogical caprice of an irrational desire? By no means. It is the intervention of an emotional postulate which takes the first step in the acquisition of new knowledge. But for its beneficent activity we should have acquiesced in our ignorance. But once an unknown transfiguration of the actual is *desired*, it can be *sought*, and so, in many cases, *found*. The passionless concatenations of a 'pure' thought never could have reached, and still less have justified, our conclusion: to attain it our thought needs to be impelled and guided by the promptings of volition and desire.

Now that such ways of reasoning are not infrequent and not unsuccessful, will, I fancy, hardly be denied. Indeed if matters were looked into it would turn out that reasonings of the second type *never* really occur in actual knowing, and that when they seem to do so, we have only failed to detect the hidden interest which incites the reason to pretend to be 'dispassionate.' In the example chosen, *e.g.*, it may have been a pessimist's despair that clothed itself in the habiliments of logic, or it may have been merely stupidity and apathy, a want of imagination and enterprise in questioning nature. But, it may be said, the question of the justification *de jure* of what is done *de facto* still remains. The votary of an abstract logic may indignantly exclaim—'Shall I lower my ideal of pure thought because there is little or no pure thinking? Shall I abandon *Truth*, immutable, eternal, sacred Truth, as unattainable, and sanction as her substitute a spurious concretion of practical experience, on the degrading plea that it is what we need to live by, and all we need to live by? Shall I, in other words, abase myself? No! Perish the thought! Perish the phenomenal embodiment of Pure Reason out of Time and Place (which I popularly term "myself") rather than that the least abatement should be made from the rigorous requirements of my theory of Thought!'

Strong emotional prejudices are always hard to reason with, especially when, as here, their nature is so far misconceived that they are regarded as the revelations of Pure Reason. Still, in some cases, the desire for knowledge may prove stronger than the attachment to habitual modes of thought, and so it may not be wholly fruitless to point out (1) that our objections are in no wise disposed of by vague charges of a 'confusion of psychology and logic'; (2) that the canons of right Thought must, even from the most narrowly logical of standpoints, be brought into some relation to the procedures of actual thinking; (3) that in point of fact the former are derived from the latter; (4) that if so, our first mode of reasoning must receive logical recognition, because (5) it is not only usual, but useful in the 'discovery' of 'Truth'; (6) that a process which yields valuable results must in some sense be valid, and (7) that, conversely, an ideal of validity which is not realizable is not valid, even as an ideal. In short, how can a logic which professes to be the theory of thought set aside as irrelevant a normal feature of our thinking? And if it cannot, is it not evident that, when reformed by Pragmatism, it must assume a very different complexion, more natural and clearer, than while its movements were shackled by the conventions of a strait-laced Intellectualism?

Secondly, Pragmatism would find an almost inexhaustible field of exploration in the sciences, by examining the multifarious ways in which their 'truths' have come to be established, and showing how the practical value of scientific conceptions has accelerated and decided their acceptance. Nor is it over-sanguine to suppose that a clearer consciousness of the actual procedure of the sciences will also lead to the critical rejection of notions which are not needed, and are not useful, and facilitate the formation of new conceptions which are needed.[1]

[1] Most opportunely for my argument the kind of transformation of our scientific ideas which Pragmatism will involve has received the most copious and admirable illustration in Professor Ostwald's great *Naturphilosophie*. Professor

In the field of Ethics Pragmatism naturally demands to know what is the actual use of the ethical 'principles' which are handed on from one text-book to another. But it speedily discovers that no answer is forthcoming. Next to nothing is known about the actual efficacy of ethical principles: Ethics is a dead tradition which has very little relation to the actual facts of moral sentiment. And the reason obviously is that there has not been a sufficient desire to know to lead to the proper researches into the actual psychological nature and distribution of the moral sentiments. Hence there is implicit in Pragmatism a demand for an inquiry to ascertain the actual facts, and pending this inquiry, for a truce to the sterile polemic about ethical principles. In the end this seems not unlikely to result in a real revival of Ethics.

If finally we turn to a region which the vested interests of time-honoured organizations, the turbid complications of emotion, and a formalism that too often merges in hypocrisy, must always render hard of access to a sincere philosophy, and consider the attitude of Pragmatism towards the religious side of life, we shall find once more that it has a most important bearing. For *in principle* Pragmatism overcomes the old antithesis of Faith and Reason. It shows on the one hand that 'Faith' must underlie all 'Reason' and pervade it, nay, that at bottom rationality itself is the supremest postulate of Faith. Without Faith, therefore, there can be no Reason, and initially the demands of 'Faith' must be as legitimate and essentially as reasonable as those of the 'Reason' they pervade. On the other hand, it enables us to draw the line between a genuine and a spurious 'Faith.' The spurious 'faith,' which too often is all theologians take courage to aspire to, is merely the

---

Ostwald is not a professional philosopher at all, but a chemist, and has very likely never heard of Pragmatism; but he sets forth the pragmatist procedure of the sciences in a perfectly masterly way.

smoothing over of an unfaced scepticism, or at best a pallid fungus that, lurking in the dark recesses of the mind, must shun the light of truth and warmth of action. In contrast with it a genuine faith is an ingredient in the growth of knowledge. It is ever realizing itself in the knowledge that it needs and seeks—to help it on to further conquests. It aims at its natural completion in what we significantly call the *making true* or *verification*, and in default of this must be suspected as mere make-believe. And so the identity of method in Science and Religion is far more fundamental than their difference. Both rest on experience and aim at its interpretation: both proceed by postulation; and both require their anticipations to be verified. The difference lies only in the mode and extent of their verifications: the former must doubtless differ according to the nature of the subject; the latter has gone much further in the case of Science, perhaps merely because there has been so much less persistence in attempts at the systematic verification of religious postulates.

III

It is clear, therefore, that Pragmatism is able to propound an extensive programme of reforms to be worked out by its methods. But even Pragmatism is not the final term of philosophic innovation: there is yet a greater and more sovereign principle now entering the lists of which it can only claim to have been the forerunner and vicegerent. This principle also has long been working in the minds of men, dumb, unnamed and unavowed. But the time seems ripe now formally to name it, and to let it loose in order that it may receive its baptism of fire.

I propose, accordingly, to convert to the use of philosophic terminology a word which has long been famed in history and literature, and to denominate HUMANISM the attitude of thought which I *know* to be habitual in William James and in myself, which seems to be sporadic and inchoate in many others, and which is destined, I believe, to win the widest popularity. There would indeed be no flavour of extravagance and paradox about this last suggestion, were it not that the professional study of Philosophy has so largely fallen into the hands of recluses who have lost all interest in the practical concerns of humanity, and have rendered philosophy like unto themselves, abstruse, arid, abstract and abhorrent. But in itself there is no reason why this should be the character of philosophy. The final theory of life ought to be every man's concern, and if we can dispel the notion that the tiresome technicalities of philosophy lead to nothing of the least practical interest, it yet may be. There is ground, then, for the hope that the study of a *humaner* philosophy may prove at least as profitable and enjoyable as that of the 'humaner' letters.

In all but name *Humanism* has long been in existence. Years ago I described one of its most precious texts, William James's *Will to Believe*,[1] as a "declaration of the independence of the concrete whole of man with all his passions and emotions unexpurgated, directed against the cramping rules and regulations by which the Brahmins of the academic caste are tempted to impede the free expansion of human life," and as "a most salutary doctrine to preach to a biped oppressed by many '-ologies,' like modern man, and calculated to allay his growing doubts whether he has a responsible personality and a soul and conscience of his own, and is not a mere phantasmagoria of abstractions, a transient complex of shadowy formulas that Science calls 'the laws of nature.'" Its great lesson was, I held, that "there are not really

---

[1] In reviewing it for *Mind* in October 1897 (N.S. No. 24, p. 548).

any eternal and non-human truths to prohibit us from adopting the beliefs we need to live by, nor any infallible *a priori* tests of truth to screen us from the consequences of our choice." Similarly Professor James, in reviewing *Personal Idealism*,[1] pointed out that "a re-anthropomorphized universe is the general outcome of its philosophy." Only for *re-anthropomorphized* we should henceforth read *re-humanized*. 'Anthropomorphism' is a term of disparagement whose dyslogistic usage it may prove difficult to alter.[2] Moreover, it is clumsy, and can hardly be extended so as to cover what I mean by Humanism. There is no need to disclaim the truth of which it is the adumbration, and a non-anthropomorphic thought is sheer absurdity; but still what we need is something wider and more vivid.

Similarly I would hint at affinities with the great saying of Protagoras, that *Man is the Measure of all things*. Fairly interpreted, this is the truest and most important thing that any thinker ever has propounded. It is only in travesties such as it suited Plato's dialectic purpose to circulate that it can be said to tend to scepticism; in reality it urges Science to discover how Man may measure, and by what devices make concordant his measures with those of his fellow-men. Now measurement is that in which ancient science failed. Protagoras alone demanded it, and Humanism need not cast about for any sounder or more convenient starting-point.

For in every philosophy we must take some things for granted. Humanism, like Common Sense, of which it may fairly claim to be the philosophic working out, takes Man for granted as he stands, and the world of man's experience as it has come to seem to him. This is the only natural starting-point, from which we can proceed in

---

[1] *Mind* for January 1903 (N.S. No. 45, p. 94).
[2] I tried to do this in *Riddles of the Sphinx*, ch. v. §§ 9-12. But I now think the term needs radical re-wording.

every direction, and to which we must return, enriched and with enhanced powers over our experience, from all the journeyings of Science. Of course this frank, though *not* therefore 'uncritical,' acceptance of our immediate experience and experienced self will seem a great deal to be granted by those addicted to abstruser methods. They have dreamt for ages of *a priori* philosophies 'without presuppositions or assumptions,' whereby Being might be conjured out of Nothing and the sage might penetrate the secret of creative power. But no obscurity of verbiage has in the end succeeded in concealing the utter failure of such preposterous attempts. The *a priori* philosophies have all been found out.

And what is worse, have they not all been detected in doing what they pretended to disclaim? Do they not all take surreptitiously for granted the human nature they pride themselves on disavowing? Are they not trying to solve human problems with human faculties? It is true that in form they claim to transcend our nature, or to raise it to the superhuman. But while they profess to exalt human nature, they are really mutilating it—all for the kingdom of Abstraction's sake! For what are their professed starting-points,—Pure Being, the Idea, the Absolute, the Universal I, but pitiable abstractions from experience, mutilated shreds of human nature, whose real value for the understanding of life is easily outweighed by the living experience of an honest man?

All these theories then *de facto* start from the immediate facts of our experience. Only they are ashamed of it, and assume without inquiry that it is worthless as a principle of explanation, and that no thinker worthy of the name can tolerate the thought of expressly setting out from anything so vulgar. Thus, so far from assuming *less* than the humanist, these speculations really must assume a great deal *more*. They must assume, in addition to ordinary human nature, their own met-empirical starting-points and the correctness (always more than dubious) of the deductions whereby they have *de facto* reached them.

'Do you propose then to accept as sacrosanct the gross unanalysed conceptions of crude Common Sense, and to exempt them from all criticism?' No, I only propose to *start* with them, and to try and see whether we could not get as far with them as with any other, nay, *as far as we may want to get*. I have faith that the process of experience that has brought us to our present standpoint has not been wholly error and delusion, and may on the whole be trusted. And I am quite sure that, right or wrong, we have no *other*, and that it is *e.g.* grotesque extravagance to imagine that we can put ourselves at the standpoint of the Absolute. I would protest, therefore, against every form of '*a priori* metaphysical criticism' that condemns the results of our experience up to date as an illusory 'appearance' *without trial*. For I hold that the only valid criticism they can receive must come in, and through, their actual *use*. It is just where and in so far as common-sense assumptions fail to work that we are theoretically justified, and practically compelled, to modify them. But in each such case sufficient reasons must be shown; it is not enough merely to show that other assumptions can be made, and couched in technical language, and that our data are abstractly capable of different arrangements. There are, I am aware, infinite possibilities of conceptual rearrangement, but their discovery or construction is but a sort of intellectual game, and has no real importance.

In point of method, therefore, Humanism is fully able to vindicate itself, and so we can now define it as the philosophic attitude which, without wasting thought upon attempts to construct experience *a priori*, is content to take human experience as the clue to the world of human experience, content to take Man on his own merits, just as he is to start with, without insisting that he must first be disembowelled of his interests and have his individuality evaporated and translated into technical jargon, before he can be deemed deserving of scientific notice. To remember that Man is the measure of all things, *i.e.* of his whole experience-world, and that if our standard measure be proved false all our measurements are vitiated; to remember that Man is the maker of the sciences which subserve his human purposes; to remember that an ultimate philosophy which analyses us away is thereby merely exhibiting its failure to achieve its purpose, that, and more that might be stated to the same effect, is the real root of Humanism, whence all its auxiliary doctrines spring.

It is a natural consequence, for instance, that, if the facts require it, " real possibilities, real indeterminations, real beginnings, real ends, real evil, real crises, catastrophes and escapes, a real God and a real moral life, just as common sense conceives these things, may remain in *humanism* as conceptions which philosophy gives up the attempt either to 'overcome' or to reinterpret."[1] And whether or not Humanism will have to recognize the ultimate reality of all the gloomier possibilities of James's enumeration, it may safely be predicted that its '*radical empiricism*' will grant to the possibilities of '*pluralism*' a more careful and unbiassed inquiry than monistic preconceptions have as yet deigned to bestow upon them. For seeing that man is a social being it is natural that Humanism should be hospitable to the view that the universe is ultimately 'a joint-stock affair.' And again, it will receive with appropriate suspicion all attempts to explain away the human personality which is the formal

[1] James, *Will to Believe* (p. ix.). I have substituted *humanism* for *empiricism*

and efficient and final cause of all explanation, and will rather *welcome* it in its unmutilated, undistorted immediacy as (though in an uncongenial tongue) the '*a priori* condition of all knowledge.' And so it will approve of that '*personal idealism*' which strives to redeem the spiritual values an idealistic absolutism has so treacherously sold into the bondage of naturalism.

With 'Common Sense' it will ever keep in touch by dint of refusing to value or validate the products of merely speculative analyses, void of purpose and of use, which betoken merely a power to play with verbal phrases. Thus Humanism will derive, combine and include all the doctrines which may be treated as anticipations of its attitude.

For Pragmatism itself is in the same case with Personal Idealism, Radical Empiricism and Pluralism. It is in reality only the application of Humanism to the theory of knowledge. If the entire man, if human nature as a whole, be the clue to the theory of all experience, then human purposiveness must irrigate the arid soil of logic. The facts of our thinking, freed from intellectualistic perversions, will clearly show that we are not dealing with abstract concatenations of purely intellectual processes, but with the rational aims of personal thinkers. Great, therefore, as will be the value we must claim for Pragmatism as a method, we must yet concede that man is greater than any method he has made, and that our Humanism must interpret it.

IV

It is a well-known fact that things are not only known by their affinities but also by their opposites. And the fitness of the term Humanism for our philosophic purpose could hardly better be displayed than by the ready transfer of its old associations to a novel context.

A *humanist* philosopher is sure to be keenly interested

in the rich variety of human thought and sentiment, and unwilling to ignore the actual facts for the sake of bolstering up the narrow abstractions of some *a priori* theory of what 'all men must' think and feel under penalty of scientific reprobation. The humanist, accordingly, will tend to grow *humane*, and tolerant of the divergences of attitude which must inevitably spring from the divergent idiosyncrasies of men. *Humanism*, therefore, will still remain opposed to *Barbarism*. But Barbarism may show itself in philosophy in a double guise, as barbarism of temper and as barbarism of style. Both are human defects which to this day remain too common among philosophers. The former displays itself in the inveterate tendency to sectarianism and intolerance, in spite of the discredit which the history of philosophy heaps upon it. For what could be more ludicrous than to keep up the pretence that all must own the sway of some absolute and unquestionable creed? Does not every page of every philosophic history teem with illustrations that a philosophic system is an unique and personal achievement of which not even the servilest discipleship can transfuse the full flavour into another's soul? Why should we therefore blind ourselves to the invincible individuality of philosophy, and deny each other the precious right to behold reality each at the peculiar angle whence he sees it? Why, when others cannot and will not see as we do, should we lose our temper and the faith that the heavenly harmony can only be achieved by a multitudinous symphony in which each of the myriad centres of experience sounds its own concordant note?

As for barbarism of style, that too is ever rampant, even though it no longer reaches the colossal heights attained by Kant and Hegel. If Humanism can restore against such forces the lucid writing of the older English style, it will make Philosophy once more a subject gentlemen can read with pleasure. And it can at least contend that most of the technicalities which disfigure philosophic writings are totally unneeded, and that the stringing together of abstractions is both barbarous and dangerous. Pedagogically it is barbarous, because it nauseates the student, and because abstract ideas need to be illumined by concrete illustrations to fix them in the mind: logically it is dangerous, because abstractions mostly take the form of worn-out metaphors which are like sunken rocks in navigation, so that there is no more fatal cause of error and deception than the trust in abstract dicta which by themselves mean nothing, and whose real meaning lies in the applications, which are not supplied.

In history, however, the great antithesis has been between Humanism and Scholasticism. This also we may easily adopt, without detracting from its force. For Scholasticism is still one of the great facts in human nature, and a fundamental foible of the learned world. Now, as ever, it is a spirit of sterilizing pedantry that avoids beauty, dreads clearness and detests life and grace, a spirit that grovels in muddy technicality, buries itself in the futile burrowings of valueless researches, and conceals itself from human insight by the dust-clouds of desiccated rubbish which it raises. Unfortunately the scholastic temper is one which their mode of life induces in professors as easily as indigestion, and frequently it renders them the worst enemies of their subjects. This is deplorable but might be counteracted, were it not thought essential to a reputation for scientific profundity at least to *seem* scholastic. Humanism therefore has before it an arduous fight with the Dragon of Scholasticism, which, as it were, deters men from approaching the golden apples that cluster on the tree of knowledge in the garden of the Hesperides.

And lastly, may we not emphasize that the old associations of the word would still connect with Humanism a *Renascence* of Philosophy? And shall we not accept this reminiscence as an omen for the future? For it is clear, assuredly, that Philosophy has still to be born again to enter on her kingdom, and that her votaries must still be born again to purge their systems of the taint of an inveterate barbarism. But some of these suggestions verge, perhaps, upon the fanciful: it suffices to have shown that Humanism makes a good name for the views I seek to label thus, and that in such extension of its meaning its old associations lose no force but rather gain a subtler flavour.

To claim that in its philosophic use Humanism may retain its old associations is not, however, to deny that it must enter also into new relations. It would be vain, for instance, to attempt concealment of the fact that to Naturalism and Absolutism its antagonism is intrinsic. Naturalism is valid enough and useful as a method of tracing the connexions that permeate reality from the lowest to the highest level: but when taken as the last word of philosophy it subjects the human to the arbitrament of its inferior. Absolutism, on the other hand, cherishes ambitions to attain the superhuman; but, rather than admit its failure, it deliberately prefers to delude itself with shadows, and to reduce concrete reality to the illusory adumbration of a phantom Whole. The difference thus is this, that whereas Naturalism is worthy of respect for the honest work it does, and has a real use as a partial method in subordination to the whole, Absolutism has no use, and its explanatory value is nothing but illusion. As compared with these, Humanism will pursue the middle path; it will neither reject ideals because they are not realized, nor yet despise the actual because it can conceive ideals. It will not think the worst of Nature, but neither will it trust an Absolute beyond its ken.

PREFACE

I am well aware that the ideas of which the preceding pages may have suggested the barest outline are capable of endless working out and illustration. And though I believe myself to have made no assertion that could not be fully vindicated if assailed, I realize most keenly that a complete statement of the Humanist position far transcends, not only my own powers, but those of any single man. But I hoped that those who were disposed to sympathy and open-mindedness would pardon the defects and overlook the gaps in this informal survey of a glorious prospect, while to those who are too imperviously encased in habit or in sloth, or too deeply severed from me by an alien idiosyncrasy, I knew that I could never hope to bring conviction, however *much*, nor to avoid offence, however *little*, I might try to say. And so I thought the good ship *Humanism* might sail on its adventurous quest for the Islands of the Blest with the lighter freight of these essays as safely and hopefully as with the heaviest cargo.

F. C. S. SCHILLER.

OXFORD, *August* 1903.

CONTENTS

ESSAY		PAGE
I.	The Ethical Basis of Metaphysics	1
II.	'Useless' Knowledge	18
III.	Truth	44
IV.	Lotze's Monism	62
V.	Non-Euclidean Geometry and the Kantian *A Priori*	85
VI.	The Metaphysics of the Time-Process	95
VII.	Reality and 'Idealism'	110
VIII.	Darwinism and Design	128
IX.	The Place of Pessimism in Philosophy	157
X.	Concerning Mephistopheles	166
XI.	On Preserving Appearances	183
XII.	Activity and Substance	204
XIII.	Humism and Humanism	228
XIV.	Solipsism	249
XV.	Infallibility and Toleration	268
XVI.	Freedom and Responsibility	283
XVII.	The Desire for Immortality	313
XVIII.	The Ethical Significance of Immortality	335
XIX.	Philosophy and the Scientific Investigation of a Future Life	351
	Index	375

I

THE ETHICAL BASIS OF METAPHYSICS[1]

ARGUMENT

The place of Conduct in Philosophy : (a) The absolutist reduction of Conduct to 'appearance'; (b) the pragmatist reaction which makes conduct primary and thought secondary. Is Pragmatism irrationalism? No, but it explains it by exposing the inadequacy of intellectualism. Ways of reaching Pragmatism (1) by justification of 'faith' against 'reason,' (2) historical, (3) evolutionary. The definition of Pragmatism. Its relation to psychological teleology. The supremacy of 'Good' over 'True' and 'Real.' Kant's *Copernican Revolution*, and the complication of the question of reality with that of our knowledge. A further similar step necessitated by the purposiveness of actual knowing. The function of the will in cognition. 'Reality' as the response to a will to know, and therefore dependent in part on our action. Consequently (1) 'reality' cannot be indifferent to us; (2) our relations to it quasi-personal; (3) metaphysics quasi-ethical; (4) Pragmatism as a tonic: the venture of faith and freedom; (5) the moral stimulus of Pragmatism.

WHAT has Philosophy to say of Conduct? Shall it place it high or low, exalt it on a pedestal for the

---

[1] This essay, originally an Ethical Society address, is reprinted from the July 1903 number of the *International Journal of Ethics* with some additions, the chief of which is the note on pp. 11-12. Its title seems of course to put the cart before the horse, but it is easy to reply that nowadays it is no longer impracticable to use a motor car for the removal of a dead horse. The paradox is, moreover, intentional. It is a conscious inversion of the tedious and unprofitable disquisitions on 'the metaphysical basis of' this, that, and the other, which an erroneous conception of philosophical method engenders. They are all wrong in method, because we have not *de facto* a science of first principles of unquestionable truth from which we can start to derive the principles of the special sciences. Plato certainly failed to deduce the principles of the sciences from his metaphysical Idea of Good, and it may be doubted whether any one has ever really deduced anything from metaphysics. The fact is rather that our 'first' principles are postulated by the needs, and slowly secreted by the labours, of the special sciences, or of such preliminary exercises of our intelligence as build up the common-sense view of life.

So what my title means is, not an attempt to rest the 'final synthesis' upon a single science, but rather that among the contributions of the special sciences to the final evaluation of experience that of the highest, viz. ethics, has, and must have, decisive weight.

adoration of the world or drag it in the mire to be trampled on by all superior persons? Shall it equate it with the whole or value it as nought? Philosophers have, of course, considered the matter, though not perhaps as carefully nor as successfully as they ought. And so the relations of the theory to the practice of life, of cognition to action, of the theoretical to the practical reason, form a difficult and complicated chapter in the history of thought.[1] From that history one fact, however, stands out clearly, viz. that the claims on both sides are so large and so insistent that it is hardly possible to compromise between them. The philosopher is not on the whole a lover of compromise, despite the solicitations of his lower nature. He will not, like the ordinary man of sense, subscribe to a plausible platitude like, *e.g.* Matthew Arnold's famous dictum that *Conduct is three-fourths of Life*. Matthew Arnold was not a philosopher, and the very precision of his formula arouses scientific suspicions. But anyhow the philosopher's imperious logic does not deal in quarters; it is prone to argue *aut Caesar aut nullus*; if Conduct be not the whole life, it is naught. Which therefore shall it be? Shall Conduct be the substance of the All, or the vision of a dream?

Now, it would seem at first that latterly the second alternative had grown philosophically almost inevitable. For, under the auspices of the Hegelizing 'idealists,' Philosophy has uplifted herself once more to a metaphysical contemplation of the Absolute, of the unique Whole in which all things are included and transcended. Now whether this conception has any logical meaning and value for metaphysics is a moot point, which I have elsewhere treated;[2] but there can hardly be a pretence of denying that it is the death of morals. For the ideal of the Absolute Whole cannot be rendered compatible with the antithetical valuations which form the vital atmosphere of human agents. They are partial

---

[1] Cp. Essay ii. on '*Useless*' *Knowledge* for its treatment by Plato and Aristotle.
[2] *Riddles of the Sphinx*, ch. x., *Formal Logic*, p. 129 *n*.

appreciations, which vanish from the standpoint of the Whole. Without the distinctions of Good and Evil, Right and Wrong, Pleasure and Pain, Self and others, Then and Now, Progress and Decay, human life would be dissolved into the phantom flow of an unmeaning *mirage*. But in the Absolute the moral distinctions must, like all others, be swallowed up and disappear. The All is raised above all ethical valuation and moral criticism : it is 'beyond Good and Evil'; it is timelessly perfect, and therefore incapable of improvement. It transcends all our antitheses, because it includes them. And so to the metaphysician it seems an easy task to compose the perfection of the whole out of the imperfections of its parts : he has merely to declare that the point of view of human action, that of ethics, is not and cannot be final. It is an illusion which has grown transparent to the sage. So, in proportion as his insight into absolute reality grows clearer, his interest in ethics wanes.

It must be confessed, moreover, that metaphysicians no longer shrink from this avowal. The typical leader of this philosophic fashion, Mr. F. H. Bradley, never attempts to conceal his contempt for ethical considerations, nor omits a sneer at the pretensions of practice to be heard in the High Court of Metaphysics. "Make the moral point of view absolute," he cries,[1] " and then realize your position. You have become not merely irrational, but you have also broken with every considerable religion."

And this is how he dismisses the appeal to practice,[2] "But if so, what, I may be asked, is the result in practice? That I reply at once is not my business"; it is merely a "hurtful[3] prejudice" if "irrelevant appeals to practical results are allowed to make themselves heard."

Altogether nothing could be more pulverizing to ethical aspiration than chapter xxv. of Mr. Bradley's *Appearance and Reality*.[4]

[1] *Appearance and Reality*, pp. 500-1.   [2] *Ibid*. p. 450.
[3] But does not this "*hurtful*" reaffirm the ethical valuation which Mr. Bradley is trying to exclude?
[4] That such is the ethical purport of this philosophic teaching is confirmed by

And the worst of it all is that this whole treatment of ethics follows logically and legitimately from the general method of philosophizing which conducts to the metaphysical assumption of the Absolute.

Fortunately, however, there appears to be a natural tendency when the consequences of a point of view have been stated without reserve, and become plain to the meanest intelligence, to turn round and try something fresh. By becoming openly immoralist, metaphysic has created a demand for its moral reformation. So, quite recently, there has become noticeable a movement in a diametrically opposite direction, which repudiates the assumptions and reverses the conclusions of the metaphysical criticism of ethics which we have been considering. Instead of regarding contemplation of the Absolute as the highest form of human activity, it sets it aside as trivial and unmeaning, and puts purposeful action above purposeless speculation. Instead of supposing that Action is one thing and Thought something alien and other, and that there is not, therefore, any reason to anticipate that the pure contemplations of the latter will in any way relate to or sanction the principles which guide the former, it treats every judgment as an act and Thought as a mode of conduct, as an integral part of active life. Instead of regarding practical results as irrelevant, it makes Practical Value an essential ingredient and determinant of theoretic truth. And so far from admitting the claim to independence of an irresponsible intelligence, it regards knowledge as derivative from conduct and as involving distinctively moral qualities and responsibilities in a perfectly definite and traceable way. In short, instead of being reduced to the nothingness of an illusion, Conduct is reinstated as the all-controlling influence in every department of life.

It may be admitted, however, that all effective ethical effort ultimately demands a definite attitude towards

---

the ingenious but somewhat flippant exposition of the same doctrine in Prof. A. E. Taylor's *Problem of Conduct*. The real problem of this book would appear to be why any one should trouble about such a theoretic absurdity as morals at all.

life as a whole, and it therefore becomes an urgent need to find a philosophy which will support, or at least will not paralyse, moral effort. The new method of philosophizing will supply this desideratum in an almost perfect way. It has been called *Pragmatism* by the chief author of its importance, Professor William James, whose *Varieties of Religious Experience* so many others besides the professional readers of philosophic literature have been enjoying. But the name in this case does even less than usual to explain the meaning, and as the nature of Pragmatism has been greatly and conspicuously misunderstood, we must try to put it in a clearer light.

We may best begin by mentioning a few of the ways in which Pragmatism may be reached, before explaining how it should be defined. For many have conceived a considerable prejudice against it by reason of the method by which William James approached it.

James first unequivocally advanced the pragmatist doctrine in connexion with what he called the 'Will to believe.'[1] Now this Will to believe was put forward as an intellectual *right* (in certain cases) to decide between alternative views, each of which seemed to make a legitimate appeal to our nature, by other than purely intellectual considerations, viz. their emotional interest and practical value. Although James laid down a number of conditions limiting the applicability of his Will-to-believe, the chief of which was the willingness to take the risks involved and to abide by the results of subsequent experience, it was not perhaps altogether astonishing that his doctrine should be decried as rank irrationalism.

Irrationalism seemed a familiar and convenient label for the new doctrine. For irrationalism is a permanent or continually recrudescent attitude of the moral consciousness, the persistent vogue of which it has always been hard to explain. It is ably and brilliantly

---

[1] He had, however, laid the foundation of his doctrine long before in an article in *Mind* (1879). And, though the name is new, anticipations of the *thing* run through the whole history of thought. Indeed, this was to be expected, seeing that the actual procedure of the human mind has always been (unconsciously) pragmatist.

exemplified at the present day by Mr. Balfour's *Foundations of Belief*, and, in a less defensible form, by Mr. Benjamin Kidd. And if, instead of denouncing it, we try to understand it, we shall not find that it is entirely absurd. At bottom indeed it indicates little more than a defect in the current rationalism, and a protest against the rationalistic blindness towards the non-intellectual factors in the foundation of beliefs. Common Sense has always shown a certain sympathy with all such protests against the pretensions of what is called the pure intellect to dictate to man's whole complex nature. It has always felt that there are 'reasons of the heart of which the head knows nothing,' postulates of a faith that surpasses mere understanding, and that these possess a higher rationality which a bigoted intellectualism has failed to comprehend.

If, then, one had to choose between Irrationalism and Intellectualism, the former would undoubtedly have to be preferred. It is less inadequate to life, a less violent departure from our actual behaviour, a less grotesque caricature of our actual procedure. Like Common Sense, therefore, Pragmatism sympathizes with Irrationalism in its blind revolt against the trammels of a pedantic Intellectualism. But Pragmatism does more; it not only sympathizes, it explains. It vindicates the rationality of Irrationalism, without becoming itself irrational; it restrains the extravagance of Intellectualism, without losing faith in the intellect.[1] And it achieves this by instituting a new analysis of the common root both of the reason and of the emotional revulsion against its pride. By showing the 'pure' reason to be a pure figment, and a psychological impossibility, and the real structure of the actual reason to be essentially pragmatical, and permeated through and through with acts of faith, desires to know and wills to believe, to disbelieve and to make believe, it renders possible, nay unavoidable, a reconciliation between a reason which is humanized and a faith which is rationalized

[1] This passage has actually been quoted by a critic as cogent evidence that Pragmatism is irrationalism! Cp. *Mind*, No. 75, p. 431, and No. 71, p. 426.

in the very process which shows their antithesis to be an error.

That, however, Pragmatism should have begun by intervening in the ancient controversy between Reason and Faith was something of an accident. In itself it might equally well have been arrived at by way of a moral revolt from the unfruitful logic-chopping and aimless quibbling which is often held to be the sum total of philosophy.

Or again, it might be reached, most instructively, by a critical consideration of many historic views, notably those of Kant and Lotze,[1] and of the unsolved problems which they leave on our hands. Or, once more, by observing the actual procedure of the various sciences and their motives for accepting, maintaining, and modifying the 'truth' of their various propositions, we may come to realize that what works best in practice is what in actual knowing we accept as 'true.'

But to me personally the straightest road to Pragmatism is one which the extremest prejudice can scarce suspect of truckling to the encroachments of theology. Instead of saying like James, 'so all-important is it to secure the right action that (in cases of real intellectual alternatives) it is lawful for us to adopt the belief most congenial with our spiritual needs and to try whether our faith will not make it come true,' I should rather say 'the traditional notion of beliefs determined by pure reason alone is wholly incredible. For is not "pure" reason a myth? How can there be such a thing? How, that is, can we so separate our intellectual function from the whole complex of our activities, that it can operate in real independence of practical considerations? I cannot but conceive the reason as being, like the rest of our equipment, a weapon in the struggle for existence and a means of achieving adaptation. It must follow that the use, which has developed it, must have stamped itself upon its inmost structure, even if it has not moulded it out of pre-rational

---

[1] Or, as James suggested, and as Prof. A. W. Moore has actually done in the case of Locke (see his *Functional versus the Representational Theory of Knowledge*), by a critical examination of the English philosophers.

instincts. In short, a reason which has not practical value for the purposes of life is a monstrosity, a morbid aberration or failure of adaptation, which natural selection must sooner or later wipe away.'

It is in some such way that I should prefer to pave the way for an appreciation of the aims of Pragmatism. Hence we may now venture to define it as the thorough recognition that the purposive character of mental life generally must influence and pervade also our most remotely cognitive activities.[1]

In other words, it is a conscious application to the theory of life of the psychological facts of cognition as they appear to a teleological Voluntarism. In the light of such a teleological psychology the problems of logic and metaphysics are rejuvenated by the decisive weight given to the conceptions of Purpose and End. Or again, it is a systematic protest against the practice of ignoring in our theories of Thought and Reality the purposiveness of all our actual thinking, and the relation of all our actual realities to the ends of our practical life. It is an assertion of the sway of human valuations over every region of our experience, and a denial that such valuation can validly be eliminated from the contemplation of any reality we know.

Now inasmuch as such teleological valuation is also the special sphere of ethical inquiry, Pragmatism may be said to assign metaphysical validity to the typical method of ethics. At a blow it awards to the ethical conception of *Good* supreme authority over the logical conception of *True* and the metaphysical conception of *Real*. The Good becomes a determinant both of the True and of the Real, and their secret inspiration. For from the pursuit of the latter we may never eliminate the reference to the former. Our apprehension of the *Real*, our comprehension of the *True*, is always effected by beings who are aiming at the attainment of some *Good*, and *choose* between rival claimants to reality and truth according to the services

---

[1] For a further discussion of the definition of Pragmatism, cp. *Studies in Humanism*, Essay i., and my article in the *Encycl. Britann.* ed. xi.

they render. Is it not then a palpable absurdity to deny that this fact makes a stupendous difference?

Pragmatism then has taken a further step in the analysis of our experience which amounts to an important advance in that self-knowledge on which our knowledge of the world depends. Indeed, this advance seems to be of a magnitude comparable with, and no less momentous than, that which gave to the *epistemological* question priority over the *ontological*.

It is generally recognized as the capital achievement of modern philosophy to have perceived that a solution of the ontological question—*What is Reality?*—is not possible until it has been decided how Reality can come within our ken. Before there can be a real for us at all, the Real must be *knowable*, and the notion of an unknowable reality is useless, because it abolishes itself. The true formulation therefore of the ultimate question of metaphysics must become—*What can I know as real?* Thus the effect of what Kant (very infelicitously) called the Copernican Revolution in philosophy is that ontology, the theory of Reality, comes to be conditioned by epistemology, the theory of our knowledge.

But this truth is incomplete until we realize all that is involved in the knowledge being *ours* and recognize the real nature of our knowing. Our knowing is not the mechanical operation of a passionless 'pure' intellect, which

> Grinds out Good and grinds out Ill,
> And has no purpose, heart, or will.

Pure intellection is not a fact in nature; it is a logical fiction which will not really serve even the purposes of technical logic. In reality our knowing is driven and guided at every step by our subjective interests and preferences, our desires, our needs and our ends. These form the motive powers also of our intellectual life.

Now what is the bearing of this fact on the traditional dogma of an absolute truth and ultimate reality existing for themselves apart from human agency? It must utterly debar us from the cognition of 'Reality as it is in itself and apart from our interests'; if such a thing there were, it could not be known, nor rationally believed in.

For our interests impose the conditions under which alone Reality can be revealed. Only such aspects of Reality can be revealed as are (1) knowable and (2) objects of an actual desire, and consequent attempt, to know. All other realities or aspects of Reality, which there is no attempt to know, necessarily remain unknown, and for us unreal, because there is no one to look for them. Reality, therefore, and the knowledge thereof, essentially presuppose a definitely directed effort to know. And, like other efforts, this effort is purposive; it is necessarily inspired by the conception of some good ('end') at which it aims. Neither the question of *Fact*, therefore, nor the question of *Knowledge* can be raised without raising also the question of *Value*. Our 'Facts' when analysed turn out to be 'Values,' and the conception of 'Value' therefore becomes more ultimate than that of 'Fact.' Our valuations thus pervade our whole experience, and affect whatever 'fact,' whatever 'knowledge' we consent to recognize. If, then, there is no *knowing* without *valuing*, if knowledge is a form of *Value*, or, in other words, a factor in a Good, Lotze's anticipation[1] has been fully realized, and the foundations of metaphysics have actually been found to lie in ethics.

In this way the ultimate question for philosophy becomes—What is Reality *for one aiming at knowing what*? 'Real' *means*, real for what *purpose*? to what *end*? in what *use*? in what context? in preference to what alternative belief? The answers always come in terms of the will to know which puts the question. This at once yields a simple and beautiful explanation of the different accounts of Reality which are given in the various sciences and philosophies. The purpose of the questions being different, so is their purport, and so must be the answers. For the direction of our effort, itself determined by our desires and will to know, enters as a necessary and ineradicable factor into whatever revelation

[1] *Metaphysics* (Eng. Tr.), ii. p. 319.

of Reality we can attain. The response to our questions is always affected by their *character*, and *that* is in our power. For the initiative throughout is ours. It is for us to consult the oracle of Nature or to refrain ; it is for us to formulate our demands and to put our questions. If we question amiss, Nature will not respond, and we must try again. But we can never be entitled to assume either that our action makes no difference or that nature contains no answer to a question we have never thought to put.[1]

It is no exaggeration therefore to contend, with Plato, that in a way the Good, meaning thereby the conception of a final systematization of our purposes, is the supreme controlling power in our whole experience, and that in abstraction from it neither the True nor the Real can exist. For whatever forms of the latter we may have 'discovered,' some purposive activity, some conception of a good to be attained, was involved as a condition of the

[1] That the Real has a determinate nature which the knowing reveals but does not affect, so that our knowing makes no difference to it, is one of those sheer assumptions which are incapable, not only of proof, but even of rational defence. It is a survival of a crude realism which can be defended only, *in a pragmatist manner*, on the score of its practical convenience, as an avowed fiction. In this sense and as a mode of speech, we need not quarrel with it. But as an ultimate analysis of the fact of knowing it is an utterly gratuitous interpretation. The plain fact is that we can come into contact with any sort of reality only in the act of 'knowing' or experiencing it. As *unknowable*, therefore, the Real is *nil*, as *unknown*, it is only potentially real. What is there in this situation to sanction the assumption that what the Real *is* in the act of knowing, it is also outside that relation ? One might as well argue that because an orator is eloquent in the presence of an audience, he is no less voluble in addressing himself. The simple fact is that we know the Real *as it is when we know it* ; we know nothing whatever about what it is apart from that process. It is meaningless therefore to inquire into its nature as it is in itself. And I can see no reason why the view that reality exhibits a rigid nature unaffected by our treatment should be deemed theoretically more justifiable than its converse, that it is utterly plastic to our every demand—a travesty of Pragmatism which has attained much popularity with its critics. The actual situation is of course a case of interaction, a process of cognition in which the 'subject' and the 'object' determine each the other, and both 'we' and 'reality' are involved, and, we might add, *evolved*. There is no warrant therefore for the assumption that either of the poles between which the current passes could be suppressed without detriment. What we ought to say is that when the mind 'knows' reality both are affected, just as we say that when a stone falls to the ground both it and the earth are attracted.

We are driven, then, to the conviction that the 'determinate nature of reality' does *not* subsist 'outside' or 'beyond' the process of knowing it. It is merely a half-understood lesson of experience that we have enshrined in the belief that it does so subsist. Things behave in similar ways in their reaction to modes

discovery. If there had been no activity on our part, or if that activity had been directed to ends other than it was, there could not have been discovery, or *that* discovery.

We must discard, therefore, the notion that in the constitution of the world we count for nothing, that it matters not what we do, because Reality is what it is, whatever we may do. It is true on the contrary that our action is essential and indispensable, that to some extent the world (our world) is of our making, and that without us nothing is made that is made. To what extent and in what directions the world is plastic and to be moulded by our action we do not know as yet. We can find out only by trying: but we know enough for Pragmatism to transfigure the aspect of existence for us.

It frees us in the first place from what constitutes perhaps the worst and most paralysing horror of the naturalistic view of life, the nightmare of an *indifferent* universe. For it proves that at any rate Nature cannot be indifferent to us and to our doings. It may be hostile,

---

of treatment, the differences between which seem to us important. From this we have chosen to infer that things have a rigid and unalterable nature. It might have been better to infer that therefore the differences between our various manipulations must seem unimportant to the things.

The truth is rather that the nature of things is not *determinate* but *determinable*, like that of our fellow-men. Previous to trial it is indeterminate, not merely for our ignorance, but really and from every point of view, within limits which it is our business to discover. It grows determinate by our experiments, like human character. We all know that in our social relations we frequently put questions which are potent in determining their own answers, and without the putting would leave their subjects undetermined. 'Will you love me, hate me, trust me, help me?' are conspicuous examples, and we should consider it absurd to argue that because a man had begun social intercourse with another by knocking him down, the hatred he had thus provoked must have been a pre-existent reality which the blow had merely elicited. All that the result entitles us to assume is a capacity for social feeling variously responsive to various modes of stimulation. Why, then, should we not transfer this conception of a determinable indetermination to nature at large, why should we antedate the results of our manipulation and regard as unalterable facts the reactions which our ignorance and blundering provoke? To the objection that even in our social dealings not all the responses are indeterminate, the reply is that it is easy to regard them as having been determined by earlier experiments.

In this way, then, the notion of a 'fact-in-itself' might become as much of a philosophic anachronism as that of a 'thing-in-itself,' and we should conceive the process of knowledge as extending from absolute chaos at the one end (before a determinate response had been established) to absolute satisfaction at the other, which would have no motive to question the absolutely factual nature of its objects. But in the intermediate condition of our present experience all recognition of 'fact' would be provisional and relative to our purposes and inquiries. Cp. *Studies in Humanism*, Essays xviii., xix.

and something to be fought with all our might; it may be unsuspectedly friendly, and something to be co-operated with with our whole heart; it *must* respond in varying ways to our various efforts.

Now, inasmuch as we are most familiar with such varying responsiveness in our personal relations with others, it is, I think, natural, though not perhaps necessary, that a pragmatist will tend to put a personal interpretation upon his transactions with Nature and any agency he may conceive to underlie it. Still even ordinary language is aware that things behave differently according as you 'treat' them, that *e.g.*, *treated* with fire sugar burns, while *treated* with water it dissolves. Thus in the last resort the anthropomorphic 'humanism' of our whole treatment of experience is unavoidable and obvious; and however much he wills to disbelieve it the philosopher must finally confess that to escape anthropomorphism he would have to escape from self. And further, seeing that ethics is the science of our relations with other persons, *i.e.* with our environment *qua* personal, this ultimateness of the personal construction we put upon our experience must increase the importance of the ethical attitude towards it. In other words, our metaphysics must in any case be *quasi-ethical*.

It may fairly be anticipated, secondly, that Pragmatism will prove a great tonic to re-invigorate a grievously depressed humanity. It sweeps away entirely the stock excuse for fatalism and despair. It proves that human action is always a perceptible, and never a negligible, factor in the ordering of nature, and shows cause for the belief that the disparity between our powers and the forces of nature, great as it is, does not amount to incommensurability. And it denies that any of the great questions of human concern have been irrevocably answered against us. For most of them have not even been asked in a pragmatic manner, *i.e.* with a determination to test the answers by the value of the consequences, and in no case has there been that systematic and clear-sighted endeavour which extorts concessions, or at least an answer, from reluctant nature. In short, no doctrine better calculated to stir us to activity or more potent to sustain our efforts has ever issued from the philosophic study.

It is true that to gain these hopes we must make bold to take some risks. If our action is a real factor in the course of events, it is impossible to exclude the contingency that if we act wrongly it may be an influence for ill. To the chance of salvation there must correspond a risk of damnation. We select the conditions under which reality shall appear to us, but this very selection selects us, and if we cannot contrive to reach a harmony in our intercourse with the real, we perish.

But to many this very element of danger will but add to the zest of life. For it cannot but appear by far more interesting than the weary grinding out of a predetermined course of things which issues in meaningless monotony from the unalterable nature of the All. And the infinite boredom with which this conception of the course of nature would afflict us, must be commingled with an equal measure of disgust when we realize that on this same theory the chief ethical issues are eternally and inexorably decided against us. Loyal co-operation and Promethean revolt grow equally unmeaning. For man can never have a ground for action against the Absolute. It is eternally and inherently and irredeemably perfect, with a 'perfection' which has lost all meaning for humanity, and so leaves no ground for the hope that the 'appearances' which make up our world may somehow be remoulded into conformity with our ideals. As they cannot now impair the inscrutable perfection of the Whole, they need not ever alter to pander to a criticism woven out of the delusive dreams of us poor creatures of illusion.

It is a clear gain, therefore, when Pragmatism holds out to us a prospect of a world that can become better, and even has a distant chance of becoming perfect, in a sense which we are able to appreciate. The only thing that could be preferred to this would be a universe whose perfection could not only be metaphysically deduced, but actually experienced: but such a one our universe emphatically is *not*.

Hence the indetermination which, as William James has urged,[1] Pragmatism introduces into our conception of the world is essentially a gain. It brings out a connexion with the ethical conception of Freedom and the old problems involved in it, which we need not here consider.[2] When we do, we may see that while determinism has an absolutely indefeasible status as a scientific postulate, and is the only assumption we can use in our practical calculations, we may yet have to recognize the reality of a certain measure of indetermination. It is a peculiarity of ethics that this indetermination is forced upon it, but in itself it is probably universal. In its valuation, however, we may differ somewhat from James, regarding it neither as good nor as ineradicable. Our indeterminism, moreover, cannot have the slightest ethical value unless it both vindicates and emphasizes our moral responsibility.

This brings us to our last point, viz. the stimulus to our feeling of moral responsibility which must accrue from the doctrine of Pragmatism. It contains such a stimulus, alike in its denial of a mechanical determination of the world which is involved in its partial determination by our action, and in its admission that by wrong action we may evoke a hostile response, and so provoke our ruin. But in addition it must be pointed out that if every cognition, however theoretical, be an *act*, and so must have a practical purpose and value, it is potentially a moral act. We may incur indeed the gravest responsibilities in selecting the aims of our cognitive activities. We may become not merely wise or foolish but also good or bad by willing to know the good or the bad; nay, our very will to know may so alter the conditions as to evoke a response congenial with its character.

It is a law of our nature that what we seek that we

---

[1] *Will to Believe*, p. ix.   [2] Cp. Essay xvi.

shall, in some measure, find. Like a rainbow, Life glitters in all the colours; like a rainbow also it adjusts itself to every beholder. To the dayflies of fashion life seems ephemeral; to the seeker after permanence, it strikes its roots into eternity. To the empty, it is a yawning chasm of inanity; to the full, it is a source of boundless interest. To the indolent, it is a call to despairing resignation; to the strenuous, a stimulus to dauntless energy. To the serious, it is fraught with infinite significance; to the flippant, it is all a somewhat sorry jest. To the melancholic, each hope is strangled in its birth; to the sanguine, two hopes spring from every grave of one. To the optimistic, life is a joy ineffable; to the pessimistic, the futile agony of an atrocious and unending struggle. To love it seems that in the end all must be love; to hate and envy it becomes a hell. The cosmic order, which to one displays the unswerving rigour of a self-sufficient mechanism, grows explicable to another only by the direct guidance of the hand of God. To those of little faith the heavens are dumb; to the faithful, they disclose the splendours of a beatific vision.

So each sees Life as what he has it in him to perceive, and variously transfigures what, without his vision, were an unseen void. But all are not equally clear-sighted, and which sees best, time and trial must establish. We can but stake our little lives upon the ventures of our faith. And, willing or unwilling, this we do and must.

In conclusion let us avow that after professing to discuss the relations of Philosophy and Practice, we seem to have allotted an undue share of our time to the former, and to have done little more than adumbrate the practical consequences of the new philosophy. In extenuation we may urge that the stream of Truth which waters the fertile fields of Conduct has its sources in the remote and lonely uplands, *inter apices philosophiae*, where the cloud-capped crags and slowly grinding glaciers of metaphysics soar into an air too chill and rare for our abiding habitation, but keenly bracing to the strength of an audacious climber. Here lie our watersheds; hither lead the passes to the realms unknown; hence part our ways, and here it is that we must draw the frontier lines of Right and Wrong. It would seem, moreover, that in the depths of every soul there lurks a metaphysic aspiration to these heights, a craving to behold the varied patterns that compose life's whole spread out in their connexion. With the right guides such ascents are safe, and even though at first twinges of mountain-sickness may befall us, yet in the end we shall return refreshed from our excursion and strengthened to endure the drudgery and commonplace that are our daily portion.

II

'USELESS' KNOWLEDGE[1]

ARGUMENT

The idealistic art of passing into 'other' worlds. A visit to Plato in a world of superior 'reality.' The difficulty of proving the reality of such experiences to others unless they lead to useful knowledge. Is the *true* always *useful*? Aristotle denies the connexion between theoretic truth and practical use, and prefers the former as higher and diviner. The Pragmatist rejection of this dogma of the superior dignity of speculation. Four possibilities as to the relation of Knowledge and Action. (1) Plato's view: Knowledge the presupposition of Action, to which it naturally leads, = the True the source of the Good; (2) Aristotle's: Pure Knowledge unrelated to Action, the highest Truth to the Good for man; (3) Kant's: the same relation, but Action ultimately superior to Knowledge; (4) Pragmatism the converse of Plato's, *i.e.* Action primary, Knowledge secondary, the Good the source of the True.

Critique of Aristotelianism.—(1) 'Truth' not superhuman, but as human as 'Good.' 'True' *means* true for us as practical beings. The recognition of 'objective truth' a gradual achievement and = the construction of a common world in which we can act together. (2) Perceived reality relative to our senses. (3) The 'eternal' truths as postulates. (4) Theoretical principles, like practical, get their meaning from their use, and are called 'true' if they prove useful. Hence 'necessary' truth only = *needful*. Implications of the dicta *the true is useful* and *the useless is false*. No knowledge really useless, for the really useless is not knowledge. *Examples*—Knowledge about the Absolute and about an 'other' world unconnected with this.

IT will readily be understood that once the idealistic art of waking oneself up out of our world of appearances and thereby passing into one of higher reality [2] is fully mastered, the temptation to exercise it becomes practically irresistible. Nevertheless, it was not until nearly two years (as men reckon time) after the first memorable occasion when he discoursed to me concerning the adaptation of the Ideal

---

[1] From *Mind*, N.S. No. 42 (April 1902), with some additions.
[2] Cp. pp. 113 note, 367-9.

State to our present circumstances[1] that I succeeded in sufficiently arousing my soul to raise it once again to that supernal Academe where the divine Plato meditates in holy groves beside a fuller and more limpid stream than the Attic Ilissus.

When I was breathlessly projected into his world, Plato was reclining gracefully beside a moss-grown boulder and listening attentively to a lively little man who was discoursing with an abundance of animation and gesticulation. When he observed me, he stopped his companion, who immediately came hurrying towards me, and after politely greeting me, amiably declared that the Master would be delighted to converse with me. I noticed that he was a dapper little man, apparently in the prime of life, though beginning to grow rather bald about the temples. He was carefully robed, and his beard and his hair, such as it was, were scented. One could not help being struck by his refined, intelligent countenance, and his quick, observant eyes.

As soon as Plato had welcomed me, his companion went off to get, he said, a garden chair from a gleaming marble temple (it turned out to be a shrine of the Muses) at a little distance, and I naturally inquired of Plato who the obliging little man was.

'Why, don't you know?' he replied, 'don't you recognize my famous pupil, Aristotle?'

'Aristotle! No, I should never have supposed he was like that.'

'What then would you have expected?'

'Well, I should have expected a bigger man for one thing, and one far less agreeable. To tell the truth, I should have expected Aristotle to be very bumptious and conceited.'

'You are not quite wrong,' said Plato with an indulgent smile, 'he *was* all you say, when he first came hither. But this is Aristotle *with the conceit taken out of him*, so that you now behold him reduced to his true proportions and can see his real worth.'

---

[1] The contents of this interview have not yet been divulged, for reasons which will appear from the course of the present narrative.

'Ah! that explains much. I now see why *you* are even greater and more impressive than I expected, and why he appears to be on such good terms with you once more.'

'Oh yes, we have made up our differences long ago, and he has now again the same keen, unassuming spirit with which he first charmed me, as a boy. Not that I was ever very angry with him even formerly. Of course his criticisms were unfair, and, as you say, his great abilities rendered him conceited, but you must remember that he had to make a place for himself in the philosophic world, and that he could do this only by attacking the greatest reputation in that world, viz. mine. But you see he is returning, and I want to ask you how you fared after our last meeting. Did you find it difficult to get back to your world?'

'I hardly know, Plato, how I managed it. And, oh, the difference when I awoke in the morning! How sordid all things seemed!'

'And did you tell your pupils what my answers were to your questions?'

'I did, and they were much interested, and, I am afraid I must add, amused.'

'And after that what did you do? Did you persuade your political men to enact laws in the Ecclesia such as those we showed to be best?'

'I fear I have not yet quite succeeded in doing this.'

'Why, what objections have you failed to overcome?'

'I have not yet even overcome the first and greatest objection of all. I have not published the account of our conversation.'

'Why not?'

'To tell you the truth, I was afraid; I feared that your arguments might fare ill among the British Philistines.'

'Why should they fare ill, seeing that, both for other reasons and to please you, I was conservative, wonderfully how, amid all my reforms, and proposed nothing revolutionary, but essayed only gently to turn to the light the eyes of the Cave-dwellers whom you mention?'

'You don't know how insensitive they are to the light.'

'Yet I was only preaching to them the necessity of self-realization.'

'I know that; but your language would have sounded unfamiliar.'

'Then you should repeat it, until it sounds familiar.'

'How splendidly you must have lectured, Plato! I hardly dare however to follow your advice. However mildly I might put them, your proposals would have shocked the British public.'

'And yet you told me that the infinitely more revolutionary and unsparing proposals of my *Republic* command universal admiration, and are held to be salutary in the education of youth.'

'Ah, but then they are protected by the decent obscurity of a learned language!'

'Surely your language is learned enough, and by the time they have passed through your mind my ideas will be obscure enough to make them decent and safe.'

'You are victorious as ever, Plato, in argument. But you do not persuade me, because there is another obstacle, even greater than that which I have mentioned.'

'Will you not tell me what it is?'

'I hardly know how to put it. But though it now seems almost too absurd even to suggest such a thing, you know everybody to whom I spoke disbelieved that I had really conversed with you, and thought that I had dreamt it all, or even invented the whole matter.'

'That, as you say, is too absurd.'

'Nevertheless, so long as people believed this, you see it was vain for me to try to persuade them of the excellence of your proposals. For I do not happen to have been born the son of a king myself, and am of no account for such purposes.'

'Still they could not have supposed that you could have invented all you said yourself.'

'I am afraid they did.'

'That was very unreasonable of them.'

'I am not so sure of that. For after all they had only my word for it that I had really met you.'

'But did they not recognize what I said, and my manner of saying it?'

'Not so as to feel sure.'

'And did they not think your whole account intrinsically probable and consistent?'

'I hope I made it appear so.'

'Surely they did not think that you could invent a world like mine?'

'I suppose they thought I might have dreamt it.'

'What, a world so much better, more beautiful, coherent and rational, and, in two words, *more real*, than that in which they lived?'

'There is nothing in all this to make it seem less of a dream rather than more.'

'Do you think they will believe you after this second visit?'

'I doubt it. Why should they?'

'It would seem, then, that we have no means of convincing these wretches of the truth.'

'I fear not; so long as they can reasonably maintain that it is no truth at all.'

'You do not surely propose to defend their conduct?'

'No, but I think it is by no means as unreasonable as you suppose.'

'I see that you are preparing to assert a greater paradox than ever I listened to from Zeno.'

'I am afraid that it may appear such.'

'Will you not quickly utter it? You see how keenly Aristotle is watching you, like a noble dog straining at the leash.'

'Let me say this, then, that though I can no more doubt your existence and that of the lovely world wherein you abide than I can my own, yet I cannot blame my fellow-men for refusing to credit all this on my sole assertion. *They* have not seen you, nor can they, seeing that you will neither descend to them nor can they rise to you. Your world and theirs have nothing in common, and so do not exist for each other.'

'You forget yourself, my friend.'

'True, I am a link between them. But what I have experienced is not directly part of *their* experience. It is far more probable, therefore, that I am lying or deluded than that I should establish a connexion between two worlds. Before they need, or indeed can, admit that what I say is true, I must show them how, in consequence of my visits to your higher world, I am enabled to act more successfully in theirs. You see, Plato, I am exactly in the position of your liberated Cave-dweller when he returns to his fellow-prisoners. They need not, can not, and will not, believe that I speak the truth concerning what I have seen above, unless I am also able to discern better the shadows in their cave below.'

'And this must surely be the case.'

'I notice that you assumed this, but you did not explain how it was that the higher knowledge of the Ideas, for example the ability to understand the motions of the heavenly bodies, was useful for enabling men to live better.'

'But surely Knowledge is one, and the True and the Beautiful must also be useful.'

'I am not denying that, although your friend Aristotle would, unless he has greatly changed his opinion; I am only saying that you have assumed this too lightly.'

Instead of replying Plato looked at Aristotle, who with a slight hesitation ventured to suggest that possibly I was right, and that he had always been of the opinion that his master had overrated the practical usefulness of scientific knowledge. Plato meditated for a while before replying.

'It is possible that there are difficulties here which escaped my notice formerly. But did I not prove that the soul attuned to the harmonies of the higher sphere of true reality was also necessarily that most capable of dealing with the discords of phenomenal existence?'

'No doubt, Plato, your spectator of all time and all existence is a very beautiful being, and I too trust that in the end you may be right in thinking that Truth and Goodness must be harmonious. But neither in your time, nor in the many years that have passed since, has it come about that the pursuit of abstract knowledge has engendered the perfect man. I greatly doubt whether you convinced even your own brothers by your argument in the *Republic*, and you have certainly failed to convince those who have deemed themselves the greatest philosophers from the time of Aristotle to the present day. They would all in private scoff at the notion that speculative knowledge was by nature conducive to practical excellence, even though a few of the more prudent might not think it expedient to state this in public, while as for the great majority, they are always crying aloud that it is sacrilege and profanation to demand practical results from their meditations, and that only an utterly vulgar and ill-educated mind is even interested in the practical consequences which theoretical researches may chance to have. And this temper we observe not only among the philosophers proper, who are few and speak a "language of the gods" unintelligible to the many, but also more patently among those who pursue the sciences and the arts, and hold that "Truth for the sake of Truth" and "Art for the sake of Art" alone are worthy of their consideration.'

'Is it true, Aristotle, that you also hold such opinions?'

'May I be permitted, oh my master, to expound my views at length, and yet briefly, as compared with the importance of the subject? You know that I do not find the method of question and answer the most convenient to express my thoughts (Plato nodded). Well, then, let me say first of all that I do not hold it true that speculative wisdom (σοφία) is the same as practical wisdom (φρόνησις), or that the latter is naturally developed out of the former. I must, therefore, with all respect agree with our critic from a lower world that you have too easily identified the two. They are quite distinct, and have nothing to do with each other.'

Then observing an involuntary shudder on my part, 'Oh, I know,' he continued, 'what you are wishing to object. How can σοφία exist without the help of φρόνησις in beings that have to act practically in a social life, seeing that it does not as such concern itself with the means of human happiness?¹ I confess to an overstatement. It is not *quite* true that σοφία and φρόνησις have nothing to do with each other. There is a connexion, because practical wisdom has to provide speculative with the material conditions of its exercise. In other words, men are too imperfect to live the divine life of contemplation wholly and always. They must to some extent busy themselves with the needs of the perishable part of their nature, and the contingencies and changes of the sublunary sphere. And the regulation and satisfaction of such needs, the whole ὕλη of things that are capable of being otherwise (ἐνδεχομένων ἄλλως ἔχειν), appertains to practical wisdom.

'Without it, therefore, speculative wisdom could not exist among men, or at least could not be self-supporting. But it does not follow that it thereby becomes dependent on practical wisdom, and still less, derivative from it. Practical wisdom serves speculative like a faithful servant. It is the trusty steward who has so to order the household that its master may have leisure for his holy avocations. It would be truer, therefore, to say that practical wisdom depends on speculative, without which life would lose its savour. But best of all is it to say that the two are essentially distinct and connected only by the bond of an external necessity.

'Having shown thus that practical and theoretical activity (ἐνέργεια) are different in kind, let me explain next why the latter is the better, and the relation between them which I have described is a just one.

'They differ in their psychological character, in their object and in their value. Practical wisdom is the function of a lower and altogether inferior "part of the soul," of that "passive reason" (νοῦς παθητικός) which we put forth only while we deal with a "matter" whose resistance we cannot wholly master. Speculative activity, on the other hand, is the divine imperishable part of us which, small as it is in bulk in most men, is yet our true self.

'Again the object of practical wisdom is the good for

¹ Cp. *Eth. Nic.* vi. 12. 1.

man and the transitory flow of appearances in the impermanent part of the universe. But the good which is the object of our practical pursuit is peculiar and restricted to man. It is different for men and for fishes,[1] and although I do not deny that man's is the higher and that therefore fishing is legitimate sport, I feel bound to point out that there are many things in the world far diviner than man. The object of speculation, on the other hand, is the eternal and immutable which is common to all. I mean to include under this not merely the eternal truths, such as the principles of metaphysics and mathematics, but the eternal existences of the heavenly bodies and the unvarying character of the perceptions which are the same for all beings, *e.g.*, those of colour, shape, size, etc.

'Whence it follows, lastly, that the value of speculation is incomparably superior to that of practice. It is not useful, and that it should occasionally lead to useful results is merely a regrettable accident. In itself it is *beautiful* and the beautiful is self-sufficient. But it is not useful, because it is exalted far above the useful, and to demand use for knowledge is, literally, impiety. For to contemplate the immutable objects of theoretical truth is in the strictest sense to lead the life divine. For it contemplates the higher and more perfect, even though it cannot grasp the absolutely perfect as continuously as God can contemplate His own absolute perfection. Still to do this, in however passing a fashion, is to rise above death and impermanence and decay. It is to immortalize oneself.

'It follows, therefore, logically and in point of fact, that any attempt to hinder or control the concern with Pure Truth, is an outrage upon what is highest and best and holiest in human nature, an outrage which the law should punish and all good men rebuke, with the utmost severity. Truth demands not merely toleration for herself from the State, but also the unsparing suppression of every form of Error, of every one who from whatever motive, whether from ignorance or sordidness or a mis-

---

[1] Cp. *Eth. Nic.* vi. 7. 4.

taken and degrading moral enthusiasm, attempts to put any hindrance in the way of her absolute supremacy.'

Towards the end of this diatribe, to which I had at various points shown myself unable to listen without writhing, Aristotle had wrought himself up into a state of fervour of which I should hardly have deemed him capable. Plato, however, skilfully provided for the continuation of the discussion by blandly remarking :—

'Bravo, Aristotle, you have spoken most interestingly, and shown not only the analytic subtlety for which you are famous, but also that true enthusiasm which proves that you are not merely a logical perforating machine for windbags and other receptacles of gaseous matter. I will leave it, however, to our visitor to answer you, partly because the question has, it would seem, grown somewhat beyond my ken, and partly because I can see that he has not a little to say, and foresee that your differences will prove most entertaining and instructive.'

'You are right, Plato, in thinking that I differ profoundly with the doctrine to which Aristotle has just given such eloquent expression. But I feel that I am hardly equal single-handed to cope with Aristotle, and I wish that Iames were present to support me and to persuade you both of what I believe to be right and reasonable.'

'And who is Iames?'

'A philosopher, Plato, of the Hyperatlanteans, very different from the "bald-headed little tinkers" who are philosophers, not by the grace of God, but by the favour of some wretched "thinking-shop," and a man (or shall I rather call him a god?) after your own heart. But, alas, he has been bridled, like Theages, by his own, and so has not yet been enabled to set forth fully the doctrine which he has named [1] *Pragmatism*, and which I would fain advance against that of Aristotle.'

'You describe a man whom I should be eager to welcome. You must bring him with you the next time you come, having told him what we have discussed.'

[1] Strictly speaking, I am reminded, it was Mr. C. S. Peirce, but it would seem to follow from pragmatist principles that a doctrine belongs to him who makes an effective use of it.

'I will if I can.'

'As for your present difficulty, you need not be afraid. You shall argue, with me as judge, and I will see to it that Aristotle obtains no unfair advantage over you.'

'You embolden me to try my best.'

'I do not think that *courage* is what you lack.'

'If I have courage, it is like yours, that which comes nearest to that of despair.'

'I never quite despaired.'

'Nor will I, though it is hard not to, to one regarding the present position of philosophy.'

'Aristotle is beginning to think that you are not going to answer him.'

'Then I will delay no longer. And first of all let me say that besides the views which have been taken by you and by Aristotle there seem to me to be two others, and that if you have no objection, I will state them, first recapitulating your own.'

'I have never an objection to be instructed.'

'I will begin with your own view then. It seemed to me to assume that there was no real or ultimate difference between the use of the reason in matters practical and matters theoretical. Knowledge was one and all action depended on knowledge, right action presupposing right knowledge. Knowledge, therefore, was useful, and there was no real opposition between the True and the Good, because the True could not but be good and the Good true. Nevertheless, Goodness was born of Truth rather than Truth of Goodness. Have I understood you aright?'

'You have put things more definitely than I did, but not perhaps amiss.'

'Aristotle, on the other hand, whom we have just heard, clearly thinks that Truth and Goodness have nothing to do with each other.'

'Pardon me, there is a goodness also of Truth, and in a sense speculative activity ($\theta\epsilon\omega\rho\iota\alpha$) is also action ($\pi\rho\hat{\alpha}\xi\iota\varsigma$).'

'Yes, I know that; you mean as exercise of function? The speculative life also is something we *do*, it is the exercise of a characteristic human activity, and so has an excellence and contributes to our happiness.'

'Precisely.'

'Very well then, what I meant was that you did not derive practical from theoretic activity.'

'Certainly not.'

'The two are as far opposed as is practically possible.'

'Yes.'

'But speculative wisdom is by far the loftier?'

'Of course.'

'And far too lofty to be useful?'

'So I maintain.'

'Very well again. Now for a third view. Is it not possible to maintain with you that the practical and the speculative reason are different and opposed to each other, but that *the former* is the superior, so that in the end we must believe and practically act on what we do not know to be true? And is not this the converse of your view, Aristotle?'

'I suppose it is, but if *that* is *your* view, I tell you frankly that I never heard anything more absurd.'

'In that case it is lucky, perhaps, that it is not *my* view.'

'Who then has been confused enough in his mind to propound it?'

'It is the view of the great Scythian, Kant, who nearly criticized the reason out of the world.'

'Ah, I know, a queer little hunchback of a barbarian! He came here once, not so very long ago, but would not stay and could not say anything intelligible. I could only make out that he was seeking the Infinite (faugh!), and was impelled by something he called a Categorical Imperative (unknown alike to logic and to grammar). Possessed by evil demons he seemed to us. Nothing Hellenic about him at all events!'

'I don't wonder at what you say, nor that Plato agrees with you. Nevertheless, he was a remarkable man, on his way, perhaps, to a higher truth, to which we may follow him, passing through the absurdity of his actual view, which is far greater than I have had time to indicate.'

'Let us go on, then, at once to something more reasonable.'

'I will go on then to the view of the Pragmatists. May one not say, fourthly, that there is no opposition between speculative and practical wisdom because the former arises out of the latter and remains always derivative and secondary and subservient and useful?'

'One may say that or any other nonsense, but if one does, one must say what one means. And one cannot always prove what one says.'

'I thought that would excite you, Aristotle. But I thought it better to reveal to you the whole aim of my argument before I proceeded to reach it.'

'You are still far from your aim.'

'I am coming to it, in good time. Meanwhile have you observed that this position which I hope to reach is the exact converse of the first, of Plato's?'

'You mean that you also deny the opposition between θεωρία and πρᾶξις, but derive the former from the latter?'

'Exactly so. I entirely deny the independence of the speculative reason. And I assert that you were quite wrong in drawing the distinctions you did between the objects of θεωρία and of πρᾶξις.'

'Do you then deny that the *good* which is the aim of practical wisdom is merely human?'

'Not at all; but I assert that the *true*, which you imagine to be in some sense superhuman, is also merely human. It is the *true for us*, the true *for us as practical beings*, just as the good is the good for us.'

'How so?'

'Why, quite simply. Are not colour and shape and size perceived by the senses?'

'Certainly.'

'And are not the senses human, and relative to us and to our needs in life, in the same way as our perception of the good and the sweet?'

'I don't see why I need suppose them to be merely human.'

'I don't see how you can show them to be anything more. How do you know that your fishes see white as you do? And even if they did, that would only show that their senses were constructed like yours, and fitted to see and avoid you when you dangle a worm before their eyes with evil intent. And, generally, how do you fancy you can refute Protagoras' great maxim " that which appears to each, is?" It is literally true, so soon as we look more exactly. Each being in the universe from your God (if indeed He be *in* the universe) down to the humblest blackbeetle, has his own individual way of perceiving his experience, and when we say that several perceive the *same* things what we really mean is that they *act* in a corresponding manner towards them. When you and I both see "red," that *means* that we *agree* in the arranging of colours, but leaves inscrutable (and indeed *unmeaning*) the question whether your experience in seeing "red" is the same as mine.

'And this agreement is both difficult, partial, and derivative. It is the fruit of much effort and of a long struggle, and not an original endowment. It has had to be carried to a certain pitch in order that it might be possible for men to live together at all. It has grown because it was useful and advantageous and those who could manage to perceive things in *practically the same* way prospered at the expense of those who could not. Thus the objectivity of our perceptions is essentially *practical* and *useful* and *teleological*. How then can you venture to ascribe to the gods, with whom you do not live, the perceptions which have come to exist as "the same" for your senses, only in order that you might be able to live with your fellow-creatures?'

'Even though our senses are different may we not perceive by their means the divine order of the same universe which higher beings perceive by such modes of cognition as are worthy of them?'

'Really, Aristotle, it astonishes me that you, living in

a more real world, should still cling to the independently objective reality of the world you have now quitted for more than 2000 years. Do you perceive it now?'

'No, but I did, and it may still be a part of the world which I no longer perceive.'

'Where then is it with reference to your present world? Is it north, south, east, or west? Or is it not in the same space with it at all?'

'Still it is in space. And I still perceive a world.'

'So does every one who dreams. Your perceiving it, therefore, is no proof that it is ultimately real. And if you had entirely forgotten what you experienced formerly, would you even be able to assert that it once was real *for you*? Would not its reality have become like unto the reality of a forgotten dream? How can you venture, then, to attribute to all beings perception of one and the same world?'

'Perhaps I was mistaken about the world in which I then lived. But this present world at least is real, and seems to me fair enough to be worthy of being perceived even by the gods.'

'It is real no doubt for you, and for me also, *while I am in it*. But you may remember that what started the argument was the difficulty I had in convincing the denizens of your former world of the superior reality of this in which we now are. And besides, how do you know that beings still higher than you, if you do not resent my mentioning such, may not enjoy the contemplation of worlds vastly more perfect even than yours?'

'Still this process cannot go on to infinity. You must at last conceive a world of ultimate reality, the contemplation of which by the supreme being would be absolute truth.'

'No doubt; you are speaking of what Plato would call the world of Ideas. But still that does not affect the argument. The world and the truth and the good we were discussing are those *relative to us*.'

'I see that I was wrong in basing my argument for absolute truth on the perceptions of the senses. But of the eternal truths of mathematics and the like one may surely affirm that they necessarily exist for all intelligences?'

'Even this is more than I can grant you.'

'How so?'

'They seem to me to be also relative to us; nay, human institutions of the plainest kind.'

'Is it not self-evident and absolutely certain that the straight line is the shortest between two points?'

'That is *our* definition of distance. It will do in the sense in which you use it, if I may add, "for one living in a spatial world which behaves like ours, and apparently yours, once he has succeeded in postulating a system of geometry which suits his world."'

'I really do not understand you.'

'I fear I have not the space to explain myself, and to show you the practical aim of our assumptions concerning "Space," even if I dared to discuss the foundations of geometry in the presence of Plato. But it really does not affect my point. What I desire to maintain is that the eternal truths are at bottom postulates, demands we make upon our experience because we need them in order that it may become a cosmos fit to live in.'

'But I do not find myself postulating them at all. They are plainly self-evident and axiomatic.'

'That is only because your axioms are postulates so ancient and so firmly rooted that no one now thinks of disputing them.'

'Your doctrine seems as monstrous as it is unfamiliar.'

'I can neither help that nor establish it fully at this juncture. Perhaps, if the gods are willing, I shall find another occasion[1] to expound to you the proofs of this doctrine, and even, if the gods are gracious, to convince you. For it seems to me that in a manner you already admit the principle of my doctrine.'

'It would greatly surprise me if I did.'

'You contend, do you not, that concerning ethical matters it is impossible to have the right opinion without,

[1] See *Axioms as Postulates*.

at the same time or before, having the right habit of action, so that, as Roger Ascham has said, "ill-doings breed ill-thinkings, and of corrupted manners spring perverted judgments"?'

'And do I not contend rightly?'

'I am not denying that your view is right, though perhaps you over-state the impossibility of separating ethical theory from ethical practice. What I should like you to see, however, is that this same doctrine may be extended also to speculative matters. Why should we not contend that the true meaning and right understanding of theoretical principles also appears only to him who is proposing to use them practically? Can we not say that the Scythian was both prudent and wise who would not grant that 2 and 2 made 4 until he knew what *use* was to be made of the admission? Just as the wicked man destroys his intellectual insight into ethical truth by his action,[1] so the mere theorist destroys his insight and understanding of "theoretical" truth by refusing to use that truth and to apply it practically, failing to see that, both in origin and intention, it is a mass of thoroughly practical devices to enable us to live better.'

'I cannot admit that the two cases are at all parallel. In practical matters indeed I rightly hold that action and insight are so conjoined as not to admit of separation, but to extend this doctrine to the apprehension of theoretic truth would lead to many absurdities.'

'For instance?'

'Well, for one thing, you would have to go into training for the attainment of philosophic insight after the fashion of an Indian Gymnosophist whom I once met in Asia and who wished to convert me to the pernicious doctrine that all things were one.'

'How did he propose to effect this?'

'Well, in the first place he declared that truths could not be implanted in the soul by argument, but must grow out of its essence by its own action. So he refused to give any rational account of his opinions, but told me

[1] Cp. *Eth. Nic.* vi. 5. 6, vi. 12. 10, vii. 8. 4.

that if I submitted to his discipline, I should infallibly come to see for myself what he knew to be true. I asked him how, and was amused to find that he wanted me to sit in the sun all day in a stiff and upright posture, breathing in a peculiar way, stopping the right nostril with the thumb, and then slowly drawing in the breath through the left, and breathing it out through the right. By doing this and ejaculating the sacred word "*Om*" ten thousand times daily, he assured me I should become a god, nay, greater than all gods. I asked him how soon this fate was likely to befall me, if I tried. He thought enlightenment might come to me in one year, or ten, or more. It all depended on me. I replied that even if I failed to get a sunstroke I should be more likely to become an idiot than a god, but that I should already be one if I tried anything so silly. You, however, seem to me to be committing yourself to the same absurdity when you try to extend to contemplation the method which is appropriate only to action.'

'But that, Aristotle, is just the point to be proved. My contention is that Pragmatism extends to the acquisition of theoretical principles a method as appropriate to them as to practice. As for Gymnosophistic, I think that your Indian friend's method was really quite different. For though he professed to reach truth by training, there was no rational connexion between the truths he aimed at and the methods he advocated, which indeed could only produce self-deception. In moral matters, on the other hand, it is, as you say, necessary to dispose the mind for the perception of truth by appropriate action. If we declined to do this we should not start with a mind free from bias and impartially open to every belief—for that is impossible—but with one biassed by different action in a different direction. So that really the training you demand is only what is needed to clear away the antimoral prejudices to which our character would otherwise predispose us. Is this not so?'

'Certainly; you speak well so far.'

'Thank you. May I point out next that the method

of Pragmatism is precisely the same in theoretic as in practical matters? In neither can the truth or falsehood of a conception be decided in the abstract and without experience of the manner of its working. It gets its real *meaning* only in, from, and by, its use: apart from its use the meaning of any "truth" remains potential. And you can use it only if you desire to use it. And the desire to use it can only arise if it makes a difference to you whether or not you conceive it, and, if so, how. You must, therefore, desire, or, as I should say, postulate it, if you are to have it at all. If, on the other hand, your practical experience suggests to you that a certain conception would be useful, *if it were true*, you will reasonably give it a trial to see whether it is not "true," and if thus you discover it and find that you can work with it, you will certainly call it "true" and believe that it *is* "true," and has been so from all eternity, and all this the more confidently and profoundly, the more extensively useful it appears. Thus it is by hypothetically postulating what we desire to be true because we expect it to be useful, and accepting it as true if we can in any way render it useful, that we seem to me manifestly to come by our principles. Nor do I see how we could really come by them in any other way, or that we should be prudent if we admitted their claims to truth on any other ground.'

'Might they not be self-evident?'

'Self-evidence only seems an accident of our state of mind and in no way a complete guarantee of truth. To none do so many things seem so strongly self-evident as to the insane. Much that was false has been accepted as self-evident and no doubt still is. Its self-evidence only means that we have *ceased* to question a principle, or not yet *begun* to do so.'

'And can you not see that there are intrinsically necessary truths?'

'Not a bit. Unless by necessary you mean needful, an intrinsic necessity seems to me a contradiction. Necessity is always dependence, and so hypothetical.'

'You blaspheme horribly against the highest beings in the universe, the Deity and the Triangle!'

'Even though you should threaten to impale me on the acutest angle of the most acute-angled specimen of the latter you can find in your world of "necessary matter" (μὴ ἐνδεχομένων ἄλλως ἔχειν), I should not refrain from speaking thus. For I want you to see the exact point of my doctrine, and where it diverges from your own.'

'Of course—I see that. If you can prove your derivation of the Axioms and show that the necessary is only the needful, the speculative reason must say a long farewell to its independence.'

'Perhaps it will be none the worse for that.'

At this point Plato interposed a question.

'Have I understood you rightly, most astonishing young man, to affirm that theoretic truth was wholly derivative and subservient to practical purposes?'

'You have.'

'In that case would you not have to regard theoretic falsehood as, in the last resort, practical uselessness?'

'You are very nearly right, Plato; the practical uselessness of the theoretic "truth" which turns out to be false is what convinces us. I am glad I have made my point so clear to you.'

'And would you contend generally that the "useless" and the "false" were not two things but one, doubly named?'

'Not quite. For the useless is not always dismissed as "false." It may also be rejected as "unreal," as is done by those who, deeming dreams to be useless, account them *unreal*. And perhaps it might be most accurate to call the "useless" "unmeaning" rather than "false." But that hardly matters, for the unmeaning will be called "false" or "unreal" as suits our purpose.'

'It seems however that you do *not* say that *the false is useless*?'

'Not until you see that when you can call it false you must *already* have discovered the limits of its use.

And certainly I would not deprive you, Plato, of all men of your "*noble lies.*"[1]

'Nor would you say that the *useful* and the *true* were quite the same?'

'Not, except in the ideal state, in which no use could be found but for the whole truth, and all were too reasonable and too well educated to desire to pursue seeming "truths" which were useless and therefore to be judged false. But might we not ask Aristotle to tell us all that logically follows from the two propositions which I am maintaining, viz. that *whatever is true is useful* and that *whatever is useless is false?*'

'Yes. I think you could assist us greatly, Aristotle, by doing this.'

'I shall do so with the greatest pleasure, that, to wit, of logical contemplation. If *whatever is true is useful* it follows that (1) *nothing true is useless,* and (2) that *nothing useless is true,* that (3) *whatever is useless is false,* that (4) *some things useful are true,* and (5) *not false,* while (6) *some things false are useless* and (7) *not useful.* But since your second proposition that *whatever is useless is false,* is the third of those which follow from your first, that *whatever is true is useful,* being indeed its "obverted contra-positive," it is clear that in this also all the others are implied.'

'What a thing it is to be a formal logician and conversant with the forms of immediate inference! I myself have never been able to break myself of the habit of trying to convert an universal affirmative simply, and I suppose I ought now to be able to guess how far you are from agreeing with a statement which I found lately in a book by one of your Oxford sophists,[2] who seemed to be discussing much the same questions, that "the false is the same as the theoretically untenable"? *You* would rather say that it was "the same as the practically untenable"?'

'Yes, the false is that which *fails* us, and causes us to fail. For I would go on to say that the theoretically

---

[1] *Republic,* 414 C.
[2] Bradley, *Appearance and Reality,* p. 155.

untenable always turns out to be so called because it is practically untenable.'

'The sophist whom, with difficulty, I read seemed to see no way from the one to the other.'

'I don't suppose he wished to. It would have upset his whole philosophy, and you know how ready philosophers are to declare inexplicable and not to be grasped by man whatever "difficulty" reveals the errors into which they have plunged.'

'Yes, there is no Tartaros to which they would not willingly descend rather than confess that they have started on the wrong track. But even you have asserted the existence of a better way rather than shown it to us.'

'I must confess, Plato, that much as I should have wished to show you that my way is both practical and practicable I have not had the time to do this. But if I had, I feel sure that I could do so.'

'Say on; there is no limit but life itself to the search for Truth.'

'That is all very well for *you*, whose abode has been in these pleasant places for so long, and to whom, it seems, there comes neither death nor change. But *I* have to go back.'

'To your pupils?'

'Yes, and already I feel the premonitory heaviness in my feet. It will slowly creep upwards, and when it reaches the head I shall go to sleep and wake again in another world far from you.'

'I am sorry; though it will interest us to see how you vanish. But before you pass away, will you not, seeing that all truth you say is practical, tell us what in this case is the practical application of the "truths" you have championed?'

'With the greatest pleasure, Plato, that is what I was coming back to. They form my excellent excuse for neglecting to tell men about your ideas.'

'I do not quite see how.'

'Why, so long as my knowledge of your world is

useless to them, it is for them, literally and in the completest way, false!'

'But surely both they and you must admit that there is much useless knowledge?'

'There is much, of course, which is so called, and actually is useless for certain purposes, but nothing which can be so for all. Much that is "useless" is so because certain persons refuse to use it or are unable to do so. Pearls are useless to swine, and, as Herakleitos said, gold to asses. And so neither ass nor hog could truly call them precious. Or, again, often what is called useless is that which is *indirectly* useful. It is useful as *logically completing* a system of knowledge which is useful in other parts and as a whole. Or perhaps in some cases the use is prospective and has not yet been discovered. A great deal of mathematics would be in this position. But if no use could be found for mathematics, they would sink into the position of difficult *games*, and then their only use would be to amuse those who liked to play with them. Or lastly, there is a good deal of knowledge which is comparatively, or as Aristotle would say, accidentally, useless, because the time spent in acquiring it might be more usefully employed otherwise. For instance, you might count the hairs on Aristotle's head, and the knowledge might enable you to win a bet that their number was less than a myriad. But ordinarily such knowledge would be deemed useless, seeing that you might have been better employed.'

'But would these explanations cover all the facts?'

'Not perhaps quite all in our world, in which there is also seeming "useless knowledge," which is not really knowledge at all, but falsely so called; being as it were a parasitic growth upon the real and useful knowledge, or even a perversion thereof, a sort of harmless tumour or malignant cancer, which would not arise in a healthy state and should be extirpated wherever it appears.'

'Still it exists.'

'As evil exists; indeed it seems to be merely one aspect of the evil that exists.'

'Are you not now extending your explanations so far that your paradox is in danger of becoming a truism? Can you any longer give me an instance of really useless knowledge?'

'Of course not, Plato, seeing that my contention is that whatever is truly knowledge is useful, and whatever is not useful is not truly knowledge, while in proportion as any alleged knowledge is seen to be useless it is in danger of being declared false! The only illustration I can give, therefore, is of knowledge falsely so-called, which is thought to be useful, but is really useless, and therefore false or, if you prefer, unmeaning.'

'Even of that we should like an example.'

'I see, Plato, that you are willing to embroil me with most of the philosophers in my world. For if I am to speak what is in my mind, I must say that knowledge of the Absolute or, what comes to the same, of the Unknowable, seems to me to be of the kind you require. Aristotle, no doubt, might speak similarly of your own Idea of the Good.'

'Oh, but I intended it to be supremely useful both in knowledge and in action.'

'No doubt you did, but because you were not able to make this plain, Aristotle would not admit it to be true.'

'We had better let bygones be bygones.'

'Very well; let me in that case give you another example, which now concerns us nearly, of knowledge which seems false, because it seems useless. I mean knowledge about the world in which we now are, regarded with the eyes of those whom in a little while I shall no longer dare to call benighted dwellers in the Cave. Until we can make our world useful to them, it is false: I am a liar and you are the unreal figments of my creative imagination.'

'You quite alarm me. Can you not devise a way, then, whereby we might prove ourselves useful, and so existent, to your friends?'

'Certainly. Could you not appear at a meeting of

the Society for Psychical Research and deliver a lecture, in your beautiful Attic, on the immortality of the soul? That would be very useful; it might induce some few really to concern themselves with what is to befall them after death, and lead them perhaps to amend their lives. I know the Secretary of the Society quite well, and I think we could arrange a good meeting for you!'

'Εὐφήμει ὤνθρωπε. I could not think of such a thing: it would be too degrading. Besides, to tell you the truth, I have long ceased to feel any practical interest in the generality of men and their world. I would do something for you, but *you* already *know* and do not need persuading. Can I not do something to benefit you personally, whether it was useful, and therefore convincing, to others or not?'

'I suppose, Plato, it is conceivable that you could, if you liked, but that it is very likely that you would not like.'

'I have already told you that I will do anything short of mixing myself up with a world like yours. I once tried it, soon after I came here, but I soon discovered that Herakleitos was right in thinking that souls retained their power of smell. Indeed, I suppose my nose must have become absurdly sensitive, for I was driven back by the stench of blood before I had got very far into its sphere. I simply could not go on.'

'I do not wonder. Things are as bad as ever in this respect, except that we have grown more hypocritical about our murders. But I can tell you how you could not only help me, but even persuade the others.'

'How?'

'By useful knowledge.'

'Of what?'

'Could you not by some divination predict to me what horses were about to win what races, or what stocks were going to rise or fall how far? Such knowledge would be most useful and therefore truest by the admission of all men: it would enable me to amass great riches, and if I were rich enough all would believe whatever I might choose to say. Money talks, as the saying is, and none dare doubt but that it speaks the truth. In this manner I might get men to credit the whole story of my visit to you. For my credit would then be practically limitless.'

'I suppose you are joking and do not seriously expect of me anything so atrocious. Besides, why should you attribute to me, or to any of those who have departed to higher spheres, any such capacity for knowing what goes on in the world we are glad to have abandoned?'

'I am sure I don't know; only that is what men commonly suppose about such matters. They think that there is far more education in death than ever there was in life, and that even the greatest fool, so soon as ever he is dead, may be expected to be *wise* enough to know all things, and *good* enough to place his knowledge at their disposal.'

'They seem to me as foolish as they are selfish.'

'No doubt; still there is that germ of truth about their action which we saw. Whatever knowledge cannot be rendered somehow useful cannot be esteemed real.'

'Alas, that it should be so!'

'I do not on the whole regret it, although I can see it must annoy you to be considered as part of the non-existent of which you always thought so meanly. But really I must be going, and return to my Cave to convince, if possible, my fellow Troglodytes that you still live and think, and to impress on them, if I can, the importance of the "two-world problem," both for its own sake and as an illustration of the truth of Pragmatism.'

III

TRUTH [1]

ARGUMENT

Importance of the question *What is Truth?* when not asked rhetorically. I. Answers logical. (1) *Truth as agreement with reality.* Breaks down over the question of the knowledge of this agreement. (2) *Truth as systematic coherence.* Open to objections on the ground (1) that not all systems are true; (2) no system is true; (3) *many* systems are true; (4) truth even if system, is more than system. (1) How about systematic falsehood? (2) How about the imperfection of all actual systems? (3) How about the possibility of alternative systems? (4) How about systems not accepted as true because distasteful, and agreeable truth accepted without being systematic? Is this last argument an invalid appeal to psychology? No, for there is no 'pure' thought, and without psychological interest, etc., thought could neither progress nor be described. The psychological side of 'system' and 'coherence.' The necessity of immediate apprehension. Coherence feelings. The infinite regress in inference, if its immediacy be denied. Non-logical 'coherence.' Interest as the cement of coherence.

II. Answers psychological. Question as to (1) the psychical nature of the recognition of truth; (2) the objects to which this recognition is referred. (1) Truth as a form of value. Valuation at first random and individual. The ultimateness of the truth-valuation. Meaning of 'simple' and 'complex' for a pragmatist psychology. Truth-valuation 'simple' for logic.

III. (2) Objectivity of truth. 'Truth' and 'fact,' 'formal' as a means to 'material' truth. Subjective truth-valuations gradually organized (1) into subordination to individual, (2) into conformity with social ends. Usefulness as the principle of selection and criterion of truth. Need for the social recognition of truth. Special cases explained.

Of all philosophic questions that of Truth is perhaps the most hackneyed and unanswerable, when treated in the usual fashion. Now the usual fashion is to indulge either in ecstatic rhapsodies about the sacredness of

---

[1] This paper was written for this volume in order to complete, with *Axioms as Postulates* and the two essays which precede it, the outline of a pragmatist theory of knowledge. It will be observed that although these four papers do not of course claim to be exhaustive, they supplement one another.

Truth or in satirical derision of pretensions to have actually attained it. Both these procedures are assured beforehand of popular applause, but both render the question—*What is Truth?* one thoroughly rhetorical, and so perhaps the one is the proper answer to the other, and 'jesting Pilate' has a right to smile at the enthusiast. Nor have the philosophers done much to improve the situation. Ever since one of the noblest Plato's 'noble lies' proclaimed the doctrine that philosophers are lovers of truth, they have been quite willing to believe this, and have often found a people willing to be deceived politely willing to admit it. But perhaps because their passion, even when most genuine, was too distantly 'platonic,' this philosophic love of truth has hardly influenced perceptibly the course of things, and it might remain in doubt whether the Pragmatist philosopher also would care and dare to obtain some more substantial token of Truth's favours, were it not that the cheapest condemnation of his enterprise is to accuse him of a malicious joy in the destruction of Truth's very notion. It becomes incumbent on him therefore to refute such slanders, and to make clear how exactly he proposes to approach, and in what sense to derive, the notion of Truth.

This essay, therefore, must examine — I. the chief current definitions of Truth, which lay claim to logical validity, and to show that they are neither tenable, nor even intelligible, without reference to its psychological character; II. to describe that psychological character; and III. to explain how Pragmatism extends and alters the traditional conceptions on the subject.

I

Under the head of unpsychological, logical, or 'metaphysical' definitions may be instanced (1) the well-known dictum that truth consists in an 'agreement' or 'correspondence' of thought with its object, viz. reality. This however speedily leads to a hopeless *impasse*, once the question is raised—How are we to *know* whether or not our 'truth' 'corresponds' or 'agrees' with its real object? For to decide this question must we not be able to compare 'thought' and 'reality,' and to contemplate each as it is apart from the other? This however seems impossible. 'Thought' and 'Reality' cannot be got apart, and consequently the doctrine of their 'correspondence' has in the end no meaning. We are not aware of any reality except by its representation in our 'thought,' and *per contra*, the whole meaning of 'thought' resides ultimately in its reference to 'reality.' Again, even if it were assumed that somehow the independent reality mirrored itself in our thought, how should we discover whether or not this image was 'true,' *i.e.* agreed with the inaccessible reality it claimed to represent? This whole theory of truth therefore would seem futile. Having started from the radically untrue and unworkable assumption that 'truth' and 'fact,' 'thought' and 'reality,' are two things which have to be brought into relation, it is inevitably driven to the admission that no such relation can validly be established.

(2) A second logical definition looks at first more promising. It conceives truth as essentially systematic coherence, the 'true' being that which 'fits' into a 'system,' the 'false' that which is discrepant with it. This has the immense advantage of not creating the chasm between 'truth' and 'reality' in which the former definition was engulfed. Both these conceptions remain immanent in the process of knowledge, which is the construction of a system of 'reality' known to be 'true' by the coherence of its parts.

This account undoubtedly brings out important features in the nature of Truth, but as it stands, it is so incomplete and misleading that we can hardly follow the fashionable logic of the day in accepting it as all we can reasonably want to know about truth. In fact, when we discount the air of mystery, the obscure phraseology and the pompous magniloquence with which this doctrine is propounded, we shall find that all it comes to is that consistency is a mark of truth, and that when we find that we can maintain our conceptual interpretations of our experiences we come to treat them as realities. But to take the pronouncement that *truth is what fits in a system* as therefore final would be ludicrously rash, and to detect the limitations of the formula, it suffices to consider what may be said in favour of a string of counter-propositions, such as, *e.g.* (1) that not all 'systems' are true, (2) that no 'system' is 'true,' (3) that *many* systems are true, and (4) that even if all truth be systematic, it is not thereby adequately defined.

(1) To define truth as systematic is at once to raise the question of systematic falsehood. For false assumptions also manifestly tend to complete themselves in a system of inferences, to cohere together, to assimilate fresh facts, and to interpret them into conformity with themselves; in short, to assume all the logical features that are claimed for 'truth.' Does it not follow, therefore, that something more than systematic coherence is needed to determine truth? As *not all systems are true*, must we not suggest a further criterion to distinguish true from false?

The reply to this objection would have to take the form largely of an acceptance thereof. It would have to be admitted that in proportion as a falsehood or a lie became more systematic, its prospects of being accepted as true grew greater, that coherent lies did often win acceptance, and that a perfectly coherent lie (or error) would be tantamount to absolute truth. Lies can be called false only when they have been found out, and they are found out just because sooner or later they do not fit into our system of 'truth.' These systematic falsehoods are never quite systematic enough, and so the mimicry of truth by false systems, so far from subverting, rather confirms the doctrine that truth is systematic.

(2) This defence paves the way for a new assault. It would be adequate if we really had an indefeasible system of absolute truth by whose aid we might detect the inconsistencies of the pseudo-systems. But where

shall we find such truth? The bodies of 'truth' which *de facto* we acknowledge in our sciences are all partial systems, incomplete in themselves and discrepant with each other. If nothing short of absolute truth is perfectly systematic, and if all our systems are imperfect, is not all our 'truth' tainted with falsehood, and must it not be admitted that *no* (actual) '*systems*' *are* '*true*'? To talk of the mimicry of true by false systems is misleading; we should remember that, in addition to the protective mimicry of Bates, there exists another form ('Müllerian') in which the mimics co-operate to advertize the undesirable character they have in common. And so our systems may all be mimicking each other and may *all* be false.

Again, I think, the contention must in substance be admitted. The actual systems of our sciences are continually being convicted of error, and cannot seriously sustain their claim to the deference due only to the perfect system. Still, in extenuation one might urge (*a*) that ignorance is not necessarily error, nor incompleteness falsehood; (*b*) that experience would seem to show that even when coherent systems of interpretation have to be recast, what occurs is a transformation rather than a revolution, reinterpreting rather than destroying the 'truths' of the older order. Though, therefore, our 'systems' may not be wholly 'true,' we may conceive them as progressively approximating to the truth. And so (*c*) we must conceive them as in the end converging in one absolute and all-embracing system which alone would be strictly and indubitably 'true.'

(3) This last defence, however, still contains a hazardous assumption. Is the ideal of a complete system absolutely true really the straightforward, unambiguous notion which it seems? Are we entitled to argue from the unity of a concept to a similar unity of the concrete ways of exemplifying that concept, and so to assume that there is *one* system *and no more*, into which all truth must finally be fitted? The assumption is a seductive one, and underlies all monistic argument. But still it is an assumption, and begs some very puzzling questions. It assumes the

absolute determination of the universe, and it is only on this assumption that the inference is cogent, that 'truth' and 'reality' can only be completely construed in one single way. If we doubt, or deny, or demand proof of, this assumption, it may well be that *many* alternative systems may be 'true,' that 'reality' can be constructed in various ways by our varying efforts. The poet may have exaggerated in suggesting

> There are nine-and-sixty ways
> Of composing tribal lays,
> And every single one of them is right;

but still the more sincerely and completely we recognize the presence of human activity in the construction of 'truth' and 'reality,' the more clearly is their contingence suggested, and the less plausible does it seem that all these apparently arbitrary procedures are foredoomed to issue in the unveiling of one single, inevitable, and pre-existing 'system.' And if we doubt the legitimacy of this assumption, it follows at once that we cannot decide the measure of truth possessed by our actual bodies of knowledge by the mere test of systematic coherence. System A may need reinterpretation into A' to fit in with system B in the final system X; but we might as well or better reinterpret B into B', so that it would fit with A into the final system Y. In such a case are we to consider $A + B'$ or $A' + B$ as ultimately true?

In short, our logic as well as our metaphysic will have to concern itself more scrupulously and less perfunctorily with pluralistic possibilities.

(4) The last objection has brought out the fact that in assuming truth to be univocally determined by the conception of a 'system,' we went too far, and uncritically settled an important issue; we have now to face a criticism urging that the conception of a system in another direction does not go far enough to determine the nature of 'truth.' To win from us recognition as 'truth,' it is not enough to have a number of coherent judgments connected in a system. The 'system' to be true must also have *value*

in our eyes; the demand for 'system' is but part of a larger demand for a 'harmony' (actual or at least ideal) in our experience; it is not merely a matter of formal logical consistency, but also of emotional satisfaction. Hence no system is judged intellectually 'true' unless it is also a good deal more than this, and embraces and satisfies other than the abstractly intellectual aspects of experience. Thus no completely pessimistic system is ever judged completely 'true'; because it leaves unremoved and unresolved a sense of final discord in existence, it must ever stimulate anew to fresh efforts to overcome the discrepancy.[1] And conversely, it is by no means rare that what impresses us as conducive to harmony should be declared 'true' with little or no inquiry into its systematic coherence; indeed, it is probably such perception of their æsthetic self-evidence that often accounts for the adoption of the 'axiomatic' postulates that form first principles for knowledge.[2]

Thus the notion of 'system' proves doubly insufficient to define 'truth.' There is 'system' which is not valued as 'true,' and there is 'truth' which is so valuable that it need not be 'system.' We need 'system' only as a means to the higher notion of 'harmony,'[3] and where we can get the latter without the former, we can readily dispense with it.

The bulk, however, of logicians would in all probability strenuously object to this last argument. They would protest against the contamination of the question of 'truth' with questions of 'harmony' and 'valuation.' To refer to these is to overpass the bounds of logic, it is to trespass on the lower ground of psychology in which thought soon gets bogged in the reedy marshes of psychical fact. No good can come of such an intermixture of psychology with logic; our criterion of truth must be logical, our thought 'pure.' To talk of desire, interest, and feeling in a logical context is sheer madness, and to require logical theory to take account of their existence is to require it to adjust itself to the alogical.

[1] Cp. p. 200.   [2] Cp. *Axioms as Postulates*, § 48.   [3] Cp. p. 189.

If the defence of logical conventions is imprudent enough to take this ground, it can meet with nothing but disaster. For we shall at once have to defy the logician (1) to produce his 'pure' thought; (2) to account for the *movement* of thought by anything but an appeal to psychological motives, desire, feeling, interest, attention, will, etc.; (3) even to describe what he conceives to happen in strictly logical terms and without constant recourse to psychology.

The first two of these points will probably be conceded by all except belated Hegelians, but the third may need some illustration, the more so as we may draw from it also an independent (fifth) reason for denying the adequacy of the conception of truth as a system. I may point out therefore (5) that the ultimate terms of this (as of every other) definition of Truth are primarily psychological. If we take it that a 'system' means a body of coherent judgments, it needs but a little reflection to see that the logical evaluation of the 'system' presupposes its psychical existence, and the previous discussion of a number of psychological questions. (1) How, *e.g.* is the system recognized? (2) What is the nature, and what (3) the cause of its 'coherence'?

As to (1) it must surely be admitted that the logical system, to be a system for us, must be apprehended as such by us. Before, that is, an alleged 'truth' can be subjected to logical reflection, it has to be actually judged 'true'; its truth has to be *felt* before it is *understood*. Even, therefore, if logic could find and reserve for itself among our conscious processes such a thing as a process of 'pure' thought, a distinct mental act would yet be necessary for its apprehension, and this act would be psychological. In other words, no truth actually occurs without, in the first place, a psychic process; hence every truth as such is conditioned by a variety of psychological influences of the kind just mentioned.

The attempt, therefore, to represent 'thought' and *a fortiori* 'truth,' as wholly an affair of mediation between self-subsistent relations fails; at every step in its progress the mediate inference has to be immediately recognized, and the mediate 'knowledge-about' rests upon and returns into an immediate 'acquaintance-with.'[1] If, therefore, we call them respectively 'thought' and 'feeling,' we shall have to say that an 'element' of 'feeling' is bound up with and accompanies every act of 'thought,' and that no actual thought either is or can be conceived as 'pure.' Moreover the *movement* of thought would have in any case to be pronounced psychological. For the *selection* of the points in the self-subsistent system, between which the thought mediated, could not be ascribed to the intrinsic nature of the system, but only to the human interest which effects the selection.

Now if such be the state of the case, why on earth should it not be recognized in logic? Logic, I presume, in the very act of constituting norms for thought, presupposes the facts of thought, and if all actual thinking, good, bad, or indifferent, is impelled by interest, then interest *ipso facto* must become a factor in the logical analysis of thought. Why, then, should we insist on tortuous and complicated misdescriptions in terms of 'pure thought' of processes which are quite simple and intelligible when we consent to regard their full psychic nature?[2]

(2) *Mutatis mutandis*, what has been said of the logical system applies also to its 'coherence.' The coherence of judgments is a psychical fact which justifies, nay demands, psychological treatment. We find accordingly that it is (*a*) a matter of immediate apprehension. However we refine upon the logical concept of coherence, we can do nothing without observing that *de facto* judgments stick together. (*b*) We observe also certain coherence 'feelings,' whose strength is best measured by that of the feeling of (logical) necessity [3] which supervenes

---

[1] James, *Princ. of Psych.* i. p. 221.
[2] All the squabbles about the 'activity' or 'movement' of thought are due to perversities of this sort. Abstract thought is not active, or even alive; it does not exist. What is active is the thinking being with a certain psychical idiosyncrasy in consequence whereof he pursues his ends by various means, among which thinking is one. The nature of his thought everywhere refers to the purpose of his thinking.
[3] See *Personal Idealism*, p. 70, note.

when we try to part the 'coherent' judgments. Truths 'cohere' when they afford us the peculiar satisfaction of feeling that they 'belong together,' and that it is 'impossible' to separate them.[1]

And (c) if the cohesion of our thoughts, the belonging together, e.g. of A — B, were not immediately felt, but had to be established by mediate reasoning, it would follow that for any two truths to cohere a reason would have to be alleged why they should do so. But this would have to be another truth, and the attempt to 'understand' the immediate psychical cohesion would have to be renewed upon this, until it became obvious that an infinite process was implicit in the simplest inference.[2] Is it not much more reasonable to suppose that the cohesiveness is a psychical feature of the thinking itself? Finally (d) it would seem that not every sort of coherence in thought was regarded as logically important. The sort of coherences, e.g. which proceed from associations and lead to puns and plays upon words are relegated to that undignified limbo in which 'fallacies' are huddled together. But if not all coherence is logical, then the logician plainly needs a preliminary psychology to distinguish for him the kind of coherence which is his concern.

(3) If logic is to make the attempt to exclude psychology, the real cause of logical coherence must be pronounced to be extralogical. For it is nothing that can plausibly be represented [3] as inherent in the nature of thought *qua* thought, *i.e.* of thought as logicians abstractly

---

[1] It is never strictly impossible to reject a 'truth,' only in some cases the cost is excessive. To accept, *e.g.* a formal contradiction, stultifies the assumption that definite meanings exist, and should consequently debar us from the further use of thinking. This is too much, and as we have an alternative we usually prefer to reconsider the thought that has ended in a contradiction. Moreover, if we desire to entertain contradictory beliefs, there is a much easier way; we have merely to refuse to think them together. This indeed is what the great majority of men have always done.

[2] For an amusing illustration of this existence of an immediate apprehension in all mediate cogency see 'Lewis Carroll's' dialogue between Achilles and the Tortoise in *Mind*, N.S. No. 14, p. 278.

[3] I am willing to suppose it just possible to translate all the features of our thinking into a completely and consistently intellectualist phraseology. Philosophers have made endless attempts to do so, but none have succeeded, though it is I suppose a merit of Hegel's to have tried more elaborately, and to have failed more obscurely, than the rest. But the philosophers' insistence on reducing everything to pure thought is merely one of their professional prejudices.

conceive it. The cause of logical coherence may be summed up in the one word *interest*, and 'thought' which is not set in motion by interest does not issue in thinking at all. If, therefore, interest is to be tabooed, the whole theory of thought becomes a mere mass of useless machinery. For it is interest which starts, propels, sustains, and guides the 'movement' of our thought. It effects the necessary *selection* among the objects of our attention, accepting what is consonant, and rejecting what is discrepant, with our aim in thinking. If, then, the *purposiveness* of our thought is its central feature, psychologically, how can a logic set it aside without the grossest travesty? How fundamental is the fact of purposive interest in mental life is apparent from the cases where the normal control of consciousness is weakened or suspended. In sleepiness, reverie, dream, delirium, madness, etc., the purposive guidance of our thought grows lax—with the result that anarchy speedily overtakes the soul. Thoughts 'cross' the mind in the most 'illogical' way, and though our mental images may still continue to mimic meaning, they have ceased to mean anything coherent, and *pro tanto* logical thinking ceases to exist.

Thus in trying to understand the doctrine that truth is system we have been driven to the conclusion that in psychology, if anywhere, the clue to the mystery of truth must lie. For not only the definitions we have examined, but all others of the sort, must presuppose a psychological treatment of the psychical facts.[1]

II

Let us turn therefore to psychology. And to begin with let us formulate our psychological questions more precisely, as (1) *what is the psychical nature of the 'recognition' of 'truth'?* and (2) *to what part of our experience is this recognition attached?*

---

[1] The definition, *e.g.* that *truth is what we are forced to believe*, obviously implies psychological presuppositions as to the nature of 'belief' and 'necessity.' Other inadequate formulas are discussed in *Riddles of the Sphinx* (new ed.), pp. 83-9.

To the first question the summary answer would appear to be that *Truth is a form of Value*, and for this reason related to, and largely interchangeable with, our other modes of valuation. Now such valuation of our experience is a natural, and in the normal consciousness an almost uninterrupted, process. We are for ever judging things as 'true' and 'false,' 'good' and 'bad,' 'beautiful' and 'ugly,' 'pleasant' and 'unpleasant.' So continuous is this habit that existence without 'appreciation,' 'fact' without 'value,' is rather a figment of abstraction than a possible psychical experience. Now it is the *de facto* existence of this habit of valuation that gives rise to the normative sciences, and the function of logic as a normative science is to regulate and systematize our spontaneous valuations of 'true' and 'false.' For of course these logical valuations also will need regulation. At first they are bestowed by individuals pretty much at random. Anything may commend itself to anybody, as 'true,' nay, even as *the* truth,[1] and there are no guarantees that any man's valuations will be consistent with any other man's, or even with his own at other times. It is only as the needs of social intercourse and of consistent living grow more urgent that *de facto* 'truth' grows systematic and 'objective,' *i.e.* that there come to be truths which are (roughly) 'the same for all.' And finally, when most of the hard work has actually been done, the logician arises and 'reflects' on the genesis of 'truth,' which, in the end, he mostly misrepresents.

It is fairly plain, therefore, that the psychical fact of the existence of truth-valuation must be the starting-point for the psychological account of truth. Whether it should be called the foundation of the whole structure, or whether it should not be likened to the intrinsic nature of the bricks of which the structure is built up, seems to be a matter of the choice of metaphors. At any rate without this valuation there would be no 'truth' at all.

Of course, however, further psychological questions may be raised about it. We may ask, for instance,

[1] Cp. the inexhaustible variety of the 'systems' of religion and philosophy.

whether the fact that we judge things true and false is psychologically simple and ultimate, or whether we could not analyse out a common element of value from our various valuations. The answer to such questions might grow long and somewhat intricate, but we are hardly bound to go into them very deeply. It will suffice to point out that the 'simple' in psychology can only mean *what it is no use to analyse further*.[1] In other words, the distinction of 'simple' and 'complex' is always relative to the purpose of the inquiry. The 'elements' out of which the 'complex' states of mind are put together do not exist as psychic facts. In the actual experiencing, most states of consciousness form peculiar and recognizable wholes of experience, which feel 'simple.' Thus the taste of lemonade is emphatically *not* the taste of sugar plus the taste of lemon; though of course it is by squeezing the lemon and dissolving the sugar that we compose the lemonade and procure ourselves the taste. The experiences which really are 'complex' to feeling are comparatively rare, as *e.g.* when we feel the struggle of incompatible desires. On the other hand, when we reflect upon our experience, it is easy enough to represent it all as 'complex,' and to break it up into factors, which, we say, were present unobserved in the experience. But the justification of this procedure is that it enables us *to control the original experience*, and the factors which the 'analysis' arrives at are whatever aids this purpose. It is in no wise incumbent on us to go on making distinctions for their own sake and from inconsistent points of view, without aim and without end. Indeed the practice of aimless analysis, though it seems to form the chief delight of some philosophers, must be pronounced to be as such trivial, irrelevant, and invalid. We have a right therefore to declare 'simple' and ultimate what it is useless to treat as 'complex' for the purpose in hand, and in this instance we shall do well to avail ourselves of this

---

[1] I owe this definition to Prof. A. W. Moore's excellent account of the functional theory of knowledge in Locke in the *Chicago University Contributions to Philosophy*, vol. iii. p. 23.

right. For an analysis of the valuation 'true' and 'false,' whether or not it is possible for other purposes, would hardly be germane to logic.

III

We are however still sufficiently remote from what is ordinarily meant by 'truth.' For truth is conceived as something 'objective' and 'coherent,' while the truth-valuations we have recognized are individual claims, and so far seem chaotic. We may have found indeed the bricks out of which the temple of Truth is to be built, but as yet we have but a heap of bricks and nothing like a temple. Before, moreover, we can venture to erect the actual structure of objective Truth we must consider (*a*) the nature of the ground over which the truth-valuation is used, (*b*) the way in which our bricks cohere, *i.e.* the 'formal' nature of truth.

As to (*a*), the use of 'truth' lies in the valuation of 'fact': 'truth' is value in the apprehension of 'fact.' The objects of our contemplation when valued as 'true' become 'facts,' and 'facts' (or what we take to be such) become available for knowledge when valued as 'true.' The system of truth therefore is constructed by an interpretation of 'fact.' But this interpretation conforms to certain building laws, as it were. It consists in the use of concepts, and postulates the fundamental principles of thought.

Hence (*b*) these result in a certain formal character of truth. Every assertion formally claims to be 'true,' and causes endless confusion if this formal claim is identified with real, and even 'absolute,' truth. Again, whatever is harmonious ('consistent') with the fundamental assumptions of our conceptual interpretation of reality is in one sense 'true.' Any non-contradictory collocation of words has formal truth. But it is truth in a narrower sense than that required for 'material' truth.[1] In its fullest

---

[1] Cp. p. 98 note.

sense our truth must harmonize, not only with its own formal postulates but with our whole experience, and it may well be that the merely formal truth of consistency is never able to attain results sufficient for our wider purpose, and so is not fully 'true.' In point of fact it is useful within limits; to show that a 'truth' follows formally is not enough to prove it *de facto* true, but tests our premises; to show that it involves a formal flaw is not enough to invalidate it, but requires us to re-word it. For we would rather renounce our conclusion than the use of our formal principles.

After premising which we may return to our problem of constructing an objective truth out of subjective truth-valuations, of, as we saw, the most varied nature. Every one of these subjective valuations is the product of a psychological interest, and aims at the satisfaction of such an interest. But even in the individual there is much regulation of his subjective valuations, and some consolidation and subordination of interests under the main purposes of his life. Hence many of his initial interests will be suppressed, and the valuations which ministered to them will tend to be withdrawn, to be judged *useless* and, ultimately, *false*. In other words, there begins to operate among our subjective truth-valuations *the great Pragmatist principle of selection*, viz. that the 'useless' is not to be valued as 'true.' The 'use' appealed to and the 'truth' extracted by this criterion are wholly psychological and, at first, only individual. But not even of the individual is it true to say that his *feeling* a thing 'true' and *calling* it so *makes* it so. His 'intuitions,' guesses, and demands have to be *verified*, and are sifted by the manner of their working. Thus the question of the *sustaining* of the valuation after it is made is a distinct one; and is perhaps the one we mostly want to raise when we inquire: What is truth?

This question becomes more intricate, but also more interesting, when we take into account the social environment. For man is a social being, and truth indubitably is to a large extent a social product. For even though every truth may start in a minority of one, its hold upon existence is exceedingly precarious, unless it can contrive to get itself more extensively appreciated. Truth is one of the few things of which no one desires a monopoly. Those unfortunate enough to have acquired and retained an exclusive view of truth are usually secluded in prisons or asylums, unless their 'truth' is so harmlessly abstruse as not to lead to action, when they are sometimes styled philosophers! Truth, then, to be really safe, has to be more than an individual valuation; it has to win social recognition, to transform itself into a common property.

But how? It is by answering this question that Pragmatism claims to have made a real advance in our comprehension of truth. It contends that once more, only more signally and clearly than in the individual's case, it is the usefulness and efficiency of the propositions for which 'truth' is claimed that determines their social recognition. The use-criterion selects the individual truth-valuations, and constitutes thereby the objective truth which obtains social recognition. Hence in the fullest sense of Truth its definition must be pragmatic. Truth is the useful, efficient, workable, to which our practical experience tends to restrict our truth-valuations; if anything the reverse of this professes to be true, it is (sooner or later) detected and rejected.

As an account of Truth this is not so much a speculative theory as a description of plain fact. Whenever we observe a struggle between two rival theories of events we find that it is ultimately the greater conduciveness of the victor to our use and convenience that determines our preference and its consequent acceptance as true. Illustrations of this fact might be multiplied without limit, because in every advance of knowledge there is always something of a struggle between the old values which seemed true, and the new, which are better. The shocking cases occur when the convenience of a science is sacrificed to that of its practitioners, and doctrines continue to be taught, like formal logic, though they are known to be false. These exemplify an illegitimate use of the pragmatic principle. As a legitimate case we may allude to the well-known fact that what decided the rejection of the Ptolemaic epicycles in favour of the Copernican astronomy was not any sheer failure to represent celestial motions, but the growing cumbrousness of the assumptions and the growing difficulty of the calculations which its 'truth' involved. Similarly when I affirm (as I have now been doing for a good many years) that the metaphysical theory of the Absolute is *false*, I only mean that it is *useless*, that it simplifies nothing and complicates everything, and that its supposed advantages are one and all illusory. And I hope that as the pragmatist way of looking at things grows to be more familiar, more of my philosophic *confrères* will allow themselves to perceive these simple facts.

Of course there still remain complications of detail about the doctrine that social usefulness is an ultimate determinant of 'truth.' It is obvious, for example, that delicate questions may arise out of the fact that not only does what works receive social recognition, but also that what receives social recognition for this very reason largely works. Effete superstitions always try to sustain their 'truth' in this way. Again, there may be old-established mental industries which have outlived their usefulness, but have not yet been condemned as false. Other truths again are intrinsically of so individual a character that society accepts, *e.g.* Smith's statement that he has a headache, or that he dreamt a dream, on his *ipse dixit*. And while new truths are struggling for recognition, it may come about that much that is useful is thought to be useless and *vice versa*, and that the discrepancy between truth as it is supposed, and as it turns out, to be, grows great. Then, again, few societies are so severely organized with a sole view to efficiency as not to tolerate a considerable number of useless persons pursuing 'useless' knowledge, or useful knowledge in a useless way. Of course there is a certain amount of social pressure brought to bear upon such persons, but it is not enough to produce complete social agreement, and the elimination of all discrepant truth. Indeed, the toleration of socially useless, and even pernicious, 'truths,' which are individually entertained, seems on the whole to be increasing. This only shows that we can afford the luxury. In earlier times the thinkers of divergent views had short shrift granted them, and so, partly as the result of much past brutality, we now enjoy considerable bodies of 'objective' truth. And considering how much use philosophers have always made of this indulgence to differ from their fellows, it would be gracious if they at least gave honour where honour was due, and appreciated the labours of their ancestors, instead of attributing the whole credit of the conformity which exists to the initial constitution of the Absolute. Or if they insist on it, they might at least, in common fairness, attempt to tell us to whom the *discredit* should attach for the discrepancy and nonconformity, which exist no less and are by far more troublesome, even if they are too indolent to help in the practical work of science, which enlarges the limits of practical agreement and constitutes objective truth.

To sum up; the answer to the question—*What is Truth?*—to which our Pragmatism has conducted us, is this. As regards the psychical fact of the truth-valuation, Truth may be called an ultimate attitude and specific function of our intellectual activity. As regards the objects valued as 'true,' Truth is that manipulation of them which has after trial been adopted as useful, primarily for any human end, but ultimately for that perfect harmony of our whole life which forms our final aspiration.

IV

LOTZE'S MONISM [1]

ARGUMENT

Lotze's proof of Monism fails because (1) he was not entitled to postulate an underlying unity of things; (2) his argument for it is unsound and contradictory; (3) it has no scientific value, nor (4) can it be equated with God; nor (5), even when it has been, does it contribute anything to religious philosophy. (1) A Unity of the Universe or Absolute, on Lotze's own showing, is not needed to explain the interaction of things, and in its sole tenable form is insufficient to refute Pluralism. Lotze's own view of Substance refutes his Absolute. (2) Lotze not entitled to hypostasize his unity, nor is its immanent causality more intelligible than the transeunt causality of things. The argument from commensurability is invalid. Can commensurability be conceived as a fortuitous growth? (3) The Absolute guarantees neither causality, nor orderly succession, nor change, nor rationality, nor the existence of spiritual beings. (4) Its identification with *God* is assumed and not proved, and really impossible. (5) It aggravates the problem of Freedom, Change, and Evil. A real 'God' must be a moral being and provable *a posteriori* from the facts of our actual world. All the *a priori* proofs worthless because too wide.

LOTZE'S reputation as a sound and cautious thinker deservedly stands so high that any attempt to question the cogency of his argument is naturally received with suspicion, and needs to be fully and clearly established before its conclusions can win acceptance. As, however, no true view is in the long run strengthened by stifling the objections against it, and no false view can in the end be considered beneficial to the highest interests of mankind without thereby implying a profoundly pessimistic divorce between Truth and Goodness, I will venture to set forth my reasons for denying the success of Lotze's proof of Monism. And while I trust that my criticism

[1] Reprinted (with some additions) from *The Philosophical Review* of May 1896.

will always remain sensible of the extent of my obligations to the author criticized, I feel it would be useless to try to conceal on that account the extent of my divergence from him, and so will commence by stating the propositions which I hope to establish in the course of this paper.

They are as follows:

I. *That Lotze had not on his own principles any ground for seeking an underlying unity of things.*

II. *That his argument in reaching it is unsound, and conflicts with his own truer insight.*

III. *That, when reached, it throws no light on any of the problems it is supposed to explain.*

IV. *That it is not essentially connected with the religious conception of a God, nor with Lotze's treatment of that conception.*

V. *That even when it is so connected, it does not contribute anything of value to religious philosophy.*

I am aware that these propositions do not mince matters, and that I shall probably be called on to explain how a thinker of Lotze's eminence should have laid himself open to such sweeping censure. I may therefore fittingly preface my remarks by a theory of the way in which such lapses are psychologically explicable. The theory I would advance is in brief that the elaborate thoroughness and detail of Lotze's discussions occasionally avenge themselves on Lotze also, by generating a readiness finally to accept the first clue out of the labyrinth which offers itself, so that at the end of a chapter full of the subtlest and minutest criticism he sometimes consents to adopt views which certainly would not have passed muster at the beginning. A similar effect produced on the reader, who is loth to believe that the display of so much acumen should be followed by momentary relapses into untenable positions, relaxes his critical attention, and so possibly explains his acquiescence in Lotze's conclusions. I have sometimes felt that the process in question is well exhibited, *e.g.* in the chapter on Time in the *Metaphysics*, and that the disproportionate abruptness and the obscurity of its conclusion are similarly conditioned by a temporary lapse of the critical faculty.

The fullest statement of the grounds on which Lotze asserts the existence of an underlying unity of things is of course to be found in the sixth and seventh chapters of the *Metaphysics* (since the *Outlines of the Philosophy of Religion* merely accepts it as established in the *Metaphysics*), and though the argument is well known, it will not be inappropriate to sketch its course in so far as it bears on the present discussion. It will be remembered that Lotze is driven to postulate a unity of things by the metaphysical difficulties discovered in the conception of Causation, taken as the assertion that one thing influences another. The impossibility of explaining such transeunt causation compels to the inference that things are not really separate and independent, but embraced in a unity which is the medium in which they exist, and renders superfluous any further question as to how change in A passes over to become a change in B. Thus by means of this unity, which in the *Philosophy of Religion* is frankly called the Absolute, all *transeunt* becomes *immanent* action, and is held thereby to have been explained. The next step, which it requires careful reading to recognize as an advance at all, is to treat this unity as prior to, and more real than, the plurality of things it serves to connect. Accordingly (*Met.* § 70) it is hypostasized as 'the single truly existing substance,' and it is explained at length how the self-maintenance of the identical meaning of this Absolute may be conceived as producing the world of experience with its regular succession of phenomena. The discussion closes with a vigorous protest against recognizing 'things' as anything more than actions of the Absolute upon spiritual beings, which, by being centres of experience, are thereby rendered independent of the Absolute (§§ 97, 98).

It seems on the face of it that the argument ends in

something very like self-contradiction, inasmuch as it seems to assert that spiritual beings are *ipso facto* independent of the Absolute, after inferring the existence of that Absolute from the fact that 'things' (in which spiritual beings are presumably included, even if they do not constitute the whole class) could not be independent.[1] But it may be shown that verbal contradictions are not the only nor the most serious flaws to be found in Lotze's argument.

I. It is in the first place by no means clear that a unity of things must be specially provided to account for the fact that things act on one another. This necessity only exists if the problem it is to solve is a valid one, *i.e.* if the fact of interaction really requires explanation. If it does not, there is no basis for any further argument. And it may be plausibly contended that it does not.

For interaction is essential to the existence of the world in a more fundamental manner than even Lotze suggests. It is the condition of there being a world at all. Without it there could be no things, no plurality, and hence no assemblage of things, no world. For each of the possible constituents of a world, holding no sort of communication with any other, would remain shut up in itself. It is easy to illustrate this by showing that in every case in which we predicate the coexistence of several things, we imply that they, directly or indirectly, act on one another. *E.g.* in the case of the gravitation of all the bodies in the universe, the interaction is direct; in the case, *e.g.*, of Hamlet and the Chimera it takes place through the medium of a mind which connects them. But interaction in some way there must be, if coexistence is to be recognized. We may therefore confidently affirm that *without interaction there is no coexistence, and without coexistence there is no world.* The existence of

[1] Lotze generally prefers to use '*unabhängig*' when proving that there must be an all-embracing unity, '*selbständig*' when showing that the unity cannot embrace the conscious centres of experience. But he sometimes, as *e.g.* in *Outlines of Philosophy of Religion*, § 18, uses *selbständig* also in the first case, so that the verbal conflict is complete. The English translation obscures the point by rendering *selbständig* by 'self-dependent' in § 98 and by 'independent' in § 69.

F

interaction is just as primary a fact as the existence of the world itself, and the assertion that things act on one another is, in Kant's phrasing, an 'analytical' proposition, which merely expands what was already asserted in saying 'there is a world.'

But is this latter proposition one which requires explanation? Have we not learnt from Lotze himself[1] that it is an improper question to ask why there should be a world at all, since the given existence of the world is the basis and presupposition of all our questionings? That has always seemed to me one of the most luminous and valuable of Lotze's contributions to philosophy, and if it is an error to attempt to derive the existence of the world, it must be equally mistaken to derive the interaction of the world's elements. For coexistence and interaction have been shown to be equivalent.

The problem of interaction, therefore, disappears. Or rather, it is merged in that of the existence of a world in general of which it is a variant. And the existence of a world is not a problem for philosophy. There is not, then, on Lotze's principles any need to recognize any unity of things other than that which consists of their actual interactions. Having a plurality of interacting things given it, our thought may distinguish a unity implied in this, viz. the possibility of their interaction. But this unity is not more real or more valuable than the plurality, but less so. Nor can it be extolled as the ground of all reality. It is merely an ideal reflection of the actual. It does not assert more than that when a thing is actual it must be conceived as also possible, and in this case we are forbidden to pry into the questions how either the actuality or the possibility came about. So far from unity in this sense therefore being a royal road to Monism, it is the common ground which Monism shares with Pluralism; nay, it is the very fact which, by implying plurality, renders possible the metaphysical doctrine that plurality is the ultimate term of all real philosophic explanation.

[1] *E.g.*, *Met.* §§ 5 and 11, *Trans.* pp. 36, 46.

Similar conclusions may be extracted from Lotze's theory of substantiality. He tells us (§ 37, *Trans.* p. 100) that the notion of a kernel of substance is a useless superstition, that "it is not in virtue of a substance contained in them that things are, they are when they are able to produce an appearance of there being a substance in them." All this is excellent and most important. For it marks the abandonment of the unknowable substrate view of substance and the return to the older and truer conception of Aristotle, that a thing *is* what it *does*, that substance is *actuality* (ἐνέργεια) and not potentiality (δύναμις).[1] But presumably this declaration is applicable also to "the single truly existing substance" (*Trans.* § 70, p. 167), and we ought then to say 'it is not in virtue of a single substance underlying them that things are; they are when they are able to produce the appearance of there being such a substance.' In other words, we have no real right to infer that there is a substantial One underlying the interactions of the Many.[2] The unity which is involved as a conceptual possibility in the actual plurality is a unity in the Many and of the Many, and must not be hypostasized into anything transcendent or more truly existent. If it is, the problem of the relations of the One and the Many at once becomes insoluble, simply because by calling it existent we are compelled to construe its existence as analogous to that of the Many, which it cannot be if its function is to be that of uniting the Many. Is not then the necessity of the One as the world-ground an illusion of the same order as that of an underlying substance?[3]

It appears, then, that Lotze sets out to find a unity which, on his own showing, he did not need to find, and finds it in a way which conflicts with the implications of his own doctrine of the self-evidence of the world's existence and of his own view of substantiality.

II. In tracing the further development of Lotze's

---

[1] See the essay on *Activity and Substance*, §§ 1, 7.
[2] Cp. p. 224, note.
[3] Cp. *Riddles of the Sphinx*, ch. x.

conception of the Unity of Things, the point of capital importance is the process whereby the unity becomes hypostasized into a real existence superior to the plurality which it unites. To explain interaction there is only needed a unity in the Many, not a One creating and embracing the Many, a union, not a unit. And, as we have seen, this union does not need explanation. Lotze, however, having failed to see that in its general and abstract form the possibility of causation needs not to be deduced, has to reject transeunt action as inexplicable and to try to substitute immanent action in its place. We are accordingly told that the interactions of things become intelligible when regarded as the ways in which the Absolute changes its states. The question as to why it is intrinsically a more intelligible conception that a being should change its own states rather than those of another is not raised in this connexion. We are merely told that *de facto* we do not " scruple about accepting it as a given fact" (§ 68, *Trans.* p. 164). Yet in § 46 Lotze had clearly seen that while we treat "this immanent operation, which develops state out of state within one and the same essential being, as a matter of fact calling for no further effort of thought," "this operation in its turn remains completely incomprehensible in respect of the manner in which it comes about." "We acquiesce in the notion of immanent operation, not as though we had any insight into its genesis, but because we feel no hindrance to recognizing it without question as a given fact." Does not this pretty decisively admit that the superior intelligibility of immanent as compared with transeunt action is not logical but merely psychological, and due to the familiarity with it which we seem to find in our own inner experience?

But is it permissible to argue that because immanent action passes unchallenged in our own case it should therefore do so likewise in the case of the Absolute?

Perhaps we shall be able to decide this when we have analysed the reasons why it seems natural to us that one state of our consciousness should be followed by another.

Let us ask then why we should change. This question may be taken in two senses, according as the stress is laid on the 'we' or on the 'change.' In the first case the question will refer to the preservation of identity in immanent change, and can be answered only by an appeal to inner experience. That A_1, A_2, A_3 are all states of A is in our own case based on our feeling of our continuity and identity. *We* can change, because we are conscious beings with a feeling of our identity. But in so far as we have here the ground for our easy acceptance of the conception of immanent action, it is evidently inapplicable to the Absolute. We can neither feel the Absolute's continuity like our own, nor even infer it like other people's on the analogy of our own. For if the Absolute can be conceived as conscious at all, its consciousness would differ radically from ours in that it would be all-embracing, not merely in the sense of having representations of all things within it, but in the sense of actually *being and feeling* the inner and unique continuity of each thing.

If, secondly, we ask why we *change*, instead of remaining as we are, our common reason seems unhesitatingly to answer, either because we are stimulated from without, or because our psychical condition is disequilibrated, is one of unsatisfied desire, so that we long to change it. In neither case do we consider ourselves subject to unprovoked and capricious changes. In the first case, immanent change in ourselves distinctly presupposes transeunt action upon us from without and consists only of our self-maintenance against such action. In the second case there is presupposed a defect of nature which puts a good we desire beyond our reach. But in the Absolute immanent change can be explained in neither of these ways. There is nothing outside it to stimulate it to self-maintenance. Nor can we not rashly ascribe to an Absolute which is to have any religious value an essential want or defect in its nature. The very considerations, therefore, that render immanent action intelligible in our own case are utterly unthinkable in the Absolute's; the very reasons which render it natural that we should change render it very unreasonable that the Absolute should. If it does change, both the fact and the manner of that change must remain wholly inexplicable facts. And if transeunt action be a mystery, immanent action in the Absolute is not only as great a mystery, but, in addition, comes very near to being an absurdity.

Taking next the argument from commensurability (*Met.* § 69), I cannot see either that it validly leads to any conclusion at all, or to the conclusion Lotze desires. It argues from the fact that all things are comparable or commensurable to a ground of this commensurability. If all things had been quite incommensurable, like, *e.g.*, sweet and red, there would have been no principle of connexion between them. There would have been no reason to expect the consequence F from the relation of two incommensurables A and B, rather than any other. For that relation would have been the same as that of A to M or B to N or M to N. Hence there would be no reason for any definite connexion whatever. Commensurability, therefore, being a fact, its origin from a single root in the permanent immanence of the elements of the world in one being is rendered probable.

Now this argument seems to lack cogency. Its very statement seems defective, and involves an 'undistributed middle' in arguing from the common incommensurability of the relation of A to B and of M to N to their identity, in spite of the fact that incommensurables may be very various. And even if we overlooked this, the logical inference from the supposition that every pair of the world's elements stood in the same relation would seem to be not to a world of a chaotic and infinite variety, but to one of eternal monotony, in which whatever combination of elements was tried the same consequence always ensued!

Nor, looking at the matter more broadly, can I see that commensurability proves anything. In a very general sense it must, of course, be granted; for if the elements of a proposed universe had turned out to be absolutely incommensurable, no world could have resulted. There cannot, therefore, be any things strictly incommensurable in the world,—even red, sweet, and loud are comparable at least as sensations,—and it is mere tautology to say that the elements forming a world must have been commensurable to form a world. Nor does this carry us beyond the possibility of interaction which we saw was implied in actual plurality.

Moreover, it would seem that by arguing from the existence of commensurability to a source of commensurability Lotze rendered his argument obnoxious to an objection which he elsewhere admits to be valid. The course of his argument here runs parallel to that of the old teleological argument, which has been so successfully challenged by Darwinism.[1] The teleological argument in biology proceeded from the given existence of adaptation in structure to an intelligent source of that adaptation —*i.e.* it argued from an adaptation to an adapter. But Darwinism seemed to show that the same result might occur without supposing any original and pre-existent fitness of structure, merely by the survival of better adapted structures. As against this objection Lotze admits that the old teleology loses its demonstrative force : he admits (*Phil. of Religion*, § 11 s. f.) that the completely automatic origin even of the most perfectly adapted system is not impossible, but only improbable, and that it is not unthinkable (*ibid.* § 12 s. f.) that an original Chaos should develop itself into a purposively ordered nature.

But if so, a logical extension of the same argument would seem to be fatal to Lotze's position here. Why should not the initial commensurability of the elements of the world itself have arisen by a process of natural selection similar to that which has guided its subsequent development? Given the necessary conditions, and the argument seems to work equally well. Just as in the biological field it presupposed the possibility of indefinite variation in all directions, so here in ontology it might, it seems, suppose an indefinite multitude of elements of

[1] See, however, the essay on *Darwinism and Design*.

possible worlds, some commensurable, the immensely greater number not. If so, it would be possible to conceive the world as constituting itself out of a fortuitous concourse of the atoms which happened to be congruous or commensurable, while those which were not would simply stay out, and appear in the actual results as little as the countless variations which did not survive. In both cases the essence of the argument would be the same, and consist in destroying the unique peculiarity of the actual result by regarding it as one out of an indefinite number of possible results. Against the atheism thus implicit in the Darwinian method Lotze's argument seems to afford no adequate protection. He cannot show that the inference he draws to an underlying unity of the world is the only one conceivable. The supposed origin of a commensurable world out of an indefinite number of commensurable and incommensurable elements is *thinkable*.

Whether, to be sure, it is also *tenable* is another question, which, personally, I would answer by a strenuous negative. For if the immense majority of things were really incommensurable with us and our world, they would be unknowable. Hence we could have no positive ground for affirming their existence. And we have no right to affirm unknowables merely for the sake of discrediting the known. Hence this bare possibility could not, to my mind, be actually propounded as an explanation of the order of nature, nor held to detract from the purposiveness we actually find there. But this protest does not help Lotze; the bare possibility of thinking such a process is enough to set aside his contention that his own solution is alone conceivable.[1] His argument moved wholly in the region of abstract metaphysics, and as an abstract possibility the Darwinian plea seems just as sound. We may not have the right to apply it to our actual world, but Lotze's argument is in no better case.

Altogether, then, it would seem as if 'not proven' was the most lenient verdict that could be passed on Lotze's derivation of the Unity of Things.

[1] Cp. *Microc.* ii. p. 598.

III. But what shall we say of the metaphysical value of this conception in the explanation of things?

(1) It has already been shown that it does nothing to solve the problem of Causation and to relieve the difficulty Lotze discovers in the action of things on one another.

(2) Does it explain, then, the orderly succession of events? Lotze labours hard to show this. He regards the changes of the world as being so ordered by the Absolute as to preserve at each moment the unchanging self-identity of the Absolute, the equation $M = M$, and to give "a new identical expression of the same meaning," in a harmony which is "not pre-established, but which at each moment reproduces itself through the power of the one existence." This hypothetical meaning of the Absolute has to explain all the peculiarities about the succession of events which Lotze finds in the world and all those he wishes to find. Nor, obviously, is it possible to gainsay him so long as that meaning is admitted to be inscrutable. One can protest only that an inscrutable meaning is no better than none at all. But for all that I would contend that the introduction of the Absolute had made events not easier to understand but harder. At first indeed it might seem, as Lotze argues (*Met.* § 72), that when one thing in the world changes, the rest must maintain the identical meaning of the world by counterbalancing changes. But what if we raise the question why anything should change at all?

(3) It will appear, I think, that no rational case is made out for the existence of change at all. The conception of the Absolute in itself contains no suggestion of change. Its sole aim, apparently, is to keep on affirming its own identity in an eternal tautology, and why it should pretend to change in doing this remains unintelligible. The only thing we know about it, viz. the unchanging identity of the meaning it preserves in the world, distinctly suggests an equal immutability for the expression of that meaning. Thus the fact of change has to be accepted as empirically characteristic of the Absolute, but it is rendered more unintelligible by the

assertion that all the changing aspects of things always mean one and the same thing.

(4) The belief that the world has a meaning, that the riddle of life has an answer, has always been the common inspiration of religious, philosophic, and scientific minds. To be disabused of it would plunge us into the deepest abyss of negation where scepticism fraternizes with pessimism. Hence it is at first reassuring to hear Lotze speaking so emphatically of the meaning of the universe as the supreme law which determines the succession of events. It is not until one attempts to work out the conception in connexion with his Absolute, that one is regretfully forced to the conclusion that the meaning of the universe is really unmeaning.

Lotze tells us that the meaning of the Absolute has to be maintained against the changes set up, we know not how, in its parts. That is the reason why B follows on A in orderly succession. But how can any action of the parts of the whole conceivably imperil the identical meaning of the whole? They have not a $\pi o\hat{u}$ $\sigma\tau\hat{\omega}$ outside the universe whence they could break in upon its order and affect its meaning or value. And if these could be in any way jeopardized, why should not any means be as competent to re-establish the equation $M = M$ as any other? Why should not C or X or Y follow as effectively on A as B? Where there is absolute choice of means, unvarying order becomes inexplicable. One would expect rather an agreeably various or sportively miraculous succession of events. Thus the introduction of an Absolute, on which no laws are binding, because it makes them all, really leaves the order of the world at the mercy of a principle which for ever threatens to reduce it to Chaos.

Nay, more; neither the existences nor the changes of the world can have any meaning if they are absolutely dependent on the Absolute, and are merely instruments in the expression of its 'identical meaning.' That meaning may be expressed by one thing as well as by another, it may be preserved by one variation as surely as by another. Thus both events and existences lose all special significance and intrinsic relation to the supposed meaning. The same holds true of the past of the world with respect to its subsequent course. The caprice of the Absolute cannot be controlled even by its own past.

(5) The foregoing will have shown, I hope, that Lotze was not very successful in avoiding the besetting sin of all Monism, whenever it is sincerely scrutinized, viz. that of reducing the Many to mere phantoms, whose existence is otiose and impotent. But a disregard of the practical absurdities that might result from too rigid a theory was not one of Lotze's weaknesses, and so when we come to the last sections of his ontology we find him saving the significance of the Many by a *volte-face* which is assuredly more creditable to his heart than to his head. He recognizes that beings which are merely immanent in the Absolute have no *raison d'être*, and so denies the existence of *things*. Spiritual beings, on the other hand, in virtue of their consciousness, detach themselves from and step out of the Absolute; they stand as it were on their own feet and become independent members of the cosmos. I heartily agree; but I am at a loss how to reconcile this with the previous course of his argument. What use was there in emphasizing the one ground of all existence, if finally everybody that is anybody is to escape and 'detach' himself from the underlying unity of the Absolute? Doubtless Lotze's doctrine is here completely in accord with the facts, doubtless it is true, as Professor Pringle Pattison says, that a spiritual being preserves its own centre even in its dealings with the Deity; no doubt also Lotze's own doctrine required such quasi-independent spirits to provoke Providence by the freaks of their free will and to generate the necessary friction in order to make the Absolute's maintenance of its identical meaning something more than child's play; but how is the incomprehensible feat accomplished?

The points mentioned should, I believe, suffice to prove my contention that the Absolute is not a principle of explanation that has any scientific or philosophic value. It resolves no difficulties, it aggravates many, it creates some of an utterly insoluble character. And by undoing his own work in the case of conscious beings and insisting on detaching them from his Absolute, Lotze himself may be considered to have afforded practical confirmation of this view.

IV. It remains to discuss the identification of the Unity of Things with the Deity. In the *Outlines of the Philosophy of Religion* Lotze accepts the Unity of Things which renders interaction possible as the basis of the conception of God, thereby making his metaphysical argument his means of proving the existence of God. One might have expected him therefore to go on to develop the consequences of this conception and to show how they agreed with the religious notions on the subject. This is not, however, what Lotze actually does. He makes no attempt to show that the Unity of Things, as discovered by metaphysics, must be susceptible of the religious predicates, must be conceived as personal, holy, just, and wise, nor that these attributes may be empirically inferred from the manner in which the Absolute unites the universe. Instead of this, he contents himself with entitling his second chapter 'Further Determinations of the Absolute,' and then goes on to prove that God cannot rightly be conceived as other than spiritual and personal. Now against the contents of this chapter I have not a word to say; his argument in it seems to me most admirable and cogent. What I do wish to protest against is the way in which he shifts his ground, is the μετάβασις εἰς ἄλλο γένος which his method at this point involves. For instead of developing a metaphysical conception, he here passes over to a criticism of popular conceptions of and objections to the nature of the Deity, and these are in every case disposed of by arguments which have nothing to do with the Absolute's function of unifying the world. Thus the spirituality of God is proved by showing that materialism is inadequate and dualism sterile; His personality, by showing that while no analogy in our experience justifies conceptions like those of an unconscious reason or impersonal spirit, our own personality is so imperfect that perfect personality is capable of forming an ideal which can be attributed to the Deity. But what has all this to do with the Unity of Things? Such arguments are quite independent of his metaphysical monism, and are not brought into any logical connexion with it merely by calling the Unity of Things God. It would have been far more to the purpose to show how the Unity of Things could be personal and moral. But this is what no monist ever succeeds in doing.

I would contend, then, that just as the hypostasization of the Unity of Things was unnecessary in the *Metaphysics*, so its deification is unnecessary in the *Philosophy of Religion*. Not even for monotheistic religions is there any necessary transition from the assertion of one Absolute to that of one God. For the unity of the Godhead in monotheism is primarily directed against the disorders of polytheism, and intended to safeguard the unity of plan and operation in the Divine governance of the world; it cannot be equated with the unity of the Absolute, unless the conceptions of plan and guidance are applicable to the latter. But this is just what we have seen they are not: the Absolute could have no plan and could guide nothing; its unity therefore has no religious value.

The reason, then, for this hiatus in Lotze's argumentation is simply this, that an Absolute is not a God and that none of the Divine attributes can be extracted from it. Hence Lotze must perforce derive them from considerations of a different kind.

V. In the sequel, moreover, this derivation of the Deity from the metaphysical unity of things is for the most part ignored, and the interesting discussions in which Lotze elucidates the nature of the fundamental religious conceptions presuppose nothing but the traditional conceptions and historically given problems of religious philosophy. Throughout the whole of this most valuable part of Lotze's book (§§ 21-70) I cannot find that he expresses any opinion rendered logically necessary by his doctrine of the Absolute, while there seem to be several, *e.g.*, the defence of Free Will, which accord with it but badly. As already stated, Lotze cannot dispense with this conception in order to uphold the conception of a Divine governance, which re-establishes the 'identical meaning' of the world against the disturbances due to free actions. And it is in this way that he explains the fact that the world exhibits a succession of phases, all of which, we are required to believe, mean one and the same thing. But the reflection is obvious that these 'free' actions also are included in the Absolute, and that their existence is one of its given characteristics. Metaphysically, therefore, we have to say that the Absolute is subject to these uncaused perturbations, which exhibit its internal instability. It is this inner instability which is the ultimate ground for change, and the question which in the *Metaphysics* (§ 83) Lotze tried so hard to put aside, viz. as to the reason why the Absolute is in motion, returns with renewed force. Lotze had there contended that the motion must be accepted as a fact and its direction likewise. But can the *kind* of motion be similarly accepted? We may not in ordinary life require an explanation when we see a man walking in the usual fashion, but when we see him staggering along as though about to fall and only just preserving his equilibrium, we think that such a mode of progression requires an explanation, and probably put it down to alcohol. Yet this somewhat undignified simile, *si parva licet componere magnis*, exactly expresses the characteristic motion of the Absolute according to Lotze. The world is ever recovering the equilibrium which is constantly endangered; it maintains itself in a constant struggle against the consequences of its own inner instability. And what we call Evil is merely one of the incidents of the struggle. If then it were true that the motion of the world required no explanation, it would be equally true that the evil of the world required none. But this is not only a conclusion monstrous in itself, but one by no means accepted by Lotze. He admits that the problem of Evil is a real one, and only regrets the failure of all the solutions proffered. But of this more anon. At present I content myself with noting that though the admission of Free Will affords a logical ground for the conception of a Divine guidance and providence, it re-arouses scruples about the Absolute which had only with difficulty been quieted.

It is not until we come to § 71 that the Unity of Things intervenes again in Lotze's discussion, and then it intervenes with disastrous effect. For it is appealed to only to refute the attempt to account for the existence of Evil by the limitations of the divine activity by the original nature of the world's constituents. But, Lotze remarks, if so, it would be necessary to assume a second superior deity in order to account for the action of the first upon such a world. And if we admit that the Deity is to be identified with the unity which makes interaction possible, it must be admitted that his objection is quite sound. But with this rejection of a Deity who can have an intelligent purpose, and a need to guide the course of the world, just because he is not unlimited in the choice of his means, vanishes the last hope of solving the problem of Evil.

The magnitude of this problem and the futility of all the solutions he mentions is quite frankly confessed by Lotze both in *Philosophy of Religion* (§§ 70-74) and in the *Microcosm* (*Trans.* ii. pp. 716 ff.). He admits that pessimistic inferences might quite well be drawn from this failure of philosophy, and does not believe that pessimism can theoretically be refuted. But pessimism is merely a cheap and easy way of getting rid of the problem, and he himself prefers to cling to the belief in a solution he cannot see, and to persevere in a search which is nobler and more difficult. Thus in Lotze also knowledge finally has to take shelter with faith and to return dejected to the home whence it set out with such sanguine hopes of making clear the riddle of existence. Lotze's language is certainly frank enough, and if frankness were all that is needed his honest declaration of his insolvency might be condoned. But one has a right to expect that a philosopher whose arguments lead him into such manifest bankruptcy should be prompted thereby to re-examine and possibly to revise his premises; and this Lotze fails to do. The suspicion that the nature of the Absolute which he has identified with the Deity may have something to do with the lamentable failure of his attempts to account for Evil never seems to enter his mind. The conclusions of his philosophy may be in the most patent conflict with the facts, but so much the worse for the facts. We are bidden to have faith in the impossible, if necessary, and pessimism is waved aside with a sneer as being too easy and obvious.

Now that a writer ordinarily so sympathetic as Lotze should have acquiesced in so flimsy a theodicy shows, I think, the desperate straits to which he was reduced, and seriously detracts from the value of his religious philosophy. I am very far from denying that an element of faith must enter into our ultimate convictions about the world; for whoever admits the reality of Evil and the possibility of its elimination thereby declares his faith in an ideal which is not yet realized. But surely we have a right to demand that our intellect should only be required to believe in a solution which it does not see, not in one which it sees to be impossible. Now the nature of faith is of the latter sort on Lotze's theory, as we shall see and as he all but admits. It may be meritorious to attempt what is difficult, but it is mere folly to attempt the impossible. Very few, therefore, whether pessimists or otherwise, are likely to be attracted by Lotze's 'faith.' And his sneer at pessimism is a little ungenerous. Pessimism may be cheap and easy and obvious *intellectually*. That is an excellent reason for meeting it with the strongest, most comprehensible and obvious arguments we can,—to prevent simpler minds from falling into it. But pessimism is assuredly *not* a cheap and easy view to hold *emotionally*. The burden of most lives is so heavy that none can desire to crush themselves down utterly by dwelling on the futility and worthlessness of it all. No one, therefore, is willingly a pessimist: every one would fain believe in a more inspiring view. But all the encouragement Lotze gives is that pessimism is theoretically tenable and any other view is extremely difficult!

Yet he is quite right; that is all the encouragement he is able to give. He cannot account for the existence of Evil; he cannot deny that it conflicts utterly with his conception of God. For he has from the very first scorned the common philosophic device of calling God a power which has no moral attributes or preferences. His God is intended to be theistic and not a mere cloak for pantheism. Yet by identifying God with the Absolute he inevitably opens the way for this very kind of pantheism. Once equate God with the totality of existence, and no one can understand how there can be in the All an element which is alien to the All. All the phases of existence, therefore, are alike characteristic of the All. God is evil as well as good, or better still, non-moral and indifferent, manifesting himself in all things alike. But this conception, to which its premises irresistibly drive Lotze's argument, no less than every other form of Monism, is certainly neither the God of what is commonly understood as religion, nor can it do the work of one. It is as impotent as a practical power as it was sterile as a theoretical principle. Its sole value would seem to have been to have drawn attention to certain incompatibilities and inconsistencies in the existing conception of the Deity.

And the importance of this service should not lightly be disparaged. If Lotze's careful, candid, and yet sympathetic examination failed to clear away the incompatibilities alluded to, we may be sure that others will not succeed, and that it is time to consider whether the requirements both of religion and of philosophy may not be better met by a different conception of the Deity. We must not be tempted by the ease with which an (unmeaning) Absolute is arrived at to accept it in lieu of the more difficult demonstration of a real God. And I believe that a clearer conception of the Deity, more clearly differentiated from the All of things, could not fail also to be of the greatest practical value. At present the conception of the Deity is not clearly defined; it melts away

G

into mist at various points; it requires a certain 'atmosphere' to be perceived. But a God who requires an 'atmosphere' has to be kept at a certain distance by his worshippers, and so is conducive neither to intimacy of communion nor to robustness of faith. This, however, is a line of thought I must leave to theologians to work out.

The general philosophical conclusion which I would draw from Lotze's lack of success in defining the conception of God is that of the futility of the *a priori* proofs of God's existence. Their common weakness lies in their being far too abstract. They are in consequence applicable to the conception of a universe as such and not to our particular world. Thus the ontological proof argues that there must be a God from the fact that there is a world at all; the cosmological, from the fact of causation taken in the abstract: the physico-theological, even, is made to argue quite generally from order to a designer thereof. Lotze's proof from interaction is of an exactly similar character. It argues generally and abstractly from the existence of interaction to a ground of interaction. It is, in fact, a form of the ontological proof, since interaction is the presupposition of there being a world at all.

Now the flaw in all these arguments is the same. They fail because they attempt to prove too much. If they hold at all, they hold quite generally and are applicable to any sort of a world. In *any* world we could argue from its existence to a God, from its change to a First Cause, from its arrangement to a designer, from its interaction to a single ground of its possibility; the argument is in each case quite unaffected by the nature of the world about which it is used. It follows that the God derived by such an argument must similarly be catholic in his applicability and indifferent to the contents of the world. The best and the worst of thinkable worlds must alike have God for their cause and for the ground of their interaction. The inference from the world to God would be equally good, therefore, in

Heaven and in Hell. The deity, therefore, inferred by this mode of argumentation must be essentially indifferent to moral distinctions, and this is the ultimate reason why the attempt to ascribe moral attributes to him in the end invariably breaks down. In Lotze's case, *e.g.*, the world would just as much imply a God whether its interactions were perfectly harmonious or utterly discordant ; and God, therefore, cannot be conceived as a principle deciding which of these thinkable cases is to be realized.

Now all this is not at all what we wanted the proofs of God's existence to do. We did *not* want a proof which held good in all thinkable universes, but one which should hold in our actual given world, and give us an assurance that whatever might be the misfortunes of possible universes, there was in our actual world a power able and willing to direct its course. But this the 'proofs' haughtily declined to do ; they mocked us instead with characterless deities 'for application to any universe.' Yet there is not, at least in the case of the cosmological and physico-theological proofs, any reason why they should not be given a specific application. On the contrary, a much stronger argument can be made for assuming a cause and beginning of its motion for *our* existing order of things than for 'a universe' as such, for interpreting the actual order and development of *our* world by an intelligent purpose than a mere order in the abstract. Even the ontological proof, if we adopt Lotze's version of its real meaning (*Phil. of Religion*, § 6), may be given a more pointed reference by making it express the conviction that the totality of the True and the Good and the Beautiful must be provided with a home in *our* world.

Thus the objections to all the proofs may be obviated by making them proofs *a posteriori*, and basing them, not on the nature of existence in the abstract, but on the nature of our empirical world. The same might be done also with the argument from interaction : it might be claimed that the peculiar nature of the interaction of things was such that a single underlying existence might be inferred in our case, although in general a unity in the

Many was alone needed. And indeed Lotze comes very near at times to seeing that this was the proper method of proving the unity of things, as, *e.g.*, when (*Met.* §§ 85, 90) he insists that his Absolute is never actual as an abstract form which subsequently receives a content, but always has a perfectly determinate and concrete value. But if so, why did he use such perfectly abstract arguments in order to prove its existence? Why did he not derive the Absolute in its concreteness from the concrete facts in which it manifests itself? Had he done so, he would have disarmed most of the above criticism and would have closed the road to many a misconception and many a difficulty. It would have been needless to ask, *e.g.*, why the Absolute should be in motion, for in arriving at it we should have had to state the reason not only for the motion but also for its amount and direction. Again, it would have been superfluous to puzzle ourselves as to how the One united the Many; for it would have been as a definite mode of combining the Many that we should have found the One.

No doubt such methods of discovering first principles are less easy, less sweeping, and therefore less attractive; the philosopher moves more smoothly in a cloudland where he can manipulate abstractions which *seem* to assume whatever shape he wills. But the philosophic interpretation of the concrete experiences of life is far safer and, in the end, more satisfying. And whatever the defects of his own practice, it is to Lotze as much as to any one that we owe the conviction that even the most imposing castles which philosophers have builded in the air have had no other source than the experience of the actual whence to draw their materials and their inspiration.

V

NON-EUCLIDEAN GEOMETRY AND THE KANTIAN *A PRIORI*[1]

ARGUMENT

Importance of geometry as a type of philosophic method, and consequently of the metageometrical ideas. I. Fallacy of the *fourth-dimension analogy*. Non-Euclidean three dimensional 'spaces,' come with Euclidean under the *genus* of general geometry. They form coherent and thinkable systems analogous to Euclid's, but so far not useful because too complicated. II. Necessity of distinguishing between *perceptual* and *conceptual* spaces. Geometrical spaces all alike conceptual constructions, and the physical world not '*in*' any one of them. III. Philosophic importance of this. The 'certainty of geometry' not peculiar, but identical with the logical necessity of consistent assumptions elsewhere. The *real validity* of geometry empirical and = its usefulness when applied. Universality and necessity of geometrical judgments as results of postulation. Kant's account of space vitiated by his failure to observe the ambiguities of the term.

FROM the days of Pythagoras and Plato down to those of Kant and Herbart the mathematical sciences, and especially geometry, have played so important a part in the discussions of philosophers as models of method and patterns of certitude, that philosophy cannot but be extremely sensitive to any change or progress occurring in the views of mathematicians. Accordingly the philosophic world was considerably startled, not so many years ago, to hear that certain mathematicians and physicists had had the audacity to question the assumptions con-

---

[1] From the *Philosophical Review* of March 1896, since when the subject has not, of course, stood still. I am painfully aware that as an account of metageometry this paper is quite inadequate, but as students of philosophy are still obfuscated with the mystical mathematics of metaphysicians, and as the capital importance of the distinction of *perceptual* and *conceptual* space is still ignored, even so slight a treatment may retain some pedagogical value.

cerning the nature of Space, which had been consecrated by the tradition of 2000 years and set forth in the geometry of Euclid. The possibilities of non-Euclidean spaces, which were as yet necessarily ill-defined and ill-understood, promptly attracted the adherents of all views for which orthodox science appeared to have no room, and no notion seemed too fantastic to become credible, if not intelligible, in space of four or more dimensions. The mathematicians themselves, who were engaged in elaborating the new conceptions, were too busy or too uncertain of their ground to resist successfully this inundation of extravagance, and the consequent discredit into which the subject fell seems to have killed the general interest in it everywhere but in France. Meanwhile mathematicians proceeded quietly with the work of analysing the new conceptions and of testing them by deducing their consequences, and thereby reached a clearer consciousness of their import. The result has been that saner views have begun to prevail, and that the sensational features of the new geometry have been mitigated or eliminated. The question has become arguable without the opposing champions considering each other respectively unintelligible cranks or unimaginative stick-in-the-muds. Not but what the rhapsodical view still periodically finds expression in print,[1] but the tendency of the interesting exchange of opinions which has been going on for the last few years in the French philosophical and scientific journals between MM. Delbœuf, Renouvier, Poincaré, Calinon, Lechalas, De Broglie, etc., seems to me to be decidedly in the direction of agreement based upon a retreat from extreme and extravagant positions on either side. In other words, the blare of trumpets which announced and advertized the arrival of the new claimant to scientific recognition is over, the pachydermatous ears of the established conservatism have recovered from the shock, and preparations are being made to assign to the newcomer a definite place in the array of the sciences.

The time then seems to be becoming opportune for

[1] *E.g.*, *Monist*, iv. p. 483.

attempting to summarize some of the results of this controversy, with a view to (*a*) bringing out the most important points established by the new 'metageometry,' (*b*) considering what light they throw on the nature of Space, (*c*) estimating what changes will have to be made in the references to geometry which philosophers have been so addicted to making. It is indeed possible that the attempt is still premature, that the parties are still too bitter to be completely reconciled, that the subject is still too inchoate and chaotic for its full significance to be determined. In that case the present writer would console himself with the reflection that his efforts can at least do no harm, and may possibly even do good by inducing philosophers to revise their antiquated notions concerning the meaning of the conception of 'Space.'

I. I shall begin, therefore, by referring to a point which the metageometers do not seem to have satisfactorily established, and that is the value of the conception of a *fourth* dimension. I say advisedly 'of the conception,' for the actual existence, or even the possibility of imagining, a fourth dimension seems to have been practically given up. The chief value of the conception seems nowadays to be situated in the possibility of making symmetrical solids coincide by revolving them in a fourth dimension. But this seems a somewhat slender basis on which to found the conception of a fourth dimension, and the same end could apparently [1] also be achieved by means of the conception of a 'spherical' space. Here then, probably, is the reason why of late the fourth dimension has not been so prominent in the forefront of the battle, and why its place has, with a great advance in intelligibility, been taken by spherical and pseudo-spherical *three-dimensional* ' space.'

It is on rendering these latter thinkable that the non-Euclideans have concentrated their efforts, and, so far as I can judge, they have, in a large measure, been successful. It has been shown that Euclidean geometry may, nay, logically must, be regarded as a special case of general

[1] Cp. Delbœuf, *Rev. Phil.* xix. 4.

geometry, and as logically on a par with spherical and pseudo-spherical geometry. It is a species of a genus, and the differentia which constitutes it is the famous 'postulate of Euclid,' which Euclid postulated because he could not prove it, and which the failures of all his successors have only brought into clearer light as an indispensable presupposition. The non-Euclideans, on the other hand, have shown that it does not require proof, because it embodies the definition of the sort of space dealt with by ordinary geometry ; and that in both of its equivalent forms, whether as the axiom of parallels or of the equality of the angles of a triangle to two right angles, it forms a special case intermediate between that of spherical and that of pseudo-spherical space. In spherical space nothing analogous to the Euclidean parallels is to be found ; in pseudo-spherical space, on the other hand, not one, but *two* 'parallels' may be drawn through any point. So while spherical triangles always have their angles *greater* than two right angles, the pseudo-spherical triangles always have them *less* than two right angles. Moreover, the Euclidean case can always be reached by supposing the 'parameter' of the non-Euclidean spaces infinitely large. So much for the possibility of a general geometry, including the Euclidean amongst others.

It has also, I think, been shown that the non-Euclidean geometries would form coherent and consistent systems, like the Euclidean, in which an indefinite number of propositions might be shown to follow from their initial definitions. They are, that is to say, thoroughly *thinkable* and free from contradiction, and intellectually on a level with the Euclidean conception of space. They are thinkable,—but (as yet) no more ; and this explains their defence against the two objections upon which their more unprejudiced opponents incline to lay most stress. It is objected (1) that there is, *e.g.*, no such thing as a spherical space, only a spherical surface. True ; but there is nothing to prevent us from *conceiving* the peculiar properties of a spherical surface as pervading every portion of the space it bounds. We can conceive a spherical surface of a constant curvature making up the texture of space, just as well as the Euclidean plane surface. This intrinsic texture would produce uniform and calculable deformation or 'crinkling' in all bodies immersed in it, and these might conceivably be aware of this deformation as they moved in a non-Euclidean space, just as they are now aware of the direction of their movements. In the 'Euclidean' case the homogeneity of Space is entire in *all* respects, in the spherical only in *some*. It is argued (2) that metageometry is dependent on Euclidean geometry, because it is reached only through the latter. But it is not clear that it may not be logically independent, even though historically it has developed out of Euclidean geometry, and even though psychologically the latter affords the simplest means of representing spatial images. And it has become clear that both the conception of a 'manifold' and that of a 'general' space admitting of specific determinations is logically prior to that of Euclidean space.

Theoretically, then, metageometry seems to be able to give a very good account of itself. But it must be confessed that this at present only accentuates its practical failure. It is admitted that Euclidean geometry yields the simplest formulas for calculating spatial relations, and even M. Calinon [1] hardly ventures to hope that non-Euclidean formulas will be found serviceable. Metageometers mostly confine themselves to supposing imaginary worlds, of which the laws would naturally suggest a non-Euclidean formulation.[2] In short, practically the supremacy of the old geometry remains incontestable, because of its greater simplicity and consequent facility of application.

II. I pass on to the second question, the light thrown by non-Euclidean geometry on the nature of Space. In this respect incomparably its most important achievement seems to have been to force upon all the distinction between *perceptual* and *conceptual* space, or rather spaces. On this point both parties are at one, and we find, *e.g.*,

[1] *Rev. Phil.* xviii. 12.
[2] *E.g.*, M. Poincaré, *Rev. de Mét.* iii. 6, pp. 641 ff.

M. Delbœuf[1] and M. Poincaré[2] stating the characteristics of Euclidean space and its fundamental distinction from perceptual space in almost identical terms. The former is one, empty, homogeneous, continuous, infinite, infinitely divisible, identical, invariable; the latter is many, filled, heterogeneous, continuous only for perception (if the atomic view of matter holds), probably finite, not infinitely divisible and variable. Both sides agree that our physical world is neither in Euclidean nor in non-Euclidean space, both of which are conceptual abstractions; their dispute is merely as to which furnishes the proper method for calculating spatial phenomena.[3] Thus all the geometrical spaces are grounded on the same experience of physical space, which they interpret and idealize differently, while seeking to simplify and systematize it by means of the various postulates which define them.

But if conceptual and perceptual space are so different, have they anything in common but the name? If the former are abstracted from the latter, upon what principles and by what methods does the abstraction proceed?

I conceive the answer to this important question to be, by the same methods as those by which 'real' or physical space is developed out of the *psychological* spaces. For, as M. Poincaré[4] well shows, we form our notion of real space by fusing together the data derived from visual, tactile, and motor sensations. That fusion is largely accomplished by ignoring the differences between their several deliverances and by correcting the appearances to one sense by another, in such a manner as to give the most complete and trustworthy perception of the object. We manipulate the data of the senses in order to perceive *things* (in 'real' space), and at a higher stage the same purposive process yields conceptual space, of course at first in its simplest form, the Euclidean. And (though I have not found this stated) all the characteristics of Euclidean space may be shown to have been constructed

---

[1] *Rev. Phil.* xviii. 11. [2] *Rev. de Mét.* iii. p. 632.
[3] Cp. Calinon, *Rev. Phil.* xviii. 12, "Sur l'indétermination géométrique de l'univers." [4] *Loc. cit.*

in this manner. Just as, *e.g.*, the varying appearances of things to the different senses were ignored in order to arrive at their 'real' place, so the varying and irregular deformations to which they are subjected at different places, when abstracted from, lead to the homogeneity of space. They are slight enough to be neglected, but if they were larger and followed some definite and simple law, they might suggest a non-Euclidean geometry. Similarly, geometrical space is one and infinite, because so soon as we abolish any boundary *in thought*, we can abolish all; it is infinitely divisible, because so soon as the division is conceived of as proceeding *in thought* the same act may be repeated as often as we please. And so on; geometrical space appears throughout as a construction of the intellect, which proceeds by the ordinary methods of that intellect in the achievement of its peculiar purposes. Nor is there anything new or mysterious about the process; no new faculty need be invoked, no new laws of mental operation need be formulated.

III. That the philosophic importance of this result is capital, is surely evident. The *certainty* of geometry is thereby shown to be nothing but the certainty with which conclusions follow from non-contradictory premisses; in each geometry it flows from the definitions. The certainty with which the sum of the angles of a triangle may be asserted to equal two right angles in Euclidean geometry, is precisely the same as that with which it may be shown to be greater or less in non-Euclidean systems.

This shows that certainty in the sense of intrinsic consistency has nothing to do with the question of the value and *real validity* of a geometry. The latter depends on the possibility of systematizing our spatial experience by means of the geometry. Our experience being what it is, we find the Euclidean the simplest and most effective system, alike to cover the facts and to calculate the divergences between the ideal and the actual results; and so we use it. But if our experience were different, a non-Euclidean system might conceivably seem preferable. In short, *as applied*, a geometry is not certain, but useful.¹

Again, the *necessity* of geometry is simply the necessity of a logical inference — hypothetical, and in no wise peculiar to geometry. Similarly, the *universality* of geometrical judgments is by no means peculiar to them, but may be explained as arising out of the *methodological* character of the assumptions on which they rest. If we decide to make certain assumptions because they are the most serviceable, we can certainly know beforehand that we shall always and under all circumstances judge accordingly. To expect us to do otherwise, would be to expect us to stultify ourselves. And certainly we have a great interest in upholding the universal validity of geometrical judgments. Is it a small thing to be able to draw a figure on paper in one's study, and on the strength of it, and by virtue of the homogeneity of space, to draw inferences about what happens beyond the path of the outmost sun? Should we not be incredible idiots, if we allowed any cheat of appearances to cajole us into a moment's doubt of so precious an organon of knowledge? It would seem, then, that the chief result of metageometry is to raise into clearer consciousness the nature of the complex processes whereby we organize our experiences, and to assimilate the case of space to our procedure elsewhere.²

But it has already become abundantly evident that a view of Space, such as that propounded, provokes conflicts with ancient and venerable views that have long adorned the histories of Philosophy. Among them Kant's conception of the apriority of Space is pre-eminent.

At a cursory glance it might indeed seem as though the new geometry afforded a welcome support to the Kantian position. If Euclidean geometry alone could prove the possibility of synthetic judgments *a priori*, could enrich us with absolutely certain knowledge absolutely independent of experience, could sustain an all-embracing,

---

[1] Cp. Poincaré's *La Science et l'Hypothèse*, pp. 66-7.
[2] Cp. *Axioms as Postulates*, §§ 40-43.

though empty, form of pure intuition, surely now that it is reinforced by an indefinite number of sister sciences, a boundless extension of our *a priori* knowledge might reasonably be anticipated. Unfortunately it proves a case of 'too many cooks' and the embarrassment of riches, rather than of 'the more the merrier.' To suppose *three a priori* forms of intuition corresponding to the three geometries is evidently not feasible, for they are in hopeless conflict with each other. If it is a universal and necessary truth that the angles of a triangle are equal to two right angles, it cannot be an equally universal and necessary truth that they are greater, according as we happen to be speaking of a Euclidean or of a spherical triangle. Clearly, there must be something seriously wrong about the assumed relation of geometry to space, or about the import of the criterion of apriority. Just as the *de facto* existence of geometry seemed to Kant to prove the possibility of an *a priori* intuition of Space, so the *de facto* existence of metageometry indicates the derivative nature of an intuition Kant had considered ultimate.

And the analysis thus necessitated rapidly discovers the seat of the error. Kant, like all philosophers before and far too many since his time, regards the conception of Space as simple and primary and the word as unambiguous. He does not distinguish between physical and geometrical space, between the problems of pure and of applied geometry. Hence he is forced to make his *Anschauung* an unintelligible hybrid between a percept and a concept, to argue alternately that 'space' could not be either, and to infer that it must therefore be some third thing. The possibility that it might be both never struck him. Still less did he suspect that each of these alternatives was complex, and that perceptual space was constructed out of no less than three sensory spaces, while it was susceptible of three different conceptual interpretations. What Kant calls 'space' therefore is not really one, but *seven*, and the force of his argument is made by their union. Confined to any one of them, the argument falls to pieces. When we see these facts as clearly as the development of metageometry has compelled us to see them, we must surely confess that the Kantian account of Space is hopelessly and demonstrably antiquated and can lend no support to the rest of his system. And should we not henceforth take care to eschew the vice of talking vaguely of 'space' without specifying what kind of space we mean, whether conceptual or perceptual, and what form of each? Even pedagogically, one would think, there can no longer be any advantage in confusing what is capable of being so clearly distinguished.

It would exceed my limits if I were to try to investigate whether Kant has not been guilty of a parallel confusion between felt succession and conceptual time in his account of the latter, still more were I to discuss whether after the withdrawal of the 'forms of pure intuition' any meaning could continue to be assigned to the Kantian conception of the *a priori*.[1] I shall conclude, therefore, with the modest hope that some of the many professed believers in the *Transcendental Aesthetic* will not disdain to define their position in face of the development of modern metageometry.

[1] Cp. *Axioms as Postulates*, §§ 10-25.

VI

THE METAPHYSICS OF THE TIME-PROCESS [1]

ARGUMENT

Significance of Dr. McTaggart's admission that the Hegelian Dialectic cannot explain the reality of succession 'in Time.' The reason of its failure, viz. that Time, Change, and Individuality are features of Reality we abstract from in our formation of Concepts. Hence abstract metaphysics always fail to account for Reality. Must we then either accept scepticism or reject a procedure on which all science rests? No; for to admit the defects of our thought-symbols for reality need merely stimulate us to improve them. As for science, it uses abstractions in a radically different way, to test and to predict experience. Thus 'law' is a methodological device for practical purposes. Science practical both in its origin and in its criterion, and ethics as the science of ends conditions metaphysics. Such an ethical metaphysic accepts and implies the reality of the Time-process. And *therefore* it has a right to look forward to the realization of its ends in time, and forms the true Evolutionism.

I DO not know whether Dr. McTaggart's interesting investigation of the relations of the Hegelian Dialectic to Time (or rather to the Time-process [2]) has obtained the attention it merits, but the problem he has so ably handled is of such vital importance, and the attitude of

[1] A reply, in *Mind*, N.S., No. 13 (January 1895), to Dr. McTaggart's articles in N.S., Nos. 8 and 10, which were subsequently included in his *Studies in the Hegelian Dialectic*, chap. v., to which Dr. McTaggart has appended a note (pp. 197-202) replying to me (so far as his standpoint permitted). His chief contention is that the 'timeless' concept is not, as I maintained, a methodological device but a necessity of thought. To which the reply is that all 'necessities of thought' are primarily methodological devices. See *Axioms as Postulates*. I have reprinted the article as it stood, in order not to blur its anticipations of Pragmatism.

[2] I prefer to use the latter phrase in order to indicate that I do not regard 'Time' as anything but an abstraction formed to express an ultimate characteristic of our experience, and in order to check, if possible, the tendency of metaphysicians to substitute verbal criticism of that abstraction for a consideration of the facts which we *mean* when we say, *e.g.* that 'the world is in Time.' To this tendency, Dr. McTaggart also sometimes succumbs (*e.g. Studies in the Hegelian Dialectic*, pp. 161-3), and it seems to me to be at the root of most of the metaphysical puzzles on the subject.

current philosophy towards it is so obscure, that no apology is needed for a further discussion of his results. That those results came upon me with the shock of novelty I cannot, indeed, pretend; for the impossibility of reconciling the truth of the Dialectic with the reality of the Time-process has long been familiar to me as the chief, and, to me, insuperable difficulty of the Hegelian position. I propose, therefore, to take for granted the reluctant conclusion of Dr. McTaggart's almost scholastic ingenuity, namely, that there is no known way of reconciling the (admitted) existence of the Time-process with the (alleged) 'eternal perfection of the Absolute Idea'—at all events until some other commentator of Hegelism has attempted to revise and refute Dr. McTaggart's arguments—and I wish to consider what inferences may be drawn from it with respect to the method of metaphysical speculation in general.

Before doing so, however, a word ought, perhaps, to be said on what Dr. McTaggart himself inclines to regard as the positive result of his inquiry, the fact namely that he has not been able to show that there is *no* possible synthesis of the Absolute Idea with the Time-process, and that he is consequently "entitled to believe that one more synthesis remains as yet unknown, which shall overcome the last and most persistent of the contradictions inherent in appearance." For faint as is the hope which nourishes this belief, and groundless as are the assumptions from which that hope may, I think, be shown to spring, one may yet congratulate Dr. McTaggart on the candour with which he distinguishes his faith in the Unknown Synthesis from the cogency of a logical demonstration, and on the diffidence with which he declines to avail himself of the easy convenience of Mr. Bradley's maxim that "what may be, and must be, that certainly is." For certainly, if one does not scruple to regard utter ignorance as the possibility that 'may be,' and the subjective need of saving one's own theory as the necessity that 'must be,' there is no difficulty which cannot be evaded by the application of that maxim and no contradiction which cannot be so 'reconciled.' My only fear would be that if such an axiom were admitted at the beginning of philosophy, it would also prove its end. Dr. McTaggart, however, is to be congratulated on having eschewed the dangers of Mr. Bradley's 'short way with the insoluble,' and on preferring to base his acceptance of conflicting views on the ancient, time-honoured and extra-logical principle of Faith. Still more admirable, perhaps, is the robustness of a faith which overlooks the curious inconsistency of denying the metaphysical value of Time, and yet expecting from the Future the discovery of the ultimate synthesis on which one's whole metaphysic depends. For myself I avow that such faith is beyond my reach. If I were driven to the conclusion that the inexorable necessities of my mental constitution directly conflicted with patent and undeniable facts of experience, I fear I should be beset by a sceptical distrust of the ultimate rationality of all things rather than solaced by visions of an 'unknown synthesis.'

But in this case I hope to show that there is no need to respect a faith one cannot share, and that Dr. McTaggart has given more to faith than faith demands.

If the contradiction cannot be solved, it can at least be exposed and explained. And unless I am very much mistaken, it will appear that the incompatibility between the assertion of the reality of the Time-process and its comprehension by any system of 'eternal' logical truth (whether Hegel's or any one else's) has its origin in very simple and obvious considerations.

Dr. McTaggart cannot find room for the reality of the Time-process, *i.e.* of the world's changes in time and space, within the limits of Hegel's Dialectic. But is this an exclusive peculiarity or difficulty of Hegel's position? Is the Time-process any more intelligible on the assumptions of any other purely logical[1] system, as, for instance, on those of Plato or Spinoza? I think the difficulty will be found to recur in all these systems. And this shows that it is not accidental, but intrinsic

---

[1] *I.e.* intellectualist.

to the *modus operandi* of all systems of abstract metaphysics.

They cannot account for the time-factor in Reality, because they have *ab initio incapacitated* themselves from accounting for Time as for change, imperfection and particularity—for all indeed that differentiates the realities of our experience from the ideals of our thought. And their whole method of procedure rendered this result inevitable. They were systems of abstract truth, and based on the assumption on which the truth of abstraction rests.[1] They aimed at emancipating philosophy from the flux to which all human experience is subject, at interpreting the world in terms of conceptions, which should be true not here and now, but 'eternally' and independently of Time and Change. Such conceptions, naturally, could not be based upon probable inferences from the actual condition of the world at, or during, any time, but had to be derived from logical necessities arising out of the eternal nature of the human mind as such. Hence those conceptions were necessarily *abstract*, and *among the things they abstracted from was the time-aspect of Reality*.

Once abstracted from, the reference to Time could not, of course, be recovered, any more than the individuality of Reality can be deduced, when once ignored. The assumption is made that, in order to express the 'truth' about Reality, its 'thisness,' individuality, change and its immersion in a certain temporal and spatial environment may be neglected, and the timeless validity of a conception is thus substituted for the living, changing and perishing existence we contemplate. Now it is not my purpose here to dispute, or even to examine, the correctness of this assumption itself. What I wish here to point out is merely that it is unreasonable to expect from such premisses to arrive at a deductive justification

---

[1] I have in this sentence purposely used 'truth' in two senses, in order to emphasize a distinction, which is too often overlooked, between the conceptual interpretation of reality, which is truth in the narrower sense, and the *validity* or practical working of those conceptual symbols, which constitutes their truth in a wider sense. In the former sense 'truth' is merely a *claim* which may, or may not, be ratified by experience (see below, p. 100, and above, p. 57).

of the very characteristics of Reality that have been excluded.

The true reason, then, why Hegelism can give no reason for the Time-process, *i.e.* for the fact that the world is 'in time,' and changes continuously, is that it was constructed to give an account of the world irrespective of Time and Change. If you insist on having a system of eternal and immutable 'truth,' you can get it only by abstracting from those characteristics of Reality, which we try to express by the terms individuality, time, and change. But you must pay the price for a formula that will enable you to make assertions that hold good far beyond the limits of your experience. And it is part of the price that you will in the end be unable to give a rational explanation of those very characteristics, which had been dismissed at the outset as irrelevant to a rational explanation. Thus the whole contradiction arises from a desperate attempt to eat one's cake and yet have it, to secure the eternal possession of absolute truth and yet to profit by its development in time! Surely this is *not* a fitting occasion for invoking that supreme faculty of Faith to which philosophy, perhaps as much as theology, must ultimately make appeal!

If these considerations are valid, the idea of accounting for the time-process of the world on any system of abstract metaphysics is a conceptual jugglery foredoomed to failure, and must be declared mistaken in principle. But there remain two questions of great importance : (1) Do such systems of abstract metaphysics lose all value ? (2) Is there any other way of manipulating the time-process so as to fit it into a coherent systematic account of the world ?

In answering the first question it will be necessary to supplement the negative criticism of the claims of abstract metaphysics by tracing the consequences of their utter rejection. I have so far contended that no abstract metaphysic could say the last word about the world, on the ground that it was *ex vi definitionis* forced to reject some of the chief characteristics of that world. But if it cannot give us the whole truth, can it give us any truth? Is not the alternative to the rejection of the full claims of Hegelism (and kindred systems) a sceptical despair of the power of the reason to find a clue out of the labyrinth of experience?

Such a plea would not be devoid of a certain plausibility. Stress might be laid on the fact that the fundamental assumption of all abstract metaphysics is the fundamental assumption also of all science, that the whole imposing structure of the 'laws of nature' is formulated without reference to the temporal and spatial environment and the individual peculiarities of the things which 'obey' these laws, and so likewise lays claim to an eternal validity. How then can Metaphysic dare to reject an assumption which supports the whole of Science? Again, it may be urged that from its very nature philosophy is an interpretation of experience in terms of thought, and must necessarily exhibit the intrinsic peculiarities of human thought. If abstraction, therefore, is characteristic of all our thinking, if all truth is abstract, it would seem that all philosophy must stand or fall with the abstract formulas in which alone our thought can take cognizance of reality, and may not dream of casting off the shackles, or denying the sufficiency, of the systems of abstract truth which the ingenuity of the past has propounded.

Nevertheless I incline to think that it is possible to steer the human reason safely through between the Scylla of Scepticism and the Charybdis of an Idea absolutely irreconcilable with experience. But to do so it is imperative to define exactly the part played by abstraction in a philosophic account of the world.

Evidently, in the first place, it does not follow that because all truth in the narrower sense (v. *note*, p. 98) is abstract, *i.e.* because all philosophy must be couched in abstract terms, therefore the whole truth about the universe in the wider sense, *i.e.* the ultimate account that can be given of it, can be compressed into a single abstract formula, and that the scheme of things is nothing more than, *e.g.* the self-development of the Absolute Idea. To draw this inference would be to confuse the thought-symbol, which is, and must be, the instrument of thought, with that which the symbol expresses, often only very imperfectly, viz. the reality which is 'known' only in experience, and can never be evoked by the incantations of any abstract formula. If we avoid this confusion we shall no longer be prone to think that we have disposed of the thing symbolized when we have brought home imperfection and contradiction to the formulas whereby we seek to express it—an accusation which, I fear, might frequently be made good against the destructive part of Mr. Bradley's "Appearance and Reality"—to suppose, *e.g.*, that Time and Change cannot really be characteristic of the universe, because our thought, in attempting to represent them by abstract symbols often contradicts itself. For evidently the contradiction may result as well from the inadequacy of our symbols to express realities of whose existence we are directly assured by other factors in experience, and which consequently are *data* rather than problems for thought, as from the 'merely apparent' character of their reality; so the moral to be drawn may only be the old one, that it is the function of thought to mediate and not to create.[1] If so, our proper attitude will be this, that while we shall not hesitate to represent the facts of experience by conceptual symbols, we shall always be on our guard against their misrepresenting them, and ever alive to the necessity of interpreting our symbols by a reference to reality. In this manner I conceive that it would be possible to utilize the terms of abstract metaphysics, whenever they seemed to yield useful formulas, without erecting them into fetishes and giving them the entire mastery over our reason. From the tyranny of abstractions there would thus always be an appeal to the immediacy of living experience, and by it many a difficulty which appals on paper would be shown to be shadowy in the field. And conversely, it would perhaps be possible for philosophy to grapple somewhat more effectively with the real difficulties of actual life.

[1] Dr. McTaggart has commented on this passage (*Studies*, pp. 110-3).

Nor can I see why philosophers should fight shy of such a procedure. For surely the admission that philosophy is an interpretation of experience in terms of thought does not preclude us from the reinterpretation of our symbols by a reference to experience wherever that may seem expedient and profitable. Why should we commit ourselves to a task which must prove either illusory or impossible, that of the rational deduction of the self-evident? It is true that philosophic explanation came into being because experience is not wholly self-explaining. But to admit this is not to imply that everything requires explanation. For all explanation must set out from certain data, which may either be accepted as facts or considered self-evident, and in no wise necessitate or justify the attempt to explain everything, an attempt which must ultimately derive everything from nothing, by the power alone of an intentionally obscure vocabulary. What the data of such an ultimate explanation of the world should be, admits, of course, of further discussion ; but I can see no reason in the nature of philosophy as such why the characteristic of Time should not be one of them. And if by a frank recognition of the reality of Time, Imperfection and Individuality we can reach a deeper, more complete and workable insight into the facts of experience, why should our philosophy be worse than one which is driven to reject them by ancient prejudices concerning the perfections which the world ought to possess?

The abstractions of metaphysics, then, exist as explanations of the concrete facts of life, and not the latter as illustrations of the former ; and the Absolute Idea also is not exempt from this rule. Nor is it to a different conclusion concerning the subordination of abstract metaphysics that we are led by the consideration of the first argument adduced in their favour, the fact that all science shares their assumption.

That all science abstracts from the particularity and time-reference of phenomena, and states its laws in the shape of eternal and universal truths, is in a sense true. But this fact will not bear the inference it is sought to draw in favour of abstract metaphysics, and must not be allowed to prejudice the inquiry into the proper method of discovering an ultimate theory of the universe. For in the first place the treatment of its initial assumption by science differs widely from that of metaphysics. Science does not refuse to interpret the symbols with which it operates; on the contrary, it is only their applicability to the concrete facts originally abstracted from that is held to justify their use and to establish their 'truth.' The mathematical abstractions which enable astronomers to calculate the path of a star are justified by their approximate correspondence with its observed position, and if there were any extensive or persistent divergence between the calculation and experience, astronomers would be quite ready to revise their assumptions to the extent even of changing their fundamental notions concerning the nature of space. But in the case of metaphysics the same principle is not, apparently, to apply. If the Dialectic of the Absolute Idea does not accord in its results with the facts of life, we are not to suspect the Dialectic. It possesses an intrinsic certainty by right divine which no failure can be admitted to impair. If the logical (or rather *psychological*) development of the Idea fails to account for the development in time, we may at the utmost postulate an 'unknown synthesis.' This *may* be philosophy, but it does not look like science.

In the second place, let us ask *why* science abstracts from the particularity of reality. Not, certainly, because it does not observe it. Nor yet because it ascribes to the deductions from its universal laws a precision which they do not possess. On the contrary, it cheerfully admits that all the laws of nature are hypotheses, represent not the facts but tendencies, and are to be used merely as formulas for calculating the facts. But why should we want to calculate the facts by such universal formulas? The answer to this question brings us to the roots of the matter. We make the fundamental assumption of science that there are universal and eternal laws, *i.e.* that the individuality of things together with their spatial and temporal context may be neglected, not because we are convinced of its theoretic validity, but because we are constrained by its practical convenience. *We want to be able to make predictions about the future behaviour of things for the purpose of shaping our own conduct accordingly.* Hence attempts to forecast the future have been the source of half the superstitions as well as of the whole of the science of mankind. But no method of divination ever invented could compete in ingenuity and gorgeous simplicity with the assumption of universal laws which hold good without reference to time; and so in the long run it alone could meet the want or practical necessity in question.

In other words this assumption is a *methodological device*, and ultimately reposes on the practical necessity of discovering formulas for calculating events in the rough, without awaiting or observing their occurrence. To assert this methodological character of eternal truths is not, of course, to deny their validity—for it is evident that unless the nature of the world had lent itself to a very considerable extent to such interpretation, the assumption of 'eternal' laws would have served our purposes as little as those of astrology, necromancy, chiromancy, and catoptromancy. What, however, must be asserted is that this assumption is *not* an ultimate term in the explanation of the world.

This does not, of course, matter to Science, which is not concerned with such ultimate explanation, and for which the assumption is at all events ultimate enough. But it *does* matter to philosophy that the ultimate theoretic assumption should have a methodological character. To say that we assume the truth of abstraction because we wish to attain certain ends, is to subordinate theoretic 'truth' to a teleological implication; to say that, the assumption once made, its truth is 'proved' by its practical working, by the way in which it stands the test of experience, is to assert this same subordination only a little less directly. For the question of the 'practical working' of a truth will always ultimately be found to resolve itself into the question whether we can live by it.

In any case, then, it appears that scientific knowledge is not an ultimate and unanalysable term in the explanation of things: Science subordinates itself to the needs and ends of life alike whether we regard its origin—practical necessity, or its criterion—practical utility. But if so, the procedure of Science can no longer be quoted in support of the attempt to found our ultimate philosophy upon abstract and 'eternal' universals. If the abstraction from time, place, and individuality is conditioned by practical aims, the next inquiry must evidently concern the nature of these practical aims, to which all theoretic knowledge is ultimately subsidiary. And if these aims can be formed into a connected and coherent system, it will be to the discipline which achieves this that we shall look for an ultimate account of the world. Is there then a science which gives an orderly account of the ends of life that are or should be aimed at? Surely Ethics is as much of a science as abstract metaphysics, and if it be the science of ultimate ends, it seems to follow that *our ultimate metaphysic must be ethical*.[1]

Let us consider next what the attitude of such an ethical metaphysic would be to the metaphysical pretensions of abstract universals and of the Time-process respectively. It seems clear, in the first place, that practical aims, or a system thereof, do not easily lend themselves to statement in terms of abstract universals. For an end or purpose seems to be intrinsically the affair of a finite individual in space and time, and the attempt to regard the timeless, immutable and universal as possessed of ends seems to meet with insuperable difficulties. If, therefore, the ultimate explanation of the world is to be in terms of ends, it would seem as though it must be in terms of individual ends, realized in and through the Time-process. Nor is there anything repugnant to reason in the conception of an end realized in a time-process that would render it difficult for a teleological explanation to admit

[1] All this seems a very fairly definite anticipation of modern pragmatism (1903).

the reality of the Time-process. On the contrary, if the transition from means to end were instantaneous, the distinction between them would vanish, and lose all meaning. Still less has it been found repugnant either to the reason or to the feelings of men to regard the Time-process as the realization of an end or even of a multitude of individual ends, *e.g.* as a process of spiritual redemption. There is, therefore, perfect harmony between an ethical metaphysic and the existence of individuals in Time and Space, while that existence is found to be irreconcilable with any abstract metaphysical formula.

We must conclude, then, that the method of explaining the ultimate nature of the world by an abstract universal formula, or a series of such, is *not* supported by the methodological use of similar formulas in the natural sciences, which, rightly considered, leads to very different inferences. What compensation then has it to offer us for its inability to take account of many of the chief data which a comprehensive philosophy has to explain? Surely the full reality which has to be explained is the individual in the Time-process. And though it will remain no trivial task to exhibit the rationality of the Real, it has yet become evident that rationality is but one of several attributes to be predicated of Reality, and that a mere rationalism or 'panlogism,' therefore, can never be anything but a one-sided philosophy.

We have to consider next the second question raised (on p. 99) as to whether by pursuing a different method philosophy is able to recognize the reality of the Time-process. And if such philosophic recognition is possible, what is the metaphysical value and methodological bearing of the reality of Time (or rather of the Time-process)? Or is there possibly, as Dr. McTaggart suggests (*loc. cit.* p. 166), "something about Time which renders it unfit, in metaphysics, for the ultimate explanation of the universe"? The prejudice to this effect is no doubt well-founded from the standpoint of a philosophy whose initial abstraction excludes Time. But if we decline to hamper ourselves by a method which fails *de facto* to account for

Time and imperfection, while its claim *de jure* had to be disallowed as ignoring the supreme practical limitations under which the whole understanding operates, the case is different. It has already been shown that an ethical metaphysic has no difficulty in conceiving the ultimate end as realizable in the Time-process. And indeed from such a standpoint it is possible to indicate an explanation even of the Becoming which is so puzzling a characteristic of the Real, and the source of all our conceptions of Time and Change—it may be ascribed to the struggle of finite existence to attain that ultimate end. Instead of being left over as an inexplicable surd at the conclusion of a metaphysical explanation, the Time-process thus becomes an integral part of that explanation, and a fruitful source of inquiry opens out to philosophy concerning its value in the discovery and estimation of ultimate truth. It would be impossible within the limits of this essay to attempt any detailed account of the metaphysical conclusions to which the admission of the reality of the Time-process would lead. Suffice it to say that I am convinced that the system we should arrive at would prove no less coherent and complete than any of the great systems of abstract metaphysics, and that the difficulties which it may at first seem to involve are due to an (inconsistent) reversion to the methods of abstract metaphysics.

There are, however, two points which it seems necessary to emphasize. The first is that a metaphysic of the Time-process will stand in the same relation to the explanation of phenomena by their *history*, as a metaphysic of abstract ideas stands to their explanation by universal laws, *i.e.* the Historical Method will represent the application in science of the metaphysical principle. But while to an abstract metaphysic the Historical Method must ultimately be foolishness, a metaphysic of the Time-process will justify that method by expressing it in a metaphysical, *i.e.* final, form. And this alone would suffice to prove its superiority; for nowadays we can as little dispense with the explanation of things by their history as with their explanation by universal 'laws.' A philosophy, then, which admits both and vindicates the use of the one, without invalidating the other (even though it regards its importance as methodological and subordinate rather than as supreme), is manifestly superior to a philosophy which absolutely rejects one of the most valuable of the working assumptions of science. And if we regard the fact that there is a development of the world in Time as the essence of Evolution, it is obvious that only a theory which accepts this Time-process as an ultimate datum will be capable of yielding a philosophy of Evolution and is worthy of the name of Evolutionism.

The second point concerns the ultimate difficulties which are left over in every known system of philosophy, and form antinomies which are insoluble for the human reason as it stands. Such on Dr. McTaggart's theory are the existence of change and imperfection, such, in his opinion, would be the beginning of the Time-process on mine. Now in face of these facts an abstract metaphysic is in an extremely awkward position. If it scorns to excuse its failure by pious phrases concerning the infinite capacity of a non-human mind to solve the insoluble, if it dreads to have recourse to the more impious $\dot{a}\rho\gamma\dot{o}s$ $\lambda\dot{o}\gamma os$ of Mr. Bradley, and to postulate an Absolute which will 'absorb,' 'submerge,' 'suppress,' and 'reconcile' all difficulties *ex officio*, in a manner no doubt highly satisfactory to itself and Mr. Bradley, two alternatives remain. Either the idea that a contradiction is a necessary proof of falsehood must be given up, and one or both sides of the antinomy must be accepted in spite of everything—in which case it is hard to say what weapon would be left wherewith to refute the most patent absurdities; or one must hope for such an enlargement of the human reason as will give it an insight into what is at present incomprehensible. For the difficulties in question have been under scrutiny too long to render it credible that any thinkable solution has been overlooked. If, however, a development of the human mind be admitted, the reality of the Time-process, in which that development takes place, can no longer be denied, and abstract metaphysic becomes indebted to it for the means to solve its difficulties. Is it not curious then to go on maintaining that the Time-process is unfit to form a factor in an ultimate philosophy?

An evolutionist philosophy, on the other hand, would not only be entitled, but bound, to await a solution of its difficulties from the secular development of the Time-process which had generated them. For its ultimate appeal is not to the abstract reason but to experience, to the Time-process in which that reason develops. It is consequently an *ignoratio elenchi* to infer that a view leading to an antimony is false, unless it can be shown that the antinomy is a permanent one. But not only is this impossible, but a solution *ambulando* may be expected on two grounds. (1) Reality, *i.e.* the data of our reasonings, may so change as no longer to suggest the antinomy. For instance, the problem of imperfection would vanish if reality attained to perfection and not even a memory remained of the imperfect. And (2) the antinomy might be resolved by such a development of the mind as would enable it to see through its present difficulties. I am aware that many of our present philosophers have a rooted objection to putting their hope in the future; yet it is only in the direction of an abandonment of the prejudice against the reality of Time that I can descry a future for hope, a future for philosophy, and a philosophy for the future.

VII

REALITY AND 'IDEALISM'[1]

ARGUMENT

Four questions about Reality—(1) how do we come to assert it, (2) its primary character, (3) its criteria, (4) its ultimate character. Epistemological and metaphysical reality. Primarily everything is real, but none of the current criteria for sifting it absolutely trustworthy in theory. Their value is practical, and practical value is really the ultimate criterion. Can we claim speculative value for such a test? Yes, if the whole process of knowing be conceived as an attempt to render our experience harmonious. At present our success is imperfect, and so divergent views may still be taken of ultimate reality. Hence it is unnecessary to regard the real as a combination of abstract universals, and quite possible to treat a plurality of individual persons as ultimate.

THE readers of Mr. Ritchie's papers will have learnt by this time that they may expect to be entertained with a clear account of his views, neatly phrased and intelligibly presented, and not disdainful of an occasional touch of humour. And in these respects they will have not been disappointed by his brilliant disquisition on—*What is Reality?*—in the May number of the *Philosophical Review*. But if they sought fresh light on one of the most puzzling and fundamental of philosophic problems, it is to be feared that they were not equally well satisfied. Mr. Ritchie's paper is polemical rather than investigatory, and he seems more concerned to make dialectical points against his adversaries than to probe his subject to the bottom. And as his adversaries' views are very various, and often have little in common but their disagreement

---

[1] From the *Philosophical Review* of September 1892. The late Professor D. G. Ritchie, whose premature demise I, in common with all his pupils, have not ceased to deplore, reprinted the article to which this is a reply in a volume of essays entitled *Darwin and Hegel* (1893), pp. 77-108.

with Mr. Ritchie's, and as, moreover, they are not stated or definitely referred to, the total effect is somewhat confusing. Nor is the confusion improved by the way in which Mr. Ritchie discusses some two or three different questions about reality in the same breath. The justification in his mind for this procedure evidently lies in the fact that they all offer a basis for objections to his own views, which he would, perhaps, not object to have called Neo-Hegelian. But this does not constitute any intrinsic kinship between the views he criticizes, and his discussion would have gained largely if he had added to his classification of the various *sorts* of reality a classification of the various *questions that may be raised about it*. It would be too much, perhaps, to expect Mr. Ritchie to excel the rest of his school as much in substance as he does in style, but it seems evident that he has, as little as they, kept clear of the Hegelian confusion of epistemology and metaphysics, to which Professor Seth [1] has of late drawn so much attention.

There are at least *four* questions, which Mr. Ritchie's paper trenches upon. They are—

I. How do we know that there is any reality at all, or how do we come to assert an external world?

II. What is reality at the beginning of inquiry, *i.e.* what is the primary datum to be explained?

III. How is it to be explained—by what criteria do we inquire into reality?

IV. What does reality turn out to be—after inquiry?

Of these, I. and III. seem to be epistemological, while II. is psychological, and IV. plainly metaphysical. Mr. Ritchie does not seem to distinguish II. from III., attributes his answer to III. without more ado to IV., and refers to I. only at the end, by way of meeting a logical objection to his view of IV. This confusion is shown also in his method of proof. His real purpose is to establish certain metaphysical views as to the nature of ultimate reality, but he treats his subject for the most part as if it were an epistemological inquiry into the criteria

[1] Now Professor Pringle Pattison.

of reality, and when, after establishing his metaphysical view of reality to his satisfaction, he is confronted [1] by the logical impossibility of identifying thought with its object, he suddenly throws us back upon the primary subjectivity of all experience. And all this without a hint of a μετάβασις εἰς ἄλλο γένος. The connexion is no doubt clear enough to Mr. Ritchie's mind, if, as must be supposed, he follows T. H. Green in his fearful and wonderful leap from the fact that all phenomena appear to some individual self to the conclusion that they are, *therefore*, appearances to a universal self; but he might at least have warned us that his opponents have repeatedly declared their inability to compass such saltatory exercises, and regard the two halves of the argument as belonging respectively to epistemology and to metaphysics, and the transition from the one to the other as a paralogism.

If, however, we refuse to take this Greenian *salto mortale*, it is evident that the first question must be settled before any of the rest can arise at all. For, as Professor Seth has so well pointed out, realism and idealism mean very different things according as they are taken in an epistemological or a metaphysical sense, and "it is possible to be epistemologically a strenuous realist and an idealist in the metaphysical sense of the term."[2] Nay, "it is only in virtue of epistemological realism that we can avoid scepticism, and so much as begin our journey towards metaphysical idealism." If, then, epistemological idealism is solipsism and "twin brother to scepticism," it must be surmounted before the nature of reality can be discussed. If it is not surmounted —*cadit quaestio*—it becomes futile to discuss whether the real is one or many, whether its criterion is consistency or what, if there is no objectivity at all. Mr. Ritchie has, of course, a perfect right to call a halt here, and to refuse to discuss anything further until his opponents have successfully emerged from the clutches of subjective idealism. But once they have been permitted to escape,

---

[1] *Darwin and Hegel*, p. 102.
[2] *Philosophical Review*, i. p. 142.

once he has conceded the objectivity of the phenomena which form the content of consciousness, he is *not* entitled to revert to the prior question. In other words, the discussion of the question—What is reality?—presupposes a settlement of the question—Is there reality?—in the affirmative. It is only when reality has been admitted to exist that we can begin to distinguish the real from the unreal, and to enumerate the different sorts and criteria of each.

It is necessary in the next place to put the primitive *datum explicandum* in the proper light. The primary psychological fact is that everything that is is real, and that the burden of proof lies on those who deny that anything is real. Nor does Mr. Ritchie dispute this, though he minimizes its importance, and apparently fails to see that reality in this sense rests on a totally different footing from all others. For it is the primary fact which all the rest are more or less complete theories to explain, and to which they must be referred in order to test their validity. If they prove capable of explaining what they set out to explain, we may reach a loftier view of reality, which will transfigure our primary datum for us, but which even so cannot be considered in abstraction from its basis; if they do not, the other 'senses of reality' are worthless. For their work is hypothetical and derivative, and if the conditions under which we ascribed reality to these interpreters of reality are not fulfilled, their *raison d'être* has vanished. But reality survives— even though its inscrutable flux of phenomena should laugh to scorn the attempts at comprehending it which it provokes.

But this unique position of primary reality Mr. Ritchie quite fails to appreciate.[1] Hence it is on the basis of an

[1] He does not even succeed in proving the unreality of dreams, by saying that they are not self-coherent nor follow in an intelligible sequence on the events of previous dreams. For their 'incoherence' is not, as a rule, intrinsic, nor anything that exists *for the dream consciousness* in the actual experiencing: it is an *ex post facto* judgment (resting usually on an imperfect memory) which is passed on them in our waking life. But awaking involves a breach of continuity, and the consciousness which condemns the dream-experience is no longer the consciousness which experienced it. And are we so sure that the coherence of our 'waking' life would survive a similar breach of continuity, such as might be

insufficient recognition of the psychological data that he proposes to consider what reality is. This question is plainly an ontological one, but Mr. Ritchie treats it as if it were epistemological, and = 'How do we know a phenomenon to be (ultimately) real?' *I.e.* he substitutes for the ontological inquiry into the *ratio essendi* of reality an epistemological inquiry into its *ratio cognoscendi* or the *criterion* of reality, and then unhesitatingly attributes to his results a metaphysical validity. Yet he seems quite unaware that such a method, even if successful, would be defective and inadequate. Even at its best, even if it could be shown that reality could be *known* only as a coherent system of thought-relations, it would not necessarily follow that reality *was nothing more*, and he would not necessarily have proved anything but the impotence of his thought to grasp reality, by reducing his symbolical expressions for reality to absurdity and contradiction. Thus his proofs cannot prove what he desires, and his refutations only recoil upon his method.

But it may be shown also that his criterion is not valid. He suggests[1] a triple test of rationality, a triple basis for the metaphysical assertion that reality is thought. (1) "The agreement between the inferences drawn from the experience of our different senses; (2) the agreement between the judgments of different persons; (3) the harmony of present experience with the results of their and our previous experience, constitute between them the test of reality." It is to be feared that

---

effected, *e.g.* by 'death' if we 'awake' after it? For comparison therefore with the intelligible sequence of successive dreams, we should require an intelligible sequence *in successive lives* to make the parallel complete. Unless, then, Mr. Ritchie has a transcendent knowledge of another life, whereby he judges our waking life to be real, because of its coherence and intelligibleness *from the standpoint of the former*, his comparison fails. It is true that we sometimes suspect our dreams while still dreaming (though as all dreams are 'near waking,' we cannot be said to be 'nearer waking' then). But does not our waking life lie under the same suspicion on the same grounds? If it is permissible for once to appeal from the 'plain man' to the man of genius, is it not 'a mad, mad world, my masters'? Have not seers, prophets, and philosophers in all ages testified that our earthly life was but a dream? And if to these divinely-inspired 'dreamers' we owe all the religions that have swayed the lives of men, must not dreams and hallucinations be accounted most real—in Mr. Ritchie's 'ethical' sense?

[1] *Loc. cit.* p. 80.

"between them" they fall very far short of giving a trustworthy test of reality.

(1) The first is open to objection as a matter of fact. It is doubtful how far the testimonies of the various senses really corroborate one another, and how far they are not rather incommensurable and referred to the same 'thing' for reasons of practical convenience. Are afterimages and overtones, which *regularly* accompany sights and sounds, to be esteemed unreal because we generally find it convenient to neglect them? And yet it is hard to say to what data of touch they correspond. Again, what can this criterion make of cases of hyperaesthesia of one sense, or of an occasional activity of some special sensitiveness? Are they to be rejected because they necessarily lie beyond confirmation by the other senses? So far as this criterion goes, there is nothing to prevent a real thing from contravening it, and an 'unreal' thing from conforming to it. Is 'Pepper's ghost' unreal because it cannot be touched? Or is a hallucination affecting several senses to be esteemed real?

(2) The second criterion is no better than the first. So Mr. Ritchie 'smells a rat,' in the case of his hypothetical mouse,[1] and limits its value by stipulating that B, C, D, and E (who do not see it) should have good eyesight. But how is it to be established that A (who does see it) does not considerably surpass them in the delicacy of his senses? In this difficulty, Mr. Ritchie proposes to call in expert opinion in the shape of "a hungry cat." (What scorn he would pour on such an appeal to the lower animals if it were a question of establishing the objectivity of an apparition!) Very good. But how if the cat side with the minority? It is to be hoped that Mr. Ritchie will prefer science to democracy, and the authoritative judgment of Athanasius and the cat against the rest of the world! If he does not, he might work out an amusing theory making the *Referendum* the ultimate test of reality. That, at least, would be a definite method of utilizing the experience

[1] *Loc. cit.* p. 80.

of others, such as is at present lacking. We act quite inconsistently in sometimes submitting to the superior delicacy of the expert's senses, and sometimes rejecting it. A room full of unmusical or inartistic people would hardly dispute about tones or colours with a single musician or painter, but an assembly of non-sensitives would probably deny that Macbeth saw a ghost (though who more qualified than Macbeth to see the ghost of Banquo?). The colour-blind, perhaps because they are in a minority, do not dispute the objectivity of colours they cannot see, but upon what logical principle should we be less forbearing towards those who claim to see the ultra-violet and infra-red rays of the spectrum, or the luminosity of a magnetic field?—In short, just as the excluding value of non-conformity was impaired in the first case by the possibility of genuine hyperaesthesia in the individual, so in the second it is impaired by the possibility of collective hyperaesthesia. And just as in the first case conformity did not exclude error, owing to the possibility of complex hallucination, so it fails in the second, owing to the possibility of collective hallucination.

(3) The third criterion at first seems more valuable—until we recollect that every new fact and every new experience is in some degree out of harmony with and contradictory of our previous experience.[1] Would it not be strange, then, to allow our own inexperience, and the stupidity of our ancestors to exercise an absolute censorship over the growth of knowledge? Besides, it so happens that in most cases when 'universal experience' is appealed to, its voice is self-contradictory. (What right have we, *e.g.* to reject countless traditions in order to prove that miracles are 'contrary to experience'?)

But perhaps Mr. Ritchie does not contend that any one of his criteria is singly sufficient as a test of reality and proposes to employ them collectively. But if so, should he not show some probability that they will

---

[1] As "Herakleitos" says (in *Mind!* p. 28), "is not the new of two things one, either itself false, or what renders all else false?"

always, or even normally, tend in the same direction? And even if they did, this would establish, not the collective theoretic certainty of criteria, each of which was individually fallible, much less a necessary basis for metaphysical inferences, but only a sort of practical probability, which it might be convenient to act upon. Thus the boasted rationality of the real reduces itself to this: upon Mr. Ritchie's own showing rationality is not an ultimate test, but resolvable into the three criteria he mentions, and in the end their value turns out to be practical!

Yet it may be that humbling the pretensions of this pseudo-rationality does good service in drawing attention to the commonest and most influential of the practical tests of reality, which may be said to have underlain and guided the development of all the rest. It lies in the fact emphasized by Professor James in his wonderful chapter on the perception of reality [1] that that is adjudged real which has intimate "relation to our emotional and active life," *i.e.* practical value. It is this criterion which has constituted the objective world of ordinary men, by excluding from it the world of dreams, hallucinations, and the transient though normal 'illusions of the senses.' It is this which accounts for the superior reality so often ascribed to feelings, especially to pleasure and pain, which Mr. Ritchie mentions.[2] It is this which absorbs into it Mr. Ritchie's fifth, or 'ethical,' sense of reality. It is this, lastly, which has moulded the whole development of the intellect, and so pervades all Mr. Ritchie's criteria and reduces them to dependence upon it. Hence if we are to speak of any 'main (derivative) sense of reality' at all, it must certainly be conceded to Professor James that "whatever things have intimate and continuous connexion with my life, are things of whose reality I cannot doubt."

But though there can be no doubt of the practical importance of this criterion, there may be much about its speculative value. The history of the practical struggle which has evolved us and our minds seems to offer but

---

[1] *Princ. of Psych.* ii. 295.   [2] *Darwin and Hegel*, pp. 82-3.

slender guarantees that our faculties should have been fitted for, and our energies directed towards, those aspects of reality which are of the greatest theoretic importance,[1] and hence arguments from practical or moral necessity, universal desires, and the like, are not usually supposed to yield the safest approach to the ultimate reality of things.

And not only must it be said that Mr. Ritchie's tests are not, properly speaking, rational at all, but it must be pointed out that he actually shrinks from mentioning in this place the test of rationality in its simplest and severest shape, viz. that of conformity to the necessary laws of our thought. The omission is surprising, and one would fain ascribe it to the perception that it would have been too palpable a begging of the issue to have made conformity with the laws of thought the *test* of reality in an argument designed to *show* that reality ultimately lay in the determinations of our thought. Or can it be due to the fact that the chief characteristic of reality is its Becoming, and that Becoming and its defiance of the law of Contradiction is what our thought has never been able to grasp? Yet the criterion is not without value. We are reluctant to admit facts and explanations which seem to contravene it, such as, *e.g.* the four-dimensionality of Space and the illusoriness of Time, and would only accept them as inferences, *e.g.* from the untying of Zöllner's knots and the alleged occurrence of premonitions, in the very last resort.

What then is the result of a critical survey of the various criteria of reality? Is it not that though all may be of service, none can be entirely relied upon as the *ratio cognoscendi* of reality? There is no royal road to omniscience any more than to omnipotence, even though we do not hold with Mr. Ritchie that the two coincide. The cognition of reality is a slow and arduous process, and of its possession we cannot be sure until we possess it *whole*. The only certain and ultimate test of reality is the absence of internal friction, is its undisputed occupa-

---

[1] Else should we not have developed, *e.g.* an electric sense?

tion of the field of consciousness, in a word, its self-sufficiency. It is because reality does *not* display this character that thought has to be called in to interpret it. If it did, there would be no distinction between real and unreal, between what is 'really' presented and 'merely imagined,' between the self and the world, and there would be no such thing as thought. As Professor James so well points out [1] a hallucinatory candle occupying the whole field of consciousness would be equivalent to a real one. But as a matter of fact the contents of consciousness present no such permanence and self-evidence; their initial state is a fleeting succession of conflicting presentations which supplant and contradict one another. Some of these are frequently followed by painful, others by pleasurable feelings, and the penalty of idle acquiescence in the flux of phenomena is rapid death. So a dire necessity is laid upon the subject to distinguish himself from the world, and to set about thinking how phenomena may be controlled. He naturally begins by ascribing to the phenomena which are followed by pains or other practically important consequences a reality not shared by the rest. This first interpretation of the chaos of presentations is probably the first for which we can have direct testimony, and represents the view of reality taken by savages and small children. It is merely an extension of this view when the 'plain man,' in the condition of 'natural realism' distinguishes hallucinations, fancies, and dreams from *true* reality.

To effect this he uses whatever tests seem most practically useful—among others those of 'coherence' and 'consistency.' Thus, the plain man's view is simply the first stage in the attempt to reach a harmony of the real. The view of the physicists represents a second and subsequent stage. And Mr. Ritchie's philosophy of the ultimate nature of reality is possibly a third. Each leads on to the other, because each is successively recognized *not* to be a coherent and consistent account of the world and *not* to eliminate the irrational and unsatisfactory

[1] *Princ. of Psychology*, ii. 287.

element in experience. The plain man's 'things,' the physicist's 'atoms,' and Mr. Ritchie's 'Absolute,' are all of them more or less persevering and well-considered schemes to interpret the primary reality of phenomena, and in this sense Mr. Ritchie is entitled to call the 'sunrise' a theory.[1] But the chaos of presentations, out of which we have (by criteria ultimately *practical*) *isolated* the phenomenon we subsequently call sunrise, is *not* a theory, but the fact which has called all theories into being.

In addition to generating hypothetical objects to explain phenomena, this process of the interpretation of reality by our thought also bestows a derivative reality on the abstractions themselves with which thought works. If they are the instruments wherewith thought accomplishes such effects upon reality, they must surely be themselves real. Hence philosophers have long asserted the reality of Ideas, and we commonly hold the triangle and the space of mathematical abstraction to be *the real* triangle and *the real* space. (Mr. Ritchie's fourth sense.) Similarly the goals to which the methods of our thought tend—its intrinsic ideals—acquire a hypothetical reality of a lofty order. For it is evident that if the real nature of phenomena is to be discovered by the way of thought, the supreme ideals of that thought must be, *or be realized by*, the ultimate reality. But it would not follow that these ideals would render reality mere thought. For they might point either at a reality which should transcend thought, or at one of which thought should be but a single activity—even as it is now the activity of real beings.

But it is needless to discuss what would happen to thought if reality had been rendered harmonious, in view of the fact that no philosophy has succeeded in doing this. The whole attempt is dependent for its validity on its success, and its success is, to put it mildly, imperfect. The scientific view of atoms goes behind the popular view of 'things,' because it holds that the latter do not construct a tenable view of phenomena. Mr. Ritchie would treat

[1] *Darwin and Hegel*, p. 91.

the atoms similarly. But would he seriously contend that he can already give an entirely consistent, coherent, and intelligible view of the whole world, giving a reason why everything is exactly what it is and not otherwise? Of course Mr. Ritchie does not lay claim to such omniscience. But if he cannot, in what respect is he better than those publicans and sinners, the 'plain men' and the realists? If he cannot, why make such a fuss about formal coherency and consistency as the test of reality? By his own admission they represent a postulate which is never actually realized, and for aught we know never can be. If he cannot, lastly, what boots it to explain that though reality is not thought for us, it is for God?[1] This free and easy appeal to the Deity, in the midst of a discussion of *human* knowledge, in order to silence an opponent and to fill up any gap in the argument, ought surely to be as severely reprobated as the mediaeval practice of ascribing any ill-understood fact or bit of knowledge to the agency of the Devil. The question is not whether to a divine mind, supposing its existence to be tenable in Mr. Ritchie's sense, Reality is Thought, but whether that assertion is a valid defence against the objection that Mr. Ritchie has given away his case when he has admitted that reality is not thought to human minds. Until, then, Mr. Ritchie can bring rather more convincing proof of his approaching apotheosis and omniscience, it must be contended that he has neither made out his assertion that rationality is the test of reality, nor its connexion with the metaphysical dogma that the real is ultimately the thought of a 'divine mind.'

This question as to the ultimate nature of reality, forming the ultimate problem of ontology, brings us to the fourth and last question which may be raised about reality. And enough has been said concerning the imperfections of our methods of interpreting reality, to render it clear that we are as yet hardly entitled to give any very confident answer to this question. From a purely scientific standpoint, I can see no reason for

[1] *Darwin and Hegel*, p. 88.

attempting to prejudge the answer. It is pre-eminently a question to be met with a *solvitur ambulando*. From other points of view no doubt several different answers may be given, and Mr. Ritchie's pantheistic doctrine doubtless remains tenable, even though its epistemological basis be insecure. But at least as much may be claimed for the doctrine which Mr. Ritchie is most anxious to refute, the doctrine which denies most emphatically that existence is ever reducible to essence, and holds that the individual is the real.

At all events it is, I think, possible to show that this doctrine is neither uncritical nor unable to maintain itself against Mr. Ritchie's objections. Mr. Ritchie regards it as the uncritical product of the popular *Vorstellung*, because it makes its appearance at a very early stage in the interpretation of reality. But this should rather speak in its favour, if it is able to reassert its validity after the fullest critical examination of the facts and of objections such as Mr. Ritchie's.

Those objections arise in the first place out of his failure to appreciate the development in our conceptions of individuality and reality which has corresponded to the evolution of the objects which they symbolize, and in the second, out of his misunderstanding the respective positions which his opponents' logic assigns to thought-symbols and that which they symbolize. To say that the individual is the real and that the real is individual, is to make a proposition concerning a reality beyond it. It draws our attention to a fact which its terms cannot fully express. It is an adjectival description of reality in terms of thought-symbols. But it is not substantival. It is no definition of reality, but a reference to it, which expresses a characteristic feature intelligibly to real beings who can *feel* the extra-logical nature of reality. Hence it does not even necessarily state the *essence* of reality;[1] for the theoretic validity (not the practical convenience) of the doctrine of essence is called in question, and the fortunes of the expression certainly do not affect the *existence* of

---

[1] I should now (1903) define 'essence' systematically in terms of purpose.

reality. But Mr. Ritchie treats it as if the sum and substance of all reality were supposed to be contained in it, and dissects it mercilessly in order to show that there is nothing in it. But in criticizing the terms of the proposition he thinks he annihilates also the reality beyond it. He is mistaken; for he tramples only on the shadow of his foe. The individual and the real (*i.e.* the thing symbolized by those symbols of our speech) are *not* a couple of categories, nor even fully defined concepts. They are just sign-posts, which to a purely thinking mind might convey no meaning, or the contradictory meanings Mr. Ritchie criticizes, but which are meant for beings who are real as well as rational. Mr. Ritchie wilfully strips himself of one of his chief means of understanding the world when he abstracts from his own reality, and is then puzzled to find that he must be either nothing or an unknowable thing-in-itself, if he be not a bundle of universal thought-relations. So he comes to the absurd conclusion that he is made up of the products of one of his own activities! Does not this remind one of the hero of Andersen's fairy tale, who became subservient to his shadow? And so it is not surprising that to one who holds that the individual is the real, his polemic[1] should appear a σκιαμαχία, which cannot grasp the logical position of reality, and results only in a series of *hystera protera*.

For example, the individual is *not* 'everything which is called one'—things are called one because we attribute to them this extra-logical character of individuality. Nor is the individual what can be expressed by a single term—because the latter is only the nearest logic can get to expressing individuality. The individual is *not* a spiritual or thinking substance—because the whole category of substance rests upon and is abstracted from the individual, is an attempt thought makes to symbolize a substantivity, which its own adjectivity never properly expresses. The individual is more than a meeting-point of universals, because universals are not individuals, nor able to form

[1] *Darwin and Hegel*, pp. 93-100.

one, however many of them meet together. But they never do meet in numbers sufficient for a quorum: the attempt to reduce the individuals to universals generates an infinite process, which is never equivalent to the finite individual.

It is not, then, any logical difficulty which compels us to modify the original sense of the assertion that individuality is an ultimate and definitely determined characteristic of reality, but the general flux of reality itself. The individual also is in process, and so individuality becomes a characteristic of which reality may be seen to have less or more. The individuality of a drop of water is very evanescent; the individuality of a schoolboy, or even of a mule, is often found to be a very stubborn fact. Once we have degrees, we can form a standard of individuality; and the scale may be prolonged inferentially beyond what is actually given. Individuality thereby becomes a hypothesis and an ideal, as well as a characteristic of reality. The atom of physics is such a hypothetical prolongation of the individual in one direction. *Monads* and the like, are prolongations in another, and, in the writer's opinion, a far more promising, direction. So we can come to say that an individual is lacking in individuality, *i.e.* shows this universal characteristic of reality too indistinctly, *seems* to lend himself too easily to 'explanation' by universals, *seems* to borrow too much from others, and the like.

But this in nowise trenches upon the value of individuality. It simply postulates that we must learn to think of the individuality of the real as we have learned to think of its reality, not as a completed *being*, but as a *becoming*, i.e. *as being a process*. That which we designate by the term individuality is a varying and growing quantity, never wholly absent, but not always fully developed. At the one end of the process are the atoms—of which we can hardly discern the individuality. At the other end are—let us say the angels—individuals so perfectly individualized that, as mediaeval doctors taught, each would form a species by himself.

And with all deference to the *magni nominis umbra*, wherewith the Absolute has overshadowed the minds of philosophers, it seems to me that it is to some such conclusion as this that the course of science tends, rather than to a single merely rational 'universal law,' from which all *existences* might be necessarily deduced by purely logical processes. Of the difficulties which the latter alternative involves Mr. Ritchie gives us a sample on page 95, which is valuable as containing a recognition by one of his school, belated and inadequate though that recognition be, of the gravity of questions that should have been considered before ever it was enunciated that reality was Thought. This is not the place to discuss what meaning, if any, can be attached to the dictum that 'Thought *realizes* (does not this covertly reassert the distinction it pretends to explain away?) itself in its Other in order to return into itself,' but it may be remarked that Mr. Ritchie's 'dilemma' which drives him to such a solution, presents no difficulties to those who hold that the real is individual. For if the universe be constituted by the interactions of real individuals, some or all of whom display as *one* of their activities what we call 'thought,' there is no such 'irrational' and 'alien' Other as troubles Mr. Ritchie; for what 'confronts thought' is merely the *whole* of which it is the *part* and the practical interpreter. Nor does thought itself ever claim more for itself than this, whether it be in its reference of every proposition to a reality beyond it, or in its recognition of the necessity that an activity presupposes a real being as its substrate, or in its ultimate foundation of all proof on the self-evident.[1]

Thus it is only an infirmity of our reason, causing us to hypostasize abstractions, which leads us to speak of 'universal laws of nature,' as if they were more than shorthand expressions for the habitual interactions of realities. But as the subtlety of our insight draws nearer

---

[1] This remark no longer seems to me adequate: the value of self-evidence seems psychological rather than logical, and proof no longer needs 'foundations,' if it can postulate its premisses and increase their probability indefinitely by the confirmations of experience. Cf. *Formal Logic*, ch. xviii. §§ 2-3.

to the subtlety of nature, the crudeness of our 'universal laws' begins to appear. We grow better able to appreciate the real individuality of things, and so substitute *specific* 'laws' for *general*. We no longer ascribe John Doe's death to the universal mortality of humanity, but get the doctor to tell us precisely why John Doe, and no other, died. As we know him better, we do not account for a friend's conduct 'because he is a man,' but by a 'because he is *this* man.' In all our explanations we seek to get down to the particular, to do justice to the individual peculiarity of things, to enlarge the part assigned to personal idiosyncrasy. On the other hand, the less we know about a thing the more confidently can we lump it together with others and the more general are the statements which the calculus of probabilities emboldens us to make about it. Hence though in the case of the lower orders of individuality such appreciation of the peculiar nature of each thing may still be an impracticable and indefinitely distant ideal, with regard to higher orders the principle is well established. We could hardly say with the poet that 'the proper study for mankind is man,' if there were not, even in the meanest, an inexhaustible store of idiosyncratic reactions,— an individuality, in short, which becomes more and more conspicuous as we pass from the lower to the higher, and looks less and less like a combination of abstract universals! Hence, if we are to hazard any assertions concerning 'Omniscience,' is it not clear that it could have no use for universals, and so far from regarding the individual as compounded of them, would apprehend the idiosyncrasy of each thing in its action, without the clumsy mediation of 'universal laws'?

In conclusion, then, let us contend against Mr. Ritchie that other views than his own of ultimate reality are tenable, that they answer the epistemological and metaphysical difficulties at least as well as his, and are at least as deserving of the name of idealism (if Berkeley retains any claim to the doctrine he discovered!), and that they are far concreter and in closer interaction with the sciences than a metempirical misconception like the Absolute. Nor need we blush to own that a view like ours would *not* prove the popular *Vorstellung* of 'persons' *wholly* false (even though it would tend to regard 'things' as being only 'persons' of a lower development of individuality), and so might prove more attractive to the 'plain man.' For it is possible to be 'critical,' *without* disregarding either humanity or reality.

VIII

DARWINISM AND DESIGN [1]

ARGUMENT

Question as to the Value of the Argument from Design in the light of Darwinism. Its theological importance; its intrinsic flaws. The Darwinian explanation of adaptation without adapting, by Variation and Natural Selection. Is it final? I. Natural Selection proves too much; it would apply equally to automata. But if intelligence is wholly inefficacious why was it developed? II. The *causes* of Variation lie beyond the scope of Darwinism, and to explain Evolution, therefore, other factors must be added. III. Natural Selection does not necessarily lead to change of species, nor exclude degeneration, nor guarantee progression. A variable factor, therefore, must be added. IV. Darwinism does not explain the origin of adaptation, but presupposes it. Nor need the struggle to adapt be more than the preservation of this initial adaptation. The struggle for bare existence brings no growth of adaptation; it is only when intelligence aims at ends and transforms the struggle for life into one for good life that improvement comes. V. The true significance of Darwinism in the discovery of Natural Selection. Indefinite variation a methodological assumption justified as a simplifying abstraction. VI. But if it is understood as a description of actual fact, it rules out teleology *a priori* and quite apart from fact. Teleology and the calculus of probability. Hypothetically it is always possible to postulate a non-teleological context to any apparently teleological event. *Per contra* it is practically impossible to disprove the teleological interpretation, and ultimately both views are postulations of a will to believe and rest on an act of faith. VII. Summary: Darwinism not incompatible with teleology if its assumptions are taken as methodological, and it is arbitrary to take them as more. It is not necessarily hostile to teleology and even indirectly furthers it by throwing into relief the miracle of progress. Evolutionism not necessarily unteleological.

THE question which is proposed for consideration in the present essay concerns the value of what has been called the Argument from Design, in the light, not so much of

[1] Published in the *Contemporary Review* for June 1897. It had been my intention to have followed this paper up with discussions of other scientific views of Evolution (which explains my success in avoiding so much as the mention of Prof. Weismann's name), and finally to attempt the philosophic formulation of

the very various and widely spread modes of thought grouped together under the name of Evolutionism, but rather of the particular form of Evolutionism which has been popularized by the labours of Charles Darwin, and not undeservedly bears his name. In face of the Darwinian theory, and the account it gives of the pedigree of life, are we any longer entitled to entertain the notion that a more than human intelligence has anywhere or in any way contributed to the making of what now exists? Is there any evidence to be found in the constitution or working of any part of nature which directly testifies to a divine creator? These are old questions which, in some form or other, men have probably asked ever since they were men, and will probably continue to ask until they have become beasts or angels. Their practical importance will readily be admitted. For clearly our attitude towards life will be very different, according as we believe it to be inspired and guided by intelligence, or hold it to be the fortuitous product of blind mechanisms, whose working our helpless human intelligence can observe but in no wise control.

Although the Argument from Design has been taken as a rough description of the subject to be treated, it will yet be convenient, at the outset, both to restrict and to expand its scope. It will be restricted in that the discussion will turn exclusively on the argument as based on *living* nature; it will be expanded, in that its subject will include the question of the action of intelligence generally in producing the present condition of things. That is to say, the possibility that though no traces of a divine intelligence are to be found in the history of the organic world, there has yet to be admitted the action of human and animal intelligence, will not be overlooked. For the world may have been brought into its present shape by *intelligent efforts*, if not by *intelligent*

---

the conception of Progress which the current science assumes and the current metaphysic denies, without comprehending its nature. But *dis aliter visum*, and the paper (to which § IV. and the end of § VI. are additions), seemed worth including even as a fragment. For a discussion of the ultimate philosophic significance of Teleology, cp. *Axioms as Postulates*, § 45.

K

direction. We are not bound to assert a divine activity so soon as we have asserted the activity of intelligence. So it has to be confessed that before the Argument from Design has any theological value, three things have to be shown—(1) that intelligence, *i.e.* action directed to a purpose, has been at work; (2) that the intelligence has *not* been that of any of the admitted existences; and (3) that from its mode of action this intelligence may fairly be deemed divine.

But if it is necessary to draw attention to a leap which the theologian's logic is too apt to commit, it is no less important to point out that the denial of the Argument from Design logically leads much further than its opponents commonly dare to go. For it would seem that a complete denial of design in nature must deny the efficacy of all intelligence as such. A consistently mechanical view has to regard all intelligence as otiose, as an 'epi-phenomenal by-product,' or fifth wheel to the cart, in absence of which the given results would no less have occurred. And so, if this view were the truth, we should have to renounce all effort to direct our fated and ill-fated course adown the stream of time. Our consciousness would be an unmeaning accident. On the other hand, if intelligence played the part in history alleged by the second theory of its action, we might still cherish a hope of steering the bark that carries our fortunes at least into a temporary harbour; if that of the first theory, we might be moved to strain every muscle at the behest of a helmsman who could envisage the goal with unerring eye.

We have, then, three alternatives, of which the old 'Argument from Design' undertook to represent one. It was a simple-minded argument, as befitted a time when the eventful history through which life has passed, and the real intricacy of its phenomena, were as yet scarcely suspected. It contented itself with observing the variety and ingenuity of the means whereby living beings attained their ends. The structure of the eye and the ear, the prescience of instinct, the processes of growth and birth, etc., provided it with inexhaustible material for respectful admiration. Surely all this could not be the result of blind chance, of unintelligent matter—it proceeded from the hand of God.

In more modern language, the Argument from Design essentially argued from the existence of adaptation to the existence of an adapter. Beings would not have been so admirably fitted for their conditions of life unless they had been intelligently 'fitted' for them. And the adaptations were so wonderful that the adapter must have been divine.

Now, it is easy to see that in this shape the Argument from Design has several weak points quite apart from the attacks which Darwinism has made on it. (1) The thought of evolution, of a cosmic process, revealing itself in the course of time, the thought that lends grandeur and strength to the modern versions of the ancient plea, was entirely foreign to it. Consequently it took the process of adapting, whereby the adaptation arose to be instantaneous and complete. Consequently it was sadly perplexed by the fact that many adaptations were far from perfect. When Helmholtz pointed out the optical defects of the eye, and the ease with which they might have been remedied, the defenders of the old teleology were at a loss to answer a sacrilegious but exceedingly awkward criticism. They could not admit what now the teleological evolutionist may say without wincing—viz. that the adaptations in themselves, and as they now exist, form a somewhat imperfect and insufficient testimony for divine agency, and no testimony at all for a divine omnipotence. And, (2) it was not shown that animal intelligence might not have constructed the adaptations actually found. This suggestion could be ruled out only so long as the belief in the fixity of species prevailed; but it became far more tenable so soon as practically unlimited time was allowed to intelligent effort to reach the degree of adaptation exhibited. And so there was nothing for it but to ascribe to the direct contrivance of the Deity every adaptation and every instinct found in the organic world, to burden, for example, the divine conscience with the fiendish ingenuity with which a sphex-wasp stings into helplessness the caterpillars it has selected to be the living food of its young. The defence of the divine intelligence, in short, was maintained at a ruinous expense to the divine benevolence.

Thus the old Argument from Design was in a bad way even before Darwinism appeared upon the scene with pretensions to deliver the *coup de grâce*. Darwin himself, it is true, did not assert that no adapter existed. But he did what was more effective; he suggested an alternative way in which adaptation might have arisen. This was not immediately fatal to the theory of intelligent effort as such; for in human beings, at least, that theory was generally admitted as a *vera causa*, and so could be co-ordinated with the Darwinian explanation. But it did leave the theory of an inferred divine adapter in the logically indefensible position of being an additional and superfluous explanation of facts already sufficiently explained in other ways.

Darwin's alternative consisted in showing that the existence of adaptations is conceivable and possible, although there has been neither an adapter nor any process of active adapting, but merely a sifting or eliminating of the 'unfitter.' To show this, he required only two of the postulates of his theory—(*a*) the existence of variability in living organisms; and (*b*) the struggle for existence among them leading to the survival of the fitter, or comparatively fit, and the elimination of the unfitter, or comparatively unfit. The variability of organisms was further conceived as of such a character as to lead to what were called 'accidental' variations in every direction. This was to indicate that no special tendency to vary in any direction more than in any other was to be assumed, and that the causes of variation, which Darwin forbore to investigate, did not favour one sort of variation rather than another. Darwin, therefore, supposed nature to start with an indefinitely large supply of variations, some adaptive, the immensely greater number not. These were sifted by the process of Natural Selection, which eliminated the non-adapted and ill-adapted, so that only the fit survived, and after a time organisms would be, in a general way, adapted to their conditions of life. The process by which these adaptations arose, therefore, was a purely mechanical one, and did not imply any intelligence. The sifting of variations by natural selection would no more imply a purposive ordering than the successive depositing of lighter and lighter detritus as a river flows out into the sea.

The anti-teleologically minded, to whom the support which biological facts had seemed to give to the belief in design had long been hateful, were naturally delighted with this easy and obvious way of disposing of the appearance of intelligent adaptation. They loudly proclaimed the disappearance of the Argument from Design, and even their critics only ventured to object that Darwinism had substituted one kind of teleology for another, and made the good (or survival) of the organism determine the conduct adopted by the race. This was a poor consolation, and, in my opinion, an illusory one. For it is not *for the sake* of the organism's good that the conduct is adopted, but it so happens that conduct can only become prevalent when it has survival-value, and that the prevalent conduct and that adapted to the conditions of life must coincide. In reality the process is not teleological, but purely mechanical. This appears quite clearly if it is supposed to act upon beings conceived to be devoid of all intelligence, and it turns out that it acts equally well. If animals were mere automata, their variations would be sifted by natural selection in just the same way, and it is quite possible and legitimate to apply Darwinian methods of argument to astronomical physics and the chemistry of the elements.

But if the Darwinian assumptions are equally applicable to automata, they are, ultimately and in principle, just as fatal to the view that animal intelligence plays any part at all in the history of life as they are to the belief in its divine direction, and this logical implication is already appearing in the ultra-Darwinian writings. It is quite consistent of them to speak of the 'omnipotence' of natural selection and to reject or minimize all other possible factors, like intelligent effort, use and disuse, physical and chemical conditions, etc., as directive forces in Organic Evolution.

If, then, Variation and Natural Selection are the alpha and omega of the matter, and adequate to account for all the facts, it would seem to be beyond doubt that there is no longer any place for any sort of teleological argument. Nevertheless, it may reasonably be contended that this inference would be entirely erroneous, for the reasons to be presently set forth.

I. The *ease* with which the Darwinian argument dispenses with all intelligence as a factor in survival excites suspicion. It is proving too much to show that adaptation might equally well—*i.e. as completely, if not as rapidly*—have arisen in automata. For we are strongly persuaded that we ourselves are not automata, and strive hard to adapt ourselves. In us at least, therefore, intelligent effort *is* a source of adaptation. And the same will surely be admitted in the case of the higher animals. How far down the possibility of such intelligent co-operation in a greater or less degree is admissible, depends very much on people's preconceived notions; but we are, at all events, unable to fix any definite inferior limit beyond which influence of intelligence cannot penetrate. Intelligence, therefore, is a *vera causa* as a source of adaptations at least co-ordinate with Natural Selection, and this can be denied only if it is declared inefficacious *everywhere*, if all living beings, ourselves included, are declared to be automata.

But should this be attempted—and it would seem to be involved, *e.g.* in the assumption of 'psychophysical parallelism'—a peculiar difficulty arises on the basis of the Darwinian theory itself. If intelligence has no efficacy in promoting adaptation—*i.e.* if it has no survival-value, how comes it to be developed at all? On the

Darwinian assumptions only those qualities can be developed which have a value for survival. This must be true also of intelligence, which, consequently, cannot be mere surplusage.

It must therefore be admitted that Darwinism is demonstrably wrong and refutes itself, if it seeks to deny the possibility of purposive adaptation and to regard *all* adaptation as the result of a mechanical natural selection. If, however, intelligence is re-admitted as a *vera causa*, there arises at least a possibility that other intelligence besides that of the known living beings may have been operative in the world's history.

II. We may scrutinize the initial assumptions of Darwinism from which the anti-teleological consequences flowed. We may ask whether variation is really as 'indefinite' and 'accidental' as represented. Is it really so impossible to say anything about its causes?

We are here entering on a battlefield of science where the reputations of experts are still being made and unmade. Hence it behoves a philosopher to be careful. Nevertheless one may venture to make some remarks on the general aspects of the question, and to assert that the matter cannot possibly be left where Darwinism would leave it. Thus (1) Darwinism puts aside the question of the origin of variations. They are 'accidental,' that is, beyond the pale of inquiry. Yet it seems to be a perfectly good and legitimate scientific question to ask— whence these variations? What, in Professor E. D. Cope's parlance, was the *origin* of the fittest? how, in Dr. J. G. Schurman's words, do you account for the *arrival* as well as for the *survival* of the fittest?[1]

(2) Darwinism assumes the occurrence of indefinite variation in every direction. That assumption is, as we shall see, essential and quite justifiable as a methodological device in examining the facts and in working out the theory of Natural Selection ; but we have a perfect right to ask whether it is actually itself a fact. That is, the study of the variations which actually occur is a perfectly

[1] *Ethical Import of Darwinism*, p. 78.

legitimate one, and as initiated—*e.g.*, in Bateson's recent work on the subject[1]—it very distinctly suggests that variation is frequently discontinuous, and that it is to these discontinuous 'sports' rather than to the accumulation of slight differences that we have to look for the origin of many new species.

In both these respects, then, the non-Darwinian evolutionists seek to penetrate deeper into the nature of Organic Evolution than Darwin needed to do when he established the reality and importance of Natural Selection, and when Darwin's followers speak of the 'omnipotence of Natural Selection,' they fail to observe that their opponents have really turned their flank. For while they do not deny the reality of Natural Selection, they go on to solve problems which, on the basis of Darwinism, cannot be discussed. Hence the Darwinians have not really any logical *locus standi*—*e.g.*, in many of their objections to the 'Lamarckian' factors in evolution. Biologists must be left a free hand in their attempts to determine the nature and source of the variations actually occurring, and in their theories to account for them. If, after admitting the existence of natural selection, they go on to say that variations are not indefinite and their causes not indeterminable, Darwinian orthodoxy has no right to interfere. Or if it mistakenly does try to interfere, its defeat is certain. For it is practically certain that some influences which can only be called 'Lamarckian' must affect both the number and the character of the variations. Living organisms are subject to the general physical and chemical laws of nature, and these render variations in certain directions practically impossible. It is very probable also that they produce certain definite effects upon the organisms exposed to them, and thus give a definite direction to variation. Thus the force of gravity imposes limits on the size to which organisms can grow upon the earth; high and low temperatures produce definite effects upon all living tissue. Starvation also will stunt the growth of all organisms. The efficacy, then, of

[1] *Materials for the Study of Variation.*

these additional factors in determining both what sort of variations can occur, and in what directions organisms can vary, can hardly be disputed. Yet this admission would seem to be a sufficient refutation of the extreme claim that Natural Selection alone is competent to account for everything and exhausts the list of the factors in organic evolution which are logically admissible.

It follows that if the Darwinian factors are not an adequate and complete account of what really happens, we are at liberty to supplement them by any additional factors we may require. Some such factors, such as geographical isolation, are, of course, admitted even by the ultra-Darwinians; others, like sexual selection and the inherited effects of use and disuse, were adopted by Darwin himself; others, again, like the sensibility of organisms and their conscious efforts to attain their ends, are at least tolerated as worth discussing. What part, if any, these factors actually play in the history of organisms is still *sub judice* and cannot here be determined. It is enough for the present argument that Darwinism is not entitled to bar them out *a priori* as methodologically inadmissible. For if they are not inadmissible, a breach is made in the iron barrier with which the original conception of a mechanically complete Darwinism shut out every possibility of teleology. It is so far attenuated that it can no longer reject *a priori* the suggestion of the possibility of one more teleological factor, viz. of a purposive direction of the course of variation. Such a purposive direction would still be hard to prove, because its action would be cloaked under a mass of other causes of variation, and because it would perhaps only display itself clearly in the occurrence of variations leading on to new species or new eras; but it would no longer be unthinkable, and that would be no slight step towards a teleology.

III. It has been shown so far that if Darwinism is, as may easily be done, made into a dogmatic denial of the share of intelligence in Organic Evolution and of the admissibility of determinable causes, of a limited number, and of a definite direction of variations, it is demonstrably wrong; we shall go on to assert that in any form it leaves unexplained the main point, the very point it was invented to explain, viz. Organic Evolution itself. This may seem a startling statement when one remembers that what led Darwin to propound his theory was precisely the evidence for Organic Evolution, the evidence of the descent of the existing forms of life from widely different ancestors. Yet the statement is made under a due sense of responsibility and with a full intention of proving it.

Darwin put forward his theory as an account of the origin of species—it is asserted that there is nothing in his theory in itself to account for the origination of species. At least, in the sense that Darwinism formulates causes which would logically lead to the evolution of new forms of life. The Darwinian factors only state certain conditions under which organisms have evolved, but they contain nothing that would necessarily cause them to evolve. They simply state that Natural Selection is a general condition under which all life exists, *whether it evolves or not*. It is equally applicable to species which change and species which do not. Every form of life is continually subject to the action of Natural Selection, weeding out the unfit and promoting the survival of the fit. But it does not follow that any particular form of life will be transformed. The conditions of success may be so various and so variable that on the whole no possible variation can obtain the victory over any other, and as a whole the species remains as it was. Let us illustrate the way in which a species under natural selection may yet persist unchanged. Suppose there is in a definite area an animal, say an anemone, which has a certain range of temperature and is variable, so that while the mass of the species is violet, it tends to vary in the direction both of blue and of red. Suppose, further, that the blue variety can stand the cold best and the red the heat, while the violet is intermediate in these respects. Now suppose a succession of unusually cold seasons. Clearly the blue anemones will flourish at the expense of the violet, and the red will nearly die out. Next suppose a succession of warm seasons ; clearly the red will recover their strength and the preponderance of the blue will be reduced. At the end of the cycle, red, blue, and violet will very likely exist in their original proportions. That is, though the Darwinian factors, variability and natural selection, have been fully and continually operative, the species has not changed. Such a case, though I have intentionally chosen an imaginary one, is not merely hypothetical; it is illustrated by a small but sufficient number of persistent species which have remained unchanged from very early geological times. Darwin himself[1] mentions the Nautilus, the Lingula, and the order of the Foraminifera, antique stick-in-the-muds literally and metaphorically, which are the Chinese of the animal world and have persisted without change from the Laurentian and Silurian ages. And over shorter periods a similar persistence under Natural Selection is the normal condition of the organic world. Indeed, specific stability is a much commoner result of Natural Selection than Evolution.

And further, not only are the Darwinian factors perfectly compatible with a changeless persistence of species, but they are equally well satisfied by change in a direction which is the reverse of that which is actually found to prevail. For not merely progressive evolution but also *degeneration* may come about under the impartial operation of variability and Natural Selection. Under certain circumstances the more lowly organized may be the fitter—*i.e.* the better adapted to cope with the conditions of life that prevail at the time ; and then the higher must either die out or degenerate. Hence biologists are familar with countless instances of degeneration everywhere. We ourselves are degenerate in far more obvious and undeniable ways than sensationalists like Nordau contend. We have lost our fur—all except a few patches on the head—our ancestral tails, our pineal eye, our sturdy claws and prehensile toes, the tapering tips of our ears and the graceful power of attentively pricking

[1] *Origin of Species*, ii. pp. 83, 90, 117.

them up; the vermiform appendix indeed remains as a joy to the evolutionist and a profit to the doctor, but to the patient the useless and dangerous relic of a *damnosa hereditas*. And all this degeneration has taken place under the action of Natural Selection.

Not but what there has also been much progression, and that in the aggregate its amount has far exceeded that of degeneration. This is just the reason why we speak of the history of life as an evolution. Life has been on the whole progressive; but progress and retrogression have both been effected under the same 'law' of Natural Selection. How, then, can the credit of the result be ascribed to Natural Selection? Natural Selection is equally ready to bring about degeneration or to leave things unchanged. How, then, can it be that which determines which of the three possible (and actual) cases shall be realized? Let us grant that Natural Selection is a permanent condition of life, from which no beings can at any time escape. But for this very reason it cannot be the principle of differentiation which decides which of the alternative courses the evolution of life will in fact pursue. It cannot be Natural Selection that causes one species to remain stationary, another to degenerate, a third to develop into a higher form. The constant pressure which it exercises on organisms does not in the least explain the actual course of evolution any more than the constant pressure of the atmosphere determines the direction in which we walk. The cause of the particular changes which have led to the existing forms of life cannot be found in an unchanging law of all life; it must be sought in forces whose intermittent action has made an instrument of Natural Selection.

It is clear, then, that to explain the changes which have resulted in the existing forms of life *some variable factor has to be added to Natural Selection*. And as to the nature of this factor Darwinism, *qua* Darwinism, tells us nothing. There may have been one or more of them, they may have been of all sorts. They may have been nothing more recondite than climatic changes or geographical isolation, to mention two of Darwin's favourite explanations when Natural Selection stands in need of something to help it out in order that it may proceed to the origination of species. Now clearly these causes of the transmutation of species, and others that might be instanced, are under the proper conditions adequate to produce *new* species—though there is no apparent reason why they should so predominantly produce *higher* species —but that does not concern us here. The point to be emphasized is that these additional factors lie beyond the scope of the peculiarly Darwinian factors, which can have nothing to say on the question whether they are to be accepted or rejected. So long as the action of Natural Selection as a permanent and universal condition of life is conceded, there is nothing further to be said by the Darwinian theory. If, then, there is no other scientific objection to it, the notion of a purposive direction of variation becomes admissible. Nay, it would be possible to combine a belief in special creation with that in Natural Selection, and claim that while Natural Selection alone could not give rise to a new species, Natural Selection *plus* special creation might account for the distribution and succession of species. We should thus reach the paradoxical result, that whereas Natural Selection was expressly invented to supersede special creation, there is no necessity to regard the two theories as incompatible! I mention this paradox merely to illustrate by it the helplessness of mere Natural Selection and the necessity of appealing to subsidiary theories in order to account for the facts of Organic Evolution.

Of course, there is an abundance of such subsidiary theories, and many of them are quite unteleological. One may, for instance, continue to object to teleology on a variety of general grounds. Only those objections will not be specially grounded in Darwinism, and so far as the latter goes, it will not be possible to rule out the supposition that the process of Evolution may be guided by an intelligent design.

IV. A further logical limitation of Darwinism is of a

still more fundamental character. We have seen that Darwinism can supply no theory of the origin of Variation. Nor does it necessarily lead to the transmutation of species. Nor does it as such involve a growth of adaptation or yield an adequate account of Progress. But more than all this, it does not even give an account of the *origin of adaptation*. A little reflection will show that a certain amount of adaptation must always be conceived to pre-exist before Natural Selection can begin to operate, the amount, namely, which is requisite to enable the organisms to exist, out of which the 'fit' are subsequently to be selected. There must be an existence of the *fit* before there can be a survival of the *fitter*, and beings must be capable of existing at all before the question of their living better and surviving can be raised. Hence the initial degree of adaptation needed for the existence of organisms in the world together must always be *presupposed* by the Darwinian theory. It must renounce therefore its claim to have accounted for adaptation as such, and so to have wholly superseded the teleological argument.

Indeed, it may be questioned whether it *ever* involves any growth of adaptation, or does more than describe the means by which an already existing adaptation is preserved through changes in the conditions of existence. It is clear that a thing must be before it can be selected. And to be, it must always be adapted to the conditions of existence. It cannot be said to grow *better adapted*, unless it actually manages to exist more copiously, or fully, or easily. But can this be said to be true of the ordinary Darwinian version of the history of organisms? Is it true that they have grown better adapted, and are better able to survive? Is not the struggle for existence, now as ever, a struggle for a bare livelihood? It boots not to suggest that many or most of the beings who now just manage to exist would have lived in comfort in a former age; for apart from the dubious truth of the assertion, it is clear the fitness of each being must be measured by its ability to exist under the conditions of its own time and place.

What seems to happen is rather this: we *start* with adaptation, with a sufficient equilibrium between the organism and its conditions of life to allow of its existence (for a season). But this equilibrium is constantly endangered by the changes in its conditions of life; hence there is constant need for an adaptive response to these changes, for novelty of adaptation. This response some somehow manage to effect, and so survive; the rest do not, and therefore perish. And it is this process which we dignify with the name of Natural Selection. But it is the name only for the mechanism which just keeps alive the sacred fire of life; it neither lights it nor improves its radiance. Nor do we come upon any incontestable traces of improvement until we come upon the traces of intelligence. It is only with beings that aim at ends, conceive *goods* and frame ideals of better living, that there begins that funding of the power over life which renders possible the pursuit, not of mere life, but of *good life*, and transfigures the struggle for existence by an ethical ideal. Natural Selection is a universal condition of life, but it is not for us a model or a guide. It is non-moral and relieves us of no moral responsibility; it remains within our power to mould it well or ill.

V. It will, perhaps, be objected that in the anxiety to invalidate the anti-teleological implications of Darwinism we have gone too far, and denied its whole scientific importance. For what is the value of Natural Selection if it does not explain Evolution? Such a result is too monstrously paradoxical to be accepted as the outcome of any argument, however solid it may seem.

This objection should be welcomed by anticipation, because it leads on to a discussion of the real scientific value of the Darwinian theory, and in so doing traces to its real source the *prima facie* conflict between Darwinism and teleology. In reality there is not involved in anything that has been said any disparagement of Darwin's tireless scientific labour, nor does anything that has been said in the slightest detract from the permanent value and immense importance of his work. What is disputed is not the valuable part of his work, nor the true meaning of his theory, and these remain intact when a misinterpretation of his theory and a misapplication of his results are controverted.

What, then, is the true significance of Darwin's work? It is *to have established once and for all the reality, universality and importance of Natural Selection as a condition of organic life.* That has been its main achievement rather than the refutation of crude theories of creation and teleology, or even the assignment of an all-sufficient cause for the changes of organic forms. It is somewhat difficult to establish this view by direct citation from the utterances either of Darwin or of the other leading Darwinians, for the reason that Darwin stumbled upon Natural Selection in the endeavour to prove Evolution, and never was greatly interested in, or even competent to discuss, the logic of his theory. Hence its fundamental conceptions are introduced quite innocently and without formal definition, as if their meaning could not possibly be mistaken; hence, also, terms like 'indefinite,' 'endless,' 'fortuitous,' sometimes only mean, respectively, 'not obviously limited,' 'in sufficient quantities,' and 'unexplored'; sometimes, as will be shown presently, they seem, quite unconsciously, to mean much more.[1] This state of things is, however, explained when we remember that there is abundant autobiographical evidence that Darwin himself elaborated his theory in support of evolutionism against creationism, and by concrete examples rather than by abstract deductions; for by such methods he would naturally not become fully conscious of its logical implications. Hence the extraction of the logical root of the Darwinian theory becomes a matter of philosophical interpretation which may be represented somewhat as follows.

Suspecting Natural Selection to play a part in the Evolution of life, Darwin had to determine what part of

---

[1] Similarly Darwinian discussions of the definition of 'higher' and 'lower,' of the persistence of lower forms and of the source of progression generally find refuge in our immense ignorance of the past, and exhibit only the reluctance of their authors to tie themselves down to precise formulations.—Cp. *Origin of Species*, ii. pp. 117, 151, 243, 274. Wallace, *Darwinism*, p. 120.

the total effect was due to the factor which he called Natural Selection. To solve this problem he adopted, no doubt instinctively, the method by which all scientific investigation proceeds in dealing with a complicated problem. This method is that of *abstraction*, of abstraction as a means of simplification. We isolate the factor of which we seek to determine the value by taking cases in which the other factors may be supposed to neutralize each other, and so to be irrelevant to the result. Our result is abstract, but, if the analysis has been carefully done, it is applicable to the concrete facts.

This is precisely what Darwin did. The phenomena of life are immensely complicated, and there was ample reason to suppose that they were affected by all sorts of influences. To lay bare the effect of Natural Selection, it was necessary to simplify them by constructing an ideal case from which other influences might be excluded.

This is the logical significance of the fundamental assumptions of Darwinism. Darwin knew that organisms varied. He did not know how much, or in what direction. But if there was a definite direction about the variation of organisms, this clearly might in various ways retard or accelerate the action of Natural Selection, and would in any event cloak it. It is obvious, for example, that if a race of elephants tend to vary in the direction of whiteness, then, though that variety may be weaker and less well equipped for the struggles of life, there will always be a certain supply of not-yet-eliminated white elephants.[1] Again the fate of the variety will be widely different, according as men consider them unlucky and kill them, or sacred and watch over them with especial care.

In order, therefore, to avoid the initial complications introduced by a possible tendency of variation in a definite direction, it was logically necessary for Darwin to assume that as a whole Variation had no definite direction. Variations occurred of all sorts, advantageous,

---

[1] It is supposed that albinos tend to be produced by in-breeding, and hence the supply is always kept up in spite of Natural Selection.

L

disadvantageous, and indifferent, hence, as a whole, Variation was indefinite. Darwin, that is, did not facilitate his task by supposing a mass of favourable variations to give Natural Selection a good start; favourable variations were no commoner than they would have been if they had been drawn at random from an indefinite supply of possible variations of all sorts.

Similarly, in order to avoid the complicating question whether these variations were not produced by definite causes, and so tended in a definite direction, Darwin said in effect—Let us suppose these indefinite variations to be accidental. That is, let us waive the question of where they came from. In this way he arrived at the assumption of indefinite accidental variation on which his theory proceeded.

It is clear, then, that this essential assumption of Darwinism was originally *methodological*, that it was a simplification of the facts assumed for purposes of analysis and easier calculation. This is, of course, an everyday procedure in all the sciences, and if a methodological assumption has been skilfully selected, it does excellent service. Now Darwin's assumption was an exceedingly skilful one : for whether or not it was true that Variation was absolutely indefinite and void of direction, it yet ordinarily seemed sufficiently indefinite to enable the ideal theoretical case to throw a most instructive light upon the actual facts.

Perhaps the character of the assumption of indefinite variation is best illustrated by a parallel methodological fiction which has also played a great part in history. I refer to the assumption of 'the economic man' in political economy. In order to build up the science of wealth, the early economists disentangled the primary laws of wealth-production by the methodological assumption of the 'economic man.' They said: Let us consider man as a wealth-producing animal ; let us suppose, therefore, that the production of wealth is his sole object in life. In that case the economic man must be taken as (1) absolutely laborious, as never distracted from his work by emotional indisposition or laziness, as a perfect wealth-producing machine; (2) he must be taken as absolutely intelligent, as always using the best means to his end, as knowing how to use his labour to best advantage, and how to sell its products in the most advantageous manner; (3) he must be taken as absolutely selfish, as absolutely disregardful of any consideration but that of how he could acquire the largest possible amount of wealth. Having thus *simplified* economic facts, let us see what will happen. So they proceeded to build up the science of abstract economics. When it was objected to them that their methodological assumption, the economic man, did not exist in reality, the wiser among them replied: 'Of course we know that, but the conditions of actual business are sufficiently close to what they would be under our ideal conditions to have much light thrown on them by the latter.' And they gave thereby a clue through the labyrinth of facts to the economists who succeeded them, and were able by means of it to calculate the effects in various departments of the inaccuracy of the methodological assumption of the 'economic man.'

Now 'the economic man' is an exact parallel to the 'accidental' and 'indefinite' variation of Darwin. They are both methodological assumptions, travesties of the truth, if taken as full and complete accounts of the actual facts, epoch-making and indispensable *organa* of science, if properly used. And the parallel extends still further. As philosophers are well aware, there is everywhere in the sciences a tendency to forget that methodological assumptions are not necessarily true because they are useful,[1] a tendency to assert as a fact what was at first assumed as an abstraction and a fiction for greater convenience in examining the facts. Alike in ordinary life and in science we are almost without exception given over, not to the adoration of an unknown god, but to the worship of forgotten abstractions and methodological

---

[1] Even so excellent a thing as Pragmatism may be overdone! In fact it usually is, *by its critics* and in popular thinking, when methodological assumptions of limited applicability are mistaken for absolute truths.

fictions, and happy is he who can avoid bending the knee to such bogeys.

For this idolatry leads to terrible confusions, as these very cases show. When 'the economic man' is taken seriously, and made a practical ideal, he leads to results which are incompatible with the maintenance of political and social cohesion, and with the sanctity of moral laws. And he provokes a reaction even worse than himself in the direction of revolutionary socialism.

So, too, with the Darwinian assumption. When it is taken as a fact and as the last word on the subject of evolution, it leaves no room for the Argument from Design, and leads to consequences entirely inconsistent with any teleology. Moreover, the misrepresentation of the principle of indefinite variation is a very easy and common one, and has been adopted in this very article in exhibiting the conflict between Darwinism and teleology. But, once it is recognized as a misinterpretation, as a case of confusing a method of examining facts with the facts themselves, the danger of any further conflict is averted.

It remains to give practical confirmation of this interpretation of the real meaning of the Darwinian principle. To do so, it may be pointed out, in the first place, that Darwin assumed the indefiniteness of Variation initially upon utterly insufficient evidence, or, rather, upon no relevant evidence at all. For he was not in the position to make any positive statements about the variations that actually occurred, and had not had the time to study them exhaustively. In fact, it is only in these days that the actual facts of Variation are beginning to be observed and recorded, and many generations of workers will probably pass away before it will be possible to state with approximate certainty what variations actually take place, and can be conceived as likely to take place. If, then, Darwin's knowledge of Variation were to be regarded as the logical basis for asserting Variation to be in fact indefinite, the foundations of Darwinism would have been extremely insecure, and Darwin ought to have begun with an exhaustive study of variations before broaching his theory. Did he, as was to be expected from so exceptionally cautious an inquirer, subject himself to this preliminary investigation? He did nothing of the sort. He simply pointed to the known variety of variations as approximately illustrative of his conception of 'indefinite variation,' and went ahead. I can find nothing more formal than a request [1] that 'the endless number of slight variations and individual differences occurring in our domestic productions, and in a lesser degree in those under nature, be borne in mind.' In other words, he did not attempt to prove the existence of indefinite variation in its literal sense; he took it for granted for the methodological reasons aforesaid. Was it wrong to do this? Not unless science is deprived of the right of making methodological assumptions. And the practical justification of Darwin's procedure is seen in the fact that his theory has in the ripeness of time provided a guiding thread and an impetus to the study of facts that might otherwise long have eluded the grasp of science.

VI. That the facts of Organic Evolution really play a very small part in producing the speculative bearing of Darwinism will appear also if we inquire into the reason of its anti-teleological action as commonly understood.

For it turns out that the destructiveness of Darwinism is a by-product of the theory which lurked in the innocent-looking phrase, 'indefinite variation.'

We have seen that, as a method of investigating the facts, this phrase is thoroughly defensible; but then in that shape it does not really touch the question of teleology at all. For if the variations are only called indefinite in order to determine the working of Natural Selection, then the possibility of their purposive occurrence is not thereby excluded.

On the other hand, let us take the phrase as a description of an actual fact. If there *are* an indefinite number of variations, and if they tend in an indefinite number of directions, it follows that the variations in any

[1] *Origin of Species*, i. p. 97.

one direction will not be more than an infinitesimal portion of the whole. It is not necessary, therefore, to adduce any special cause for those particular variations; they need not be regarded as due to anything more than chance, that is, to causes which do not in any intelligent way discriminate in their favour. That advantageous variations should occasionally occur is no more remarkable, or in need of explanation, than that by throwing dice long enough we should occasionally throw sixes. If, then, indefinite variation be an actual fact, no special intelligence need be assumed to account even for the most abnormal variation. In other words, *a principle has been adopted which rules out the hypothesis of intelligent direction a priori*, if we forget or fail to perceive that indefinite variation is a methodological assumption. And being *a priori*, the principle would rule out the hypothesis whatsoever the facts were, and however much they might suggest the action of intelligence. Intelligence is nonsuited by the way in which the question is put, and irrespective of the facts of the case.

Yet all this is due to nothing more mysterious than an application of the calculus of probabilities, for, as all who are even slightly familiar with this calculus are aware, even the most improbable result may be expected to occur if a sufficiency of cases be given. It is highly improbable, for example, that any one should, by fair dealing, acquire a hand containing thirteen trumps at whist. But if he had played some 640,000,000,000 hands, he might fairly expect to hold all the trumps on one occasion. Everything that happens *may* be due to chance, and no matter how improbabilities are multiplied, we never altogether eliminate the infinitesimal probability that everything *is* due to chance. Supposing we were to try to persuade an obstinate materialist that our conduct was dictated by a purpose and due to intelligence, and was not the action of an automatic mechanism which had by some strange chance put on a delusive appearance of purposiveness. However intelligently we acted, we could not convince our adversary, if he were permitted to regard our action as one out of a series of actions displaying no intelligence. He would cheerfully admit that the action seemed intelligent, and by itself would justify the inference to a real intelligence behind it. But he would urge, if I take it as the one intelligent action out of an indefinite number of unintelligent actions, there is nothing in it that need cause surprise or calls for the assumption of real intelligence. We might try to convince him by multiplying the symptoms of intelligence, but in vain. For, though he would admit the growing improbability of such a continuous series of apparently purposive actions, he could still expand the context of non-purposive actions rapidly enough to maintain his theory of their chance origination.[1]

If, therefore, an indefinite number of non-adaptive variations be really granted, no adaptations, however numerous and complete, can ever prove an intelligent cause of variation. Even if all the known facts testified aloud to the operation of an adapting intelligence, the Darwinian assumption might still be used to disprove all teleology, if unbounded license were given for the invention of hypothetical variations! Now, of course it is not contended that variations as known are all obviously adaptive; it is claimed rather that we do not know enough about them to say what their actual character is. But it must most strenuously be asserted that the Darwinian theory cannot be quoted as destructive of the action of purposive intelligence in organic evolution until the occurrence of indefinite variation has been raised from the position of a methodological device to that of an incontestable fact.

Even then it may be doubted whether the fortuitous character of the facts could ever be rendered incontestable. To defy refutation by the facts the teleologist has merely to adopt a device analogous to that of his opponent. Just as the latter could always assume a non-teleological extension of what seemed a teleological ordering, so the former can always assume a secret

[1] Cp. pp. 71-2.

teleology within the seeming chance. This he can do in several ways; most thoroughly by assuming that the order purposed *exactly* coincided with the results of a fortuitous distribution, and was intended so to do. This ingenuity, however, would somewhat overreach itself. It would have to conceive the intelligence immanent in the world's order as one *aiming at concealment*. For our only method of discriminating between the results of 'design' and 'chance' is to observe a *deviation* from the fortuitous distribution (which betrays no preference for any particular result) in the direction of what may be conceived as a *more valuable* result. Hence in the case supposed, the deviation being nil, we should have no reason to suspect the presence of intelligence. And generally, one would have to hold that a supposition which rendered the results of 'design' and 'chance' undistinguishable abolished also the difference between the two conceptions; a world governed by such an intelligence would be *no better* than one wholly due to 'chance.'[1] By supposing, therefore, that the 'design' *makes no difference*, the teleologist would defeat his purpose.

But he can assume the intelligent deviation to be of whatever magnitude the facts demand, and by assuming it to be *small enough* he can suppose a purposively guided order which mimics chance, just as the anti-teleologist could explain 'design' as a mimicry by chance. And so he can conceive a (really) teleological order infinitesimally different from one merely fortuitous, and the mere tabulation of statistics will never decide its actual character. The mere record of the throws will never tell us that once in a hundred throws the dice came up sixes by intelligent design (of a nefarious kind). And yet that single throw might have sufficed to win the game! Now in the history of Organic Evolution the really valuable events which help on progress are certainly of the extremest rarity. It is only once in an aeon that

[1] Cp. James, *Varieties of Religious Experience*, pp. 443-7, and *Philosophical Conceptions and Practical Results*, pp. 9-11.

an 'accidental' variation distinguishes itself from a myriad others by lifting organic structure permanently on to a higher plane. It is only once in centuries that a genius is born who does the same for social progress: the great events in history are utterly unique, and turn the course of things so thoroughly that they need never be repeated. But all uniqueness makes a mock of Science, which 'explains' by finding uniformities.

Hence the teleological and the anti-teleological interpretation of events will never decide their conflict by appealing to the facts: for in the facts each finds what it wills and comes prepared to see. And yet the facts will not *wholly* bear out either, so long as they present traces of what we can describe as disorder in the one case, or order in the other. The decision therefore needs an act of choice; it eminently calls for the exercise of our 'will to believe'; it rests, like all the ultimate assumptions of our knowledge, upon an act of faith.

VII. The position, then, is this: 1. If we take the Darwinian assumptions as methodological, they are perfectly legitimate, most fruitful and valuable, and establish the fundamental biological law of Natural Selection. But there is no conflict with the belief in teleology, and the Argument from Design remains unimpaired.

2. If we take the Darwinian assumption as representing a fact, it is certainly destructive of all teleology. But the fact is not established and is open to grave doubts on scientific grounds, while its destruction of the teleological argument is simply a foregone conclusion *a priori.*

3. If, while admitting that indefinite variation has not been shown to exist, we yet contend that it is the sole working assumption by which the facts can be investigated, and that the possibility of a purposive guidance must be rigidly excluded from Science, we simply beg the question. For certainly, if all the evidence is to be interpreted in accordance with such canons, no evidence for teleology can ever be found. One need not object to people wearing blue spectacles if they like—they are in fact

often useful, if not ornamental—but it is ludicrous to maintain that everything is blue because we insist on looking through the spectacles.

This ought to constitute a sufficiently explicit answer to the question, Is Darwinism, properly understood, necessarily hostile to teleology? Not only have we been able to answer that question by an emphatic negative, but we have uncovered the source of the misunderstanding which led to the question. We might go on to raise rather the opposite question, and ask, Does Darwinism in any way tend to strengthen the Argument from Design and the belief in teleology? That would, perhaps, be asking too much; its services in this respect seem to be mostly of an indirect sort. It is often invigorating to be attacked, especially when the assult can be successfully repulsed, and perhaps in this sense the Argument from Design is the stronger for having been impugned in the name of Darwinism.

More can perhaps be extracted from another point brought out by Darwinism — viz. from the fact that Natural Selection is a universal law of life operating indifferently, whether there is stagnation, degeneration, or progression. From this it may be inferred that the ghastly law of struggle for existence, the cruel necessity which engages every living thing in almost unceasing warfare, while not itself the cause of progression, is yet capable of being rendered subservient to the cause of progression. The progress, the adaptations, actually found, are certainly not due to Natural Selection: yet neither does Natural Selection form an obstacle to their occurrence. Nay, we may conjecture that the power which makes for progress, a power which we may divine to work for nobler ends, is lord also of Natural Selection, and can render it a pliable instrument of its purpose, a sanction to enforce the law of progress, a goad to urge on laggards.

What that power may be Darwinism cannot directly tell us. Before we could ascribe to it a pronouncedly teleological character, we should have to measure our strength against a number of possible factors in Organic

Evolution as 'mechanical' as Darwinism. But I believe it could be shown that all these mechanical laws of Evolution, from Spencer's law of differentiation downwards, fail just where Darwinism pure and simple failed—viz. in accounting for the historical fact of progress. Either, therefore, we should have to admit that an as yet unformulated mechanical law of Evolution accounted for progression, or that it was due to an agency of a different order, to the guidance of an intelligent and purposive activity. It may be suggested, however, that a critical examination of the current mechanical theories of Evolution must distinctly strengthen the belief that there has been operative in the history of life an intelligent force to which we must ascribe the progression and direction of the process of Evolution. And inasmuch as Darwinism occupies a leading place among these mechanical theories, its examination will greatly conduce to that result.

We have discussed so far only mechanical theories of Evolution. But in itself Evolution is not necessarily bound to be mechanical; it is perfectly possible to regard it as the gradual working out of a divine purpose. And once we adopt the evolutionist standpoint, it is clear that the Argument from Design is materially and perceptibly strengthened. (1) Positively, because Evolutionism lets us as it were behind the scenes and shows us how means are adapted to ends in the gradual process of Evolution. This renders easier and more comprehensible the belief underlying all teleology in a power that intelligently adapts means to ends. (2) Negatively, Evolutionism greatly weakens the objection to the teleological argument based on the imperfection of existing adaptations. We are no longer compelled to proclaim everything already perfect; it suffices that we can find nourishment for the faith that everything is being made perfect.

If, then, Evolutionism strengthens the Argument from Design, the latter indirectly owes a debt of gratitude to the theories which have facilitated the adoption of the Evolutionist standpoint. And among these Darwinism stands pre-eminent. Evolutionism was as old as one of the earliest of Greek philosophies;[1] but it was not until Darwinism made it a household word that it could force its way into the consciousness of men at large. And as a philosopher who regards Evolutionism in some form as affording the most hopeful method of approaching the mystery of existence, I am inclined to hold that when historical perspective has cleared away the molehills we have made into mountains, it will be here that will be found Darwin's most momentous and enduring service to knowledge and to mankind.

[1] That of Anaximander : see *Mind I* p. 129.

IX

THE PLACE OF PESSIMISM IN PHILOSOPHY[1]

ARGUMENT

To prove that Pessimism is an ultimate attitude of will.
(1) It is not merely disappointed hedonism. (2) It may result from the breakdown of any ideal of value. Now any system of values may be judged (*a*) adequate, (*b*) inadequate, (*c*) inapplicable, to Life. Similarly in judgments of Fact, reality is judged (*a*) knowable (*b*) unknowable, (*c*) inexhaustible. But the 'critical' solutions (*c*) reduce themselves to (*b*). All our modes of Valuation stand and fall together, and 'Truth' is among them. Hence Optimism and Pessimism become ultimate alternatives. Still Pessimism is secondary. Practical value of this issue.

THE aim of this essay is to show that logically Pessimism should be taken in a far wider and more fundamental sense than is commonly assigned to it, and that when this is done, it forms an attitude towards the ultimate questions of philosophy which is not susceptible of being resolved into any other, and cannot be refuted, but only accepted or rejected. It forms one of those ultimate alternatives the choice between which rests essentially upon an act of will.

In attempting to establish this view, it will be convenient to start by determining what we are to understand by the term Pessimism. It has been customary to subordinate the treatment of the subject too much to the particular views of representative pessimist writers, and to pay too little regard to the logical connexion of the pessimist positions. Hence, a belief has become current that Pessimism might be summed up in the assertion that life was not worth living, because in it the

[1] Reprinted (with a few additions) from the *International Journal of Ethics*, for Oct. 1897.

pains predominated over the pleasures, and the whole question was thus reduced to one of the possibility and result of the hedonistic calculus. Now, it is true that the doctrines of Schopenhauer and von Hartmann lend themselves to such a narrowing of the issue, but I believe that it is possible to demonstrate the essential shallowness and logical inadequacy of a transition which is psychologically so easy as to have been made almost universally.

In the argument that life is not worth living because it involves an excess of pain, the second clause states a reason for the first, and, if it is proved, the conclusion clearly follows. What has not been observed, however, is that even if it should *not* be proved, the conclusion may yet be true, because it may rest on other reasons. To argue that because one ground for a conclusion is unsound, the conclusion itself cannot be established, would evidently be nothing else than the familiar logical fallacy of denying the antecedent—until it has been shown that no other grounds are possible. But this is not the case here. The condemnation of life, which Pessimism essays to pronounce, does not necessarily rest on a single basis: it forms an attitude of thought which has been linked with the assertion of the predominance of pain by a mere accident of historical development. It is quite possible to condemn life on various grounds without holding it to be predominantly painful. It is possible to condemn it, not because it has too little pleasure, but because it has too little of the other ends which are recognized as good in themselves, because it has too little virtue or knowledge or beauty or duration. Life may shock us into a denial of its value also by its moral, its aesthetic, its intellectual deficiencies: it may seem so brief, so nauseatingly petty and contemptible that the game is not worth the candle. In all such cases the Pessimism cuts itself adrift from its supposed hedonist basis; and, even where the hedonist standard is retained, it need not be of an egoistic character. It may be sympathy with the misery of others that tempts us like the Buddha, like the Preacher in Thomson's *City of Dreadful Night*, to condemn life.

Again, it is possible to argue, more subtly, that the unhappiness is the effect rather than the cause of the worthlessness of life. It is "not that life is valueless because it is unhappy, but that it is unhappy because it is valueless."[1]

But what enables man thus to apply to life the standards by which it is itself condemned? Nothing surely but the fact that he is capable of framing an ideal of worth, an ideal of something worth striving for and of holding it up to reality as a mirror in which to behold its deficiencies. It is because we systematize our valuations and so form ideal standards which alone bestow true value upon life, that we can condemn it because it nowhere allows us to attain perfect happiness or full knowledge or complete goodness or aesthetic harmony.

Now it is evident that the deficiencies in life which the formation of these ideals enables us to detect will act as a potent stimulus to progress so long as the deficiencies seem comparatively small and the ideals appear attainable; if, however, we allow our ideals to outgrow our means of reaching them, the chasm between them and the actual will become too deep to be bridged by hope; we shall despair of attaining our heart's desire and bitterly condemn the inadequacy of the actual. Thus Pessimism will ever hover like a dark cloud over the path of progress, ready to oppress with gloom alike the cowardice that despairs and the temerity that outstrips, prematurely and recklessly, the limitations of the practicable. It is a natural and almost inevitable phase in spiritual development, which results whenever any object of desire is found to be unattainable, and it has no exclusive affinity for the details of a pettifogging calculation of probable pleasures and pains. The sole reason why the question of Pessimism has mostly been debated on a hedonistic basis is because Happiness is the one ideal which is universally comprehended, which allures by its elusive glitter even the coarsest and most commonplace of men.

Having thus freed Pessimism from its entanglement in

[1] *Riddles of the Sphinx*, p. 99.

hedonistic disputes, we may proceed to determine its deepest nature. This nature would seem to consist in the denial of the *value* of life, in whatever terms and by whatever standards it may be formulated. If Pessimism springs from the experience of pain, it will deny the value of life because happiness is unattainable; if from moral indignation, because goodness is unattainable; if from aesthetic disgust, because beauty is unattainable; if from scepticism, because knowledge is unattainable. But in each case the value of life will be denied. It makes no difference to Pessimism whether a man despair because the world is so miserable, or so bad, or so hideous, or so inscrutable.

It follows from this that Pessimism is essentially a certain definite attitude towards the great and well-recognized class of judgments which are known as judgments of Value (*Werturteile*). Now, judgments of Value are possible about everything that is experienced, and are usually contrasted with judgments of Fact in that they do not inquire what a thing *is*, but what it *is worth*. And, like the primary judgments of Fact, alike whether they are ethical, aesthetical, or merely emotional or affective, they are primarily relative,—*i.e.* they assert that something has value for this purpose or that, for this aspect or that, of human nature. But just as the logical judgments must ultimately be accommodated in a coherent *system* of Truth, so the judgments of Value must ultimately all be referred to some supremely valuable end of action, or *Summum Bonum*. It will be possible then to estimate life as a Whole by this supreme standard of Value, and to discuss whether it satisfies it or not. If, as the outcome of such discussion, it shall appear that no coherent system can be framed, and that our valuations fail, their failure will create the situation on which Pessimism forms the emotional reaction.

Now as the result of such discussion, only three alternatives seem thinkable:

I. We may conclude that Life is adequate to the attainment of the supreme end of action, and that, consequently, it has value and is worth living. This is the position taken by every form of Optimism.

II. We may decide that Life is inadequate to meet the requirements of the standard applied to it; that, consequently, it has no value, and so is not worth living. This is the conclusion implied in every form of Pessimism.

III. We may object on principle to the attempt to answer the question, and contend that it should not be raised, arguing, *e.g.*, that it does not follow from the fact that the value of everything in life may be determined, that we can determine the value of life as a whole. This may be called the *agnostic* or—with a reference to the Kantian denial of metaphysics and its analogous answer to the ultimate question of knowledge — the *critical* answer.

It is worth pointing out that these three modes of treating the ultimate question of Value correspond exactly to the ultimate modes of answering the question as to the ultimate Fact. We answer the final problem of theoretic knowledge also in three ways: (1) We may declare that existence is ultimately knowable, and explain its nature in more or less tentative systems of constructive metaphysics. (2) We may deny that in the end anything can be known. This is the sceptical attitude. (3) We may protest that human knowledge is not competent to solve its ultimate problems, and has no right to raise the question. This is the attitude of a ' *Criticism* ' which shrouds the ultimate metaphysical truth in the unfathomable obscurity of the Thing-in-itself, and yet Tantalus-like, is ever tormented by the phantom of a satisfaction which it believes to be hopelessly beyond its reach.

Whichever kind of ultimate question, then, we raise, whether that of the nature of ultimate facts or that of their valuation, three alternatives seem possible. But we can hardly avoid asking further whether they are all equally tenable. That is a difficult question which I cannot here discuss exhaustively. The proper academic thing to do would be, I suppose, either to evade an answer altogether or to decide in favour of the third alternative,—which is nearly as unsatisfactory as no answer at all,—and to finish up with a learned sneer at those who venture on 'dogmatic' conclusions. But, for once, I should like to dare to be dogmatic—at least to some extent—and to indicate some reasons at least for eliminating that third alternative.

For it seems to me that it reduces itself to the second, that the emotional value of 'no answer' is equivalent to an answer in the negative. Nor can I see why, if judgments of Value are rightly and properly made, they should not be applicable to the scheme of things as a whole. Certainly we make this assumption in the case of the judgments of intellectual Value,—*i.e.* in determining the value of our judgments of Fact. We assume that because judgments of relative truth and falsity are made, the former can ultimately be fitted into a coherent and congruous system of Truth. That is, we recognize that in the end *Truth too is Value*,[1] and decline to predicate the 'truth' of any 'fact' which seems discordant with our system. Indeed it is by such a reference to logical values that we discriminate among the 'facts' which claim reality, and grant or refuse their application.

But if we are entitled to hold that there is Truth, and not merely judgments relatively true,—in other words, that is, that our logical valuations may be combined into a system, and that the ideal of Truth is applicable to Reality and controls it,—why should we not be equally entitled to affirm similar validity for the ideals of Goodness and Happiness?[2] If Experience as a whole can be judged true or false, coherent or incoherent, why should it not be judged as a whole good or bad? At all events, it cannot be taken for granted, without attempt at argument, that human judgments of 'good' and 'bad' mean nothing to the whole, while (equally human) judgments of 'true' and 'false' may be appealed to to extract its inmost mysteries.[3]

[1] Cp. pp. 54-5. [2] Cp. pp. 345-6. [3] Cp. pp. 9-10.

Moreover, the attempt to draw such a distinction would seem to break down even on the theoretic side. Granted that our theoretical account of the world had denied to all the judgments of Value, except those which use the predicates of 'true' and 'false,' all ultimate significance, yet the fact would remain that such judgments were made and formed an integral part of life. They would remain, therefore, as an inexplicable factor in the world. And the more we realized the importance of this factor and the manner in which it permeates all our activities and directs even the intellect when it is seeking to deny it, the more doubtful should we become whether we had explained anything while this was left inexplicable. That is, we should inevitably be impelled towards scepticism on the theoretic side, and the practical reflex of scepticism is, as I have elsewhere shown, nothing else than Pessimism.[1]

It remains to ask whether the problems of Value or of Fact are more ultimate, and whether ultimately the one may not be subordinated to the other. I believe that they may and must, and that the antithesis between them is ultimately pernicious because *all values are facts* and *all facts are values*, *i.e.* products of one or other of our modes of valuation.[2]

But once more I can only very briefly indicate the ground for this conclusion. I shall here confine myself to observing that mere intellection is impotent (ἡ διάνοια αὐτὴ οὐθὲν κινεῖ), that the human mind is essentially purposive, that in its activity the judgments and ideals of Value supply the motive power to the judgments of Fact, and that, in the absence of anything valuable to be reached by them, no reason can be assigned why such judgments should be made. Hence if judgments of Fact, in spite of their illusory logical independence, seem psychologically to be rendered possible by and rest on

[1] *Riddles of the Sphinx*, ch. iii. and iv.
[2] The issue raised by Pragmatism here may be stated as being whether *logical* valuations alone shall be allowed to constitute 'facts,' or whether this privilege may not, under the proper conditions, be extended to the rest. And however the question is decided, it is obvious that the conception of 'Truth' needs further scrutiny and can no longer be naïvely taken for granted.

judgments of Value, does not the question—What is life worth?—become the most ultimate of all? Thus, with respect to this question, Optimism and Pessimism seem to supply the sole alternatives; nor does it seem feasible still further to reduce their multiplicity to unity by alleging any formal ground for subordinating Pessimism to Optimism. For, as we have seen, the same ideals which, while they are regarded as attainable, confer Value upon existence, once they are despaired of, plunge us into irremediable Pessimism. The most that can be said is that just as in logical judgments negation results from the failure of an affirmation, just as scepticism springs from a painfully achieved distrust of knowledge, so Pessimism is always *secondary*, and results from the breakdown of some optimistic scheme of Value. But even so it would seem to follow that Pessimism must be theoretically possible so long as such a scheme of Value can be felt to be inadequate and rejected; that is, so long as there persists a breach between the ideal and the actual.

What, then, is the practical conclusion to which the argument conducts us? It has vindicated for the question of Pessimism a position of paramount theoretic importance which would entail a far more serious treatment than is generally accorded to it in the teaching of Philosophy. And in view of the vast accumulations of unco-ordinated and uncorrelated knowledge which Philosophy has in these days to think over and digest, in order that mankind may not utterly lose its bearings in the cosmos, philosophers may well shrink from taking up the burden of a problem of such magnitude and difficulty as that of Pessimism. But even if Philosophy could renounce its task of giving a rational account of every phase of experience, we might yet hesitate to hold that its acceptance of this problem would be pure loss, or in the end would prove detrimental to its true interests. To assume responsibility is potentially to acquire power, and no question is better calculated than this of Pessimism to make Philosophy a power in human life, for none can bring it into closer contact with the actual problems of men's lives. And does not the whole history of its past show that Philosophy has never been more flourishing and influential than in periods when it has seemed to make some response to the outcry of the human soul, to the question—What shall I do to be saved? If, then, Philosophy takes courage to do its duty, if it addresses itself to the question of the Value of Life and grapples with the Demon of Despair that besets the souls of many, who shall say that there is not still in store for it a career of unprecedented splendour among the forces that may mould the destinies of man?

X

CONCERNING MEPHISTOPHELES

ARGUMENT

M. the real hero of *Faust*, but his character concealed behind his 'masks.' He is really a philosophic pessimist who knows his opposition to be futile. His pessimism compared with Faust's. How he has grown cheerful and an intellectualist. The meaning of Gretchen's criticism. M. as the *Schalk*. Not seriously concerned to win Faust's soul. Absurdity of the vulgar interpretation. M. as Faust's redeemer. But he has recourse to miracle; which spoils the argument from Faust's redemption. The possibility of redeeming M.

IT has often been remarked that the Devil tends to become the real hero of any work of art into which he enters. However that may be, he is certainly the hero of the greatest poem in modern literature, of Goethe's *Faust*. Properly to appreciate Mephistopheles, it is fortunately not necessary to depreciate the other chief characters of the drama, to minimize Gretchen as an episode which usually comes earlier in the history of a German student, and to disparage Faust as an effete pedant, who, even when saved by the might of the Devil and the gracious permission of the Deity, remains to the end essentially commonplace and thoroughly deserving of eternal reunion with so excellent a *Hausfrau* as Gretchen would doubtless have developed into.

But there certainly is a touch of paradox about the assertion that Mephistopheles is the real hero of *Faust*, and so it becomes necessary to clear away the prejudices that have obscured his character. We must try to understand Mephistopheles himself, to understand, that is, why he has become a rebel against the divine order, to reconstruct his history, to conjecture how he became the Devil he is, to perceive wherein his devilry consists. What we need is, in short, a sympathetic study of his personality and point of view, which, without daubing him with luminous paint in the hope of representing him as an angel of light, shall do justice to the interest of his character and function, and to the brilliance of his achievements. Indeed, we may even generalize and say that a sympathetic appreciation of the Devil is always an essential of every real Theodicy, of every vindication of the Divine Justice which scorns to stultify itself by effecting an illusory reconciliation of God and the Devil by means of their common absorption in the Absolute, and to reduce them, along with everything else, to vapid 'aspects' of that all-embracing but neutral unity.

Let us examine therefore the fascinating personality of Mephistopheles, whom every man and most women (other than a sweet innocent like Gretchen) must surely have preferred to *Dr. juris Faustus*, and with whom the more experienced Helen of *Part II.* has clearly to the discerning eye a secret understanding.

The chief difficulty in understanding Mephistopheles arises from his fondness for disguises. He is always masquerading. He masquerades as the dutiful attendant in the courts of Heaven, whose antics almost wrest a smile of approval from the gravity of God;[1] he masquerades as an unattached poodle in search of a master,[2] as a travelling scholar,[3] as a nobleman in gorgeous robes of gold and crimson,[4] as a capped and gowned professor,[5] as a limping charlatan,[6] as a king of beasts,[7] a ratcatcher,[8] a magician,[9] a financier,[10] a showman,[11] a prompter,[12] a doctor,[13] a Phorkyad,[14] a duenna,[15] a strategist,[16] a minister,[17] and a fool.[18] And he knows his weakness and several times alludes to it, *e.g.*—

---

[1] *Prologue in Heaven.*
[2] Scene ii.
[3] *Study*, Scene iii.
[4] Scene iv.
[5] *Ibid.*
[6] *Cellar*, Scene vi.
[7] *Witches' Kitchen*, Scene vi.
[8] *Street*, Scene xix.
[9] Part II. Act. I.
[10] *Ibid.* Scene iv.
[11] *Ibid.* Scene vi.
[12] *Ibid.* Scene vii.
[13] Act II. Scene i.
[14] *Ibid.* Scene iii.
[15] Act III.
[16] Act IV. Scene ii.
[17] Act V. Scene iii.
[18] Act V. Scene vi.

> Komm, gib mir deinen Rock und Mütze,
> Die *Maske* muss mir köstlich stehn.

and again—

> Mein *Mäskchen* da weissagt geheimen Sinn ;
> Sie fühlt, dass ich ganz sicher ein Genie,
> Vielleicht sogar der Teufel, bin.

But after all the subtlest of his disguises, his most habitual mask, is one which deceives all the other characters in *Faust, except the Lord*, and has, so far as I know, utterly deceived all Goethe's readers except myself. I mean his disguise as a mediaeval devil. That of course is his great part, and he plays it very well, with an exquisitely humorous perception of its absurdity. For of course he knows quite well that he is nothing of the sort. Indeed, he is often telling us so, either because he wearies of the grotesqueness of the disguise imposed on him by universal prejudice, or because he knows that he will warn in vain a besotted audience which insists that he shall appear in horns and hoofs and full regimentals as a devil.

And yet the success of this mask constitutes the real tragedy of his situation. To have to play the part of an obscene and silly mediaeval fiend, even in jest, renders him ridiculous. It impedes the expression of his genius, it obscures the spiritual grandeur of his attitude, and in the end conducts him to what seems a most grotesque conclusion. For, like Job, he is ignominiously smitten with boils, and leaves the scene as the vanquished victim of an overpowering literary tradition.

To appreciate therefore the real subtlety and depth of his spirit we must strip off this mask also and recognize his real genius. For Mephisto is a genius, as even Gretchen, a highly prejudiced witness, must admit.

And what is rare in a genius, he is also a wit and a philosopher, of the profoundest, and this combination renders the *Faust* the finest study of philosophic Pessimism in any language. Not one of the professed pessimists, not even the Buddha, not even Schopenhauer, not even James Thomson, has succeeded in expressing the dire philosophy of negation more effectively and consistently than the poet in his sketch of Mephisthophelianism. Clear, candid, and consistent, Mephistopheles records his incisive and uncompromising protest against the whole order of the world, and scorns to practise any concealment of his meaning. If his doctrine has escaped detection, it has been by reason of his Bismarckian frankness in divulging it. One can only suppose that people have been too much distracted by the show of his diabolism to perceive this, too greatly fascinated by the horns and hoofs of his ruminant mask to recognize beneath his pranks the corroding wit, the *Galgenhumor*, of a despairing sage.

Yet from the first his words were plain. In his very first interview with Faust he reveals himself—

> Ich bin der Geist, der stets verneint,
> Und das mit Recht ; denn alles, was entsteht,
> Ist wert, dass es zu Grunde geht ;
> Drum besser wär's, dass nichts entstünde.

And similarly in the *Prologue in Heaven* he had protested against the misery and futility of existence, and when the Lord asked him whether he would ever come only to bring accusations against his creation and to disapprove of everything—

> Kommst du nur immer anzuklagen ?
> Ist auf der Erde ewig dir nichts recht ?

he at once replies—

> Nein, Herr ! ich find' es dort, wie immer, herzlich schlecht.

It is this conviction of the intrinsic worthlessness of existence that turns him into an agency of destruction. Not-being is preferable to Being, and so it is good to destroy. But it is unnecessary to hate : Mephisto, though as a good pessimist he heartily wishes our extinction, is *not* the enemy of mankind. Nay, he even *pities* the wretches whose torment is his function, and sickens of his job—

> Die Menschen dauern mich in ihren Jammertagen,
> Ich mag sogar die Armen selbst nicht plagen.

Mephisto then is perfectly clear about his position. And he also sees its hopelessness. He is too complete a pessimist to suppose that his protest can be of avail. He is well aware that he cannot destroy the world he condemns, either wholesale or in detail.

> Und freilich ist damit nicht viel getan.
> Was sich dem Nichts entgegen stellt
> Das Etwas, diese plumpe Welt,
> So viel als ich schon unternommen,
> Ich wusste nicht ihr beizukommen.

If he evades therefore Faust's retort

> So setzest du der ewig regen,
> Der heilsam schaffenden Gewalt
> Die kalte Teufelsfaust entgegen,
> Die sich vergebens tückisch ballt!
> Was anders suche zu beginnen,
> Des Chaos wunderlicher Sohn!

it is not that he is under any illusion. He, the Lord, and Faust all *agree* that his work for evil is futile and productive of good. He has therefore every right to announce himself as

> Ein Teil von jener Kraft,
> Die stets das Böse will und stets das Gute schafft.

Nor does he deny the Lord's description of his beneficent and stimulating, but from his own point of view futile, activity—

> Des Menschen Tätigkeit kann allzuleicht erschlaffen,
> Er liebt sich bald die unbedingte Ruh';
> Drum geb' ich gern ihm den Gesellen zu,
> Der reizt und wirkt und muss, als Teufel, schaffen.

It is instructive to compare this pessimism with that to which Faust had succumbed at the beginning of the action, and to see how much deeper it cuts. Faust's discontent with the cosmic scheme is quite a petty, personal, and superficial affair. In Faust's first soliloquy the jaded old professor, who has exhausted all the knowledge of his age and finally himself, has, naturally enough, discovered that all is vanity. His lowered vitality can no longer sustain even the ideal to which he had sacrificed his life. So he despairs even of knowledge. As a last wild attempt he tries the short cut of magic. But the spirit world does not open out its splendours to the invocations of lassitude and fear. Faust shows himself deficient in the daring needed to meet the Earth-spirit as an equal, and so he is repulsed. Then in humiliation and disgust he turns to question the worth of life—in the characteristic phrases of a bookworm!

> Soll ich vielleicht in tausend *Büchern* lesen,
> Dass überall die Menschen sich gequält,
> Dass hie und da ein Glücklicher gewesen?

He makes a first, and therefore ineffectual, attempt to poison himself, but (a true German!) is restrained by sentimental reminiscences of the faith of his childhood. This scene alone would be enough to prove that he has in no wise overcome the love of life. He does well, therefore, to confess—

> Zwei Seelen wohnen, ach, in meiner Brust!

whereof the one clings closely to his earthly life. It is hard to suppose that his life is in serious danger; so feeble an attempt at suicide is not the symptom of a serious pessimism.

In his second interview with Mephisto, Faust is more impressive. His *tedium vitae* rises to the superb denunciation of life which begins

> In jedem Kleide werd' ich wohl die Pein
> Des engen Erdenlebens fühlen,

and culminates in the comprehensive curse which ends

> Fluch sei der Hoffnung! Fluch dem Glauben!
> Und Fluch vor allen der Geduld!

This forms the high-water mark of Faustian pessimism. But even here the skilled psychologist will note an undertone of nervous irritation and impatience which stamps it as a passing ebullition, provoked, perhaps, by the stimulating presence of Mephisto.

It is clear, then, that in point of profundity Faust's pessimism cannot vie with that of Mephistopheles; you might string together the woes of a dozen Fausts and yet fail to fathom the clarified depths of Mephisto's world-negating indignation. And Mephisto's pessimism is not merely profound; it is also individual. It is neither the regulation abstraction of the text-books, nor derived from any bookish source whatever. It takes its peculiar colouring from his personal character.

Mephistopheles is essentially a cheerful pessimist. Cheerful pessimism sounds paradoxical, and I hardly think that an abstract logic, scorning the lessons of psychology, would credit its existence. But if we consider the point psychologically it will seem natural enough. It is only in its primary form that pessimism is incompatible with cheerfulness; the lapse of time here, too, may work the strangest transformations. Now Mephistopheles is very old; indeed, it is mainly his preternatural age that renders him a supernatural being. His pessimism, therefore, is likewise very old; it has confronted the inane spectacle of life's nothingness for aeons. If therefore we would understand him, we must seize this clue:

> Bedenkt der Teufel, der ist alt,
> So werdet alt ihn zu verstehn.

Now in ordinary life the pessimist rarely grows old enough to grow cheerful. Pessimism is not a creed conducive to longevity. But even within the narrow limits of ordinary life it seems hardly possible that pessimistic emotion should long retain the intensity of its first outburst. Here, as elsewhere, time must surely dull the sharpness of the initial agony. If we can endure to live on at all we must always somehow adapt ourselves to life. Passionate pain must smoulder down into settled sentiment, which becomes less emotional and more intellectual as it grows older. Now Mephistopheles has long survived the discovery of the vanity of life. For untold ages he has lived with, and despite, this thought, as a critical spectator of all life's futile cruelties. And so he has grown accustomed to its presence—

> O glaube mir, der manche tausend Jahre
> An dieser harten Speise kaut.

His wounds are scarred over, though their memory remains. Is it not natural then that he should long have ceased to feel the misery of life, and long have replaced it by a merely intellectual conviction, which would scarce impede the pleasurable exercise of his faculties? We are often told that with a hard heart and a good digestion a man can stand much: how much more a demon who could certainly dispense with a heart, and probably with a digestion? And so he is *not* personally miserable. The note of personal suffering mingles no longer with his indictment of the world: nay, he may even feel relief at having cast off all personal responsibility for the senseless spectacle. Well may he be serene, and even gay—his pessimism, like his witches' elixir, is very old and defecated—

> Das auch nicht mehr im mindsten stinkt.

In a word, Mephisto has become a thorough intellectualist, and complete intellectualism is perhaps the most diabolical thing we can conceive. For to evil-doing, as to all other carnal pleasures, cometh satiety at the last. Moreover our possibilities are limited. But not so to evil thinking: to the idle curiosity of intellectual contemplation nothing is good, nothing evil, nothing sacred, nothing shocking, but everything is food for a reflection, cold and unending and unsparing. It peeps and pries upon a mother's grave; it is equally at home in Heaven and in Hell. Once therefore it has judged and passed its condemnation, there is no obvious reason why any recrudescence of feeling should lead it to reverse its verdict.

It is this intellectualism which Gretchen has detected in Mephisto, and which forms the really valid ground for her otherwise thoroughly feminine dislike. Not that of course we should be justified in taking Mephisto altogether at her valuation. Indeed, there is a preposterous incongruity in the thought of judging the cosmic spirit of negation by the feminine intuitions of a little *grisette*, who is madly in love and furiously jealous of the ascendency which a more powerful mind has over her lover. We must allow a large discount for a woman's instinctive mischief-making when she intervenes between man and man.

> Es tut mir lang schon weh,
> Das ich dich in *der* Gesellschaft seh'.

Gretchen fears and hates him because she suspects in him, and rightly, a danger to her love, an obstacle to a *mésalliance* which would have domesticated Faust and unfitted him for further ventures. And so she insinuates all she can, and has apparently succeeded in getting her view accepted by the public.

> Wo er nur mag zu uns treten,
> Mein' ich sogar, ich liebte dich nicht mehr

is her last and unfairest appeal.

That too is an old, old story, as old as the way of a man with a maid.

Still in a way Gretchen is right—despite the defects of her grammar—

> Man sieht, dass er an nichts keinen Anteil nimmt;
> Es steht ihm an der Stirn geschrieben,
> Dass er nicht mag eine Seele lieben.

Only that is Mephisto's intellectualism. He himself sees clearly that the struggle is for the control of Faust, and that if the *liaison* with Gretchen is to come to a respectable conclusion there is an end of his designs on Faust (or rather of the Lord's designs whereof he is the instrument). And so he takes ruthlessly effective steps to bring about a separation. Gretchen is an obstacle in his path, and so she is removed. But he never expresses the least hatred for her: the expression of her hate he interprets as a tribute to his intellectual eminence, and takes quite coolly—

> Sie fühlt, dass ich ganz sicher ein Genie,
> Vielleicht sogar der Teufel, bin.

The paradox of Mephisto's combination of cheerfulness with pessimism is thus explained by the recognition of his age and intellectualism. But these very features seem to render more urgent another difficulty. Mephistopheles is far too clear-sighted not to see that all his efforts are futile, that he is ever being overruled by a higher power and turned into another's agent.

Why then does he persist in his activity? The readiest reply to this would doubtless be—Why should he not? If all things are futile, why one thing more than any other? To a thorough pessimist what does it matter what he does?

In general this reply is sound enough, but I hardly think that it explains the peculiar features of this case. I should incline rather to question whether after all it is so sure that Mephistopheles *does* persist in efforts whose futility he recognizes. The answer will depend on how seriously you take him.

If you take him quite seriously, you must certainly answer—Yes. He professes to the end to busy himself with Faust's damnation. But are you intended, or even entitled, to take him seriously? It seems to me that we have the highest authority for holding that Mephisto is *not* serious. The Lord himself tells us that Mephisto is the *Schalk*, the imp or merry-andrew, among fiends—

> Von allen Geistern, die verneinen,
> Ist mir der Schalk am wenigsten zur Last.

And throughout the play he acts up to this character. Hatred, gloom, and gravity are foreign to his nature. It was by eschewing these that he escaped from the miseries of his pessimism. He no longer despairs of life, because he has trained himself to laugh at it, forming thus the counterpart of the Lord, *der sich das Lachen abgewöhnt*, who has seen the high seriousness of all things. So Mephistopheles laughs at a world he cannot alter, or abolish. His satisfaction comes from satirizing all the world, from the unimpeded exercise of his sarcastic wit. He mocks at God, men and angels, nay, even at professors! Nor does his mockery spare himself. He is as ready to make a fool of himself as of any one. But withal he is always good-tempered and good-humoured: not even Faust's very trying temper ever leads him on to lose his own.

Is it at all likely then, that he should be grimly in earnest about his diabolic mission? Is it his serious ambition to capture the soul of Faust?

Why then should he, in the very act of engaging in his wager with the Lord, ostentatiously proclaim that he cares nought for the dead?

> Für einen Leichnam bin ich nicht zu Haus.

A remark by the way, the truth of which is fully attested by his preference of earth to hell as a place of residence. Or, again, does he seriously believe that a contract signed with blood is needed? Why, then, does he turn the whole thing into farce? Once more, does he really want Faust's services in hell? What for? What possible use could he have for a more than middle-aged German professor? And would a serious-minded and conscientious devil allow himself to be cheated of his prey, by a sheer lapse of attention? And why finally, if he desired to see Faust damned, did he not leave him severely alone? Had he done so, would not Faust eventually have committed suicide, and so have inevitably fallen into his domain?

Surely these questions answer themselves. The vulgar interpretation of Mephistopheles is absurd. The truth is that *Mephistopheles is never serious*. He knows that the whole conception of a soul-hunting devil is a mediaeval anachronism. He knows also that he can do nothing, that however reluctant, his freedom is but semblance, that he is a helpless instrument in the hands of a God who tells him outright *Du darfst nur frei erscheinen*. And so being deprived of every other satisfaction, he derides the cosmic order which constrains him. Wherefore he plays the fool throughout. He is bent on *amusing himself*;

not on ruining Faust, or capturing souls by methods whose crudity would shame a Hottentot magician. Had he been serious, would he ever have dreamt of accepting the impossible bet which the Lord proposes?—

> Zieh' diesen Geist von seinem Urquell ab.

Would he have assented to the preposterous conditions Faust imposes on him? For Faust—so little does he know wherein to seek satisfaction of soul—proposes to consider himself *damned* when he shall consider himself *satisfied*, and demand the continuation of the present moment:

> Werd' ich zum Augenblicke sagen,
> Verweile doch, du bist so schön!

is to be the signal for his *damnation*!

The absurdity of this is plain: A man who is capable of declaring himself *satisfied* is not *damned*: he is *happy*—or a liar. And if Heaven be the satisfaction of desire, he has *ipso facto* attained Heaven. It was philosophically impossible, therefore, that the story should end in anything but the salvation of Faust.[1]

Thus it is that the encounter with Mephisto sets Faust's feet upon the pathway of salvation. *Mephistopheles is Faust's real redeemer.* He it is who rescues Faust from the fatal listlessness into which he had fallen and revives his interest in life. Faust is never nearer damnation than *before* Mephistopheles appears. Not that, as we saw, he was really likely to commit suicide just yet. He would doubtless have pursued his theoretical study of the subject a little further first, and perhaps, *e.g.* have tried to read through the *Sacred Books of the East*. But the inanity of his life would have continued to prey upon him, and after a few more fits of depression and a few more attempts, he might have succeeded. For, as he justly says, he was at a critical time of life; too old to amuse himself, too young to refrain from yearning and trying—

---

[1] Unless, indeed (as Vischer, the witty author of the *Third Part of Faust*, suggested), Faust's severest trials only begin after he has got to Heaven, and has to act as pedagogue to the 'blessed boys' (*selige Knaben*) mentioned in the final scene.

Ich bin zu alt um nur zu spielen,
Zu jung um ohne Wunsch zu sein.

Then Mephistopheles enters his life and revives his interest in it, by telling him about the worlds unrealized which cannot be read up in books. Before they start together Faust has recovered the use of the imperative, and demands to be initiated into every form of human experience. Mephisto laughs at the psychological impossibility involved, and has difficulty in dissuading Faust from reverting to his old hankering after the infinite. But he slowly makes a man of him. Faust scorns the animal pleasures of the coarsest debauchery. He escapes lightly from the snares of the affections in the brief tragedy of Gretchen, which scars his soul with mingled memories of ecstasy and guilt. He pays his homage to the aesthetic ideal by his descent into the fairyland of Art. But even Helen cannot paralyse a spirit [1] so astutely guided: he returns, to be initiated into the realities of politics. Thus in the end Mephistopheles bridges for him the gulf 'twixt word and deed which he had once imagined could be traversed by a trick of mistranslation.[2] And so Faust finds his real life's work in action. It is working and ruling that mature him and make him ripe for the life eternal. But to what, I should like to know, does he owe this whole career, if not to the unwearying aid of Mephistopheles? How else could the philosopher have become king, the obscure pedant a prince of the Empire?

Not that on this account we need ascribe to Mephisto any special merit, or suppose that his motives will bear scrutiny. Mephisto knows no doubt that he is redeeming Faust; but he does not help him in order to save him, any more than he attends him, in order to tempt him. The truth is that tempting is not seriously in his line: amusing is, and indeed I suspect that if the tradition be true that cards are a diabolic invention, it may well have

---

[1] Wen Helena paralysirt,
Der kommt so leicht nicht zu Verstande.
[2] Cp. *Scene in the Study*.

been to Mephisto that we owe them, but rather to his ingenuity in amusing *himself* than to his desire to ruin *others*. He seems to make his one solitary attempt at tempting in the excursion into Auerbach's cellar, but even there a doubt remains. If Mephisto meant it as a serious temptation to drunkenness, how are we to explain the incorrigible frivolity with which he sacrifices all prospect of success by playing pranks upon the worthy topers? Does he not here, as always, prejudice his alleged design by a reckless pursuit of the moment's joke? And after that Mephisto only obeys orders, and finds the ways and means for the whims of Faust.[1] His position is indeed sufficiently abject. He is ruled by Faust, and overruled by the Lord, and perfectly aware of it. But he manages none the less to get some fun out of his servitude, and is never in better form than when, quite gratuitously and without the least advantage to his supposed design, he is taking Faust's pupils for him and playing the professor. And after all, as he knows that in any case he can accomplish nothing, he does not greatly care what he does. Nevertheless, it is somewhat curious that he does not play the fool still more extensively, stays so long with Faust, and abstains from wrecking the joint enterprises in which they were engaged. I can only suppose that he must have found Faust personally amusing, and that his restless striving was interesting to a mind which could never delude itself into thinking any end worth the attaining.

Nevertheless, it is very remarkable that even Mephistopheles cannot save Faust without a miracle. That is the great flaw, psychologically speaking, in the poem. The Faust we meet at first has sunk to such a state that a moral miracle alone can save him. He has almost, if not wholly, lost the taste for life, the faith in life, and the vitality to respond to the new vistas which Mephisto's art displays. To offer such a man all the delights of

[1] It is true that, as in tradition bound, he takes Faust with him to the *Walpurgisnacht*. But was not Faust by this time wearying of Gretchen and ready to desert her? So Mephisto points out with calm scorn in repelling Faust's coarse reproaches (scene in the *Field*).

earth is as futile as to crown a dyspeptic king of Cocagne, or to equip a blind man with the ring of Gyges. He is too old to enjoy, too young to be indifferent.

At his first interview Mephistopheles attempts to reawaken Faust's love of life by conjuring up seductive dreams. But at their second meeting Faust receives him with imprecations on life. This convinces Mephistopheles that a miracle is necessary. Faust must be rejuvenated. By drinking the witch's potion he rids himself of the infirmities which thirty years of study have heaped upon his body and his spirit. This is the turning-point of the plot. Without this renewal of youth could Faust have captivated Gretchen or eloped with Argive Helen? And what *savant* of fifty-five would not trust himself, even without the devil's aid, to achieve great things, nay, perhaps, to realize the Platonic dream of the domination of the wise, if he could suddenly find himself restored to the vigour of five and twenty?

But such a miracle must hopelessly break up the natural course of psychological development, and so Goethe's *Faust* does not answer the practical question which Pessimism forces on our notice, the question, namely— What to do with those for whom life has lost its savour? I must confess that so far as human sight as yet extends this problem seems insoluble. Perhaps a good rest, a dip in Lethe, and the resumption of a more attractive life might be therapeutic agents of sufficient power, and something of the sort may possibly yet be found to be among the resources of Providence.

But how about Mephisto's own salvation? His case is very different, and it has to be considered, without the poet's aid,[1] merely by a study of his character. We must note first that his pessimism is not of Faust's type; his vitality is not exhausted, nor has he wearied of the world or of himself. He is still willing to be amused, and is certainly amusing. So far therefore from sinking into

---

[1] In private conversation Goethe seems however to have realized that the spiritual problem he had chosen required to be completed by the salvation of Mephistopheles. Only he did not think his contemporaries were enlightened enough to tolerate this notion.

the inaction of despair, he is the stimulus to progress in a world which, but for him, would grow inert. Says the Lord

> Des Menschen Tätigkeit kann allzuleicht erschlaffen ;
> Er liebt sich bald die unbedingte Ruh' ;
> Drum geb' ich gern ihm den Gesellen zu,
> Der reizt und wirkt, und muss, als Teufel, schaffen.

There is activity enough about Mephisto and to spare; but it is of the wrong kind. It is frivolous, for all the pessimism out of which it grew. It has no serious purpose of its own, and now aims only at an intellectual play with a scheme of things it confronts without approving. And this is just the reason why it is impotent, why it becomes subservient to an alien end. Aiming at nothing, Mephistopheles, the unbelieving scoffer, cannot but become a servant of the Lord. But he is a bad servant and an unwilling, and remains a blot upon a universe which condones such service, and so reveals its imperfection and its impotence. Impotent though he seems, his mere existence indicates the limitation of what we fondly deemed Omnipotence.

The redemption, therefore, of Mephisto is the postulate of a complete Theodicy, on grounds both metaphysical and moral. Our moral sensibility demands that there shall be no hopeless evil. And our reason enforces this demand by showing that we cannot call good a world of which *any part* is evil, without destroying the whole meaning of good. For metaphysics the ultimate solidarity of things is such as to demand universal salvation. No universe is perfect in which any part is imperfect ; for the suffering of any part that is imperfect must produce a sympathetic tremor in the whole. But these are topics which perhaps transcend the bounds of literary criticism ; though they might well provide food for thought for the theologians who have prided themselves on the popularity of their hells, and for the philosophers who have too easily proved the perfection of the world by excluding from its notion all that makes 'perfection' worth the having.[1]

[1] Cp. p. 3.

It is clear, then, that Mephisto must be saved. But he can be saved only by working on his actual character. He must be led to remould himself. He must be driven out of his idle intellectualism, out of his critical *rôle* of an unconcerned spectator of all time and all existence, including his own actions. It is here that the real difficulty lies. If he were merely inert, he could, like man, be forced into action. But he is active enough; only he feels no responsibility for his actions, which he regards as dispassionately as the operations of natural forces.

The only chance therefore would seem to be to get him to take up his personal responsibility, to reverse the policy which has driven him into his attitude of passive and futile, but unanswerable, protest. He must no longer be overruled in every action; he must no longer feel that

> Du darfst auch da nur frei erscheinen,

that his spontaneous agency is mere illusion. Give him real freedom to choose alternatives, real power to try his hand at shaping a world that will realize his ideals, and he may then convince himself, that it is better to help on the Divine purpose than to thwart it. Whether he will or not remains uncertain, as in the case of every one of us; but it is from this contingency alone that the real interest and tragic significance of the cosmic drama spring. This much at least seems clear, that a theodicy which strives to oppress opposition by omnipotence must overreach itself: sheer force can overcome Mephisto as little as Prometheus.

XI

ON PRESERVING APPEARANCES[1]

ARGUMENT

I. Mr. F. H. Bradley's antithesis of 'Appearance' and 'Reality' as a catchword. II. His criterion of the 'non-contradiction' of ultimate reality. But (1) the criterion not ultimate, and used too recklessly. It is applied to merely verbal difficulties. It is meaningless to call an unknowable Absolute real, and this explains nothing about appearances. Nothing even apparently real can be really contradictory. Non-contradiction is only a special form of Harmony, and the rejection of contradiction is only a form of the struggle towards satisfaction. Other modes of reaching harmony. Harmony a postulate. (2) The criterion stultifies itself by condemning everything, nor is it saved by the doctrine of 'Degrees.' III. A valid doctrine of the relation of appearance to reality must eschew the transcendence which renders Mr. Bradley's Absolute futile. Necessity of retaining a grasp on reality throughout. The growth of reality: (1) the reality of immediate experience our starting-point and end. (2) 'Higher realities' inferred to explain it, but remain secondary. Their variety and relativity to purpose and need of a final synthesis in (3) ultimate reality. IV. As to this, five principles to be laid down: (1) Ultimate Reality must be made a real explanation. (2) 'Appearances' must be really preserved. (3) Primary reality of immediate experience to be recognized. The reality even of dreams. The reality of the higher world of Religion. How Idealism makes a difference. (4) The greater efficiency of the higher reality. (5) Why Ultimate Reality must be absolutely satisfactory. Because otherwise it would not be regarded as ultimate. Why truth cannot be evil. If it were, its pursuit would cease. Only complete satisfaction would bring finality of knowledge, and that only if not merely conceived, but actually experienced. The 'beatific vision' as the ideal of knowledge.

I

THE ambition of this paper is not, as might perhaps wrongly be conjectured from a hasty perusal of its title,

---

[1] This essay appeared in *Mind* for July 1903 (N.S. No. 47). The chief additions are in IV. (3), (4), and (5). The constructive problem it deals with is that indicated at the end of *Axioms as Postulates* (*Personal Idealism*, p. 133).

to provide an Outline of Cosmetic Philosophy, and still less to carry owls to Athens by exhorting philosophers to an observation of social proprieties they have rarely shown any tendency to set aside. Its aim is rather to examine the nature and scope of the familiar antithesis between 'appearance' and 'reality,' the vogue of which I cannot but regard as the chief constructive result of the work of the greatest of English sceptics, Mr. F. H. Bradley. In Oxford, at all events, this antithesis has been an immense success. It is ever hovering on the tongue alike of tutor and of tiro in philosophical discussion, and provides them with a universal solution for the most refractory of facts. It seems to have become the magic master-key which opens—and closes—every door, the all-accommodating receptacle into which every mystery may be made to enter and to disappear; in short, it is just now the greatest of the catchwords wherewith we conjure reason into topsy-turvydom and common sense out of its senses. If its Olympian author ever deigned to look upon the struggles and contentions of lesser and lower mortals, he would doubtless be vastly amused to see what an Alpha and Omega of Philosophy had sprung invulnerable from his subtle brain. But being myself immersed in the struggle of teaching and having a certain responsibility in seeing to it that what is called thought involves thinking and affords proper training in mental precision and clearness, I find that this antithesis has become to me a considerable nuisance, and also, it must be confessed, a bit of a bore. I propose, therefore, to probe into it a little, and to examine its pretensions, with a view to seeing whether the relation of 'appearance' to 'reality' cannot be put on a different and, to me, more satisfactory footing.

II

I must begin however by raising a very general, and, I think, very fundamental, objection to Mr. Bradley's method of constructing the wonderful edifice of his metaphysics. I venture to assert with the utmost trepidation, and at the risk of being crushed, like Mr. Bradley's other critics, by a sarcastic footnote to his next article, that in putting forward his fundamental assumption that 'ultimate Reality' is such that it does not contradict itself, and in erecting this into an absolute criterion, he builds in part on an unsound foundation which has not reached the bottom rock, in part on an airy pinnacle, a sort of what in Alpine parlance is called a *gendarme*, which will not bear the weight of the mountains of paradox which are subsequently heaped upon it.

(1) By the first charge what I mean to convey is that the ultimateness of Mr. Bradley's absolute criterion has been taken for granted far too easily. But before adducing reasons for this contention, I must disavow every intention of impugning the validity of the Principle of Contradiction as such. I accept it fully and without reserve; nay more, I use it every day of my life. But my intellectual conscience impels me to ask—*As what must I accept it?* And *in what sense?* To these questions Mr. Bradley's criterion of non-contradiction appears to supply no obvious answer. It is enunciated quite abstractly, and it is not clear to me that, as stated, it has a sense adequate to bear the metaphysical structure put upon it, or indeed any sense at all.[1]

The meaning of Mr. Bradley's 'absolute criterion' (as of everything else) must therefore be sought in its applications. But Mr. Bradley's applications seem to warrant the utmost suspicion, if not of the principle in the abstract, yet of the sense in which it is actually used. A principle which asserts itself alone *contra mundum*, and convicts the whole universe of self-contradiction may surely give pause to the most reckless. There is no need, therefore, to question the principle in

---

[1] As Mr. Alfred Sidgwick well says, "every fact that changes its character in the least degree proves to us daily that the 'Laws of Thought,' those pillars of elementary logic, are too ideal and abstract to be interpreted as referring to the actual things or particular cases that names are supposed to denote."—*Distinction and the Criticism of Beliefs*, p. 21. Cp. my *Formal Logic*, ch. x.

the abstract: in the abstract it may mean anything or nothing. But in the particular way in which Mr. Bradley proceeds to use it, it is open to much exception, and I find myself unable to admit its claim to ultimateness, while it is obvious that Mr. Bradley has for once simply taken over his allegation from the classical (and intellectualist) tradition of Herbart and Hegel. I shall discuss however only the former point, as it is clear that if the Principle of the impossibility of self-contradiction in the Real can be shown not to be ultimate, it will follow that Mr. Bradley was wrong in taking it to be such.

My first question must be to inquire what shall be held to constitute such self-contradiction as will render a supposed reality amenable to the jurisdiction of the absolute criterion? Mr. Bradley appears to hold that any quibble will suffice to bring an aspirant to reality before the revolutionary tribunal of his incorruptible philosophy, and that an unguarded phrase, such as ordinary language can scarcely abstain from, is evidence enough for ordering off to instant execution the wretched 'appearance' which had dared to simulate 'reality.' But surely justice should require some more decisive proof of iniquity than the fact that something which claims to be real can be formulated in what appear to be contradictory terms? For may it not be the contradiction rather than the reality which is 'appearance'? Yet such apparent contradiction is all that Mr. Bradley's negative dialectics seem in the great majority of instances to prove. It is a result which does not astonish me, but seems to be of little value. *In words* everything can be made to look contradictory, and Mr. Bradley has but completed the work of Gorgias and Zeno, with his own peculiar brilliance and incisiveness. But I do not see that this necessarily proves more than that language has not yet been rendered wholly adequate to the description of reality.

And it ought not to be necessary to remind serious thinkers that to dazzle the spectators by a display of dialectical fireworks is not to explain the universe. The most illusory of seeming realities is worthy, not merely of being ridden down and 'riddled with contradictions' and left for dead upon the field, but also of being *understood*. And I am at a loss to see how to call it self-contradictory and then forthwith to invoke a self-subsistent, inaccessible Absolute, which includes all appearances and transcends all apprehension and inexplicably atones for the incurable defects of our actual experience, is to explain it, or anything else whatsoever.

As against such cavalier methods I should protest that only propositions are properly contradictory, that only a reasoning being can contradict itself, and that it is an abuse of language to describe our use of incompatible statements about the same reality as an inherent contradiction in the reality itself. Indeed, I should combat Mr. Bradley's contention that everything sooner or later turns out to be self-contradictory with the axiom that *nothing which exists*, in however despicable a sense, can really be contradictory. The very fact of its existence shows that the 'contradictions,' which our thought discovers in it, are in some way illusory, that the reality 'somehow' (to use Mr. Bradley's favourite word in this connexion) overpowers, swallows, reconciles, transcends, and harmonizes them.[1] If therefore it appears 'contradictory,' the fault is ours. It is, in Herbart's language, a *zufällige Ansicht*. It can be purged of its apparent contradiction, and it is our duty to effect this and to interpret it into a harmony with itself which our mind can grasp. Only of course I can see that this purification may require something more than a dialectical juggle with terms: we may need a real discovery, we may have to make a real advance, before the refractory ore of 'appearance' will yield us the pure gold of 'reality.'

I have intentionally used a word which seems to me to give the clue out of the labyrinth into which Mr. Bradley has beguiled the fair maid, Philosophy. The conception of *Harmony* seems to me to be one legitimately applicable to ultimate reality and to contain a meaning

---

[1] Unless indeed the internal conflict which is described as a 'contradiction' be the essential nature of all reality as such—as some extreme pessimists have contended.

which I vainly look for in that of 'contradiction.' It forms a postulate higher and more ultimate than that of non-contradiction, which indeed seems to be only a special case thereof, viz. that of a harmony among the contents of our thought. The contradictory involves a jar or discord in the mind, which most people in their normal condition feel to be unpleasant (when they perceive it), and this is the first and immediate reason why we avoid contradictions and reject the contradictory. The second reason is that our *Thinking* rests on the Principle of Contradiction, and that if we admitted the contradictory, we should have (if we were consistent) to give up thinking. But thinking is too inveterate a habit (at least in some of us), and on the whole too useful, to permit of the serious adoption of this alternative.

Thus the struggle to avoid and remove contradictions appears as an integral part of the great cosmic striving towards satisfaction, harmony, and equilibrium, in which even the inanimate appears *more suo* to participate.[1] In this struggle the intellectual machinery which works by the Principle of Contradiction plays an important part, and we should fare but ill without its aid.

But it is not our sole resource. An apparent contradiction can be cleared out of the road to harmony by other means than a course of dialectics terminating in a flight to an *asylum ignorantiae*, miscalled the Absolute. (1) I would venture therefore to remind Mr. Bradley of many excellent things he has himself said about the immediacy of feeling. (2) It would seem that in certain modes of aesthetic contemplation the so-called self-contradictions of the discursive reason may vanish into a self-evident harmony. (3) It is well known that our immediate experience enables us to accept without scruple or discomfort, as given and ultimate fact, what philosophers have vainly essayed for centuries to construe to thought. The fact of *change* is perhaps the most flagrant example. But in the last resort our own existence, and that of the world, is similarly inconceivable and

[1] See p. 214.

underivable for a philosophy which makes a point of honour of systematically denying the factual, and labours vainly to reduce all immediate 'acquaintance with' to discursive 'knowledge about.' And lastly, (4) if the worst should come to the worst, the solution *ambulando* —which in this instance we may translate 'by going on' —is always open to a philosophy which has not wantonly insisted on closing the last door to hope by assuming the unreality of 'time' (*i.e.* of the experience-process).[1]

For these reasons then I am forced to conclude that Mr. Bradley, in appealing to the principle that the Real is not self-contradictory, has not succeeded in expressing it in its complete and ultimate form. His 'absolute criterion' is not the whole truth, but a part of the greater principle of Harmony. And inasmuch as our experience is plainly not as yet harmonious, it is clear that the principle is a Postulate. We must conceive the Real to be harmonious, not because we have any formal and *a priori* assurance of the fact, but because we desire it to be so and are willing to try whether it cannot become so.

(2) My second charge can be dealt with more summarily. It concerns the immense disproportion between the foundation of Mr. Bradley's system and the superstructure he has built upon it. Mr. Bradley argues from his absolute criterion to the conclusion that everything which is ordinarily esteemed real, everything which any one can know or care about, is pervaded with unreality, is 'mere appearance' in a greater or less degree of degradation.[2] In this Mr. Bradley appears to carry the policy of 'thorough' to an excess which renders his whole

---

[1] Cp. p. 109.

[2] I cannot here criticize this 'doctrine of degrees' as fully as it deserves. It appears to be the only obstacle to our accounting Mr. Bradley's philosophy the purest scepticism (or rather nihilism), but I cannot but regard it as thoroughly indefensible, and even unintelligible. For, as Capt. H. V. Knox has pointed out to me, it seems impossible even to state it without recurring to a number of the lower categories which Mr. Bradley had previously invalidated. Otherwise the consideration of the different *amounts* of rearrangement required for the 'conversion' of 'appearances' into the Absolute, of the greater or less *intervals* separating them from it, of the varying lengths of time *needed* to see through an appearance, would seem to be simply irrelevant, and unable to establish the distinctions of kind among appearances which are aimed at. Yet strangely enough, Time, Space, and Quantity have themselves been written down as 'mere

method unendurable. If only he had exempted a few trifles, like religion and morality, from this reduction to illusion, we might have tolerated his onslaughts on the abstractions of metaphysics; as it is, there is nothing that can withstand the onset of his awful Absolute.

Now if anything of the sort had happened to a philosophic argument of my own, I should have been appalled. I should have felt that something had gone wrong, that some secret source of error must have sprung up somewhere, or that I must somehow have misunderstood my principle. If the result of my intellectual manipulations of the world had been to convict it of radical absurdity, I should have regarded this as a reflection, not on the universe, but on the method I had used. I should have felt I had *failed* intellectually, and must try again in another way.[1] I should never have dared to condemn the universe in reliance on so tenuous an argument from so narrow a basis. In the last resort I might even have doubted the validity of my principle. I should certainly have doubted its application. Mr. Bradley, apparently, is exempt from any such scruples, but, at the risk of making a deplorable exhibition of the crassest 'common-sense,' I must submit that a system which culminates in so huge a paradox thereby discredits its foundations. And so Mr. Bradley's final Ascension from the sphere of Appearances and Reception into the bosom of the Absolute reminds me of nothing so much as of the fabled 'rope-trick' of the Indian jugglers.

III

Only a strong conviction of its necessity, together with a habit of outspokenness learnt from Mr. Bradley's

---

appearances' (*Appear. and Real.* pp. 362, 364, 369, etc., first ed.), and Mr. Bradley makes no attempt to show how the reality of appearances can be rehabilitated by a reversion to points of view which themselves are appearances. It is as though to atone for his haste in calling all men liars, the psalmist had proceeded to accept the testimony of the most egregious liars to the veracity or the rest.

[1] Mr. Bradley's critical canon is apparently the reverse of this. *E.g.* in discussing the sense in which the self is real, he argues that "if none defensible can be found, such a failure, I must insist, ought to end the question."—*App. and Real.* p. 76.

own example, could have embarked me on so painful a criticism of the cardinal doctrine of Appearance and Reality. Before proceeding from it to the easier and more congenial task of expounding what I conceive to be the real relation of these conceptions, I must however add a word on a point already hinted at, viz., that Mr. Bradley has not really extricated us from that slough of agnosticism, to which their more porcine instincts are ever drawing back even philosophers to wallow. Indeed, his facetious remark about Spencer's Unknowable,[1] that it is taken for God "simply and solely because we do not know what the devil it can be," might, with quite as much propriety, be applied to his own Absolute. For though he has reserved for it the title of Sole and Supreme Reality, it is only used to cast an indelible slur on all human reality and knowledge. It absorbs,' 'transcends,' 'transmutes,' etc., all our knowledge and experience. It is therefore quite as unknowable as Spencer's monstrosity, and adds insult to injury by dubbing us and our concerns 'mere appearances.' And after all the scorn we have seen poured on the futility of an unknowable reality as the explanation of anything, it passes my comprehension how these consequences of his doctrine should have escaped the notice, I do not say of his disciples, but of Mr. Bradley's own acuteness.

It is useless however to speculate how far Mr. Bradley knows himself to be a sceptic, until he chooses to confess, and we had better concern ourselves with the true relation of reality to appearance. Mr. Bradley's fundamental error seems to be his $\chi\omega\rho\iota\sigma\mu\acute{o}\varsigma$, the separation he has effected between them by violently disrupting their continuity. Once we do this, we are lost. The 'reality' we have severed from its 'appearances' can never be regained, and we remain, as Mr. Bradley holds, enmeshed in a web of appearances, and impotent to attain a knowledge or experience of Reality. But all this appears to be the consequence of a gratuitous error of judgment. We should never have admitted that in

---

[1] *App. and Real.* p. 128, footnote.

grasping a higher reality we were abandoning the reality of the lower. In the ascent to Truth we can never lose touch with a continuous reality. I should liken the advance of knowledge to a severe rock-climb on which we must secure our handhold and our foothold at every step. Rightly used, the rope of metaphysical speculation is an added safeguard which unites the workers at their different posts; it must not be made into an instrument to juggle with. Mr. Bradley, on the other hand, seems to tell us that we can never reach the summit of our ambitions unless we can throw our rope up into the air and climb up after it into the hypercosmic void.

We must begin therefore with reality as well as end with it, and cling to it all the way as closely as we can. We must not argue, 'if appearance, not reality,' but 'though appearance, yet reality.' Unless we do this any ultimate Reality we may vainly imagine will effect no contact with our knowledge and our life, but float off into the Empyrean beyond our ken.

Now the only reality we can start with is our own personal, immediate experience. We may lay it down therefore that *all immediate experience is as such real, and that no ultimate reality can be reached except from this basis and upon the stimulation of such immediate experience.* From this we start; to this, sooner or later, we must in some way return, under penalty of finding all our explanations shattered, like bubbles, into emptiness.

In other words, the distinction of 'appearance and reality' is *not* one which transcends our experience, but one which arises in it. It does *not* constitute a relation between our world and another, nor tempt us to an impossible excursion into a realm inexorably reserved for the supreme delectation of the Absolute. It always remains relative to our knowledge of our world.[1] And it in no wise warrants any disparagement of 'mere appearances.' The most transparent of appearances, so long as it exists

---

[1] If I am quibbled with I will even say that *for me* it remains relative to *my* knowledge of *my* world. And I will *deny* that this means solipsism.

at all, retains its modicum of reality, and remains, from one important point of view, fundamentally real.

For let us consider how we proceed to ascertain the higher realities which are rashly thought to abrogate the lower. We start, indubitably, with an immediate experience of some sort. But we do not rest therein. If we could, there would be no further question. Our immediate experience would suffice; it would be the sole and complete reality. Appearances would *be* the reality and reality would truly appear. In heaven, no doubt, such would be the case. But our case, as yet, is different: *our* experience is woefully discordant and inadequate. In other words, our experience is *not* that of a perfect world. We are neither disposed, therefore, nor able, to accept it *as it appears to be*. Its surface-value will not enable us to meet our obligations: we are compelled therefore to discount our immediate experience, to treat it as an appearance of something ulterior which will supplement its deficiency. We move on, therefore, from our starting-point, taking our immediate experience as the symbol which transmits to us the glad tidings of a higher reality, whereof it partly manifests the nature.

The 'realities' of ordinary life and science, such as the 'external' world and the existence of other persons, are all of this secondary order: they rest upon inferences from our immediate experience which have been found to work.[1] They are thus pragmatically true, and the process of reaching them is everywhere the same: we experiment with notions which are suggested to our intelligence by our immediate experience, until we hit upon one which seems to be serviceable for some purpose which engrosses us. We then *declare real* the conception which serves our purpose, nay more real, because more potent, than the immediate experience for the satisfaction of our desire. Only, as life is complex,

---

[1] Of course I do not deny, and indeed in a different context I should even insist, that the assumption of these higher realities *alters* our immediate experience for us. That indeed is the chief proof of their value: assumptions which make no difference are otiose and so invalid. And we should hardly get where we want, if we could not each day start a little higher up.

its sciences are many and its purposes are various; so there will be a multitude of such higher realities conflicting with each other and competing for our allegiance. And, superficially, they will look very different. Nevertheless, the ultimate realities of the physicist, whether they be atoms or ions or vortex-rings or electrons, have reached their proud position by no other process than that by which the savage has devised the crudities of his Happy Hunting Grounds or the old-fashioned theologian the atrocities of his Hell. They remain on the same plane of interpretation, and all alike are attempts, more or less successful, to supplement some unsatisfactory feature or other in our primary experience.

It is easy to see how from this point we may reach the conception of an *Ultimate* Reality. The 'higher realities' are conceived differently for the purposes of our various sciences and various pursuits, and so there will arise a need for an adjustment of their rival claims, and a question as to which (if any) of them is to be accepted as the final reality. Is the 'real world,' *e.g.*, the cosmic conception postulated by geometry, or by physics, or by psychology, or by ethics? Is it a whirl of self-moving 'matter,' or a chaos of mental processes, or must we assume a Prime Mover and a Self? Again, it is obvious that a higher reality may afford very imperfect satisfaction from some points of view and may have to be transcended by one still higher, and that this process cannot cease until we arrive at the conception of an Ultimate Reality capable of including *and harmonizing* all the lower realities. And this, of course, would contain the final explanation of our whole experience, the final solution of our every perplexity.

IV

Thus the struggle to attain a glimpse of such an Ultimate Reality forms the perennial content of the drama of Philosophy. But that struggle is foredoomed to failure, unless we can manage to avoid certain pitfalls and to hold fast to certain guiding principles.

(1) The Ultimate Reality must be made into a *real explanation*. It must *never* therefore be allowed to become transcendent, and to sever its connexion with the world of 'appearances' which it was devised to explain. There must always be preserved a pathway leading *up to it* from the lowest 'appearances' and *down to them* from the Throne of Thrones, in order that the angels of the Lord may travel thereon. If this be neglected, the ultimate reality will become unknowable, incapable of explaining the appearances, and therefore invalid.[1]

(2) The 'appearances' must be really preserved. They must not be stripped of their reality or neglected as mere appearances, merely because we fancy that we have seen *in them* glimpses of something higher. So long as they exist at all, they are real. The world *really* is coloured, and noisy, and hard, and painful, and spacious, and fleeting, notwithstanding the objections of our wiseacres, and there is excellent sense even in maintaining that the earth is flat (some of it) and that the sun does rise and set. Even a nightmare does not become less real and oppressive because you have survived, and traced it to too generous an indulgence in lobster salad.

For (3) it must never be forgotten that the immediate experience is after all in a way *more real, i.e. more directly real*, than the 'higher realities' which are said to 'explain' it. For the latter are inferred and postulated simply and solely for the purpose of 'explaining' the former, and their reality consequently rests for us upon that of the former. Or in so far as the higher realities are more than inferences, they become such by entering into immediate experience and transfiguring it.[2]

The dependence of all ulterior reality upon immediate

---

[1] It is clear that this objection alone would justify the rejection of Mr. Bradley's Absolute. But, so far as I can understand it, it seems to be constitutionally incapable of complying with any of the conditions I am laying down.

[2] The simplest example of this is the way in which the results of thought attain immediacy in perception.

experience is easy to illustrate. I sit in my armchair and read, what I will call one of the more severely scholastic works on philosophy. There appears to me my friend Jones who has come to tell me that my friend Smith has been arrested on a charge of bigamy and wants me to bail him out. I have no reason to doubt the veracity of Jones or the reality of the situation. I feel therefore the urgent necessity for instant action, and, hastening to the rescue, I—awake with a start! It was all a dream, you will say. On the contrary, I reply, it was all a reality. While I lived through it, the experience was as vivid and real as anything I ever experienced. It is so still : the thought of Smith's bigamy—he happens to be the primmest of old bachelors—still affords me uncontrollable amusement. It is true that I have now modified my opinion as to the order of 'reality' to which the experience belonged. I had thought that it belonged to our common waking world ; I now regard it as belonging to a more beautiful dream-world of my own.[1] We see, therefore, how the 'higher' reality depends on the immediate. The reality of Smith's excessive susceptibility, of Jones's visit, and of the bigamy itself, rested upon and was relative to that of my dream-experience. When my experience changed, I was no longer entitled to infer the existence of my previous realities in the world of my waking life.[2]

The application of this principle is quite general. A change in any particular 'appearance' may entirely invalidate the argument for the 'reality' which served to explain it in its previous condition; its annihilation would destroy the ground for the assumption of *this* reality ; and the annihilation of all appearances would obviously destroy all the reasons for assuming *any* reality.[3] The principle is one of considerable speculative importance, for it enables us to conceive how we should

---

[1] And possibly also of Jones, if (as sometimes happens) he also dreamt the story he told me.
[2] Cp. pp. 18, 32, 43, 369.
[3] Hence we may say that Mr. Bradley's maltreatment of 'appearances' destroys all 'reality.'

think the reality of a 'lower' to be related to that of a 'higher' world of experience, if and when we experienced such a transition from one to the other. And to Religion, of course, this is a point of capital importance. For unless we can conceive how the higher or 'spiritual' world can transcend and absorb, without negating, the lower or 'material' world, the postulates of the religious consciousness must continue to seem idle fairy tales to the austere reason of the systematic thinker.

Moreover this dependence of derivative realities on primary experience has a most important bearing on the philosophic status of Idealism. At present Idealism remains in the position of an unprofitable paradox, because none of those who have professed a theoretic belief in it have cared or dared to act upon their theory. And so the argument for it is among those which, in Hume's phrase, admit of no answer and carry no conviction; and yet, strangely enough, idealist philosophers, so far from being disconcerted by it, seem to be rather proud of this fact. Why else should they perpetually be apologizing for what they conceive to be the paradox of their doctrine, and explaining that it really leaves the empirical reality of things entirely untouched? Idealism, they say, opens no royal roads to higher realms: it makes no practical difference to the reality of anything, save, perhaps, that it enables the philosopher to recoil at will upon a point of view not understanded of the vulgar.

To all of which, as humanists, we must reply, that this defence but aggravates the charge. It proves Idealism to be either worthless or pernicious: the latter, if its sole function is to gratify a philosophic pride; the former, if it really makes no difference. And while a temporary air of paradox is not unbecoming to the youth of a novel view, it is the plain duty of every doctrine that seriously pretends to maintain itself as truth before the public to turn itself into an accepted truism as quickly as it can. *If therefore Idealism really means anything, it must enable the idealist to regard reality differently from the realist,* and to act differently in virtue of his truer insight. To say that Idealism makes no difference is thus to pronounce its utter condemnation. It is to admit that it is the same thing as Realism, variously named, *i.e.* to render it a useless subtlety. And must we not as pragmatists concede, that if it were really *useless*, it would incontestably be *false*?[1]

To be true at all, therefore, Idealism *must* make a difference, but what shall we say it is? It seems to me that if Idealism is right in its fundamental contention that existence is experience, and if we really try to live up to this insight, the difference which it *ought* to make is quite clearly this: that while the idealist does not deny the *relative* reality and pragmatic value of his actual experience, he does not feel bound to commit himself in his inmost soul to the assertion also of its *absolute* reality. That is, he will make a certain inward reservation as to the ultimate reality of an imperfect world; he will hold himself free to contemplate with a certain irony the brute facts of an experience he cannot wholly master, free also to uphold in their despite the ultimate validity of the ideals his spirit craves; in short, he will possess a reserve of strength not open to his rivals, wherewith to meet the buffetings of circumstance. Practically also he will be more alert to seize upon whatever chances offer to effect improvements in an actual order he does not hold to be definitive; he will hold himself prepared to advance to worlds of a higher and more harmonious order,[2] and to welcome whatever indications of their possibility may float within his ken. The vision of the realist, on the other hand, conceiving himself to be cognizant of a final, rigid, and independent reality, should be undeviatingly fixed upon and bounded by the 'brute' facts of his actual experience; this he must regard as final, and he will thus debar himself from all experiments that might extend its borders or transform the context, and so the texture, of his universe. As for the *soi-disant* idealists who can draw no inference from their creed, we must contend that

---

[1] Cp. pp. 38-40.   [2] Cp. pp. 18, 22, 368.

they have really failed to grasp its meaning, and are unworthy of the name they have assumed. For the bow of Odysseus belongs to him alone who can bend it, and, if need be, use it upon the enemies of truth.

(4) The reality of the 'higher reality' must be made to depend throughout on its *efficiency*. This follows implicitly from what we have already established. Immediate experience forms the touchstone whereby we test the *value* of our inferred realities, and if they can contribute nothing valuable to its elucidation, their assumption is nothing but vanity and vexation of spirit. For what started the whole cognitive process was just the felt unsatisfactoriness of our immediate experience; our inferences must approve themselves as specifics against this disease, by their ability to supplement the actual, by the *power* they give us to *transform* our experiences. The transmutation of appearances therefore must not be represented as an inscrutable privilege of the Absolute; it must be made a weapon mortal hands can actually wield. This in fact is what we are continually doing; it is the whole aim of our conceptual manipulation of experience. If to 'think' it left 'reality' the same, we should not waste our lives upon what is to most a painful and irksome business; but in point of fact our thought *ministers to our perceptions* and so alleviates the burden of life. The results of our past thought enter into and transform our immediate perceptions and render them more adequate as guides to action. And this is what we want our thought to do and why we value it. Intellectualist prejudice indeed has interpreted this process into an excuse for 'analysing' perception into 'thought'; it is better regarded as a proof of the practical value of thought and of the teleological character of conception.

What will in the last resort decide, therefore, whether an inferred reality really exists or is merely a figment of the imagination, is the way it works, and the power which its aid confers. The assumption, *e.g.*, of the earth's rotundity is 'true,' and preferable to the 'flat-earth' theory, because on the whole it works better and accounts better for the course of our experience. Similarly, if I am comparing the merits of the scientific theory that the transmission of light is effected by the vibrations of a hypothetical reality called the 'ether' with those of a more poetic theory that it is due to the flapping of equally hypothetical cherubs' wings, my decision will certainly be affected by the consideration that I can probably discover regular ways of manipulating the ether, but can hardly hope to control the movements of the cherubs.

An assumed reality, then, approves itself to be *true* in proportion as it shows itself capable of rendering our life more harmonious; it exposes itself to rejection as *false* in proportion as it either fails to affect our experiences, or exercises a detrimental effect upon them. Knowledge is power, because we decline to recognize as *knowledge* whatever does not satisfy our lust for *power*.

It follows (5) that *Ultimate Reality must be absolutely satisfactory*. For that is the condition of our accepting it as such. So long as the most ultimate reality we have reached in thought or deed falls short in any respect of giving complete satisfaction, the struggle to harmonize experience must go on, lead to fresh efforts, and inspire the suspicion that something must exist to dissolve away our faintest discords. We cannot acquiesce therefore in what we have found. Or rather our acquiescence in it would at most betray the exhaustion of despair. To this we might be reduced for a season, but the hope would always rise anew that somehow there was something *better, truer and more real* lurking behind the apparent ultimates of our knowledge. For illustration I need merely appeal to the well-known fact that an 'other' world is always conceived as a 'better' world. The absolutely satisfactory alone would rise superior to such doubts. It would be *psychologically impossible* to suspect it of bearing hidden horrors in its breast. The thought is no doubt abstractly conceivable, but a human mind could hardly be found seriously to entertain it. Similarly we might play with the idea of a progress in knowledge which should not only fail to be a progress in harmony, but should reveal fresh horrors at every step, until by the time absolute truth had been reached the cumulative cruelty of what we were forced to recognize as ultimate reality surpassed our most hideous imaginings as far as our knowledge surpassed that of a Bushman. Now I do not for a moment suppose that common sense can be terrified with such suggestions into regarding them as more than the nightmares of a mind distraught, and I venture to think that a pragmatist philosophy can show that common sense is right. For there is a serious fallacy in the notion that the pursuit of Truth could reveal a chamber of horrors in the innermost shrine, and that we could all be forced to acknowledge and adore an ultimate reality in this monstrous guise. If this were truth, we should decline to believe it, and to accept it as true. We should insist that there must be some escape from the Minotaur, some way out of the Labyrinth in which our knowledge had involved our life. And even if we could be forced to the admission that the pursuit of truth necessarily and inevitably brought us face to face with some unbearable atrocity—an undertaking which seems so far to have overtaxed even Mr. Bradley's ingenuity—a simple expedient would remain. As soon as the pursuit of truth was generally recognized to be practically noxious, we should simply give it up. If its misguided votaries morbidly persisted in their diabolical pursuit of 'truth regardless of the consequences,' they would be stamped out, as the Indian Government has stamped out the Thugs. Nor is this mere imagining. The thing has happened over and over again. All through the Middle Ages most branches of knowledge were under black suspicion as hostile to human welfare. They languished accordingly, and some of them, such as, *e.g.*, Psychical Research, are still under a cloud. It is hardly necessary to allude to Comte's drastic proposals for the State regulation of science, and every teacher knows that the Civil Service Commissioners in the last resort prescribe what shall be taught (and how) throughout the land. In short the fact is patent to all who will open their eyes that in a thousand ways society is ever controlling, repressing, or encouraging, the cognitive activities of its members.[1]

And not only would this be done, but it would be an entirely reasonable thing to do in the case supposed. If the pursuit of knowledge really aggravated, instead of relieving, the burden of life, it would be *irrational*. If every step we took beyond 'appearances' were but an augmentation of the disharmony in our experience, there would be no gain in taking it. The alleged knowledge would be worse than useless, and we should fare better without it. We should have to train ourselves therefore to make the most of appearances, to make no effort to get behind them. And natural selection would see to it that those did not survive who remained addicted to a futile and noxious pursuit. This then would be the worst that could happen; the frivolity and thoughtlessness of the day-fly might pay better than the deadly earnest of the sage. But the day-fly would have become incapable of assenting to the extravagances of ultra-pessimism, simply because it would not think of what was coming.

From the worst possibility let us turn to the best. The best that has been mentioned is that by Faith and daring we should find an experience that would conduct us to the fortunate thought of an ultimate reality capable of completely harmonizing our experience. And a merely intellectualist philosophy would have no reason, I presume, to ask for more than this. But just as before we conceived the principle of non-contradiction to be a form of the wider principle of harmony, so now we can hardly rest content with a reality which is merely *conceived* as the ground of complete satisfaction. For so long as it remains a mere conception, it must remain doubtful whether it could be realized in actual fact. To remove this doubt, therefore, our ultimate reality would have *actually to establish* the perfect harmony. By this achievement alone, *i.e.* by returning to our immediate experience and transmuting it into a form in which doubt would have become impossible, would it finally put an end to every doubt of

---

[1] Cp. pp. 58-60 and 342-4.

its own ultimateness. But by this same achievement it would have dissolved our original problem. The antithesis of 'appearance' and 'reality' would have vanished. Ultimate reality having become immediate experience the two would coincide, and we should have entered into the fruition of their union.

And so should we not finally catch a glimpse of an ideal which, in its own way, theology has dreamt of as 'the Beatific Vision'? The ideal of knowledge, as of the life to which it ministers, would not be an infinitely complex system of relations about which one might argue without end, but the *vision*, or *immediate* perception, of a reality which had absorbed all truth and so had become, as it were, intellectually transparent, and in which the whole meaning of the cosmic scheme was summed up and luminously comprehended—not only *understood*, but *seen* to be very *good*, and more than this, to be supremely *beautiful*. In other words, the bliss which Aristotle tried so hard to attribute to a Deity scornful of all communion with a suffering universe, could never be derived from a discursive 'thinking upon thought';[1] it would have to take the form of an *aesthetic* contemplation of the perfect and all-embracing harmony.[2]

---

[1] Not that Aristotle's νόησις is really discursive. His thought (though not always his language) has really quite outgrown the Platonic antithesis of sensation and thought.

[2] For suggestions as to how this Beatific Vision can be conceived as attainable, see the next essay.

XII

ACTIVITY AND SUBSTANCE [1]

ARGUMENT

Need for a reconstruction of the conception of Substance by means of the Aristotelian conception of 'Ενέργεια.
I. *Its historical antecedents.* The antithesis of the Process and Permanence view of existence, Eleaticism — Heracliteanism — Platonism. Aristotle's criticism of Plato's οὐσία as mere potentiality—his advance in forming the conception of ἐνέργεια.
II. *Aristotle's statement of his doctrine.* 'Ενέργεια as Substance—not a form of κίνησις but *vice versa.* When perfected it no longer implies 'motion' or 'change.' Hence the Divine activity is continuous and eternal and ἐνέργεια ἀκινησίας.
III. *Its consequences.* Perfect happiness—the transition from Time to Eternity—'Ενέργεια ἀκινησίας a *scientific* conception of 'Heaven.'
IV. *The paradoxes of the doctrine.* How can there be activity, life, or consciousness without change?
V. *Their explanation.* The difficulty not in the facts but in the arbitrary interpretation we have put upon them. Thus (1) the equilibrium of motions is conceivable as the perfection, not as the cessation of 'motion,' (2) perfect metabolism would transcend change, and (3) so would a perfect consciousness.
VI. *Advantages of so conceiving Activity.* Rejection of 'Becoming' and 'Rest' as ideals. Conceivableness of 'Heaven' and 'Eternity.' Avoidance of the 'Dissipation of Energy.' Spencer's see-saw as to the interpretation of 'equilibration.'
VII. *The old theory of Substance worthless.* If 'Substance' is conceived as the substratum of change it becomes unknowable and explains nothing. Berkeley detected this in the case of material, Hume in that of spiritual 'substance.' Psychology has recently found it out in the case of the 'Soul' and physics in that of 'matter.' 'Energy' as the only physical reality. Lotze's criticism and reconstruction of substantiality.
VIII. *The Activity without motion as the ultimate ideal of Being.* Activity the sole substance—how it produces the illusion of a substratum in which reality is never found. It is in proportion as the real actualizes its possibilities in a harmonious form that it assumes the features of an ultimate ideal. The value of such an ideal.

---

[1] The greater part of this appeared in *Mind*, N.S. 36, Oct. 1900, under the title of *The Conception of* 'Ενέργεια 'Ακινησίας. But it has been revised and considerably expanded.

My aim in this essay is to throw out some suggestions for a reconstruction of the conception of Substance which the work of the sciences so sorely needs, but to which modern philosophy, although Hume had cleared the ground by showing the worthlessness of the old notion of substance,[1] has as yet contributed little of a really constructive character.[2] This aim I hope to achieve by going back to Aristotle and extricating from an unmerited obscurity the Aristotelian ideal of Being, which seems to me to have formulated the only useful and tenable conception of Substantiality nearly 2300 years ago. I am aware that this sounds incredible, and would be so, if that conception had ever been properly understood. But this has never been the case; for reasons arising partly from the facility with which appearances generate the vulgar notion of Substance as the unchanging substratum of change, but also not unconnected with the brevity of Aristotle's extant utterances on the subject. The worst of packing truth in a nutshell is that, so bestowed, it cannot safely navigate the stream of time and will at best float down it without notice.

My first task, therefore, will be to expound more fully the Aristotelian conception of *Energeia*, to show how it culminates in an activity which transcends change and motion (ἐνέργεια ἀκινησίας), and to remove the paradoxes which this seems superficially to involve. I can then proceed to show that this conception completely supersedes the vulgar notion of Substance, that it alone is of service in the sciences and competent to satisfy the intellectual and emotional demands we must make upon our conception of ultimate Being, and thereby not only removes a number of misconceptions which have been a constant source of trouble in science and philosophy, but goes far to relieve philosophy from the opprobrium of terminating in inconceivable mysteries.

---

[1] I refer of course to his criticism of the Self in the *Treatise*.

[2] For, of course, the Kantian assertion that Substance is an *a priori* 'category' by which we recognize the permanent in change is unprofitable verbalism. It explains neither the *formation* of the notion, *i.e.* how we come by this ideal, nor its *meaning*, *i.e.* what in concrete fact it is to persist through change, nor its *application*, *i.e.* how we discern 'substances' and discriminate them from things which only seem so.

I propose to trace, therefore, (1) the historical antecedents of Aristotle's doctrine, (2) his own statements of it, (3) its consequences, (4) the objections to it, (5) the answers to these, (6) its advantages over rival theories of substance, (7) the worthlessness of the latter, and finally (8) the value of the Aristotelian conception as an ultimate ideal.

I

The history of thought, like that of politics, has largely been the history of great antitheses which have kept up their secular conflict from age to age. In the course of that history it may often have seemed that the one side of such an antithesis had finally triumphed over the other, but in the next generation it has often appeared that its rival had rallied its forces and restated its position to such effect that the preponderance of opinion has once more swung back to its side. Perhaps the most important metaphysically of these antitheses is that which has at different times been formulated as that between Γένεσις and Οὐσία, Ἐνέργεια and Ἕξις, Becoming and Being, Change and Immutability, Process and Permanence, and it will be necessary to cast a rapid retrospect over its varying fortunes in order to appreciate the full significance of Aristotle's doctrine.

It will suffice for this purpose to start with the metaphysic of the Eleatics, taking it as the extremest, crudest, most abstract, and therefore most impressive, representative of what we may call, for purposes of reference, the *permanence*-view of the ultimate nature of existence. In the Eleatics the affirmation of Being took the form of a rigid immutable Ὄν, whose uncompromising unity reduced all motion, change and plurality to an inexplicable illusion, and remorselessly crushed out the whole significance of human life. This uncanny Monism was defended with a dialectical ability which has never since been equalled, and Zeno's proofs of the impossibility of motion are still full of instruction for philosophers of all schools.

But in the philosophy of Herakleitos Nemesis overtakes the Eleatics. Herakleitos affirms against them the ultimate reality of Becoming, the unlimited all-pervading *Process*, which unremittingly surges in the circling road, the ὅδος ἄνω κάτω, wherein all things stream away (πάντα ῥεῖ καὶ οὐδὲν μένει). In spite of the somewhat sinister denial of permanence implied in this addition, Heracliteanism may well have seemed to restore to the universe the life which Eleaticism had made impossible.

But in Plato the pendulum swings back again to the side of οὐσία. Rightly or wrongly, he detected in Heracliteanism consequences which seemed to him fatal to the possibility of knowledge, and instead of seeking to determine the actual limits of the Flux and betaking himself to the practical methods science has since elaborated in order to know it, he preferred to reject Heracliteanism and to propound a revised, and greatly improved, Eleaticism. He points out our need of a ποῦ στῶ, which is not swept away in the Flux, of a fixed standard whereby to measure and render knowable the flow of Becoming, and in his theory of Ideas he conceived himself to have supplied this demand. In it plurality is, in a manner, recognized in the plurality of the Ideas, united though they are in the Idea of the Good, while the phenomenal world is admitted not to be wholly illusory, being μεταξὺ τοῦ ὄντος καὶ μὴ ὄντος, intermediate between the Ideas and the principle of impermanence, the mystery of which Plato seems to have thought he could resolve by calling it the 'Non-Existent.'

In the end, however, the Idea remains the only true reality, and the Idea as such is unchanging Being, out of Space and Time. Hence to call anything, *e.g.*, Pleasure, a 'Becoming' (γένεσις) is *ipso facto* to cast a slur upon its reality and to disqualify it for the position of the Chief Good which must be, he thinks, an abiding 'ousia.'

In Aristotle the tables are once more turned. To Aristotle the real world, *i.e.* the world whereof we desire an explanation, is after all the world of change in which we move and live, rather than the system of immutable and timeless 'laws' which we devise for its explanation. Hence Plato's changeless 'ousiai' seem to him too distant and divorced to explain the world. A conception of Substance which is to explain the facts of the world must not subsist in an impassible immutability in the super-celestial seclusion of a transcendent τόπος νοητός : if Substance meant no more than this, it would be a mere potentiality (δύναμις). If οὐσία, therefore, is not immanent and does not assert itself in the world of phenomena, but remains an inert and secluded δύναμις, it is lifeless and worthless. For the potentiality owes its visibility, its value, nay, its very existence, to the glow shed upon it by the actual exercise of function (*energeia*). Hence the 'universal' (καθόλου), if it is to be truly valuable either for science or for practice, must be in the world and pervade it ; or, in his technical phrase, must display itself in *actuality* (ἐνεργείᾳ) by the way it *actually* works. Not that Aristotle denies the validity of the considerations which led Plato to frame his conception of οὐσία ; he denies only its adequacy. In his anxiety to escape out of the Heraclitean flux Plato had overshot the mark : he had committed himself to a conception of Being too rigid and remote to explain the Becoming of phenomena. The highest conception must be Ἐνέργεια and not Δύναμις, the *actual* functioning of a substance whose real nature is only so revealed.

This too is the ultimate reason why, in his *Ethics*, Aristotle denies that ἀρετή is the Good, and contends that the Good, Εὐδαιμονία, must be the *exercise* of the ἕξις (δύναμις), ἐνέργεια κατ' ἀρετήν. A merely statical treatment of the truly valuable will not suffice : the Good is not merely ἀγαθὴ φύσις, it is ἀγαθὴ φύσις in exercise, and a disposition (ἕξις) is only valuable as the basis and potentiality of an ἐνέργεια. In this way the whole of Aristotle's philosophy, both in its constructive and in its critical aspects as a reply to Plato, may be enunciated in the one word, '*Enérgeia*.' It has indeed always been more or less recognized that into this technical term

Aristotle has packed all that was most distinctive, most original, most fundamental, and most profound in his philosophy. Now in philosophy all real originality is *constructive*—for you cannot pull down without a standing ground whence to effect the operation—and all real constructiveness is also *critical*, for, as the earliest Pharaohs already knew, the most effective and unanswerable way of abolishing your rival's constructions is to use them up in your own. Hence it is that Aristotle's conception of *Energeia* constitutes both his really effective criticism of Plato, a criticism whose massive weight is far more crushing than the querulous and dialectical quibbling which he so often seems to substitute for serious appreciation of his master's work, and also the really decisive step in his advance beyond Plato. But the step was such a great one, and advances into regions so remote from our habitual modes of thinking, that not even the lapse of twenty centuries has rendered it easy to follow in his footsteps.

II

It follows from his rehabilitation of the Process-view of the world that Aristotle has (*a*) to establish the superiority of his conception of ἐνέργεια over the Platonic conception of οὐσία, (*b*) that he has to distinguish it from the conception of κίνησις or γένεσις, which had succumbed to the Platonic criticism.

The first point is of course easy enough to establish. It suffices to point out that a substance apart from its activity is an abstraction, or, in Aristotle's words, that the actuality is naturally prior to the potentiality, that to *be* is to *be active*.[1] This simple truth, that a substantiality which *does* nothing *is* nothing, is now of course familiar enough, and perhaps best known in the Herbartian formula, 'without causality no substantiality,' though it lies at the roots also of Hume's criticism of substantiality. But the very fact that it has so often to be reaffirmed

[1] Cp. esp. *Eth. Nic.* ix. 7. 4 (1168 a 6) ἐσμὲν δ' ἐνεργείᾳ.

P

shows the strength of the natural prejudices against which it has had to contend.

The same remark applies with tenfold force to the second point, viz. the difficulty of grasping the constructive aspect of the conception of *Energeia*. It has not ceased to appear paradoxical to us because of our inveterate, but quite illogical, habit of regarding a 'function' (ἐνέργεια) as a sort of 'process' (γένεσις), or even—when we try to be particularly 'scientific'—as ultimately reducible to a sort of 'motion.' In other words, we ordinarily subsume Aristotle's ἐνέργεια under the conception of what he would have called κίνησις. And if we do this, his notion of an activity without motion (ἐνέργεια ἀκινησίας) must seem the very height of paradox, a paradox whereof the edge has not been blunted by the progress of two thousand years.

But the fault is ours; we have unwittingly employed conceptions which are the precise opposite of the device whereby Aristotle turned the flank of the Platonic criticism of Becoming and established his own conception of Ἐνέργεια. In superseding by it the Platonic οὐσία he could not, of course, merely revert to the earlier conceptions of 'becoming' and 'motion' whose logical annihilation Plato had effected. He was bound to provide something new in his conception of *Energeia*, and to distinguish it from both its precursors. And he does it. He does not fall into the trap to which we succumb when we regard a 'function' (ἐνέργεια) as a sort of 'process' (γένεσις), or, materialistically, try to reduce all things to 'matter' in 'motion.' He does the very opposite. Instead of classifying ἐνέργεια under κίνησις, he simply makes ἐνέργεια the wider and supremer notion, and subsumes κίνησις under it as a peculiar species, viz. an *imperfect* ἐνέργεια.[1]

---

[1] Cp. *e.g. Physics*, iii. 2, 201 b 31, ἡ κίνησις ἐνέργεια μέν τις εἶναι δοκεῖ ἀτελὴς δέ, viii. 5, 257 b 8, ἔστιν ἡ κίνησις ἐντελέχεια κινητοῦ ἀτελής. *De Anima*, ii. 5, 417 a 16, ἔστιν ἡ κίνησις ἐνέργειά τις, ἀτελὴς μέντοι: iii. 2, 431 a 5, φαίνεται τὸ μὲν αἰσθητὸν ἐκ δυνάμει ὄντος τοῦ αἰσθητικοῦ ἐνεργείᾳ ποιοῦν · οὐ γὰρ πάσχει οὐδ' ἀλλοιοῦται (*sc.* τὸ αἰσθητικόν), διὸ ἄλλο εἶδος τοῦτο κινήσεως · ἡ γὰρ κίνησις ἀτελοῦς ἐνέργεια ἦν · ἡ δ' ἁπλῶς ἐνέργεια ἑτέρα ἡ τοῦ τετελεσμένου. *Metaph.* Θ, 6, 1048 b 29 πᾶσα γὰρ κίνησις ἀτελής.

Cp. also *Eth. Nic.* x. 3, 1174 a 19, where it is explained that ἡδονή is not κίνησις, because it does not need perfecting (being indeed what itself perfects ἐνέργεια), while κίνησις does.

Κίνησις, that is, arises from the longing of the imperfect for the perfect, of the 'matter' (ὕλη) for the 'form' (εἶδος); it is simply the process whereby it reaches whatever degree of perfection the inherent limitations of its nature concede to it.

Ἐνέργεια, on the other hand, does not essentially or necessarily imply motion or change. In fact in the typical case, the perfect exercise of function by the senses, there is neither 'motion' (κίνησις) nor 'change' (ἀλλοίωσις) nor 'passivity' (πάσχειν); the appropriate stimulus rouses the organ to activity and the organ functions naturally in grasping it;[1] when this process is free from friction ('impediment') perception is perfect and accompanied by pleasure (ἡδονή).

Man, unfortunately, only catches brief glimpses of this happy state of things: our activity cannot be sustained, because, owing to the defectiveness (πονηρία or φαυλότης) of a composite nature adulterated with 'matter' (ὕλη), we grow weary and allow our attention to wander and cannot be continuously active (συνεχῶς ἐνεργεῖν).[2] But God is not so hampered; his is a pure and perfect nature; he is pure Form, unimpeded by Matter, and always completely and actually all that he can be. Hence the divine ἐνέργεια is kept up inexhaustibly,[3] and ever generates the supreme pleasure, simple and incorruptible, of self-contemplation (νόησις νοήσεως), which constitutes the divine happiness. It follows, as a matter of course, that this ἐνέργεια is above and beyond κίνησις; it is ἐνέργεια ἀκινησίας or ἠρεμία. Hence in a famous passage—whose fame is yet unequal to its merits[4]—we are told that "if the nature of anything were simple, the same action would ever be sweetest to it. And this is the reason why God always enjoys a single and simple pleasure; for there is not only an activity of motion, but also one void of motion, and pleasure is rather in constancy[5] than in

---

[1] *Eth. Nic.* x. 4. 5, 1174 b 14.   [2] *Ibid.* x. 4. 9, 1175 a 4.
[3] This is true also of the heavenly bodies, by reason of their more perfect ὕλη. Cp. *Metaph.* 1050 b 22.
[4] *Eth. Nic.* vii. 14. 8 (1154 b 25-31).
[5] ἠρεμία cannot be translated 'rest' without misleading. For 'rest' to us = non-activity, which to Aristotle is tantamount to non-existence. He uses the

motion. And change of all things is sweet, as the poet hath it, because of a certain defect."[1]

The immense significance of this passage has been strangely overlooked and the commentators say singularly little about it. Thus, of the two latest editors of the *Ethics*, Prof. Stewart accuses Aristotle of waxing poetical, while Prof. Burnet finds nothing to say about it at all; and as this has occurred after I had vainly attempted to call attention to it,[2] I think I may assume that still further comment is needed to help modern minds to grasp the beauty and importance of Aristotle's thought.

III

It follows from the above that the perfect or divine life is one of unceasing and unchanging activity, which is also an eternal consciousness of supreme happiness. And yet nothing *happens* in it. It is eternal, not in the illusory sense in which geometrical triangles and epistemological monstrosities (like *e.g.* Green's *Eternal Self-Consciousness*) are put out of Time by a trick of abstraction, but because it can be shown to have a positive nature, which precludes the conditions which engender time-consciousness. For, as Aristotle was well aware, (objective) Time is a creature of Motion; it depends on the motions whereby alone it can be measured; it is the 'number' of motion (κινήσεως ἀριθμός). If then κίνησις arises out of the imperfection of an ἐνέργεια, the perfecting of an ἐνέργεια will necessarily involve the disappearance of Time, together with that of Motion. Or, as I have elsewhere expressed it,[3] Time is the measure of the impermanence of the imperfect, and the perfecting of the time-consciousness would carry us out of Time into Eternity. In other words, the conception of Ἐνέργεια Ἀκινησίας is a *scientific* formulation of the

---

word in order to express the steady and effortless maintenance of a perfect equilibrium. Cp. *An. Post.* ii. 19, where the same word is used to describe the emergence of the logical universal, *i.e.* of the *constancy of meaning*, out of the flux of psychological 'ideas.' [1] Cp. also *Metaph.* Λ. 7, 1072 *b* 16.
[2] *Riddles of the Sphinx*, p. 443, new ed. p. 424.   [3] *Ibid.* ch. ix. § 11.

popular theological conceptions of Heaven and Eternity. We have merely to add that this motionless functioning is suffused with a glow of aesthetic delight, to get a complete conceptual interpretation of what theology has called the *Beatific Vision*.

IV

But of course all this sounds unfamiliar and fantastical and is not quite easy to grasp—if it had been, the notions of Heaven and Eternity would hardly have become targets for so much cheap scorn. And it is needless also to deny that there seems to be a paradox here which demands a defence.

The paradox is that it has been implied that there can be activity, life, and consciousness *without* change, imperfection, or decay. This seems an utter paradox because in our actual experience consciousness is a succession of mental states or processes, because life is sustained by a continual metabolism, and activities are recognized only by the changes which they exhibit. We are therefore accustomed to regard a changeless activity as equivalent to *rest, i.e.* as cessation of activity, as death.

About these facts, of course, there is no dispute. All motions are measured by the unequal rates of change, and when bodies maintain the same position relatively to each other, they are taken to be at rest. Similarly, it is not to be denied that vital function consumes living tissue, and no one would dream of disputing that consciousness is a continuous flow of experiences.

The only question is as to what *inferences* we are entitled to draw from these facts, and by what conceptions we are to interpret a transcending of change such as is *conceivable*, though not *imaginable*.

Accordingly I propose to show: (1) That we are *not* entitled to infer from the facts the impossibility of an ἐνέργεια ἀκινησίας; (2) that it is by this conception rather than by that of 'rest' that the ultimate ideal of existence should be interpreted. I shall consider the conceptions of Motion, Life, and Consciousness in turn.

V

(*a*) It has long been admitted that *Motion* tends to equilibrium, and that in a perfect equilibrium there would be no (perceptible) motion and no available energy.

Under the name of the dissipation of energy this fact of its equilibration has become notorious. It is the great bugbear of physics which has given rise to the gloomiest vaticinations concerning the inevitable decadence and ultimate doom of the universe.[1]

This whole difficulty arises out of our habit of contemplating equilibration as cessation of Motion or 'Rest.' An equilibrated universe cannot change and its latent energy cannot be used to change it. *Ergo* such a universe is 'played out.'

But why should we not regard this situation as a case of Ἐνέργεια Ἀκινησίας, as a *perfecting* of Motion until it has everywhere become perfectly regular, steady, smooth and frictionless? Logically, in fact, this seems a far preferable alternative.

Suppose, *e.g.* an equilibrium of temperature. If two bodies are at equal temperatures, does that mean that they have ceased to have temperature? Have they ceased to radiate out heat, or (to put it in terms of the current theory about heat) to exhibit the molecular

[1] Strictly the 'degradation' or 'dissipation' of energy is said to apply only to finite portions of the universe, and consolation is sometimes sought in the thought that the universe is possibly infinite, and that in an infinite universe anything may happen. Now it is true that the doctrine of the dissipation of energy ceases to apply to an infinite universe, but the reason is merely that in view of an actual infinity, all propositions become unmeaning. And an infinite universe or whole involves a contradiction in terms, and is a pseudo-conception which can be reached only by a confusion of thought. (Cp. *Riddles of the Sphinx*, ch. ix. §§ 2-9.) Emotionally too the worthy people who regard infinity as something delightful and magnificent seem to have not the faintest notion of what an infinite universe would really be like. What it means is that in no conceivable way, from no conceivable point of view, would it exhibit any finality or security of any kind. It would be what Prof. James calls a *nulliverse*, an indefinite *plurality* of things, which could never be *got together* into a unity, an amorphous *heap* whose conduct would be utterly incalculable.

vibrations which appear to our temperature-sense as heat? Surely not: it means that each body receives as much 'heat' as it radiates, that the 'molecular motions' proceed with entire regularity and constant velocities. But if so, is it not a condition of Activity (ἐνέργεια), not of Rest?

(*b*) In the case of *Life* it is much easier to conceive perfection as a changeless activity, because we are more inclined to regard life as depending on a harmony of changes rather than on their mutability, on the mere instability of organic processes. Thus if with Spencer we conceive life as an adjustment of internal to external relations ('mutual adjustment' would be better!), it is evident that the success of life will depend on the degree of *correspondence*, however attained, between the organism and its environment. Perfect correspondence therefore would be perfect life, and might be conceived as arising by a gradual perfecting of the correspondence until the organism either adapted itself completely to an unchanging environment or instantaneously and *pari passu* to a changing one, in such wise that the moment of non-adaptation (if any) was too brief to come into consciousness. In either case the relation of the organism to its environment would be unchangingly the same. It would persist therefore in being what it was, in expressing its nature in its activities, without alteration or decay, gaining nothing and losing nothing, because of the perfect equipoise of waste and repair.

That such an equilibrium is not unthinkable may be illustrated also by the conceptions of a balance of income and expenditure, of the 'stationary state' of economics and of perfect justice as a social harmony in which each maintains his own position in society without aggression on others. Surely in none of these cases could it be asserted that there was a *cessation* of social or industrial relations. Once more, does not the apparent paradox arise merely out of the habit of interpreting ἐνέργεια ἀκινησίας as a cessation of activity?

Yet it is this latter view which is really unthinkable,

as may be illustrated by taking a hypothetical case, that of an adaptation or harmony on the verge of the perfection, the possibility of which is in dispute.

It must be admitted that in the stage *immediately preceding* perfect adaptation the organism is very much alive, and moreover carries on its life with a minimum of friction and a maximum of success. In such a life difficulties would exist only to be overcome, and no *process* of adapting would be more than momentary.

Now suppose it to become *instantaneous*. We are required to believe that in the very instant when the last trace of maladaptation is eliminated, life suddenly and inexplicably ceases, and the organism, which but the moment before had been rejoicing in its might, is, with scarce a noticeable change, suddenly smitten with metaphysical annihilation!

Is not this incredible? Could a catastrophe like this be paralleled by anything in nature or literature except the tragic fate which overwhelmed Lewis Carroll's Baker "in the midst of his laughter and glee," when the Snark he had so successfully chased turned out to be a Boojum, and he "softly and silently vanished away"? And so, does not the principle of continuity compel us to think the ἀκινησία of perfect adaptation, to which all κινήσεις point, as life and activity (ζωὴ καὶ ἐνέργεια), as Aristotle has contended.

(*c*) To *Consciousness* it seems at first harder to apply this same interpretation. For what most impresses us about consciousness is the flux of Becoming, which is the world's aspiration to Being. Consciousness flows with a fluidity which is quite incapable of precise, and almost of intelligible, statement. It is a perpetual transition from object to object, not one of which it can retain for a fraction of a second, and in which nothing ever occurs twice. To suggest, then, that it may persist, in an eternal fixation of unchanging objects, would seem to be the very acme of insanity.

Nevertheless, the Aristotelian theory here also has no quarrel with the facts: it only contends for their better and more logical interpretation. To infer from the facts the 'relativity' of all consciousness and Hobbes' dictum *sentire semper idem et nil sentire ad idem recidunt*, appears to it either a truism or an error, and in no wise decisive.[1] It is a truism, if it asserts that sensation *in time* involves change, and that all *our* experience is in time. It is an error, if it is taken as the starting-point of an argument which either proposes to conduct us out of consciousness and to represent it as an unmeaning accident in a scheme of things which when perfectly equilibrated would transcend it, or even to bind us Ixion-like on an unresting wheel of change.

For the facts are susceptible of a better interpretation. May we not regard the flow of appearances as a *defect*, not as a merit, of consciousness, engendered as an adaptive response to the vicissitudes of a defective world? May not impermanence in consciousness (as elsewhere) mark the πονηρία of a φύσις impotent to function without ceasing (συνεχῶς ἐνεργεῖν)?

At all events it seems to be the case that (1) we strive to prolong and retain pleasant states and objects of consciousness; (2) the fluttering of attention is protective, and necessary to survival under conditions which render it unsafe to become too much absorbed by the object of our attention (or attentions), lest something to which we have failed to attend should absorb us in a too literal sense; (3) even where practical exigencies do not compel us, we have to shift the objects of our attention because they are never found to be *wholly* satisfactory. May it not be argued also that the unsatisfactoriness is the cause of the impermanence, and not *vice versa*? But could we once attain an object of contemplation which was wholly satisfying, should we not seek to retain it in consciousness for ever? If he had achieved the Best (τὸ ἄριστον), could any one be mad enough to wish to change it, for the worse? if he had passed the gates of heaven, could he lust again for the impurities of earth?

Surely it follows, as Plato saw, from the very notion of

[1] Cp. *Riddles of the Sphinx*, ch. xii. § 5.

the Good that it must be a permanent possession; it follows also, as Aristotle saw, that if we are to be conscious of it at all (and if not, how can it be a *good*?), it must be as an ἐνέργεια ἀκινησίας. I suspect, therefore, that the objection to ἐνέργεια ἀκινησίας is at bottom one to the whole notion of an attainable Good. But whether the advocates of this objection are naïvely optimistic enough to imagine that an *unattainable ideal, recognized as such*, continues to be an ideal a rational being can aim at, or whether they are pessimistic enough to renounce all ideals altogether, it is *their* notion and not that of ἐνέργεια which involves a fundamental paradox.

But, as before, let us test the rival interpretations by examining consciousness in the moment immediately preceding its hypothetical fixation. It would have to be reached, of course, by a progressive development of consciousness in fulness and intensity and power of attention, and by the gradual suppression of all interruptions and discords. There can be no doubt, therefore, that it would be consciousness of a very high order, *i.e.* a contemplation, most pleasant and unimpeded, of whatsoever most delights the soul. If now we eliminate the last faint source of trouble and unrest and disturbance, the last distraction which prevented us from concentrating our attention wholly upon what most it loves to dwell upon, why should consciousness go out rather than go on? Will it not become rather absolutely constant and continuous, and remain conscious *sensu eminentiori*?

VI

An 'Activity void of Motion' then is conceivable, if only we will make an effort to see through the confusions of our vulgar view. Nay, in the end it would seem that it alone was conceivable as the ideal of Being.

For of the alternatives none are ultimately thinkable. The conception of Becoming, as philosophers have been driven to recognize from Parmenides to Hegel, is infected with insoluble contradictions, which disappear only if we follow Aristotle in conceiving it as essentially imperfect, as ἐνέργεια ἀτελής. To do this renders it intelligible, for we can then regard all the processes we actually observe as pointing forward to an ideal of a perfectly and equably self-sustaining activity, to attain which would relieve them of their contradictions.

The ideal of Rest, on the other hand, is wholly illusory: there is no rest anywhere attainable for the virtuous any more than for the wicked. It is non-existent as a fact, and it is non-existence as a conception. For if anything could really cease to be active, it would *pro tanto* cease to be.[1] The only *Weltanschauung* therefore which could appropriately take up the ideal of Rest would be one like Mainländer's, which regards the world's history as the long protracted agony of the Absolute's suicide.

Compared with these, the advantages of the conception of Ἐνέργεια Ἀκινησίας are manifest.

It enables us to give a scientific interpretation of the religious conception of Heaven and to differentiate it from that of Nirvâna (= 'bliss conceived as rest'). It involves a positive conception of Eternity and explains the transition from 'Time' to Eternity.

We avoid, moreover, sundry difficulties. We may, *e.g.*, dismiss the apprehension that an equilibration of cosmic energy must be regarded as the final destruction of cosmic activity. We may thus avoid henceforth Spencer's strange see-saw in regarding equilibration now as universal death, now as perfect life, according as physical or biological analogies come uppermost in his mind.

The chapter on this subject in *First Principles* is most instructive. It affords an admirable example of the confusion engendered by a lack of the conception of ἐνέργεια ἀκινησίας, and so it may be useful to trace Spencer's utterances in detail. It will be seen that he keeps on contradicting himself as to the character of equilibration on alternate pages, and speaks with a double voice throughout.

(*a*) By the first voice it is conceived as *death* or

[1] Cp. *Riddles of the Sphinx*, ch. xii. § 6.

cessation of activity. Thus § 173: "there finally results that complete equilibration we call *death.*" § 176: "the final question of Evolution is ... incidental to the universal process of equilibration; and if equilibration must end in complete *rest* ... and if the solar system is slowly dissipating its forces ... are we not manifestly progressing towards omnipresent *death?*" He answers that even though the "proximate end of all the transformations we have traced is a state of *quiescence*," an "ulterior process may reverse these changes and initiate a new *life.*" (Hence, too, the see-saw of Evolution and Dissolution is deduced in ch. xxiii.) Again in § 182 he asks, "Does Evolution as a whole, like Evolution in detail, advance towards complete *quiescence?* Is that motionless state called *death*, which ends Evolution in organic bodies, typical of the *universal death* in which Evolution at large must end?"... "If, pushing to its extreme the argument that Evolution must come to a close in complete equilibration or *rest*, the reader suggests that, for aught which appears to the contrary, the *Universal Death* thus implied will continue indefinitely, it is legitimate to point out" that we may "infer a subsequent *Universal Life*" if we suppose equilibration to be again upset, or (more properly) unattainable. In short, equilibration = 'death.'

(*b*) The above seems unequivocal enough until we listen to the second voice, which exactly inverts the valuation of equilibration and non-equilibration, and implies the equation, 'equilibration = life.' *E.g.* § 173 (*init.*), death is explained as due to a *failure* of equilibration. § 173 (*s.f.*), the *life* of a species depends on an equilibration between the forces that tend to increase and to destroy it. § 174, an equilibration or correspondence between idea and fact is the end of mental evolution, and "equilibration can end only when each relation of things has generated in us a relation of thought" ... and then "experience will cease to produce any further mental evolution—there will have been reached a *perfect* correspondence between ideas and facts; and the intellectual *adaptation* of man to his circumstances will be complete." So, of moral and emotional adaptation — "the limit towards which emotional adaptation perpetually tends . . . is a combination of desires that corresponds to all the different orders of activity which the circumstances of life call for" . . . and this "*progressive adaptation* ceases only with the establishment of a *complete equilibration* between constitution and conditions." Again, § 174 (*s.f.*), "Thus the ultimate state . . . is one in which the kinds and quantities of mental energy generated . . . are equivalent to, or in equilibrium with, the various orders . . . of surrounding forces which *antagonize* such motions." § 175, Equilibrium is held up as the economic ideal from which the fluctuations of over- and under-production depart. It is the all-inclusive *ne plus ultra* of the adaptation of "man's nature and the conditions of his existence." It is also the social ideal, and limits the process towards heterogeneity—"the ultimate abolition of all limits to the freedom of each, save those imposed by the like freedom of all, must result from the *complete equilibration* between man's desires and the conduct necessitated by surrounding conditions." And compare lastly the sublime conclusion of the chapter (§ 176), in which equilibrium, guaranteed by the Persistence of Force, secures to us the prospect of perfect happiness by affording "a basis for the inference that there is a gradual advance towards harmony between man's mental nature and the conditions of his existence," and "we are finally bidden to believe that Evolution can end only in the establishment of the greatest *perfection* and most complete happiness"!

The italics, of course, are mine throughout. As for the contradiction, it is striking, but easily explicable. The suppressed middle term, which connects the two conflicting views of the value of perfect equilibration, is the absence of motion or change. This being a characteristic both of 'death' and of complete adaptation, the interpretation wavers in the most tantalizing way. But no one who has grasped the doctrine of *Energeia* can doubt that 'equilibration' must be conceived as Life and as the perfection of Activity.

VII

And now what shall we say of Substance? Is it not plain that we have acquired of it a conception which will help it out of the mire in which it has floundered over long? A brief reminder of the history of the conception may suffice to make this clear, and perhaps impress on us the tragic slowness with which truth prevails. As its very name implies, it has been usual to regard 'substance' as a permanent substratum which persists through change and constitutes the real 'essence' or 'being' of a thing, that which makes it what it is. It is the thing itself or 'in itself,' the hidden core of its intrinsic nature which is the real source of its behaviour, however thickly it may seem to be overlaid with variable states, the 'accidents' which the exigencies of its interaction with other things may impose upon it. And there can be no doubt that the behaviour of things renders this thought extremely plausible. For some features in the behaviour of things are so much more persistent and characteristic than others that we cannot but esteem them differently. The distinction, therefore, of the perdurable 'substance' and the fleeting 'accidents' is natural, and, in the first instance, of great practical value. But as formulated in the conception of Substance, the distinction overshoots the mark. It fails to express the very difference it was intended to bring out, and when it is thought out, it lapses into impotent absurdity.

For the distinction was not really meant to be one between what was accessible and inaccessible to observation, nor is a hard and fast line to be drawn between 'essential' and 'accidental' attributes. So soon as we inquire, therefore, what is the nature of Substance as it really is in itself and apart from its accidents, the futility of our conception is revealed. It appears that, strictly speaking, all we know about a thing is its 'accidents,' and that we cannot comprehend how even its most essential properties 'inhere in' its substance. The substance thus becomes either a needless nullity or an unknowable, an inscrutable substratum which is conceived to underlie everything, but explains nothing, just because it is unknowable and can neither be experienced nor examined. In this form, therefore, the conception of Substance has no value for any purpose whatsoever, either philosophic or scientific.

But philosophers have been slow to find this out, though it is a melancholy satisfaction that, even so, they have anticipated the scientists. Berkeley, arguing from the current notion of Substance, had the genius to perceive that 'material substance' was a philosophic superfluity. Hume promptly extended this argument to the destruction of 'spiritual substance.' He pointed out that *apart from its states* there was no self or soul. So he resolved the self into the sequence of its states of consciousness.[1]

Both Berkeley and Hume were fully justified in their criticism. How right they were the sciences proceeded to discover on their own account. In the last thirty years it has become quite a commonplace in psychology to proclaim 'soul-substance' useless, and to conceive the mind as consisting of a 'stream of consciousness.' And at the present moment physicists seem to be finally making up their minds that the 'matter' which had lingered on in physics as the substrate of physical phenomena is mere 'scaffolding,' and that all scientific facts can really be more simply and conveniently conceived as transformations of 'energy.' Now it would not yet be true to say that the conception of 'Energy' in modern science coincides with the ancient conception of 'Energeia.' But they agree in rejecting the old notion of 'substance' as a substratum. It is clear, moreover, that they are akin in spirit, and that in the hands of a master like Prof. Ostwald [2] the conception of 'energy' is rapidly

[1] J. S. Mill similarly sees that Substance is only postulated as a support for phenomena, and that if we think away the support and suppose the phenomena to remain without any agency but an internal law, every consequence, for the sake of which Substance was assumed, will follow without Substance.—*Exam. of Hamilton*, p. 252.

[2] See his admirable treatise on *Naturphilosophie*.

approximating to that of 'Energeia.' Indeed the chief difference at present is that whereas 'Energeia' avowedly and consciously stands for a theory of substance, 'Energy' still seems to crave for a backbone of substantiality. Thus the scientific auguries seem favourable to a reform of the conception, while an inveterate error may well be judged to be decrepit when its patrons discover it to be of no avail.

Alike in philosophic and in scientific circles then, it seems to be pretty generally agreed that the old view of Substance is worthless. It lingers on chiefly because reconstruction has not kept pace with criticism. And yet Lotze's criticism of Substantiality brings him (unconsciously it would seem) very close to the Aristotelian conception. After pointing out the uselessness of the substratum view he declares[1] that "it is not in virtue of a substance contained in them that things are, they are when they are able to produce the appearance of their being such a substance." It is thus out of the behaviour of a thing that we construct its 'essence,' and this should properly be regarded, not as an intrinsic power but rather an immanent and *individual law* which maintains its identity and guides its varying reactions in its dealings with the other members of the cosmos. Lotze's construction is excellent so far as it goes, but still entangled in polemic against the catchwords which it is striving to supersede. And so he hardly makes plain what is this 'individual law,' and how the illusion of an underlying substance is produced. It is better, therefore, to start at once from Aristotle on the straight road to truth, than to attain it after devious wanderings among the paths of error.

VIII

The Aristotelian conception of *Energeia* is our best starting-point because it affords no foothold for an unknowable substratum. Indeed of such a view of

[1] *Metaphysics*, § 37.

substance it is the final refutation. For it a substratum could only be the potentiality of an actuality which was the true substance, and so far from explaining the latter would need it for its own explanation. As ἐνέργεια is prior to δύναμις, so is the behaviour of a thing to the 'substance' conceived to render that behaviour possible.[1] The truth therefore is that *the activity is the substance* : a thing *is* only in so far as active. So it is the activity which *makes* both the 'essence' and the 'accidents,' both of which are as it were 'precipitated' from the same process of active functioning. The 'essence' is merely such aspects of the whole behaviour as are selected from among the rest by reason either of their relative permanence or of their importance for our purposes.[2] And so we may define the 'substratum' which we have feigned as the hidden source of substantiality as being nothing but an attempt to express the thought of *a permanent possibility of activity*. But true reality does not reside among the tangled roots of things. We have no need to dig down vainly to a 'subject,' which 'is' not thought or will or feeling, but only 'has' them, in derision, in order to discover our true self. To find true 'Being' we must look upwards to the Ideal, not downwards to the unknowable. Our true self is not what underlies thought, will and feeling, but what combines them in a perfect harmony.[3] Reality is not what transcends experience but what perfects it.

Let us once conceive, therefore, a 'Being' which has

---

[1] This principle really involves the rejection of several popular superstitions in philosophy. For instance, the so-called '*a priori* element in knowledge' stands in the relation of δύναμις to actual knowledge, and, so far from explaining it, needs to have its assumption justified by its convenience for the purposes of actual knowing. Similarly, the ultimate reason why we may not argue monistically from the *actual plurality* of things to the higher reality of an all-including world-ground is that the plurality is actual (ἐνεργείᾳ), while the unity is only implicit (δυνάμει), and rests on our experience of the former. It is, therefore, of secondary reality and value. Cp. p. 67.

[2] These two criteria are, of course, convergent. For a permanent aspect is naturally one which it is important for us to take into account, while an important aspect is naturally one which we try to render permanent. J. S. Mill (*Examination of Hamilton*, p. 239) recognizes the first only when he says that the sensations answering to the Secondary Qualities are only occasional, those answering to the Primary, constant.

[3] Cp. *Riddles of the Sphinx*, p. 140.

realized all its potentialities, and our difficulties disappear. For we shall then have transcended the conditions which engender the illusion of an inscrutable background of 'substance.' At present our existence seems immersed in a sea of possibilities which are the objects of our unceasing hopes and fears: nothing is ever quite all that it is capable of being; nothing can ever wholly realize itself in any single moment. Hence the potential everywhere extends beyond the actual, and the shadow of an incalculable and inexplicable Thing-in-itself is cast over the whole of experience and obstructs the portal that should lead from knowledge to reality. At present, then, we must admit that nothing is ever all it might be. If, however, we imagined any being overcoming this defect and attaining to a complete and harmonious self-expression in its activities, how could it any longer even suggest a shadowy region of possibilities bound up with its actual self and inhering behind the scenes in a substratum which is the substance both of the actual and of the potential? In the coincidence of the actual and the potential which the realization of the latter would involve, there would vanish our antitheses of 'essence' and 'accident,' of 'ideal' and 'real,' of 'appearance' and 'reality.' For the 'appearance' would have become the 'reality,' and the real would have fully appeared.

Such is the ideal of 'Being' Aristotle has attributed to the divine perfection, such the full import of his ἐνέργεια ἀκινησίας. Nor is there any reason for confining this perfection to the Deity: we can quite well conceive a cosmos composed of beings whose activities had thus transcended change. Indeed, I cannot see how in the end perfection is conceivable in any cheaper way: it is only in a universe made up of a finite number of constituents, each of which is individually perfect, that perfection can be predicated of the whole, and that the perfection of any part can be secured against the irruption of intrusive discords. Whether of course there is any possibility of actually realizing any such ideal is quite another question, and no one could be more keenly conscious than myself of the bitter contrast between such dreams of metaphysics and the stern facts of our daily life. But once upon a time our fairest facts, our most uncontroverted truths, were but the visions of a dream, divined by a prescience that slowly hardened into science ;[1] and so perchance even dreams like these may come true, or rather may be made to come true, if we try. It is, moreover, certain that if we dismiss such thoughts as idle dreams, dreams they will remain, and no end will ever come to the conflict and the friction that wear out our world ; whereas, if we consent to look for possibilities of harmony, our willingness may be the first condition of success. And even for the proximate purposes of ordinary life, there is perhaps some practical value in the contemplation of a metaphysical ideal which can stimulate us to be active, and to develop all our powers to the utmost, while at the same time warning us that such self-realization must assume the form, not of a hideous, barbarous, and neurotic restlessness, nor of an infinite (and therefore futile) struggle, but of an activity which, transcending change and time, preserves itself in an harmonious equipoise.

[1] See *Axioms as Postulates, passim.*

XIII

HUMISM AND HUMANISM[1]

ARGUMENT

I. Humanism resembles Humism in being an anti-*apriorist*, pragmatist empiricism; but II. differs in being neither scepticism nor intellectualism. Nor does it surrender to Hume's criticism of Causation and Activity. III. Cleverness of Hume's criticism of the Volitional theory of Causation. IV. Its unsoundness and inconclusiveness. V. Inability of Rationalism to refute Hume: Voluntarism as the alternative.

THE human mind, by nature, abhors novelties far more than a vacuum, and when they are forced upon it by the course of its experience, its natural instinct is to close its eyes to their existence or to explain them away. Now this is as easy as it is natural. For nothing is *absolutely* new. Everything, therefore, can always be conceived as an old thing in a new guise, and, with a little stretching of the one and carving of the other, be classified under the existing rubrics. In this way we are enabled to blind ourselves to the vicissitudes of science and to retain our comfortable belief in the uniformity of nature.

But though it is practically certain that, so soon as it is seriously attempted, accommodation will always be found (or made) for novelties within the fabric of any science, their classification at first is somewhat uncertain and goes frequently astray. It behoves, therefore, those who are interested in them to see to it that they are classified correctly.

Hence it will be useful and enlightening to discuss the attempt to classify the new Humanism as an extended

[1] Republished with a few additions from the *Proceedings of the Aristotelian Society*, 1907.

form of Humism. As in all such cases, there is some logical foundation, as well as much psychological excuse, for the attempt to apperceive the new in terms of the old. It contains some truth, and is partly right. But it is also largely wrong.

To consider this classification in its former aspect first; it is obvious that Humism and Humanism are both *empiricisms* of a pronounced type, and that this constitutes an important resemblance between them. Again, there seems at any rate to be a certain likeness in their attitude towards the metaphysics of the period. The fascinating style and the more than Socratic irony of Hume do indeed render it difficult to determine the exact motives of his philosophizing. But we shall not, probably, go far wrong, if we suppose that his opposition to dogmatism, alike whether it took the form of religious bigotry or of philosophic narrow-mindedness, gave zest to his interest in philosophy. Hume seems to take an impish delight in upsetting religious and philosophic orthodoxies, and his own doctrines seem rather to be selected with this purpose than held with any absolute assurance of their intrinsic worth. Hume is quite willing to admit their defects: after they have served their purpose and done their emancipating work, he is quite ready to disavow his instruments and to affect an attitude of gentlemanly unconcern about the abstruse inanities of theologians and metaphysicians. This temper, indeed, would appear to be the essence of his 'scepticism.' Psychologically regarded, it does not lie in his doctrine, but in his attitude towards theoretic difficulties.

Now, superficially regarded, the Humanist attitude may seem quite similar. It is somewhat lacking in that reverence for academic dogmas, technicalities and shibboleths, which it is often supposed to be desirable and possible to inculcate into the young. It is certainly critical of very deep-rooted assumptions which have hitherto passed current without challenge. It is singularly modest in the claims it makes for its own principles. It makes no attempt to represent them as 'absolute' truths, but puts them forward tentatively as practically efficient working principles, which are worthy of being tried but susceptible, nevertheless, of unceasing improvement. And to a dogmatic metaphysician this hardly seems to be claiming truth for them at all. He finds it easy, therefore, and natural to treat Humanism as a mode of scepticism, and as involving a denial of truth altogether. Then again the humaneness and urbanity of allowing every one a vote in the making of truth, of allowing every mode of experience and of aspiration to count for what it may turn out to be worth, seem monstrous laxity, which must be fatal to the discipline of the intellectual world, and can proceed from nothing but infamous indifference to the sanctity of truth. Thus Humanism, to dogmatically biassed eyes, not only seems to introduce universal suffrage into the philosophic world, but to enable Plato's 'democratic man' to usurp the throne of the Philosopher-King.

So, however strenuously Humanists may disclaim evil designs, there is one belief which they can hardly hope to eradicate all at once, viz. the hoary tradition that universal experience shows that relativism and 'subjectivism' must end in scepticism and anarchism.

I

Such are, I believe, the feelings and reasonings of those who, without being hopelessly committed to some self-contradictory and untenable form of intellectualism, look upon the new philosophy with suspicion, and conceive it as a revival of Humism. And yet, now that we have indulged their misgivings to this extent, we may fairly call upon them to notice in their turn the important and deep-seated differences, both in attitude and in doctrine, which exist between the theories they are seeking to classify together. (1) For one thing, the Humanists are not distinguished amateurs, concerning themselves with philosophy only to clear out of the way an obstacle to worldly wisdom, but hard-working professionals, themselves leading the academic life, and exposed to all the rigours of the academic atmosphere. (2) They do not themselves draw the sceptical conclusions attributed to them, but protest that their doctrines mean a rescue and a reform and an advance of philosophy. (3) Such a reform, they declare, is rendered necessary by the deplorable state to which metaphysics has been reduced by the collapse of idealism into scepticism, while an advance is no less urgently required if philosophy is to keep pace with the developments of the sciences, particularly of psychology and biology. As regards doctrine, again, the differences are at least as well marked as the resemblances. For though both Humanism and Humism may be classified as empiricisms, there is evidently ample room for divergence within empiricism.

It is not too much to say that the philosophic character of an empiricism depends entirely on how it conceives 'experience.' Now Humanism manifestly conceives 'experience' very differently from Humism. (1) It does not accept Hume's psychology with its associationism and its sensationalism. Its voluntaristic is essentially different from his sensationalistic empiricism, and by comparison with the latter may even be called a sort of apriorism. For a postulate, however much it may have been suggested by experience, is still an anticipation of nature, which we bring to the facts. It has to be assumed *before* it can be 'proved.' Even though it was meant for application to experience, it was assumed because it was desired, even though it serves as a guide in experimentation and a major premiss in argumentation, it is clearly prior to the experience we try to organize thereby. It becomes, therefore, from one point of view, a merely verbal question how the Humanist voluntarism should be classified, and if the form of intellectualism against which it had to contend had been sensationalistic instead of rationalistic, it would doubtless have laid more stress on the very real affinities of the postulate with the *a priori*.

In fact its epistemological achievement may be said to

have destroyed the old antithesis between 'empiricism' and 'apriorism' by rendering both terms ambiguous, and propounding a middle way which forms a third alternative to the epistemological dilemma. Of the dogma 'all knowledge comes from experience' it inquires, 'aye, but from a *passive* experience or an *active*?' Of the dogma 'all knowledge implies an *a priori*,' it inquires 'but *how a priori*? Is it prior as a mere fact of our (present) mental constitution, and so powerless to guarantee its own future continuance, or as an intelligent act of faith?' Clearly, then, a voluntarist *a priori*, adopted upon the bare suggestion of experience for its methodological value, and established by its continued working, does not fit into the old classification at all.

(2) Humanism does not accept Hume's criticism of causation and his denial of activity, as all intellectualisms are (more or less unwillingly) compelled to do. (3) It is not naturalistic; because it regards the mechanical conception of nature as itself a construction for human purposes, which is valuable and valid because, and in so far as, it subserves these purposes. (4) It is not deterministic, as rationalisms are logically bound to be, but libertarian.

Thus it agrees with Hume only (1) in the belief that the course of events has something to teach us, and brings real enlightenment, because it cannot be predicted with absolute certainty, *i.e.* in a common empiricism; it agrees (2) that no apriorism can ever give the guarantee it aims at, and assure us of the future, because any 'necessity of thought' may change if human nature changes; it agrees (3) in a common pragmatism, *i.e.* in their agreement that practical efficiency of a conception is relevant to its truth, and may be pleaded in answer to apparent theoretical defects. But even here the differences are very marked. Hume's pragmatism hardly seems to be sincere; it is always suspiciously suggestive of a blind to disguise his scepticism. Again, Hume's appeal to the pragmatic principle is quite arbitrary and capricious: he uses it to save the face of common sense and (perhaps) of science, but not to rehabilitate philosophy or religion. Lastly, he neither generalizes the principle nor claims for it any *theoretic* validity: *i.e.* for Hume, as for the rationalist, and as for Kant, there is still an implicit dualism between theory and practice, and a sort of 'independence' of the former, even though this redounds only to its own confusion.

II

On the whole, therefore, it can hardly be contended that the classification of Humanism as Humism is either a very exact or a very fruitful way of assimilating the new to the old. Nay, we may go farther and maintain that upon some of the most important points of philosophical debate there is a profound antithesis between Humism and Humanism, and a very marked congruity between the former and Rationalism. To illustrate by three typical cases: (1) Rationalism and Humism are both intellectualism; Humanism is not; (2) both deny the conception of Activity, which Humanism emphasizes and exploits; (3) Rationalism has in consequence to accept Hume's criticism of Causation, whereas Humanism is enabled to reject it.

The first of these points is really so obvious that a simple statement would suffice for it, if it did not lead to far-reaching consequences which have not yet been observed. As it is, it may be well to point out that, from a voluntarist standpoint, the differences in intellectualisms are quite secondary. Rationalism and Sensationalism can always strike up an alliance against Voluntarism which is cemented by their common appeal to a dark, dumb, irrational, and inexplicable background of 'feeling.'[1] In the shadow of vague terms, whose inveterate ambiguity extends back to the days of Plato,[2] all voluntary action

---

[1] Mr. Sturt (*Idola Theatri*, ch. v. and ix.) has done good service by pointing out how essentially this conduces to the "passivism" of a rationalistic intellectualism like Mr. F. H. Bradley's.

[2] Who in the *Theaetetus* (156B) includes pleasure, pain, and, desire in the list of αἰσθήσεις.

may be reduced to 'feeling,' which can be equated with 'sensation,' which, again, can be taken as purely cognitive, whenever it is convenient, until every trace of man's free and self-directive activity is wiped out from the philosophic picture. Hence, both intellectualisms can agree on the essential points that (1) intellection is the only philosophically valuable human function; that (2) nothing but intellection is necessary to cognition; that (3) the purer the intellection, the less alloyed with whatever other elements are reluctantly admitted into our nature, the truer and more trustworthy its results; that (4) cognition means rendering the mind *passively receptive* of an already determined, rigid and independent object, variously denominated 'reality' or 'truth'; that (5) in consequence of all these considerations, anything in the nature of human activity or initiative can only (if it exists) exercise a malign and disturbing influence on our cognitive procedure, and must therefore be abstracted from in scientific theory, and repressed in practice.

Humanism, on the contrary, maintains (1) that intellection is not the only valuable function in human life, nor the source of its value; (2) that not merely does 'intellection' not suffice to explain cognition, but that it does not even explain itself, for the reason that real knowing is never a 'purely intellectual' process, but essentially presupposes such non-intellectual aspects as desire, interest, and purpose, which enter into and control all cognitions; that (3) it is frequently not true to say that the 'purer' the intellection, the more valuable the results; that (4) in consequence cognition, whether perceptual or conceptual, is never a merely passive recognition of an already made object, but always an interaction with a reality which is still capable of being moulded to some extent by our action; (5) that human activity, therefore, is nothing science need be ashamed of or metaphysics frown upon, but is rather the fountain-head of philosophic understanding, which can neither be ignored nor repressed. It will subsequently appear that this difference of attitude towards human activity, which is deducible from the general standpoint of intellectualism, foreshadows the welcome it has accorded to Hume's attack upon the conception of activity.

III

Hume's criticism of the conception of power or activity is quite as clever, and quite as paradoxical as his criticism of the conception of cause. It is even more essential to his naturalism and more radically destructive in its philosophic effects. Yet, strange to say, it has provoked no remonstrance. The champions of the *a priori* make no fuss about it, the bodyguard of the Pure Reason raise no hue and cry: it is silently and tamely acquiesced in. It is never denounced in lectures as one of the twin pillars of Hume's all-corrupting scepticism; its consequences are never dwelt on; it is never criticized! This extraordinary state of things seems to be due simply to the domination of intellectualism, which has neither the interest nor the ability to contest the assumptions lurking in Hume's ingenious argument.

The argument itself does not occur in the body of the *Treatise of Human Nature*.[1] In writing the *Treatise*, Hume appears to have been chiefly concerned to puzzle the philosophers; so he deals chiefly with the opinions of the learned. Now as these were then, much as now, still under the spell of the intellectualist tradition traceable to Plato, Hume took no notice of the common-sense explanation of the source of the notion of power or agency. He conceives himself to be contending throughout against a metaphysical *a priori* knowledge of causation by means of which effects could be predicted with certainty prior to all experience. His problem is to find a connexion such that "from a simple view of the one" we can "pronounce that it must be followed by the other."[2] It is to such

---

[1] It is astounding, but characteristic, that, in view of this, the preface to T. H. Green's edition of Hume should contain the assertion that the "only essential difference" between the *Treatise* and the *Enquiry* is "in the way of omissions" made in the latter.

[2] *Treatise*, ed. Selby-Bigge, p. 161.

philosophic accounts of causation that he addresses his triumphant challenges, when he "desires to have pointed out to him" the impression from which the idea of necessary connexion could possibly be derived.

But after publishing the first volume of the *Treatise*, Hume was bound to come across remonstrances based on a primitively human view of causation which may fairly be called the original philosophy of mankind. This is the *volitional* theory of causation, which models itself on the voluntary control of the bodily organs and accepts the immediately experienced sequence of volition and motion as all we need know of the 'inner nature' of causation. Upon this view the 'impression' which gives rise to the idea of causal efficacy would be simply the every-day experience of voluntary motion, and this simple answer to Hume's theory would be easily and obviously fatal to his whole position.

Hume, therefore, was bound, if possible, to invalidate this theory, and nothing testifies more strikingly to his supreme cleverness than the way in which he meets this difficulty. He promptly inserted in the *Appendix* to the *Treatise* a short passage, in which he points out, very lucidly and consistently, that there is no reason why the sequence of volition and motion should be treated (by him) differently from any other, or regarded as more intelligible.[1] But how seriously he took this volitional theory is attested by the elaborate refutation bestowed on it in the *Enquiry*.[2]

Its gist may be summed up as follows: (1) Hume starts, as in the *Appendix*, from his own analysis of causation as an established truth, and points out that the supposed immediate experience of causal agency is nothing more than a regular sequence, which must accordingly engender the 'custom' or expectation which *is* the causal nexus.

(2) He clearly states his presupposition that real

---

[1] Green and Grose barely mention the fact in their edition, but make no comment.
[2] §§ 51-53 and note to § 60.

knowledge of causal efficacy must be prior to experience: "were the power or energy of any cause discoverable by the mind, we could foresee the effect even without experience."[1]

(3) He argues specifically that the feeling of power which accompanies voluntary motion is illusory, because (*a*) the union of soul and body and the operation of the one on the other is avowedly a mystery; because (*b*) voluntary control varies greatly with the various organs. Why, on this theory, "has the will an influence over the tongue and fingers and not over the heart or liver?" Again, a man suddenly paralysed is as conscious as ever of a power to command his limbs, though the usual motions no longer ensue. As, however, consciousness never deceives (a comically scholastic maxim!) it never really testifies to any real power. "We learn the influence of our will from experience alone." (*c*) Volitions are not the immediate antecedents of voluntary motions. There are a number of intermediary processes in the brain and the nerves and the muscles, of which we are not conscious. Ergo, the original power felt, the 'sentiment' or 'impression' or 'sensation' of *nisus*, or endeavour, is no proof of a power to move the limbs.

Hume proceeds to argue similarly that neither the felt effort in overcoming the resistance of bodies, nor the voluntary control of our conscious states, can have given rise to the idea of power; but the latter of these need not be considered by us, as primitive reasoners cannot certainly be credited with introspectiveness enough to have observed it.

IV

The extreme brilliance of this argument is undeniable, but this hardly explains the acceptance it has won from philosophers of all schools, as different as Reid, Hamilton,

---

[1] Ed. Selby-Bigge, p. 63; cp. also p. 78, note: "These sensations" (of effort) "which are merely animal, and from which we can *a priori* draw no inference, we are apt to transfer to inanimate objects."

Mill, and Kant.[1] It is difficult not to believe that its success was largely due also to their intellectualist prejudices and their unawareness of its real scope. For in itself Hume's argument, though brilliant, is by no means invulnerable. Indeed, with a little care, we may detect in its proof several flaws and gaps.

Hume's analysis of the way 'causes' are imputed by us does not go nearly deep enough.

(1) He had no right whatever to start with 'events' and their 'sequences,' and to assume that the problem was how to *connect* them. Human activity penetrates more deeply into the making of objects of knowledge than either Hume or Kant suspected. It not only turns 'sequences' into 'consequences,' but singles out 'sequences' and 'events' by selection of the relevant, in a way that is always *risky*, and must always seem 'arbitrary' to an intellectualism which is looking for a fool-proof method of absolute cogency. Hume's empiricism takes over uncriticized the pragmatic realities of common sense, which has analysed experience into a coming and going of things and persons in space and time, and tries to distinguish them still further into a series of 'impressions' of which each is to be a 'distinct existence.' But to a more radical empiricism 'experience' presents itself as a continuous flow, out of which 'events,' 'effects' and 'sequences' have to be singled out by strenuous efforts, and the causal principle is an instrument of *analysis*. The determinate 'sequences,' therefore, for which 'causal connexions' have to be discovered are themselves creations of human attention and interest, and do not exist as such, apart from our volitional activity. Hence they cannot validly produce a basis for a *denial* of that activity.[2]

(2) It seems to be profoundly vitiated by a confusion between the historical origin and the logical validity of

---

[1] Cp. J. S. Mill, *Logic*, III. 5, § 11. Mill, like Hume, assumes that the volitional theory cannot be true, if it is not certain 'previous to trial.'

[2] Cp. *Formal Logic*, ch. xx. § 3. It is clear that in correcting this fundamental error of Hume's we dispose also of all the philosophies which have assumed with him that the task of philosophy is to find principles of *synthesis*. Kant's whole problem, *e.g.* disappears altogether.

the volitional theory of causation. Hume argues, very plausibly, that the theory is not valid, and infers that it could not have served as the prototype of our causal notions. But this is clearly an *ignoratio elenchi*. Obviously it is no answer to an account of the origination of a belief to show that the belief arrived at is wrong. Still less is it this to show that a further belief derived from this erroneous belief is also wrong. For our truest and most valuable beliefs have frequently originated in what are now despised as childish errors. The confusion grows worse when we observe that Hume professedly was not inquiring into the validity but into the origin of the belief in causal efficacy. His explanation thereof rested on the psychological impossibility of suggesting any other source for it but uniformity *plus* expectation; not on the logical defects of the proposed alternatives. Hence he involves himself in verbal contradictions which are almost comical. On the same page he declares [1] both that "every idea is copied from some preceding impression or sentiment, ... there is nothing that produces any impression, nor consequently can suggest any idea of power" and also that we *have* a "sentiment of a *nisus* or endeavour" and "*feel* a customary connexion between ideas" and transfer these "feelings" (or "sensations") to objects.

Whether, therefore, the volitional theory be right or not, Hume's case, as presented by himself, is fatally damaged by the mere suggestion that the immediate experience of voluntary motion was the source whence men first derived their notion of causal efficacy. That historically this was the origin of the belief is nowadays beyond doubt, nor does Hume really deny it. Men and the higher animals all begin their intellectual careers as animists, and animism means that all motion is interpreted on the analogy of voluntary agency, which is a familiar experience to us all long before it is analysed, reflected on or explained away. If, however, Hume had explicitly admitted this as the historical origin of the idea of causation, he would have found himself compelled to face

[1] Ed. Selby-Bigge, p. 78.

the voluntaristic and humanistic interpretation of experience as a whole, and would have found a way to his own associationism blocked or lengthened.

(3) The argument that the volition-motion sequence is like any other, and explicable in the same way, is valid enough if Hume's assumption is granted. But if it is not, it is simply a *petitio*. And voluntarists are in no wise bound to grant it.[1] They may reasonably reply:—'You must not calmly beg the question of the nature of sequences in a sense favourable to yourself. The real question is *which* sequences are to be chosen as clues to the interpretation of the rest. As to this we and you differ. *We* start *ab intra* from the sequences which we most directly experience, and, treating them as typical, logically arrive at the conceptions of causal efficacy and necessary connexion. We admit, of course, that our method is sheer "anthropomorphism." But then we are Humanists, and know it. *You* on the other hand only cripple yourself by trying to ignore the human character of your intelligence, and refusing to acknowledge the validity of your immediate experience. You insist on starting *ab extra* from the sequences which you observe in the outer world. You assume, that is, that you can know *no more* about yourself than about any one else. And lo, you have no difficulty in showing that you can know *as little* about yourself as about any one else! But what have you gained? You have only rendered *all* the happenings in the world opaque to your intelligence. And what have you proved? Only that the facts are obligingly ambiguous enough to submit to either interpretation. This we do not dream of denying, and we think your interpretation very clever. But it is quite arbitrary, wrongheaded and superfluous. Moreover, it is vain, because it has *not* refuted ours, on the advantages of which we forbear to enlarge.'

(4) The assumption that knowing a cause supplies also *a priori* knowledge of the effect may have been made by rationalists who (more or less inconsistently)

---

[1] Cp. *Studies in Humanism*, p. 230.

held also the volitional view of causation. If so, Hume's reply that the limits of our voluntary control of bodies have to be ascertained from experience is so far valid. But it clearly is not self-evident that if volition is the true type of causation this must be known to us before experience. And so Hume's argument does not touch voluntarists who are also empiricists. For these will naturally disclaim any *a priori* knowledge of causes and regard it as the most natural interpretation of experience to suppose that the consciousness of power is not only the source of the notion, but also good evidence in its favour until there is reason to reject it. They will simply say—'what causes are, and wherein and to what extent we are causes, and what effects we can produce, all this we learn only from experience. And why on earth should we not? Why should we not all, from the baby to the paralytic, have to find out the limitations of our powers from experience? Surely you would not have us assume that we must be born with a complete *a priori* idea of power and a similar knowledge of all that we are and can? Such an assumption would be enough to make nonsense, not only of our theory, but of any theory on any subject whatsoever!'

(5) The most solid part of Hume's argument, however, is that which disputes the value of the psychological consciousness of agency on physiological grounds, and thus leads on to the epiphenomenal view of mind and the reduction of conscious beings to automata. Indeed it is difficult to see what reply was open to voluntarists at the time. At present, however, thanks to the development of evolutionary and genetic views of life, adequate replies are easily forthcoming.

For example, we may say that the general principle underlying the gradations and variations of voluntary control of different parts of the body is the welfare and efficiency of the organism as a whole. Also that it is in general beneficial to concentrate consciousness (which is connected with what are physiologically the most expensive functions of the higher brain centres) upon

R

those functions which have to be performed in a variable manner, and consequently need the aid of reflection. Functions, on the other hand, which are regular and can be performed in the same way, can be allowed to become automatic, and even unconscious, at least under normal circumstances. It will then appear that these biological principles amply explain " why the will has influence over the tongue and fingers, and not over the heart and liver."[1] The functions of the one must be conscious, those of the other are better carried on by mechanisms.

The same principles suffice to deal also with the lapsed intermediaries between the volition and the motion, which now escape our consciousness. Historically all these intermediate processes may be regarded as mechanisms which have been developed for the better performance of the motions or the better husbanding or directing of the consciousness. They have, therefore, no interest for themselves, and there is no reason why their normal functioning should be conscious.[2] Primitive organisms, however, manage to perform all the vital functions, for which we now have specialized organs, *without* such mechanisms. We must suppose, therefore, that in their case there are *no* intermediaries involved in voluntary motion, and that so the testimony of consciousness was once literally accurate. It is substantially accurate also in the higher organisms. For if it is generally true that function moulds structure, and if all structures are acquired, then the organism is made by the mode of life it has *chosen*, and as a whole, with all its mechanisms, it is best regarded as an *embodied will*.

As for the failures of voluntary control which are due to morbid degenerations in the organs, how can they prove voluntary control to be unreal? Surely the

---

[1] The existence of individual variations in the extent of this voluntary control is a strong confirmation of this explanation. There are well-attested cases on record where even the beating of the heart could be arrested at will, and it is well known that some people can wag their ears, while others have this power only over their tongue.

[2] In most of these cases, however, the withdrawal of consciousness is not absolute. For *disturbances* of normal functioning are usually felt as *pains*.

breakdown of a machine does not prove that it was *not* constructed by intelligence? It proves only that the intelligence was not unlimited.

V

On the whole, therefore, Hume cannot be said to have refuted the volitional theory of causation. It yields an answer to Hume which is much simpler, directer, completer, more congruous with common sense and better supported by historical and anthropological evidence than any other. Why, then, has no rationalist even attempted to answer Hume along these lines? Why do they all continue to torment themselves, and to excruciate their readers, by devising devious, obscure, ambiguous, far-fetched, complicated theories to vindicate so simple and successful a human practice as that of postulating causes *ex analogia hominis*, the more so that the 'answers' they achieve always fail to answer the essential point,[1] or at best wander away into metaphysical principles so remote from our experience that they cannot even be applied to it, and so answer neither Hume's nor any other question, and in no wise vindicate our actual human practice? One can hardly believe that the reason was wholly an instinctive hatred of Humanism, a reluctance to recognize man as a measure of things, and human activity as a real force and a real clue to the nature of the world.

The reason in part cannot but have been a failure to realize the full significance of Hume's results. For this is far more than the refutation of an 'uncritical' theory of causation, far more than the substitution for it of Hume's own theory, far more even than the establishment of a naturalistic and mechanical treatment of the human mind. That a thorough-going Naturalism follows logically and at once from Hume's proof that the conception of human agency rests upon an illusion, is indeed a matter of course.

---

[1] In Kant's case I take this to be the question why in the end the data given *to* the mind should be, and ever continue to be, such that the mind *can* construct a cosmic order out of them.

But for this very reason too much importance should not be attached to it. It follows indeed that it is a sad waste of energy for psychologists and epistemologists, who have in principle assented to Hume's assumptions, subsequently to contend for the recognition of mental activity in any shape or form. For even though mental activity were (as I believe it to be) the most real and essential and all-pervasive and ineradicable fact in our nature, and implicit even in the very theories which seek to set it aside, it would yet be vain to try to extort a recognition of its existence from the Humian assumptions, or to describe it in naturalistic terms. How can any one, *e.g.* confute a polemic which begs the point at issue with the superb audacity of Hume's argument in the Appendix to the *Treatise*?[1] First he professes a desire to find a 'perception' on which the causal connexion could be based; then he assumes (1) that "if perceptions are distinct existences, they form a whole only by being connected together"; (2) that "no connexions among distinct existences are ever discoverable by human understanding." Whence it would clearly follow that, even if we *had* a 'perception' of causal connexion, it could not, *ex hypothesi*, serve as *a principle of connexion*, by the very fact of its being a 'perception,' and so doomed to remain a distinct and disconnected existence![2]

Thus the very attempt to prove the existence of activity to those who insist on taking up a point of view from which it cannot be seen, is a mistake. The true retort to their attitude is to show that it is arbitrary, and does not go deep enough, and that better alternatives exist. Mr. Bradley, however, is quite right from his own point of view, as an intellectualist, as a logician, and as a pupil of Hume, to wage war upon the concept of Activity: he is wrong only in imagining that a conception which has been expunged from psychology and expelled from

---

[1] P. 635, ed. Selby-Bigge.
[2] It is not so clear why "the connexion or determination of the thought to pass from one object to another" which "we only feel" should not yield the "internal impression" required; but Hume's large and loose way of equating 'impression,' 'sensation,' and 'perception,' greatly helps him in ruling out this possibility.

science can be restored by metaphysics without a monstrous paradox.

But, after all, Naturalism in psychology is a small and comparatively harmless affair. It has its uses, and as a temporary expedient may even be salutary for the restricted purpose of a special science. There is nothing, therefore, in its use that need alarm philosophy. It can always be regarded as methodological, and need not be taken as true beyond the point at which it ceases to be useful. If the Humian denial of Activity merely meant Naturalism, philosophy could well survive the demonstration.

There are, however, other consequences implicit in Hume's denial which might well appal all but the extremest sceptics, or rather nihilists. If we have the courage to work out the implications of Hume's philosophy completely, it will be seen to come to much more than a revised notion of causation, or than scepticism about some 'axioms' of science. What it comes to is an utter cancellation of all ideas of agency, activity, cause, power, efficacy, force, energy, not only in us, but throughout the Universe. All these terms, it should be noted, are not merely inexact adumbrations of more efficient truths, unsuited for the clear thinking of the sciences; they are essentially illusory and unmeaning, and to be wiped out of the vocabulary of those who would see reality as it truly is. The whole world would thus be reduced to a mere sequence of events, to a flow of uncomprehended happenings within us and without us, of which we should be the impotent spectators, inscrutably endowed with a consciousness which might be written off the ledger of the Universe without affecting its sum total in the least degree. To ask—what makes the Flow flow?—is futile; to control it, is impossible; to observe it, is vain; all we can do (if we can *do* aught) is to let ourselves *drift*, and to cultivate as much equanimity or indifference as we can muster towards what is fated to befall us. In short, the systems of all the sciences are shattered, and the world, whether psychical or physical, relapses into Chaos.

For it would be a great delusion to imagine that the conceptions of the physical sciences can escape from the general *débâcle* of the products of the human intelligence. Their fundamental conceptions, when they are analysed, always, sooner or later, imply ineradicable references to human experiences which have been declared illusory. Thus 'matter' ultimately refers to our feelings of resistance. So does 'force.' 'Motion' involves 'place,' and place human experience of the difference between 'here' and 'there' and of 'voluntary' change of place, in default of which we should have no ground for ascribing the changing appearances to the motion of unchanging bodies in space rather than to alterations in the appearances themselves. 'Energy' involves both the 'motion' and the 'work' experience. And so forth. The physical realities, therefore, being dependent on what have become psychical illusions, are themselves rendered illusory. In no place and in no sense have we a right to use any of the tabooed illusions.

The only mystery which apparently remains over is one which the theory disdains to notice, viz. how all these incriminated terms have come into being at all, and why, if they signify nothing and are not true, they are so useful and indispensable. Can it be that some demon, more humorous than Hume himself, is compelling us to believe, or at least to behave as if we believed, what we know is not true? This difficulty, however, may be respectfully left for intellectualism to contemplate with care. Our Humanism, by the simple expedient of starting from our immediate experience, and declining to admit that it is deceptive and invalid, merely because Hume has exercised his ingenuity to make it appear so, dissolves the whole *mirage* of Humian magic.[1]

If only rationalists would follow our example, what a relief it would be to students of philosophy! For whatever the more than Spartan fortitude with which we endure the difficulties of our subject, do we not all suffer from the paradoxes which its concessions to Hume have

See James on 'The Experience of Activity,' in *A Pluralistic Universe.*

imposed on rationalistic philosophy? Should we not confess in our candid moments that it would be a relief to get rid of the paradox, for example, that in the whole universe there either is no agency or activity at all, or that such agency resides solely in the whole *to the exclusion of its parts*?

What again of the Kantian 'answer to Hume'? What a giant paradox it is! How strange that the slur of subjectivity which Hume has cast upon our notion of causation should be held to be removed by extending its scope! And all in vain, because after all the mind does not 'create' the world it makes, and remains dependent on experience for the means to discriminate between a 'casual' and a 'causal,' an 'objective' and a 'subjective' sequence. Why then does it not find its material refractory? How does it know that it will not become so in the future? Perhaps it may. But if so, are we not back in complete empiricism, and might not the whole *a priori* machinery just as well be flung upon the scrap-heap? It is, however, nowadays being pretty widely recognized that Kant's answer to Hume is no real answer at all; but the reason why Kant could not excogitate any real answer is capable of being elucidated. It becomes, at any rate, much clearer when we perceive that having missed the only real answer, viz. the volitional, he had to have recourse to the paradox of ascribing to a being who has been deprived of all agency, power and initiative, the power of enacting rules *a priori* to which the course of events must conform! But is it not clearly impossible to combine the Kantian assertion of the reality of mental activity with an acceptance of the Humian denial of all human activity?

It would seem then that in this case, as in that of the Humian psychology, Kantian Rationalism is unable to shake off a humiliating dependence upon an insidious doctrine which has managed to beguile it into positions whence an effective rejoinder is no longer possible. It would be interesting to trace out in detail the final fiasco of rationalistic intellectualisms in their controversies with sensationalism, starting from Plato's *Theaetetus*; but this would be to re-write the history of philosophy with a proper attention to the existence of voluntary activity. Enough, at any rate, has been said to show, not only that the affiliation of Humanism to Humism is extremely misleading, but also to suggest, perhaps, that in reality the boot is on the other leg, and that it is intellectualism alone which is groaning or grovelling in the grip of Hume.

XIV

SOLIPSISM[1]

ARGUMENT

The argument from action to belief proves the sincerity of Humanist disclaimers of solipsism. But there are transitions to solipsism from (1) absolute, (2) subjective idealism, (3) Aristotelianism, (4) most modern philosophies, even (5) the 'New Realisms.' These become crypto-solipsistic, because they ignore the processes by which the knower arrives at 'objects' and compares them with his former objects and those of others, and overlook the selectiveness of thought and the existence of error. (6) The interdependence of subject and object also leads to solipsism.

The Humanist rejection of solipsism and its pragmatic confirmation. It is not theoretically cogent, but the appeal of solipsism to the analogy of dream life is false. The dreamer and the maker of dreams. The pragmatic refutation of all practicable solipsism.

"SOLIPSISM is the most detestable form of wickedness that ever entered into the mind of a philosopher." This pronouncement, the *solipsissima verba* of an intelligent undergraduate, once occurred in an Oxford examination paper. It should afford philosophers much food for reflection. At first sight it seems to evince only an insufficient apprehension of the philosophic mind's capacity for crime. There is a not ignoble apologia for the Speculative Life in the suggestion that if philosophers were not allowed to indulge in it they might be committing murders instead of paralogisms. Even so the

---

[1] When one considers what an appalling amount of time and energy is annually consumed in Examinations, and how little any of the parties to them have to show for it, it is surprising that they are so rarely utilized for the purpose of gauging the trend of current thought upon the subjects examined on. That they can be made to afford instruction to others than the examiners will, I hope, be a conclusion distinctly suggested by the present article, which is largely inspired by the answers to a question set in 1908 in the Oxford School of *Literae Humaniores*, and is reprinted from *Mind*, No. 70.

Philosopher-Villain has been, as Plato himself has testified,[1] a good deal commoner than the Philosopher-King. Possibly however the writer was desirous only of complimenting his tutor (who was one of the examiners) and of taking an optimistic view of his character. But supposing him to have been sincere, why should he have regarded so practically innocuous a thing as Solipsism as an offence, and have classified it as a form of wickedness, however mild? And what did he mean by Solipsism?

These questions are worthy of investigation, and I feel myself peculiarly fitted for the task. For though not myself a solipsist, I have been repeatedly mistaken for one. I may be presumed therefore to hold views sufficiently akin to Solipsism to appreciate it fairly, and yet to be interested in distinguishing myself from it.

Inherently of course Solipsism is an absurd predicate to fasten on to a Humanist philosophy. Humanism is essentially social, and therefore pluralistic. But for this very reason it cannot treat the problem of Solipsism with that curious mixture of *hauteur* and frivolity to which monistic philosophies are driven. It may honestly admit and sympathetically examine the case for Solipsism, and gather therefrom much instruction about the processes by which individual valuations acquire social currency. A monistic philosophy on the other hand is always haunted by the dread that if the One which alone truly is should turn out to be in any real sense spiritual, it may be driven to admit that Solipsism is the ultimate truth. It is tempted, therefore, to hedge, and to obscure its logical implications, and to fix a gulf between the theoretic meaning of its principles and its practical consequences.

A Humanist can afford to be more candid—because no logical necessity impels him. He is quite free in the matter. If he wanted to be a solipsist he could be. If he were, he need not hesitate to say so. He would be afraid of no one, for he would see that there was no one to be afraid of. But if he did not want to be a solipsist,

[1] *Republic*, 487 D.

and denied that he was, this assurance should suffice, because it would yield a trustworthy guarantee. And if it could be observed that in his actions he did *not* ignore the existence of others, but recognized them as beings with thoughts, wills and tempers of their own, for which he was both unable and unwilling to undertake the responsibility, the guarantee would be complete.

For it is a unique peculiarity of a Humanist's philosophy that in it it is possible to argue back from a behaviour to the belief that underlies it. He holds that the reality of a belief depends on, and is tested by, its applicability. His beliefs therefore must be acted on, and he cannot afford the luxury of theoretic beliefs, which cannot be acted on in practice. If he acts on a belief, he must hold it true; if he does not act on it, he does not truly believe it. In all other philosophies the 'highest' truths may be unpractical and inapplicable to life, while the beliefs implied in action may be secretly despised as 'practical makeshifts.' Hence arise endless possibilities of nonsense, ambiguity and misconstruction, not to say disingenuousness. For if what is believed to be the highest 'truth' should be nonsensical verbiage, it cannot be detected by the test of practice, which can eliminate only errors that are acted on. Errors that remain *purely* 'theoretical' cannot be got rid of, because they cannot be tested in the only final way. It cannot, therefore, be inferred that if such a philosopher behaves as if his fellow-men were other than himself, or he himself were other than God, he really believes this. He may only be pretending, or finding it necessary to convey a false impression for practical purposes, because in his philosophy there is no necessary connexion between theory and practice. Now in practice no one actually behaves as if he not only owned the world, but also *was* the world; but whereas in the humanist's case it is possible to infer from his actions that he does not believe that he is the world, in the case of other philosophers it is not. Humanism, therefore, may safely be believed when it disavows Solipsism; other philosophies may be Solipsisms at heart, though they do not avow this in their behaviour.

But what is Solipsism? It may best be defined perhaps as the doctrine that all existence is experience, and that there is only one experient. The Solipsist thinks that *he is the one*.

Now if this is thought out, it will be seen that very many sorts of philosophers are ultimately solipsists or as good as solipsists. When they do not themselves see this, they may fitly be called crypto-solipsists. Crypto-solipsism may also be ascribed to any view which needs Solipsism for its logical completion, and so the various sorts of Solipsism add up to a formidable total.

1. That the 'absolute idealist' is a solipsist need only be barely stated. For the matter has been threshed out elsewhere.[1] He is a solipsist because he believes that the Absolute is the sole experient, and that he is himself the incarnate Absolute. A good many absolute idealists, moreover, see this, and are proud of being the Absolute.[2] But it is needless to linger over this distressing sort of philosophic megalomania, as its nature is so clear.

2. 'Subjective idealists' are classed as solipsists, almost by acclamation; and yet this attribution seems in their case far more disputable. For a good many of them are also charged with pluralism, and it is hard to see how one can be both a pluralist and a solipsist. Why moreover should not Berkeley's pluralistic universe of 'Spirits' be taken by us as seriously as it was intended? It may have been a mistaken compliment to the Deity to impose on him the duty of lurking behind every particle of 'matter,' but this is no reason for denying the communion of spiritual beings. The only difficulty Berkeley's system here presents is that of explaining how the individual comes to suspect a transcendent cause

---

[1] Cp. *Studies in Humanism*, Essay x.
[2] We learn however from one answer that when the writer (under ether) dreamt that he was the Absolute 'and that in fact Solipsism was true,' he felt 'very lonely and miserable.' Could one be sure of this, it would avenge on the Absolute its callous indifference towards the sufferings of the world.

beyond the flow of appearances; but this difficulty is common to nearly all philosophies, so that we should be ill-advised to press the point.

3. Aristotle on the other hand is clearly a crypto-solipsist, and if Aristotelians took their master seriously and tried to live up to his precepts, they should all be solipsists. For though at first sight Aristotle seems a perfect type of common-place realism, he has a queer streak of romance at the bottom of his mind, which nearly always in the end transfigures his conclusions. And so it ought not to surprise us that he has put up Solipsism as his supreme ideal. He makes his God into an incorrigible solipsist. For he is completely wrapped up in the contemplation of his own experience (νόησις νοήσεως), in the ecstatic enjoyment of his own eternal perfection. God thinks only of himself, not of the world; αὐτὸν ἄρα νοεῖ, Aristotle gleefully declares, and the rest of the world does not exist for him. Unlike Olympian Zeus, he is non-social, and leads a βίος μονώτης, like a beast. Nevertheless Aristotle thinks we ought to imitate and emulate his God; he insists that such imitation is not futile flattery, but the best and highest thing we can do. Thus the Theoretic Life and the injunction ὅπως μάλιστα ἀθανατίζειν mean—'be as solipsistic as you can, as your imperfect ὕλη will allow.' The concluding romance of the *Nicomachean Ethics*,[1] therefore, means that Solipsism is the highest truth.

4. If it is permissible to consult the opinions of the young and to accept them as omens of the future, we shall have to say that most of the historically famous philosophies are logically solipsisms, or at least will hereafter be treated as such. For the answers to the 'Greats' question mentioned at the outset unequivocally teach that the ranks of the Solipsists include Berkeley (without a scruple), Hume (despite his annihilation of the self), Locke (despite his belief in external reality), Descartes (because he is supposed to have started that pernicious falling away from Aristotle which is called

---

[1] Book x, ch. 7 and 8.

modern philosophy), Fichte and Lotze (because they were German idealists), all personal idealists, pragmatists and humanists *en bloc* and as a matter of course, and last, but not least, Dr. Rashdall, who was even said to be 'the typical solipsist.' Evidently, if these *voces populi* are to be believed, the solipsists are a very formidable band, both here and in Hades. On the other hand some may perversely think that these dicta are not so much contributions to the history of philosophy as reflections upon the way this subject is taught in Oxford.

5. Still Solipsism is strangely insinuating, beyond doubt, and, especially when disguised as Crypto-Solipsism, worms its way into the most unlikely places. It has for example a curious affinity for the New Realism. To illustrate this it will happily not be necessary to examine all the New Realisms *seriatim* ; for their name is legion, and they agree in little but this that none of them can find any obvious escape from the old difficulties of the Old Realism. It will suffice therefore if we try to understand the reason of this affinity, and then trace its working in two or three of the most notable brands of New Realism.

To attribute solipsistic leanings to New Realisms seems at first a paradox which is not adequately vindicated by the common experience of the meeting of extremes. But there are in this case real logical grounds for the coincidence. The New Realist gets so absorbed in his object that he entirely neglects his subject, and so is not on his guard against *his own* subjectivity. Hence his account of the Real becomes *de facto* his own private view of it, which cannot be accommodated to any one else's and is at bottom a fabrication of his own idiosyncrasy. Thus Solipsism finds it easy to enter into New Realisms and to possess them in at least four distinct ways.

(1) New Realisms are mostly uncritical because they are so unpsychological. Despising the study of the history and pedigree of mind, the New Realist accepts as real whatever he thinks he perceives, without inquiring as to how he came to perceive it. Consequently he is hardly

conscious that he is not infallible, but is frequently forced to correct his first perceptions by subsequent experiences. His trust in the perception of the moment blinds him to the need of withholding his assent from his 'objects,' of recognizing how his 'ideas' pervade them, and of amending both by long and painful testing. He falls a prey to the 'intuitions' of the moment, and never inquires how 'true' intuitions are discriminated from 'false.'

(2) In consequence of never comparing his perceptions at different times with each other, he never asks himself how his perceptions accord with those of others. Hence he fails to notice the social and human character of truth, and to discover that the most imperative reason for assuming the existence of subjective 'ideas' lies in the necessity of a social compromise. When A and B perceive reality differently, it is easier, humaner and better to ascribe to both an 'idea' of reality than to assert the unreality of one of these perceptions and to leave them to fight out *which* one it is. Reality is thus cleared of a contradiction which can be treated as 'merely subjective.' New Realism on the other hand, after ruling out the problems of intersubjective adjustment as psychological irrelevance, unwittingly bases its analysis on the single case of a knower knowing *his* world, without regard to the worlds of others. And this procedure is naturally and essentially solipsistic.

(3) Even this case of a single mind at a given moment it cannot analyse effectively for lack of psychological interest. Hence it fails to perceive the all-pervading selectiveness of all thought, and to reflect on the important fact that whatever is perceived has been conditioned by the direction of attention upon it, and preferred to something else that might have been perceived if the attention had been directed otherwise. About the totality of reality an infinity of truths may be enunciated or perceived; hence the one which is enunciated or perceived is necessarily the outcome of an enormous amount of selection. And it is obvious that the ground of this selection cannot lie in the reality as such, but must proceed from the

interests of the selecter. The facet of reality which is affirmed cannot have been selected by itself. For alike in active and in passive experiencing reality is always present as a whole. Hence the mere perceiving of any particular reality already implies an immense adjustment or cutting down of reality to subjective interests, which if unchecked may easily develop into Solipsism.

(4) Being of a trustful and dogmatic character, the New Realism does not expect to be deceived and misled into error. It is consequently ill-equipped to deal with the deceitfulness of nature in a world in which everything genuine is mimicked, protectively or aggressively, and even a childlike faith in absolute truth is no guarantee of infallibility. Hence so long as the New Realist refuses to be critical and to study this whole apparatus of deception, he will accept all its results as real just as they appear to him, and once more glides into an unwitting Solipsism.

But it is high time to illustrate these generalities by their application to three selected cases of New Realism. All of these appear to be psychogenetically joint products of incapacity to reply to Mr. G. E. Moore's 'refutation of Idealism,' and of unwillingness to carry Kantian principles out completely into a consistent account of mental activity, for fear of lapsing into 'subjectivism'; but as two of these have not yet appeared in the philosophic arena, they must be described anonymously as secret doctrines endemic in two of our leading colleges.

(*a*) The first of them is the more lively, or less stable, form, and varies perceptibly from year to year. It is convinced that the troubles of dogmatic philosophy began when Locke introduced 'ideas' into it, and that if ideas are abolished all will be well. It has no ideas, therefore, in its theory of knowledge. It starts from a definition of knowledge as an immediate apprehension of what is. It perceives realities, and not 'copies' of them. There is, therefore, no 'gap' between subject and object, and no need to interpose ideas between the mind and reality and to puzzle oneself vainly about their 'correspondence.' The mind is caught fast in the embrace of that which is, and nothing can divorce them. By thus shutting out 'ideas' it hopes to leave no loophole for the demon of subjectivity to enter in.

The theory has its difficulties, doubtless, especially when asked to explain the nature of error, but on the whole it is very reminiscent of Aristotle and seems very sensible. It reproduces, almost completely, the view of reality initially taken by an unsophisticated human mind.

And yet its weak point lies just here. It is good for *a* human mind. But not for more. So soon as the problem is complicated by the introduction of a second mind, its solution ceases to satisfy. For the second mind also perceives reality quite as spontaneously, confidently, intuitively. Only it does not perceive quite like the first. Each naturally maintains that it perceives rightly, and the other wrongly. The result is a row. To allay this disturbance, and to render social life possible, therefore, a compromise has to be affected between the conflicting claims of divergent minds. Common sense rules that to avoid quarrels *neither* shall be deemed to be in direct contact with the object as it really is. For if both had an immediate and inerrant apprehension of what is, the actual divergence between its results would plainly be impossible. But both are supposed to recognize one and the same object in their own subjective way. The common world of reality is variously reflected in the various individuals that cognize it. Thus to avoid greater evils a subjective factor is introduced into all knowing; the 'ideas' of various minds are interpolated between the mind and the realities it tries to know, but can never apprehend immediately. All perception of reality thus becomes representative, and is subject to subjective distortion, and how far this may go can never be determined *a priori*.

Hinc illae lacrimae; hence the long agony of the theory of knowledge, from Descartes to Kant and from Kant to Humanism. For the whole problem of what it means for two minds to know the same thing, and of how it can be

S

called the same if they know it differently, rushes back upon us.

For Humanism indeed the coast remains clear and the answer simple. It merely bids us complete the work of Kant (most infelicitously called by him Copernican) by describing the psychical functioning to which our data are conformed *in their integrity*, *i.e.* without mutilating, depersonalizing and sublimating them by fictions of a *Bewusstsein überhaupt*. The 'subjectivity' which was thought to vitiate cognition and refused to be eliminated, is a blessing not a curse; for it is really that which gives the needful cue to the 'objective' ordering of the initial mess of crude experience. It is the importance of some of its contents for the purposes of human life which confers upon them a superior reality; it is the usefulness of some ideas which leads to their (intersubjective) recognition as 'true' and objectively valid, and effectively discriminates them from the vagrant fancies that are rejected as worthless and therefore remain 'merely subjective.' For a mind, however, which has become replete with fixed ideas that the thinker's personality must at all costs be ignored, that the study of psychical fact is incompatible with that of physical order, that the genesis of knowledge has no relation to its nature, and that once science condescends to take note of the individual it is for ever debarred from noticing anything else, this Humanist way of producing 'objectivity' will seem to demand far too radical a rethinking of old prejudices. It will be rejected doubtless; but what will be done about the problem?

It may be suggested to the New Realist that the simplest way of maintaining his original position and escaping from the difficulties of this whole criticism is to turn solipsist. He cannot find room for the objects of other minds, but he can get rid of the other minds. If he will systematically refuse to recognize the other minds that seem to disagree with him, he avoids the complication which such recognition inevitably introduces. He is left alone with his objects, and no one can question the rightness of his perceptions. In words perhaps this position may be thought to fall short of Solipsism, because there are still realities for him to perceive. But he has become the autocratic judge of this whole reality; and this is in substance Solipsism. He is the only mind in the world, of which he is the sole experient. Οἶος πέπνυται, τοὶ δὲ σκιαὶ ἀΐσσουσιν.[1]

(*b*) The second type of New Realism seems less extreme, and one might prognosticate for it a longer life. It makes attempts to account for the existence and correction of error, and for the growth and improvement of knowledge. To do so it has to admit the presence of a subjective contribution in our perceptions of reality; but it regards this as the source only of error and 'opinion.' Between 'opinion' and 'knowledge' it fixes a great gulf, like Plato in the *Republic*. Knowledge is of the object, and though it involves a relation of the mind, it must not be supposed to alter the nature of its terms. Hence the object *in* the cognitive relation is just as it was (or would be) in itself, and nothing about it is dependent on the mind's knowing it. This last corollary is of course somewhat difficult to defend, when it is questioned. So is the gulf between opinion and Knowledge. It might prove hard to adduce an unequivocal example of 'Knowledge,' and to show that what is so called is ever more than 'opinion,' and, of course, if no Knowledge can be found, its total effect is sceptical. Again the theory is hard put to it to assign a tolerable position to a good many facts, *e.g.* those of colour-perception.

But it is when confronted with the facts of error and difference of opinion that this New Realism most clearly seems to falter. When A and B both claim to apprehend reality, but differ irreconcilably as to what reality is, it is at a loss to decide which of them is right. And yet the need for such decisions cannot lightly be denied. For such differences are deep-seated and persistent. Two men may even agree entirely as to the facts, so far as

[1] *Odyssey*, x. 495.

human science can express them; yet they may still be worlds apart in their attitude towards them. What the one hails with joy, the other may recoil from with abhorrence. For example, one may worship the syllogism, and another despise it, though both may agree upon the perfection of its form. One man may shrink from immortality, another from extinction. To one the belief that all is one may be an inspiring gospel, to another the paralysis of all effort and the grave of all interest in life. Does it not seem piteously inadequate, then, to decree all such differences out of existence by calling them differences of *opinion*, proving only that there is no *Knowledge* of the matters they concern? Moreover it is vain; for men differ as to the truth about all things (even about mathematics so soon as one gets beyond the merest verbal trifling),[1] and differ most signally about the matters of the highest import, such as God, Freedom and Immortality, and the meaning and value of life. This New Realism, therefore, has either to confine itself to the abstract enunciation of the veriest platitudes, such as that everything either is or is not, though no one can tell which, or to exclude from the realm of knowledge proper everything that is really important and therefore in dispute, and to assume an agnostic attitude on such questions as, *e.g.*, whether God exists and the like.

Hence once more a great temptation comes upon the New Realist. He could treat the whole body of his own opinions as 'Knowledge,' if only he could suppress the pestilent opinions that conflict with his. This he could do in two ways, either practically or theoretically. Of these the practical way would doubtless be preferable in itself, were it not impracticable; however much he may desire to produce unanimity by the old effective methods, ruthless persecution for the sake of establishing a philo-

---

[1] Nay, Prof. Poincaré has recently declared (1912) that the difference between the pragmatist, and the 'Cantorian' attitude in mathematics is theoretically insoluble, because it proceeds from a difference in mental type. As, however, it is part of the pragmatists' case that such differences exist, and can only be evaluated practically, this is in effect a verdict in their favour. Cp. *Studies in Humanism*, ch. xii. § 10.

sophic theory of knowledge would not be tolerated in these days.

In theory, however, Solipsism grants him the means to achieve his end. If he can persuade himself that he alone experiences, he can hold that whatever he feels certain of is Knowledge, and the 'opinions' of others need no longer contradict his. He can treat them as illusory equally with themselves, and he will consistently ignore the opinions and cut their authors.

The difference between this type of New Realism and the first will be plainly this, that whereas Solipsism was a *necessity* for the truth of the theory in the first case, in the second it is only a *convenience*.

(c) A third crypto-solipsistic form of New Realism has been promulgated by Prof. S. Alexander in his presidential address to the Aristotelian Society (1908). Like so many realists, he has assumed the chief crux, viz. that perception is unequivocally of the object, and that the object is not mental but physical. It is assumed also that perception makes no difference to the object, and that therefore a hundred persons may all see the same tree. So far this is only naïve Realism, and not obviously untenable. But what are we to think of the further doctrine that the memory also of the tree is a physical object? Do the hundred persons have the same memory-object, or does each have his own, and are there as many objects as there are memories? If so, the one perceived tree has magically blossomed into a hundred remembered ones, and these must all be related to the tree and to each other. And what of the changes memory-objects undergo? Are they too all 'physical' and not mental? The only way to reduce this plethoric wealth of 'physical objects' to something like a manageable compass would seem to be that of Solipsism, and this might also relieve the theory of the embarrassments in which its obvious and avowed inability to account for error at present involves it.

6. One more example of a constructively solipsistic doctrine may complete our survey. The doctrine that

Subject and Object are mutually interdependent is crypto-solipsistic. It begins, tamely enough, by holding that the Object must exist for a Subject, and no subject can exist without objects. This doctrine, in its proper meaning, is a purely verbal truth, an affair of definitions, stating the meaning of the words 'subject' and 'object.' But in Oxford it is, for some inscrutable reason, still regarded as important; and strangely enough is credited to 'idealism,' instead of being classed as thoroughgoing relativism.

At any rate the doctrine becomes either Solipsism or nonsense so soon as an attempt is made to apply it. If it seriously means to affirm that the existence of the Object is conditional upon that of the Subject, it implies that whenever a subject dies the world of objects must be annihilated with it. But this is clearly not what happens to our common world whenever one of us dies. It follows therefore either that the death of a subject is inconceivable and impossible, or that what died was not a subject, or that the common world is not an object, or that what was annihilated was not the common world and so that the latter is *not* dependent on its relation to a subject. But the first of these alternatives seems contrary to fact, while the last is contrary to the theory; the others render it irrelevant to the problem of knowledge. For what we wanted to know was what happened to the 'objective' world when a 'subject' died, on the 'idealistic' assumption that a 'subject' is implied in the persistence of every 'object.' Clearly if this is so, the persistence of the Object after the death of a subject shows that the Subject which sustained it does *not* die when one of us dies (alike whether that death means our extinction or our transfer to a different world). We, therefore, and our world are not Subject and Object in the sense required by the theory. The Subject is not one of us, but must be a category, or a Cosmic Ego, or what not. But if so, how is it, and its Object, relevant to the nature of our knowledge? There is on the one hand the deathless Subject of an indestructible world, and on the other we, who are not subjects in this sense, perceiving objects after our kind; and between the two there is no real connexion. The Subject, doubtless, may continue to perceive the changeless world which forms its Object throughout all the mischances of our mortal life; but we never perceived that world, and to our questions about the relation of our world to our minds we get no answer. The whole doctrine has thus become an irrelevant speculation concerning a Subject and an Object about which we only know that they are not human, nor humanly knowable; it leaves unexplained and unintelligible the position of the pseudo-subjects and pseudo-objects which surround us.

Once more the only way of really making the theory mean anything and of really correlating subject and object is to construe it solipsistically. The consistent idealist must hold that since with the Subject there would pass away the Object, it is only if, and so long as, *he* is a subject that a world of objects can endure.

It is possible that by this time the force of the argument may be producing an impression that for company's sake every philosopher, who cannot bear to stand alone and to lead the βίος μονώτης, had better own to Solipsism. But such intimidation will not daunt the Humanist nor cause him to desist from his endeavour (1) to refute Solipsism and (2) to solve the solipsistic puzzle.

(1) The Humanist's refutation of Solipsism is simple and sufficient. He is not a solipsist, because he chooses to believe in the existence of others. He believes this not so much for the sentimental reason that he does not want to be alone in the universe, but because he does not want to regard himself as the author of his whole experience. He will not take the responsibility of being all there is in a world such as is now provided. He does not desire to be any or all of the other minds, nor the totality of reality. He sees that he cannot be the Absolute without being also the Devil (and an insane Devil at that!), and so he prefers to be neither Absolute nor Devil.

Now this position seems eminently reasonable, but if any one declines to accept it, the Humanist cannot *compel* dissentients to adopt it. He cannot compel them not to be solipsists, if they prefer to regard him and everything else as just creatures of their disordered imaginations; nor does it follow from the nature of his theory that he should have this power. Whereas to a solipsist it must appear extremely puzzling, as well as annoying, that he should not be able to avoid contradiction and resistance at the hands of what *ex hypothesi* are his own creatures.

The Humanist refutation of Solipsism, then, begins frankly with a postulate. Into the origin of this postulate it is no more necessary to inquire here than in other cases. For it seems unmeaning to discuss the antecedent reasonableness of a thing not yet in existence. The human reason must have something to reflect on before it can discuss the value of anything. A postulate, therefore, has to be made before it can be justified. The 'origin,' therefore, of our fundamental postulates can only be deduced in a 'mythical' form. But we are not really concerned with it. Whether it was an inspiration or a random guess, the postulate that there are others has come into existence. Once made, it has of course been tested by its working. And it will hardly be disputed that it has worked very well. It is therefore accounted reasonable and true by the generality of mankind, who are not philosophers. And a Humanist philosopher at any rate is not easily persuaded that in so vital a point the experience of mankind is wrong. He will therefore claim the right to hold the postulate true, because, and so long as, it works.

It will be noticed that the refutation of Solipsism by the success of this postulate is thoroughly pragmatic. It is neither *a priori* nor absolute. It does not rest on presuppositions about the possibilities of all experience. It does not profess to show that Solipsism is unthinkable. It is willing to allow that Solipsists may exist, and even flourish. It is willing to listen to what they have to say for themselves. It makes no higher claim for its own postulate than that it seems to provide a congenial and adequate way of handling the facts of human experience. If that experience should alter, it admits that it might be necessary to revise our postulates. But while it endures as it is, a successful postulate is as true and as reasonable as truth can be.

But does not this concede too much and admit that a reasonable Solipsism also may be possible? To deny this possibility *a priori* would be to deny that there may be legitimate differences of opinion, conditioned by the deep-seated differences of human personalities. It would imply a relapse into that absolutistic intolerance, which has provoked so many inhuman attempts to reduce all thought to the level of a mechanical uniformity, and renders the pretensions of metaphysical system-mongers so ludicrous a series of failures. It does not follow then from the fact that Solipsism may reasonably be denied that it may not reasonably be upheld. This latter contention therefore demands distinct examination.

(2) If the belief in other minds is a postulate, any one may, if he chooses, try to dispense with it. But he still remains under the obligation of devising an alternative scheme for the conduct of his life. Let him, therefore, try. His position is that his whole experience is like a dream, and he interprets his waking experience by his dream experience, instead of *vice versa*, like the generality of men. He believes that he makes his dream and all the creatures in it, and this belief he extends to all the incidents of his life.

There seems to be nothing theoretically absurd or untenable about such Solipsism: it may even claim the merit of greater consistency as compared with the vulgar view that interprets solipsistically dreams alone.[1] But the solipsist would have of course to adapt his theory somehow to his practice. He must not for example be led to imagine that because life was a dream of his, he could know beforehand how the dream was going. For if he imagined this, events would soon refute his theory.

[1] Cp. *Studies in Humanism*, ch. xx. §§ 16-18.

In other words his Solipsism would have to be *empirical*, and not *a priori*, precisely as is our ordinary solipsistic interpretation of dreams.

A Solipsism so conceived would seem to be harmless. It would make no practical difference. Our solipsist would have to recognize in the persons and objects of his 'dream' quite as much 'independence' and ability to resist the control of his will as the most benighted pluralist. He would have to treat them as other than his dreaming self. We all usually pay this amount of respect to the creatures of our dreams. If the solipsistic theory of their nature is to be retained, it is on condition that it remains a mere theory which is not allowed to affect conduct. Should it be allowed to do so, it would of course spell disaster, and would refute itself in the one really final way, viz. by the elimination of its holder.

Nevertheless it is a point deserving of consideration whether theoretic exception should not be taken to an assumption which Solipsism shares with Common Sense. Both assume it as self-evident that the solipsistic interpretation of dream life is valid, *i.e.* that the self that *has* the dream is identical with the self that *makes* the dream. This, however, may be disputed. The dreamer is the victim, and not the maker, of the dream which surprises and torments him. Hence every dreamer, and every solipsist, is not really *one* but *two*. The strange possibilities of such an inherent duality in the 'self' are vividly illustrated by the famous 'Beauchamp' case so graphically recorded by Dr. Morton Prince,[1] in which, apparently, the 'maker of dreams' obtained control of the body. If then after the fashion of Miss 'Beauchamp' every solipsist is accompanied by his 'Sally,' it might become a subtle question whether the dreamer or the maker of dreams was really entitled to be a solipsist, and how sincerely the former could really take a solipsistic view of his complex personality. But it will probably be vain to raise this point; metaphysicians have always been too neglectful of ordinary people's dreams to be critical of

[1] *The Dissociation of a Personality* (1906).

their own; and besides the subject is too recent, too sensational, and above all too psychological, to appeal to them.

For a philosophy, however, which is content to stop short at the theoretic level there is no other way of refuting the Solipsism which we have described. But for a philosophy which insists that theoretic doctrines must be capable of application to practice the last word is not yet said. It will fasten on the very feature in this Solipsism which exempted it from theoretic refutation, and justify thereby its final condemnation. A Solipsism, it will say, which must in practice recognize other minds and acts *as if* they were real and makes no practical difference in the solipsist's behaviour, does not logically differ from the view it simulates in practice.

On pragmatic principles this objection seems sound and insuperable. If a solipsism admits that it must in practice behave as if other beings were real, then it has plainly passed into its other, and can no longer boast of a separate existence: it has suffered the same fate as an offensive ghost which, according to Plutarch, once made itself a nuisance in the Plataean territory. When it declined to yield to entreaty or exorcism, the Plataeans simply caused an image of it to be placed over the spot it haunted, and then, though no doubt it continued to occupy the same space, it was no longer a supernatural, but merely an aesthetic, eyesore—a hideous statue being something wholly natural. To any solipsism, on the other hand, which will not in practice admit the existence of other minds, the sufficient reply is that it is impracticable. And the fact that neither of these retorts constitutes a conclusive refutation of Solipsism in the eyes of philosophies which have assumed a different conception of the relation of theory to practice, leaves Solipsism a thorn in the flesh (or perhaps a squib in the vitals) only of those other philosophies.

XV

INFALLIBILITY AND TOLERATION[1]

ARGUMENT

The claim to infallibility is logically involved in the belief in absolute truth, and is held by the Pope in a less extreme form than by the philosopher. It legitimates intolerance and leads to persecution and social discord. Common sense evades its practical absurdities by assuming that no human truth is ever absolute. But this leads to scepticism.

It is better, therefore, to drop the absolutist assumption altogether, and to *humanize* truth, making it mean the *best* view devised up to date. This legitimates and promotes toleration and social harmony. But it shocks all dogmatists. And so the Roman Church will probably suppress Modernism, and refuse to give up its dogma-enacting powers, baleful as they have proved even to itself.

A DETACHED spectator of the follies of mankind could not but be profoundly impressed by the widespread interest which has been aroused throughout the world by the Pope's Encyclical against what is called Modernism. In many quarters the Papal condemnation is regarded as a sort of Congo atrocity in the spiritual world. But no reason is given why Protestants and Agnostics, Jews and Infidels, should interfere, even in thought, with the way in which internal discipline is administered in a Church which has always proclaimed its resolution to prescribe with authority and to enforce unquestioning obedience. Why should sympathy be lavished on persons who are oppressed because they refuse to liberate themselves by leaving an institution which excommunicates them? In these days when no Church is strong enough to persecute effectively, and it has become quite an arguable position that the best way of furthering the spiritual development

[1] This paper appeared in the *Hibbert Journal* for October 1908. For further light on the genesis of intolerance cp. my *Formal Logic*, ch. xxv.

of mankind would be to break up all ecclesiastical institutions, why should Roman ways of enforcing discipline be denounced with indignation? Why should not those who do not relish them be left to make their choice between submission and departure? They have been surreptitiously trying to combine the advantages of an ancient and highly picturesque community with those of an unrestricted freedom of individual thought; they have been detected and sharply called to order. Why then should they be pitied and paradoxically helped from outside to stay inside by people who would gladly welcome them if they would come out?

In other quarters the Pope's procedure meets with strong approval, and rationalist philosophers may be heard condemning Modernism as fervently as Pragmatism. The perplexities of the controversy, moreover, are only deepened when one observes how curiously vague and general are the Modernist's replies to the Papal accusations. It is all very well to denounce the obscurantism of the Vatican and to prophesy the disastrous failure of the Papal policy; but it would have been more to the purpose to show how any other course would have been consistent with Papal authority.

Thus the whole situation forcibly suggests a suspicion that the facts have not been fully put before the public. Modernism is clearly suspected of being something far more dangerous and subversive than the Pope's examples prove; and both its allies and its enemies appear to think that there is more at issue than merely the domestic question of what latitude of thought the Roman Church can tolerate.

A belief that this is truly so, that this suspicion is amply justified, that the issue is really one of vital importance to the whole human race, and that this can be, and ought to be, made clear, is the *raison d'être* of this essay.

What is really at stake and what really arouses so much interest is the old conflict between the claim to infallibility and the right to persecute on the one side, and the freedom of thought and the duty of toleration on the other. This it is that evokes so much feeling on both sides, when it is (more or less clearly) perceived; and rightly, for the question is plainly one of universal import and worth fighting over. It should, however, have been explained that the decision of this question does not rest with popes and theologians, but with philosophers and scientists: for it depends ultimately on the view that is taken of Truth.

Very few have understood the claim to infallibility. Nearly all would scout the idea that we may all be infallible, even the silliest of us, if we will only equip ourselves with a suitable view of Truth. In non-Catholic countries it is commonly supposed that the infallibility of the Pope is the acme of theological extravagance, and that the Vatican Council of 1870 irretrievably stultified Romanism for ever in the eyes of reason by its enunciation of this monstrous dogma. In point of fact, infallibility is an essential postulate implicit in all rationalistic philosophy, and the dogma of the Roman Church is merely the religious formulation of a belief which it shares with nearly all its critics. The infallibility of the Pope differs from that of the philosopher and the common man only in being limited, relatively reasonable and couched in singularly guarded and moderate terms. For the Pope, when he claims to be infallible, does not believe himself to be infallible on all and sundry subjects, but only when speaking on matters of religious faith, and that solemnly and in his capacity as head of an infallible Church. And he takes great care *not* to say *when* he is speaking in this capacity, so that practically the dogma is comparatively innocuous. Whereas the common man claims infallibility for every thought that may chance to come into his head at any time, whether or not it agrees with what he said a moment ago. He attributes, moreover, to every one else a similar endowment with infallibility, regardless of the consequences.

It is true, no doubt, that the man in the street is unaware of the monstrous claim he makes. But this

xv INFALLIBILITY AND TOLERATION

does not alter the facts that both he and the Pope believe themselves to hold the same theory of Truth, and that this theory implies a claim to infallibility. The sole difference is that whereas the Pope draws its consequences consistently, cautiously, and with moderation, the man in the street does so inconsistently, wildly, and extravagantly. And then the latter turns upon the former and roundly accuses him of demanding what is repugnant to reason!

Yet the Pope and the man in the street both profess belief in the existence of absolute truth. Both also believe in their own capacity to enunciate it. But an absolute truth is one which could not under any circumstances become false. Whoever enunciates it, therefore, could not (so far) possibly be wrong. But what is this but to claim infallibility?

As ordinarily assumed, however, this claim is wildly absurd. For when men fail to agree in enunciating absolute truths, each has as good a right to think himself infallible as the other. Every man, therefore, who in good faith makes a statement he believes to be true, and believes that truth is absolute, must claim infallible truth for his statement, and infallibility *pro tanto* for himself, its maker. He becomes a little pope *in posse* in his own eyes. And he must insist on enforcing his rights. All must agree with him. The facts that his pronouncements do not meet with universal acceptance, and indeed that no two men ever quite agree, cannot affect the theoretic validity of his claim. Nor can it be impugned by the fact that others put forward conflicting claims with equal assurance. Each must abide by his own vision of absolute truth. Whoever does not see the same as he does must be either a fool or a knave: a fool if he cannot see it, a knave if he will not admit that he sees it. He must be made to see it, therefore, by fair means or foul. The social consequences may be imagined. There must be war unceasing and unsparing upon earth, until one and the same Truth, immutable, infallible, and absolute, is established upon it, and is seen and accepted by all without exception. Thus persecution becomes a duty and tolerance a crime.

Common Sense, of course, would be the first to shrink with horror from the consequences of its own doctrine. For, unlike philosophy, it will never press logic to absurdity. It will decline, therefore, to take the claim to infallibility with such tragic earnestness in practice. It will much prefer to point out that while no doubt it is imperative to believe that absolute truth exists, it would be decidedly presumptuous to suppose that any one had got it. In fact there is no very urgent necessity to regard absolute truth as anything but an ideal. In practice no one can really work with it. Not only does it lead to endless quarrels when different men all claim to be absolutely right, but even the same man entangles himself by enunciating incompatible truths with equal absoluteness at different times. And so it will finally be suggested that perhaps this inconvenient infallibility had better be dropped, and even smile approval on a paradoxical philosopher who, perceiving the awkwardness of the situation, comes forward with proposals to attenuate its virulence by contending that though every judgment any one makes is necessarily infallible for the time being, yet there is nothing in this to prevent any one from superseding and annulling his infallible judgment by another equally infallible, and as shortlived, the moment after.[1]

It is clear, however, that reluctance to follow out the logical consequences of an unpalatable doctrine is not strictly the right way to atone for its initial ferocity. It is far more consistent to interpret absolute truth absolutistically than to draw its fangs in such a lax and easy-going democratic way. It will never do to let common sense steer us straight into scepticism, by surrendering the belief that some one must have absolute truth. If, we should argue, absolute truth exists, it is clear, no doubt, that the common man has not got it.

---

[1] Such is actually the purport of Mr. F. H. Bradley's doctrine of the infallibility of the last judgment (cf. *Mind*, N.S., No. 66, and my comments in No. 67, pp. 373-6).

But some one must have it, else it would not exist, and then there would be no truth at all. Even if it is among the prerogatives of deity, it is reasonable to suppose that it has been deposited with some human representative. Let us search the world, therefore, for one whom we can regard as such a depositary of absolute truth, and submit to his authority. And whom shall we find to satisfy these conditions better than the Pope? His infallibility is infinitely more credible than that of the man in the street.

Such a train of thought must surely appeal very powerfully to all who feel a spiritual craving to submit themselves to authority, who long to shuffle off the responsibility for their acts, and to find some one who will guide and direct them. And their name is legion. If, therefore, there were no Pope, he would have to be invented for such souls. His Holiness need not fear that his faithful will desert him. There is no reason to think that the *anima naturaliter Vaticana* is becoming extinct. He must, however, eschew the restriction of his claim to faith and morals. The absolutistic view of truth logically demands that truth be fully unified. A plurality of authority implies a plurality of truth; and this is inadmissible. The Pope, therefore, must be the infallible authority in art, politics, and science, as well as in religion. There is, moreover, a practical reason for this arrangement. If there is no single infallibility to cover the whole realm of thought, if there are a number of authorities all claiming to speak infallibly in the name of their respective sciences, it is impossible to avoid conflicts and collisions between them; and this must discredit, weaken, and perhaps destroy, the whole principle of authority as such.

Before, however, this unification of authorities is finally achieved, it is easy to predict that a prolonged period of painful contention must ensue. The world at present contains a great number of conflicting authorities, of which it is by no means clear that the Roman Church is the strongest and best fitted to survive; it contains also many recalcitrants against all authority, and an appreciable number of philosophers who, though they insist on the absolute authority of 'Reason,' will admit no reason but their own. It seems improbable, therefore, that this doctrine of the infallibility of those who speak in the name of absolute truth will make for social peace and quiet. For all parties are in duty bound by their allegiance to absolute truth to wage war unflinchingly upon all views but their own, and wherever they can to oppress, suppress, and persecute by all means in their power. History, therefore, will repeat itself. Its bloodstained pages tell too eloquently how thoroughly man has tried to live up to his supposed obligations, and the psychological intolerance which has become so natural in man shows how deeply the corollaries of his belief in the absoluteness of truth have sunk into his soul.

Is it not possible, therefore, to pay too high a price even for absolute truth? In modern times there is probably a growing number of men to whom the price to be paid will seem excessive and such consequences seem repulsive. It is time, therefore, that for their benefit we considered the alternative which, apprehended with various degrees of clearness, underlies the modern revolt against mere authority, the Modernist attitude towards religion, and the extensive sympathy therewith.

Let us return to the practical but illogical compromise whereby Common Sense robbed the intolerant belief in the absoluteness of Truth of all its terrors. A single step beyond it in the same direction will take us into a new world, a very paradise of freedom. Common Sense was willing to admit that in point of fact absolute truth was not in any man's possession, and that however confident men might feel about the truth they had, they were often, if not always, victims of an illusion, and might as well allow for this possibility in their behaviour towards their fellows. For its immediate purpose of mitigating the acerbity of absolutist theory and securing social intercourse this compromise is plainly adequate. It works well enough in practice. Theoretically, however, it is more than dubious. It is most unpleasantly and directly suggestive of sceptical inferences. If it is held that most men most of the time are deluded when they suppose themselves to be enunciating absolute truth, if it is impossible to show that any one ever succeeds in enunciating such a thing, what does the doctrine of absolute truth become but a subtle and insidious means of discrediting all human truths? Is not this the explanation of that paradox of philosophic history, viz. that consistent rationalism always in the end collapses into scepticism?

It is clear then that absolute truth is not really an operative idea. It is an ideal that ever recedes into the distance when we try to grasp it. Men are not really infallible, and cannot treat each other as such. The truths they actually deal in are not absolute. The common-sense belief that they are is really an ill-considered prejudice.

Let us candidly confess, therefore, that not only do we not have absolute truth, but that what we have is enough to content us. Let us boldly say that we do not need absolute truth, that it is a superfluity and an encumbrance, and get rid of it in theory as well as in practice. Let us frame a new conception of Truth. Let us strip her aegis of the rigours and terrors that compelled reluctant assent but rendered her unapproachable in her warlike armour, and teach her to dwell peaceably in our midst, to speak our language, and to interest herself in our life. Let us, in a word, *humanize* Truth, instead of idolizing her as a goddess who is more than half a demon. Let us define the true no longer as what is cogent and compulsory and irresistible, but as what is attractive and valuable and satisfying. Let Truth mean whatever can satisfy our cognitive cravings, whatever can answer a logical problem. And let it mean our *best* answer for the time being. Let it be conceived, that is, as essentially progressive and *improvable*, and therefore as superseded by new truth and turning into 'error' so soon as something superior to the old dawns upon any human soul.

Thus Truth will no longer shine upon us from afar with the dim glimmer of an infinitely distant nebula. It will no longer dazzle us with the delusive flashes of a will-o'-the-wisp that is really 'error.' It will be a torch kindled by human will and wielded by human hands (or rather a succession of such torches, each rekindled as the last expires), always lighting the way for man as he passes onwards. The objects it illumines will come into its sphere as man's life requires them; they will drop back into the limbo of the useless, out of which they were drawn, as they are used up or improved upon.

From such a reconstitution of the idea of Truth it is clear that man must gain immensely. And, apart from the glamour of words, even Truth will lose nothing. Even its 'absoluteness' is not wholly lost. It is only avowed to be what it is—an ideal, the culmination of Truth's working value, the perfect satisfaction of every cognitive ambition. As such it may still yield the remote and emotional consolation which was all it could afford before, when the illusions of verbiage were purged away. The human truth which alone we have and alone we need, on the other hand, will be a very real and potent influence. It must enormously enlarge the liberty of thought. It must enormously enhance humaneness of discussion. It must utterly explode the foundations of dogmatism and intolerance.

For nothing at first can be 'true' but what can commend itself to some one and satisfy some spiritual need. Conversely, whatever can do this can claim 'truth'; it has a claim to be heard and tested, even though it be merely the fleeting inspiration of a moment. Every man has a vote in the making of truth; any man's truth may be elected, any man's vote may decide the election. But no man has a right to use force; no man has a right to impose his convictions on any other: superior attractiveness alone effects conversions in the conflict of opinions. Nor has any one a right to argue that because he is right every one else must be wrong: Truth is plural, and can adjust herself, like a rainbow, to every man's sight and point of view. Hence an indefinite variety of truths may be valid relatively to a variety of differently constituted and situated persons. Toleration mounts the throne left vacant by Infallibility.

But what a blasphemous travesty of Truth, what a hideous anarchy it must all seem to absolutists, dogmatists, pedants, authoritarians of all sorts! How it must seem to them to shiver into atoms the whole edifice of Truth and the foundations of all intellectual order! No wonder they must support Rome against the inroads of such modernity! No wonder they are almost speechless with horror and incoherent with indignation! For the *mirage* of an absolute Truth in the skies is dissolved beyond recall, and its worshippers are left desolate. To them it seemed the real thing. It never was the real thing, and they have lost nothing but an illusion. But they do not, and perhaps will not, see this. All that was of real value remains. The terrestrial realities remain of which the celestial phantasmagoria was the reflection. There remains the practical necessity of living together and agreeing upon the conditions of a common life. Man remains with his gregarious nature, his lack of originality, his respect for tradition, his easy acquiescence in the habitual, his dislike of innovation, his preference for order and system, his eagerness to think the world a cosmos— in short, with all the forces that weld society together.

More than enough remains, therefore, for the compacting of our intellectual order. The 'real' and 'objective' becomes that which it is socially convenient to recognize, in a rich variety of senses. 'Objective truth' will be that which all or most can agree on, and fits in best with the course of their experience. It articulates itself into systems of truths which are more substantial, more useful, and probably more durable, than the transcendent vision which was sacrificed. Certainly these systems are at present plural, not because Truth cannot be conceived as one—for the plural truths can easily be conceived as converging towards a single consummation—but because men do not, in fact, agree. Whether they *can* agree remains to be seen; they have every motive to agree, and have lost the strong stimulus they had to insist obstinately on their individual infallibility. But, on the other hand, the notion of agreement has itself become less exacting: men can 'agree to differ'; they can maintain all individual views which do not clash with those of others or lead to social discord. In short, the existing situation will be altered only by the infusion of a more tolerant temper into all opinions.

But has not all this carried us far away from the Modernist movement in the Church of Rome? Not at all; it has brought us to its core. Modernism, in its philosophic forms,[1] is essentially the recognition by certain more enlightened or sensitive clerics of the intellectual forces which are drawing men in religion, as in science and philosophy, towards the humanistic conception of Truth which we have sketched. They have perceived at last what the lives of laymen have always dumbly attested, that religion is not primarily a matter of theology but of religious experience, and is nowhere reducible to a rigid chain of incontrovertible syllogisms. They have therefore abandoned the intellectualistic travesties of religion, which kill its spirit to embalm its letter, and offer long strings of pseudo-rational propositions as a satisfaction to a reason which easily detects their imposture and is itself seeking for something more nutritious than pure intellect. But such dogmas, as M. Leroy has shown, are utter failures as purely intellectual propositions: they neither can nor do *compel* assent; as such, they can neither be defended nor even made to mean anything that matters. So to understand the meaning of dogmas and the nature of religious beliefs is a fatal mistake. They are not really intellectual products at all, and therefore cannot be attacked (or defended) as such. No religion really rests on the

---

[1] Its historical criticisms of ecclesiastical tradition are quite a different affair. Here the trouble arises out of the attempt to reduce religious truth to historical, and history to science. But historical truth differs fundamentally from scientific in that the evidence on which it rests cannot be multiplied at pleasure. And to assume that religious truth rests *solely* on historical testimony is to beg some vital questions.

impersonal support of pure reason; nor can it be kept from moving with the times by chains of rusty syllogisms. For the truth is that dogmas are essentially secondary expressions of the vital value of a religion, the by-products of a spiritual life that was never nourished on pure intellect. They are, as it were, the lifeless fossils of a living faith, and remain unmeaning marvels unless they are re-enveloped in the life which grew them. That life, moreover, is primarily an individual attitude of soul: however closely it is wrapped in a spiritual environment, each soul must nourish itself and grow in its own congenial fashion.

The chief paradox of the situation is that these facts of the spiritual life should have been so intensely perceived in the Roman Church. For at first sight they look such a supreme vindication of Protestantism, such a sanctioning by psychologic science of the evangelical or mystic. But it must never be forgotten that, like all science, psychology is catholic and impartial. Every religion may be vindicated by the psychologic tests in so far as it is genuine, *i.e.* really nourishes the spiritual life. It speaks well for the intelligence of the Catholic Modernists that they should have discovered this. But they had discovered also that the idea of a Church, of an historical association with a corporate confidence in the truth of its position, has very great religious value. They were probably not wrong in thinking that the Roman Church could flourish exceedingly on Modernist lines.

But will it ever prefer to do so? It is very hard to say. It must be a very hard question to decide for the astute directors of Papal policy. Superficially, no doubt the present indications are that this bold and novel policy will not be adopted. Ancient institutions, whether they are called Churches, bureaucracies, or universities, never do adopt a bold and novel policy: they are always under the control of men too old to *run the risk* of such a policy. Modernism, therefore, will be crushed, and Medievalism will prevail; a mechanical uniformity will be enforced, even at the cost of schism. But appearances are nowhere more deceptive than in matters ecclesiastical, and history does not confirm the view that the Pope always knows his own business best. It is quite conceivable that in due course, when the more cautious sympathizers with modern thought have risen by dint of years to the higher posts in the hierarchy, and the pressure of circumstances has convinced the less fanatical conservatives that something must be done, some successor of Pius X. will be moved to issue another Encyclical which, after splitting a vast number of hairs to prove that what is now sanctioned is not identical with what was condemned before, will define the sense in which a Modernist attitude may be permitted, and concede the substance of what has lately been denied.

There would be both psychological and historical warrant for this prophecy. The opposition to any novelty of thought is always largely a matter of individual psychology. The human mind becomes less open to new impressions as it grows older, and in all institutions the high authorities are always old, and often stupidly conservative. Progressiveness and open-mindedness are tender plants which must be carefully cultivated, and often forced. Historical analogy points to the same conclusion. The making of dogmas usually ends by making orthodoxy a razor-edge between two opposite heresies which have been successively condemned. It is formulated so as to conceal the facts that when new ideas arose the old men in authority conservatively condemned them, and that when, nevertheless, they triumphed, words had to be found that would not break too abruptly with the old traditions.

Such, however, are what may be regarded as the normal psychological and political obstacles to the progress of human thought, and they are in no wise peculiar to the Roman Church. What complicates the situation in her case is that there are other serious objections to innovation which render her the least likely of the Churches to modernize her basis. By so doing she could probably purchase an ignoble peace and enduring prosperity, but only at the cost of two things which have hitherto been very dear to her. In the first place, she would have to renounce *the right to persecute*. Truly a trivial matter this, it may be thought, seeing that it cannot nowadays be exercised. But it is one thing to suspend it in practice and for prudential reasons, and quite another to give it up in theory and on principle. Principles which cannot be carried into practice often grow all the dearer for their pathetic impotence, as is proved by intellectualist philosophies. Moreover, to renounce this right would not only break with much historical tradition, but would also sacrifice the ambition of recovering the lost power of the Church.

Secondly, the right of making dogmas (of the old quasi-rational sort) would have to be abandoned. The Church would have to follow the example set by Science and, more recently, by philosophy. Science for some time past has been too busy and too rapidly progressive to find it worth while to formulate into fixed dogmas her working theories, which, in the words of Sir J. J. Thomson, form "a policy and not a creed." It has grown accustomed to use them merely for what they are worth, and so long as they are worth it. In philosophy the discovery of the proper attitude towards dogmas has been of slower growth, though philosophic Humanism is quite clear as to their value and the mischief they have wrought.

But religion hitherto has always stood for the eternal fixity of dogma, once it has been defined. In most Churches, indeed, this power of making dogma has long been in abeyance. They have been too tightly wedged into an antiquated creed which none of its members could construe literally, or tied to some paralysing political *concordat*, or too loosely organized to act corporately. But this inability has usually been construed as a disability, and the power of making dogma has seemed a mark of the superior progressiveness and unity of Rome. Acceptance of Modernism, however, would mean the sacrifice of this flattering prerogative.

Here again, however, it might be argued that the apparent loss would be a real gain. For the making of dogma is always a perilous business. In making dogmas it is hard to avoid making heretics. And the more heretics a Church makes the less 'catholic' does it become. It is extraordinary what losses the Roman Church has incurred by her indulgence in the dogma-making instinct. Was a disagreement about the calculating of that most inconveniently migratory festival, Easter, worth the bisection and permanent weakening of Christendom? Was the defining of the Trinity and the Incarnation—in terms which however satisfactory they seemed to the 'orthodoxy' of the time have long changed their meaning so as to have become unintelligible —worth the loss of Africa and Asia to Mohammedanism, and the destruction of the best of the Northerners, the Arian Goths? The world in all probability would long ago have been Christian, the Roman Church would have been truly 'catholic,' but for the disastrous practice of defining dogmas, and the intolerance of which this was the cause and the effect. Will history repeat itself? Will dogma be made though the angels weep? Will Rome decide in accordance with her past traditions, *fiat dogma, ruat coelum*? It will be immensely hard to break with them, and the traditional policy will necessarily have immense strength. But who can say? Not even Pius X. But the situation is very interesting, though decidedly more comfortable for those who can watch from without the distractions of an embarrassed Church.

XVI

FREEDOM AND RESPONSIBILITY[1]

ARGUMENT

I. Does Determinism blot out the criminal's responsibility for his crimes? And would he fare better at the hands of Science, if he were treated as irresponsible? If he cannot help offending, can society help punishing? Belief in social reform presupposes an alternative and better course of events. Is, then, a belief in 'Freedom' irrational, and should Determinism make no difference to practice?

II. The scientific value of Determinism as a methodological postulate. 'Law' as the instrument of prediction. But this ignores *novelty*, and our postulate's confirmation is only empirical. The value of Determinism diminished by our ignorance, and largely sentimental. The caricaturing of Libertarianism. 'Free' choice not motiveless. Freedom demanded and explained by the moral struggle, and so thinkable and possible. The clash of rival postulates leaves us free to choose between them. Does this *prove* 'Freedom'?

I

IF the Social Revolution should ever pass from the region of vague sentiment into that of crude and cruel fact, there is at least one class of learned men whose extinction may be prophesied with as great confidence as that of priests and kings. When the amiable exhortation of the French revolutionist has been acted on, and the neck of the last king has been constricted with the entrails of the last priest, the last millionaire will no doubt have been smothered with the unsaleable remainders of the last professor of philosophy.

Such at any rate is the estimate of the value of philosophy Mr. Robert Blatchford's pamphlet, *Not Guilty, A Defence of the Bottom Dog*, very distinctly manages to

[1] This essay appeared in the *Oxford and Cambridge Review* for November 1907.

convey. It is an appeal on behalf, not merely of the downtrodden and unsuccessful, but also of the degraded and criminal classes, and an indictment of what is, or passes for, 'justice,' human and divine. He defends his clients on the ground, mainly, that they are the helpless victims of heredity and environment, whose brute instincts have been further brutalized by the horrible conditions under which they have been nurtured. And he denies *in toto* the right of society to condemn and to punish those who could not have been other than they are.

In other words, Mr. Blatchford (and with him presumably the whole party of militant Socialism) is essentially concerned with the old philosophic theme of Freedom and Responsibility, complicated though it is no doubt for modern minds with the problems of atavism, heredity and variation. But he scorns to seek the aid of technical philosophy. He is weary of the learned who darken counsel with technical verbiage. He has no use for useless learning, for "the tangle of Gordian knots tied and twisted by twenty centuries full of wordy but unsuccessful philosophers" (p. 169), nor can he understand (p. 16) why "the world is paying millions of money and bestowing honours and rewards in profusion upon the learned and wise and spiritual leaders who teach it to believe such illogical nonsense" as a man's responsibility for his acts. He prefers instead to argue the whole matter out again for himself, to reiterate the old fallacies, to repeat the old inconsequences, to be stopped at the old deadlocks.

Mr. Blatchford would possibly be surprised to find how much precedent there is for all his positions, if he had the curiosity and leisure to trace them back to their origins. Even his condemnation of the futility of philosophy is no new thing, and is mild compared with the things which philosophers have been in the habit of saying of each other. The opinion which the greatest philosophers have entertained of the efforts of their colleagues has usually been a low one. Herakleitos, the great Ephesian, used all his predecessors as illustrations of his maxim that much learning did not teach intelligence. And the philosopher-pedant has never been denounced more brilliantly and incisively than by Plato.

As for the use of Determinism as an excuse for the bad man, it has been one of the earliest inferences to be drawn from moral philosophy. No sooner had Socrates put forward the suggestion that virtue was (a sort of) knowledge, and thereby laid the foundation of a scientific study of morals, than this dictum was improved into a *reductio ad absurdum* of morality. It was at once pointed out that if virtue was knowledge, then vice must be ignorance, and that no one was vicious willingly, any more than ignorant. Vice, therefore, was involuntary, and no one should be blamed for being vicious. The retort, fixed for us in the *Ethics* of Aristotle (iii. 5. 17), that by the same reasoning virtue might be proved involuntary, could not arrest the controversy: it had merely to be accepted (as it promptly was by the Stoics) to bring upon the scene full-blown Determinism, and to inflict upon ethics a perennial problem which the majority of philosophers at the present day probably regard as insoluble, to wit that of reconciling the strict determination of every event with the moral demand that it *shall*, nevertheless, be possible to break the chain of circumstance in order to choose the right.

Clearly, therefore, Mr. Blatchford's contentions have abundant plausibility as well as many precedents. There is much excuse also for the lapses of his logic. The spectacle of human folly, crime, and misery is so harrowing that only the coolest intellects can bear coldly to criticize and carefully to examine proposals that promise a wholesale alleviation of the burden of man. And yet unless Mr. Blatchford's clarion is merely to create confusion and dissension in the ranks of the army with which man is battling with his secular foes, these are just the points to be scrutinized. The chief source of human suffering is not social. It is not a consequence of man's imperfect control of his own nature, nor of the imperfect development of his social sympathies and the resulting inhumanity to his kind. It springs from our inadequate control of the forces of nature, and can be relieved only by the gradual growth of the knowledge which is power. If the Socialists could prevail upon the nations of the earth to abandon the folly of their internecine strife, to put down their monstrous armaments, and to devote a tithe of their annual cost to scientific research, they would achieve more for the advancement of humanity, and even for their own aims, in twenty years, than they are likely to accomplish by centuries of merely political agitation.

But, even in dealing with those evils which are either social in their nature or capable of being mitigated by social expedients, we must be cautious. We must beware of letting our sentiment run away with our logic, and of adopting a philosophy which would ultimately stultify and sterilize all efforts at reform. We must not, therefore, allow our sympathy for the weak to unman us. We must not allow our pity for the degraded to drag us down. In making allowances for the victims of unfavourable circumstances we must seek to brace, and not to relax, their powers of resistance. We must, therefore, preach Freedom to them and not Fatalism, Effort and not Acquiescence. Still less must we ourselves begin by acknowledging the omnipotence of Fate. We must not despair of victory. We must vindicate the power of our persistent efforts to reshape the world within us and without us. In other words, we must uphold the reality of Human Freedom.

It is not, therefore, from any lack of sympathy with the humanitarian aspects of Mr. Blatchford's argument that it seems to us open to criticism. What we desire to attack is the logical inconsequence of his position. What we desire to show is that Robert Blatchford the Determinist cuts the throat of Robert Blatchford the social reformer. And what we desire to establish is that, whatever politics we favour, any advocacy of practical interference with the existing order of nature, nay our whole rational life, presupposes and implies the reality of our Freedom and

XVI   FREEDOM AND RESPONSIBILITY   287

the rejection of Determinism. But, of course, it is one thing to exhibit the practical importance and necessity of Freedom and another to establish its theoretical validity as a philosophic interpretation of the facts of life, and in this larger undertaking we shall have to encounter the arguments of many of the philosophers of the past and nearly of all the present.

We may, however, at once proclaim that there is an enormous logical gap between Mr. Blatchford's theoretical position, and the practical consequences he seeks to draw from it. If we grant the former, we not merely need not, but cannot, assent to the latter. If we contend for the latter, we must begin by ignoring the former.

If it is true that "no man is answerable for his own acts," because he has had "no part in the creation of his own nature" (p. 10), if it is true that "law is based upon the false idea that men know what is right and what is wrong, and have power to choose the right," whereas really men are not good or bad, but merely weak or strong, fortunate or unfortunate (p. 19), if it is true that wrong-doers are "ignorant" or "diseased" or "insane" or "mentally deformed," and hark back "atavistically" to the savage and the beast, if it is true that our social conditions are bad, and acting on bad natures, create much vice and crime, if it is true that our "justice" is imperfect and ineffectual, and that our "punishments" largely fail either to reform the criminal or to protect society—if all this is true, does it follow that "all praise and blame are undeserved," and that no one ought to be punished (p. 203)? And does it follow that Mr. Blatchford's client, the "Bottom Dog," would fare better if he were transferred from the jurisdiction of morals to the tender mercies of Science, and were "entitled to be judged by the standard we apply to beasts" (p. 207)?

Mr. Blatchford is very confident: he defies us (p. 209) to deny one statement he has made, "to break one link of the steel chain of logic I have riveted upon our metaphysicians, our moralists, our kings, our judges and our gods," and tells us that "if all those (inferences) are not true, this book is not worth the paper it is printed on" (p. 203).

Well, let us see. Let us appraise the value of human beings according to the new ideals, with the coldly commercial and unsentimental eye of natural science, regarding no man as an end in himself and every one merely as an instrument to social well-being, and let us see where the "Bottom Dog" will come out.

The answer is not hard to get. For Sir Francis Galton has studied the social value of the different types of human being. He has calculated that the average value to the community of an Essex labourer's baby at birth is about £5, *i.e.* that moderate sum would be the 'present value' of the surplus of his production over his consumption of wealth during an average life. A baby genius (or even talent) would, of course, be worth buying up at many thousands of pounds by an intelligent society, and the new science of Eugenics has for its ultimate aim an increase in the natural supply of such valuable infants. A baby criminal, on the other hand, or idiot, or lunatic, or weakling, or wastrel, clearly possesses only negative value for social purposes. Such creatures are a dead loss to the community, which has to keep up prisons, asylums and hospitals for their sakes, and to employ judges, doctors, clergymen and policemen to cope with them. Not only do they fail to enrich the community by useful work, but they are a heavy burden upon it, and probably have to be supported for the greater part of their lives at the public expense. Clearly, therefore, society would be better without them, and if Science could prevent their birth, it would unquestionably do so; if it could detect them after birth, it would extinguish them as speedily as possible. No sentiment of pity or prejudice about justice and right would impede its mercilessly reasonable calculations. The darker the colours in which the wretchedness of the "Bottom Dog" is painted the more urgent would become the case for his scientific and systematic suppression.

But would this conclusion commend itself either to Mr. Blatchford or to his client? Yet he comes very near to confessing that such, on scientific principles, would be the right and rational way of dealing with the criminal. If the criminal is a recrudescence of the beast in man, and comparable to a tiger or a shark (p. 213), why on earth should he not be treated as such? Surely Mr. Blatchford would not preserve him from extermination merely in order that he might provide sport for our judges and our police? In one passage (p. 215) Mr. Blatchford admits that "although the prisoner ought not to be punished, it is imperative that he be restrained.' Quite a sensible conclusion, no doubt; but as an argument for leniency how verbal and how feeble! Mr. Blatchford can, of course, insist on reserving the word "punishment" for the retribution inflicted on misdeeds, and deny the application of the name to the treatment which aims at the protection of society and the reclamation of the offender. But would not such a defence savour of the hair-splitting of the philosophers whom Mr. Blatchford so despises? Besides, has he a right to ignore the facts that the actual treatment of anti-social conduct is largely inspired by the preventive, and even by the reformatory, views of "punishment," and that even a spice of vindictiveness, if there is fore-knowledge that the commission of a crime will lead to social execration, may act as a powerful deterrent from crime.

If, moreover, it is admitted to be "imperative" to "restrain" offenders, surely the cheaper and more effective the means the better. Science could certainly suggest modes of prevention far more efficacious than the punishments now in vogue, while at the same time cheaper and socially more advantageous. But it is probable that they would strike us all as strange and cruel. For example, it would be cheaper to brand or to mutilate than to imprison, and far more terrifying to vivisect than to hang. Moreover, in cases where even this deterrent failed, society might console itself with the thought that it would reap great benefits from the advance of knowledge derivable from scientific executions. In the present state of moral sentiment, while the criminal is regarded as a responsible person who can to some extent control his actions, there is little or no prospect of any such scientific revision of punishments. But on what grounds could Mr. Blatchford object to schemes of this kind? Surely by appealing from current morality to Science he has precipitated his *protégé* from the frying-pan into the fire.

But even this is not all. Mr. Blatchford has fallen into what is logically a still graver inconsequence. He has so far argued—and we, to humour him, have joined with him—quite in the ordinary common-sense way, as if the mode and amount of the punishment of offenders were an open question and dependent on the arbitrament of society. *But this whole mode of reasoning involves the assumption of human freedom and a denial of Determinism!* He and we have both assumed that even though the criminal could not but commit his crime, yet society at least was free to punish him, or to pardon, or to send him to a hospital. But if Determinism is the true philosophy, this assumption is utter nonsense, and an alternative to the punishment is just as unthinkable as to the crime. Society can no more help itself than the criminal. Whatever is and happens, must be and happen. Nothing could possibly be otherwise. The murderer must commit his crime, the police must catch him, the jury must convict, the judge must condemn to death, the executioner must hang, Mr. Blatchford must take society to task and scold it and denounce its institutions, and fail to carry conviction; he must contradict himself and use just the bad arguments he does—and all this must have been predestined from all eternity!

It is astonishing that so good a reasoner as Mr. Blatchford should not have perceived the incongruity; but like most Determinists he has tacitly assumed freedom enough to grease the wheels of justice and to retain a meaning in responsibility.

Hence it is by no momentary lapse that he falls into an affirmation of Free Will. He is forced repeatedly to use arguments which are nonsense unless Freedom is real, because his whole case requires him to use them.

He could not be a social reformer without them. How else could he argue that the social order can and should be changed, or assert that disease may be prevented (p. 9), or say that we *ought* not to blame or punish (pp. 19, 99, etc.), or declare (p. 236) "man cannot be blamed : society cannot be blamed. But both can be *altered* : by environment," or bring forward any measures for the altering and improvement of the social order? For all these things imply that at least two courses of events are possible—*possible really* and not merely to our ignorance—and that it depends on human choice and action which of them is to be realized. But in a fully determined world whence are they to come? It is vain to suggest that somewhere or other there may be "a man with reason and knowledge and inclination for the task of improving society or the individual by *teaching* one or both."

If such a being exists, he will be one of the determined forces of the universe, and as powerless as any of the rest to alter its predestined course. The universe is destined to be saved or to be damned—we do not know which. And if we did know, it would not matter, seeing that we could not act otherwise than we do. That, inexorably, is the implication of Determinism. If we wish, then, to think the world as alterable for the better, as capable of varying its course, we must introduce some free agency into it to infuse some indetermination into it. A very little will suffice. A very little freedom will falsify the doctrine that everything is foredoomed in one single and inevitable way, and that nothing can change its character. Once there are real alternatives, and real choices, and real freedom in the world, man can master his fate and remould himself.

This is the ennobling faith which every reformer must hold; but it is *not* Determinism. It is utterly incompatible with Determinism of any sort or kind; and if Mr. Blatchford wishes to be consistent, he must choose between it and Determinism. His choice will be a free and most momentous one, but this need not prevent him from weighing the alternatives which are put before him.

If he chooses Determinism, he renounces the attempt to 'alter' society and to guide its fated course. But he may think that he has saved himself and the world from the taint of irrationality which the belief in Freedom would set upon it. But this surely would be a delusion. If it is impossible and irrational to choose, then his very choice of Determinism commits him to at least one irrational act of choice. If he replies that this seeming 'choice' too was determined, and that he could not have chosen otherwise, then the belief that he did really choose at least was an illusion.

Moreover, he will find that although he, by some fortunate necessity, was impelled to think (what he believes to be) the truth, others are by that same necessity constrained to remain deluded and to believe in a freedom which is irrational and impossible. Thus, one way the world has of exhibiting its rationality to a Determinist is to engender necessary errors and delusions!

Again, in spite of his enlightenment, he will find it just as impossible as heretofore to avoid relapsing into forms of speech and modes of thought which have meaning only if the freedom they imply is *not* an illusion. To be consistent, Determinism should erase from language all such terms as 'can,' 'may,' 'ought,' 'should,' 'need not,' 'if,' 'either . . . or,' 'perhaps.' Nor is this a mere question of words; when we use them, we really mean them and really imagine, however mistakenly, that we are speaking of real possibilities and alternatives. But this is all wrong, if Determinism is right. We should cleanse our minds of the attitudes of thought which correspond to all this Libertarian language. Doubts, hypotheses, possibilities, choices and alternatives should be as impossible in thought as they are in reality. If, however, as is probable, Mr. Blatchford also should despair of clearing his mind of these delusions, must he not resign himself to regard a universe which *of necessity* engenders and harbours them as truly expressive of the nature of things? But why in this case should a universe which fosters such illusions strike him as particularly hopeful or rational?

If on the other hand he chooses to believe in Freedom and prefers a world in which there can be real alternatives, he will choose a world which can (perhaps) be altered and improved. In such a world, of course, the desire for reform can be rational, and the ordinary assumptions of his words and thoughts and acts will not be stultified.

But he will not, even so, escape from the charge of irrationality. For the first move of the Determinist will be to bring this indictment against the 'free' universe. Such a universe cannot, he contends, be fully determined; and if there is to be detected anywhere within it the slightest trace of indetermination, its rationality is compromised beyond redemption. If, he declares, there is anything anywhere of which the behaviour is undetermined, to however small an extent, the rational order of the world is irretrievably ruined. Everything must be absolutely fixed; or else everything must get so loose as to dissolve itself in chaos. The menace is so terrible, the danger is so imminent, that it would seem to need the recklessness of a sceptic to reply that since the irrationality of the universe was manifest in either case, he at least considered himself free to choose whichever form thereof best pleased him; while it would require an unusual amount of philosophic courage to resist intimidaation and to dare to question the conclusiveness of the deterministic plea.

Here then we come to the great antithesis of Freedom and Determinism, which may well claim to be the 'blue-ribbon' problem of philosophy. Its claim to this proud position rests in the first place on the fact that it is one of the few philosophic problems which are capable of interesting the ordinary man. Every one is capable of feeling its central difficulty, the conflict and compulsion of motives and the apparently 'free' decision of the 'will.' Every one also can perplex himself with the apparently unanswerable arguments for Determinism. And so, secondly, the problem seems a typical example of the inherent debility of human reason, which here is driven to assert the impossibility of what seems plain fact, and involves itself in irrationality, whichever of the alternatives it chooses.

This, however, is by no means wholly displeasing to the ordinary man, who readily reconciles himself to a situation which puzzles the professors of philosophy. He can the better enjoy this speculative deadlock, that it causes hardly any practical inconvenience. For in practice we all agree to use language which (as we saw) implies the reality of possibilities, alternatives and free choices. The Determinist no doubt uses (or should use) all this phraseology with a mental reservation. He believes it to be an illusory consequence of our mortal ignorance, and consoles himself with the thought that if he knew everything, all this evidence of Freedom would disappear. But this pious hope cannot be said to make any practical difference. As an agent he must, in the actual state of his knowledge, behave *as if* there were real freedom in the world.

Hence it has been, very plausibly, contended that the whole question is devoid of practical importance. If, whatever the speculative position we may prefer, whether we are Libertarians, Determinists or Sceptics, we are all bound in our action to assume that some acts are free and some alternatives real, while others are determined and calculable, what need is there to solve the theoretic problem? Has it not practically solved itself? What difference does it make which theory is true, if they all lead to the same behaviour? Nay, upon the latest and most approved principles of 'pragmatic' logic, must we not hold that theories which lead to the same results in practice are not really different at all, but only verbally various ways of saying the same thing?

This attractive way, however, of cutting the Gordian knot appears to rest upon a misconception. The believer in Freedom at least cannot admit that his belief makes no difference to his acts, nor believe that the Determinist's belief has no influence on his behaviour. He must point out that if it is true that the alternative theories make no practical difference the reason is that one of them, viz. the Determinist, cannot be acted on, and that therefore the pragmatic test cannot be applied to it. If and so long as the Determinist acts *as if* he were free and able to choose between alternative possibilities, the theory his acts imply cannot be discriminated by its results from that implied in the Libertarian's acts. But so soon as the Determinist *feels* that he has no choice, and acts on his belief, the Libertarian holds it *will* make a distinct difference in his action. He will subject himself to all the paralysing influences of Fatalism. He will abandon the attempt to control his impulses. He will relax his efforts to overcome the 'natural' tendencies of his character, and to resist the pressure of his environment. And if one considers what the natural tendencies of the average man at present are, it does not seem probable that the effect of such self-indulgence will in the main be good and elevating or even conducive to the survival of Determinists. Thus the preaching of Determinism may do much harm, by relaxing the fibres of men's moral nature and by tempting them to let themselves drift upon a current of lazy habit, which they take to be the irresistible stream of Fate. No doubt in practice a consistent Determinist will hardly be found. But this is not to show that Determinism is harmless, nor is it an argument in its favour: and even temporary fits of 'slackness' may be morally disastrous.

Of course no harm will come of a merely theoretic Determinism. To be refuted by its results a theory must be acted on. Until it is acted on, its truth remains in suspense, as a claim which has not been tested, or as a plaything of idle speculation. And to show that it *cannot be acted on* is to show, not that Determinism is harmless, but that it is meaningless.

It would be too much, however, to expect Determinists to assent to this conclusion. For it follows logically from *their* assumption that no moral revolution will result from the adoption of Determinism, because no man is free to adopt it, or not, as he pleases. Whatever view any one adopts, he was fated to adopt. Whatever the moral degeneration or dissolution the future may have in store for us, it was preformed and predestined by the immutable order of the universe. Hence it must seem idle to a Determinist to deprecate or to deplore what no skill or thought could have averted. It is silly to resent the inevitable, and this does not become less silly if we perceive also that our very resentment was inevitable too.

We come, therefore, finally upon one of the most remarkable peculiarities of the 'Free-Will' controversy, namely the fact that an argument which is valid and cogent for those who have adopted one set of assumptions has no cogency at all for those who have adopted the other. Superficially this seems a paradox which lends itself to sceptical conclusions: and these have accordingly been drawn by most of the philosophers who observed this singularity. But this is really a mistake: the true significance of the fact is quite different. In the end it turns out to be a legitimate consequence of the reality of choices. It merely means that, when we have chosen, we can abide (up to a certain point) by the consequences of our choice, and keep at bay the interpretations which would stultify it. Hence we must expect to find that in a sense a consistent Determinism cannot strictly be refuted, refuted that is by the purely, or merely, intellectual considerations which it would itself accept as a conclusive refutation. But we shall also find that the demand for such refutation is itself an error, and that the possibility of a wilful (and not necessitated) Determinism is quite consistent with the reality of our Freedom. We shall also strive to vindicate the plain man's faith in Freedom by explaining what is the real nature of our Freedom, and by showing how it may be conceived as a rational doctrine.

II

We have shown so far not only that it is grossly inconsistent in a Determinist to propose to reform the world, but also that he could not act, either rationally or at all, except on the assumption of Freedom. But we made no attempt to explain either the truth contained in Determinism and the reason of its plausibility, or the real nature of Freedom, nor did we try to answer the case against Freedom as it is commonly presented. The whole question, consequently, seems to have been left in a thoroughly inconclusive and unsatisfactory condition.

We may now begin by considering the truth in Determinism. Why is it that we all so frequently assume that the future is fixed, that events can be calculated beforehand, and that predictions can be made which will come true? Why is it that so many philosophers go further still and assume that *all* events are in this way fully determined, and regard the idea that any event should still be indeterminate, uncertain, incalculable or as they technically say 'contingent,' as fatal to science and as the very height of irrationality and absurdity?

The answer to this question will easily be found by any one who has trained himself to note that the 'truths' we assume are always relative to some purpose in which we are interested, and are not asserted aimlessly and at random. Now mankind has always been intensely interested in forecasting the future—for the best and most cogent of reasons. For had we been unable to devise methods of prediction, we should have remained the helpless sports of circumstance. It is very unlikely that we could have survived, and it is certain that we could not have prepared for and controlled the course of experience, even to the extent we now can. Hence foreknowledge of the future is man's capital achievement, an achievement of the greatest practical and vital value. Man is distinctively the animal that 'looks before and after,' that observes the present, and studies the past, in order to control the future. Naturally enough, his intelligence has been adjusted to and moulded upon this vital necessity. And not only his intelligence, but his whole nature. He has grown a strong intellectual and emotional bias towards any idea that helps him to achieve his purpose. He is willing and eager to hail it as 'true.' Hence there has arisen a desire for prediction, a passion for certainty, which in some selected spirits (philosophers to wit) may be over-developed and rise to quite unreasonable and self-defeating heights.

But how was this desire to foretell, and so to control, the future, to find its satisfaction? Well, mankind did not know; but mankind was willing to try. It tried in all sorts of ways, and very queer and superstitious most of them now seem to us. What oracle have human faith and human craving left unconsulted, what mode of divination have they failed to think of, from what mode of propitiation have they shrunk, to what mode of magic have they scrupled to immolate their dearest and their best? A potent array of institutions and observances, a long list of pseudo-sciences, an astounding record of irrational absurdities and atrocities, attest the reality and persistence of the human desire to lift the veil of the future. For this purpose the noblest of the ancients did not disdain, as augurs to watch the flight of birds, as haruspices to inspect the sacrificial entrails; they were proud to keep the Sybil's prophetic books or to trick the fates and to pamper the prescience of the sacred chickens with cunningly diluted gruel. No sooner had man looked at the stars than the thought at once occurred to him that these wonders of the sky must be fraught with significance for his terrestrial fortunes. And so he proceeded to conceive the marvels of their rhythmic motions as instruments of calculation, until the wisest of the ancients did not deem it a waste of time to observe the conjunctions of planets that determined the fates of men, or the portents of flimsy comets that were supposed to take a keen interest in the fortunes of the solar system. Modern astronomy is as much indebted to astrology for its birth as to the practical necessity of determining the length of the year and so the recurrence of the seasons and the right time for the exercise of agricultural foresight. Most of the ancient modes of divination, such as chiromancy, geomancy, catoptromancy, rhabdomancy, sortilege and incubation, have become merely learned names to most of us. But their equivalents still survive, sustained by their occasional success in satisfying human desires. The law, even now, does not think it derogatory to its majesty to persecute the poor palmists and fortune-tellers who try to make a precarious living out of the curiosity of those who despair of calculating their personal future by more scientific means. And whenever a gathering of undergraduates has inspirited a table to turn, it is always asked to indicate what horse is going to win whatever is the next important race.

But it must not be thought that the history of human credulity is merely a sickening and abject record of human folly, which has no value for Science. For out of all this mass of wild experimenting experience has selected what was workable. By outcasting superstitions Science segregates itself. Magic is the mother of Science, much as Error is of Truth; it is inferior to its offspring, not in its conception or its pedigree, but in its efficiency. Science is a system of magic formulas, which after many trials and with many tribulations man has made. But the formulas (or 'laws') of Science really and habitually work, and so verify themselves and are accepted as true: those of its unsuccessful and discarded rivals are only occasionally supported by a 'coincidence' or by the psychic tendency of many beliefs to verify themselves.

A scientific formula which does not work is impossible by definition. For if a formula fails to work when applied to the phenomena it was devised to control, it is condemned as false, and we seek to supersede it with a better. Nevertheless the fundamental ideas of Science are the same as those of pseudo-science or of magic. They are all ineradicably and intensely human, as befits the descendants of the human passion to control experience. Astrology, for example, rests on the same assumption as the most scientific Determinism, and only carries it one step further. It represents as calculable fact what Science as yet is content to treat as an unattained ideal, and so far from being intrinsically absurd the claim of astrology should be what every man of science must in theory aspire to. For if it is true, as Science assumes, that the universe is a fully determined and connected system, it ought theoretically to be possible to start in it from any changes which occur at any point, and, if we know them well enough to trace out their connexions, to calculate out the determinate alterations they must entail at any other point. Why not, therefore, observe the wanderings of the planets, and predict thereby whether our neighbour's dog is destined to recover from the mange? Nothing can be so lofty as to tear itself away from the causal connexion wherewith Science grasps it, nothing so mean as to escape from its clutches. Scientific 'law' cares for the least as for the greatest.

The conception then of 'law' has proved our magic passport to the order of nature. It has worked so well that many of us have quite forgotten its homely and human origin, and abstracting it from its context, have grown to regard it with superstitious reverence. It is often looked upon as a magical and *a priori* thing, which has no origin in the experience it controls and no dependence on the nature which 'obeys' it. We even hope by thus exalting it to extract from it a guarantee that the course of nature, which has heretofore behaved conformably with our idea of 'law,' will for ever continue to show itself thus amenable to our needs. But we may postulate and proclaim *a priori* necessities of thought as much as ever we please; we cannot prove that it is an *a priori* necessity of thought that the course of nature should for ever conform to our *a priori* necessities of thought. And even if it were, it would not set at rest the question as to what can guarantee a complete harmony between our thought and things.

But of all such *a priori* thinking our wishes are the

fathers. The truth is much simpler and more prosaic. We have found that by assuming all events to be determined by 'laws' which (by a process of continuous approximation) we can 'discover' and formulate, we can reduce chaos to cosmos, and control our lives. But *Law means Determinism*. It means that there are series of events such that, once we know their law, we can start from A and predict B, and then C, and then D, and so on for ever, in an absolutely certain sequence. If we choose to believe that anything was able and likely to follow upon anything else, the conception of law would be abrogated. But if we choose to believe in law, we believe that the course of events is in principle calculable and predictable. And if we 'discover' enough 'laws,' *i.e.* hit upon formulas which work, we can, more or less approximately, forecast what is going to happen and take measures accordingly.

This then is the true reason why we all have a bias towards Determinism, in so far as we sanction and pursue the aim of Science. We will to believe in law, and law involves determination, so that Determinism seems to become the price of prediction. So whenever we want to forecast the future, we turn Determinists, and calculate as though the future were already determined. We must do this, or give up the attempt at prediction. In so far as a thing is 'free' to act thus or otherwise, its action is unpredictable. This then is the meaning of calling Determinism the universal postulate of Science as such.

But are the postulates of Science true? Of this nothing can assure us but experience, and experience pursued to the point at which nothing new can happen any longer. In our experience this is not (yet?) true. Novelties are still intruding on us daily. And so in point of fact our scientific guesses are often wrong in detail, and deficient in exactitude. In all the sciences 'laws of nature' are being rejected, re-enacted, revised and re-modelled daily. They are 'true' only in so far as they work, and are able to anticipate results which experience confirms.   There is no more mystical nor higher test of their truth.

Nor does the general postulate that there are specific laws really rest upon any other ground. It too is held to be true, because it works. And no cunning of philosophic system-building can really safeguard it any other or any *a priori* truth. Our postulate might cease to work at any point or time. However dear and indispensable it had been to us, however deeply we had grafted it upon the roots of our being, however strenuously we might protest against a failure that would put us to intellectual confusion, we should have to submit to the rulings of experience and to recognize the *de facto* limitations of our principle. In point of fact our intellectual *débâcle* would not be quite so terrible as is often represented. If our postulate ceased to be usefully applicable to our experience, we should say that it had only seemed to be true, but was not, and search for some more tenable assumption. Or again it might work for some things and not for others. There is nothing *inconceivable* in a universe only partly 'subject to law.' It would be *inconvenient*, no doubt, especially if we were uncertain about the limits of its law-abidingness, and we should therefore admit the existence of this defect only in the last extremity. Some heroic souls might even persist to the last in their faith that the whole *must* be subject to law, though no mortal vision could ever detect its laws. But the majority of men would judge it better to get half a loaf than no bread, and would content themselves with believing the world as calculable as they could practically make it, and would not declare the world irrational and Science vain, merely because they could not calculate everything.

If then the world, or any part of it, happened to be 'free' and therefore incalculable, we should so far find it inconvenient. But the inconvenience need not be considerable, if in point of fact the sphere of Freedom is restricted and its amount is not great. Hence the inconvenience of abandoning a complete Determinism may easily be less than that of believing our direct experience of Freedom, our immediate consciousness of the reality of choices, to be quite illusory. For, as we saw in the first part, Determinism also, by implying this consequence, administers a severe shock to our faith in the rationality of existence.

In point of fact and as things stand, the inconvenience of the belief in Freedom is wholly sentimental from the standpoint of the Determinist, and wholly imaginary from that of the Libertarian. For all practical purposes the belief in Freedom does not cause the slightest inconvenience. For owing to the limitations of our actual knowledge, there is always a great multitude of events which we consider to be theoretically calculable, but either cannot calculate at all in practice, or can calculate only so roughly as to leave extensive scope for what might be 'free' variations. If, therefore, some of these events were really incalculable, it would make no practical, but only a sentimental, difference to us. For, alike whether we thought them true or not, we should of course continue to treat as calculable all of them we wanted to calculate, and so should score as many successes as heretofore.

Secondly, and this is a still more important mitigation of the alleged inconvenience, we often as it is find ourselves in the position of having to deal with what we believe to be fully determined events, but with a knowledge of their nature so imperfect that we cannot but distrust the accuracy of our forecasts. But we do not on this account despair of calculating. For it is often possible, nevertheless, to calculate within what limits the actual result is likely to lie, or again to work out the alternatives which the defects of our knowledge leave open. In both these cases, therefore, all that is affected is, not the deterministic method of calculation, but only the confidence with which we regard its results.

If now we abstain from conceiving Freedom (wrongly) as an agency which is by nature infinite and unlimited, either in its power of breaking down habit and upsetting expectation, or of suggesting alternatives, what reason is there why the admission of a certain flavour of Freedom, of a certain degree of indetermination, should seriously interfere with our actual practices of calculation? Consider *e.g.* the case of human action. There is no practical difference in the way we regard it, despite the tremendous contrast of our theories. As it is, both Determinists and Libertarians are fully aware that they hardly ever know the character and circumstances of their fellow-men well enough to make sure of foreseeing their exact behaviour. Both agree also that it would be preposterous on this account to regard human actions as utterly incalculable. Both parties are agreed that whether there is freedom in human action or not, human action is more or less calculable; both parties hold that it presents to our knowledge a finite number of alternatives and a limited extent of possibilities. And both parties are fully entitled by their theories to come to this practical agreement. Which is of course the reason why both parties can live together sensibly in society.

The Libertarian, however, would be disposed to declare the whole inconvenience an imaginary bugbear of the opposing theory. For he would deny the necessity of conceiving 'free' acts as quite incalculable. He would claim that his theory also was fully competent to satisfy the practical and the scientific demands for a foreseeing of events, even though it was bound to reject the metaphysical theory into which they had been perverted.

For why after all, he might urge, should Freedom be conceived as an infinite and uncontrollable force which is radically disruptive of all rationality and order in the universe? Because certain philosophers desire to conceive it so for controversial purposes? Because Determinists cannot bear to be deprived of a bogey which forms their sole argument against Freedom? Why should what he believes to be the truth be sacrificed to the interests of a philosophic party? How thoroughly characteristic of a certain type of philosopher! Your philosopher is a most exacting creature. If you give him an inch, he at once

takes an ell, and claims the all. He must have all or
nothing. He will not compromise with the clearest facts.
If the facts confute his favourite theory, he denounces the
'scepticism' of their upholders. So here. A world that
is not absolutely determined, he is determined to treat
as a chaos. Nothing like our actual world can satisfy
any of his demands. For he is never satisfied to use a
principle just for what it is worth and in cases where
experience shows it to be applicable. He is always
wanting to make it absolute, and to apply it to the
universe without reservation and discretion, dogmatically
and *a priori*. And it is little enough he knows about
the universe! His 'metaphysical' knowledge is a gigantic
bluff. For it is one of his oddities that the less he knows,
the more confident he grows. If, for example, there is
the least ground in his experience for holding that the
world is (in some *one*) sense one, his imagination will
forthwith proclaim it as a universal and necessary truth
that the universe is one also in innumerable other senses
and is under an *a priori* pledge to behave itself according
to his desires and expectations also in a multitude of
other respects, which he has not inquired into and about
which he knows nothing! Those, of course, who love
the philosophic type of mind will understand engaging
little idiosyncrasies such as these, and make allowance
for them. But to the plain man's common sense they
must often prove perplexing and alarming.

In this case, moreover, the metaphysician's 'logical'
temper works very unjustly. He refuses to regard the
forecasting of human action as a matter of practical convenience and its principle as a matter of scientific method.
He insists on taking it as something absolute and metaphysical, as an indefeasible revelation of the ultimate
nature of things. So he is not only driven to misconceive
its meaning and to exaggerate its scope, but is blinded
to obvious facts which every one else has no difficulty in
seeing, and beguiled into a most outrageous and indefensible travesty of the indeterminist position.

During the last thirty years quite a number of dis-

X

tinguished British philosophers have set out to discuss the question of Freedom. Most of them have confused the issue by playing upon the different senses of the word. Not a few of them have attempted to hoodwink the public by assurances that 'self-determination' was the only kind of Freedom thinkable or ethically needed. But every one of them has propounded the same caricature of the freedom of indetermination. And not one of them has made the slightest attempt to show that the doctrine they denounced was actually held by any Libertarian, or formed a logical deduction from which no Libertarian could escape.[1]

Now the caricature of Freedom which is in vogue for controversial purposes is, briefly, this: If you allege that there can be anything, however slightly, undetermined about any action, you allege the reality of motiveless choice. But this, so far from safeguarding responsibility, really renders responsibility impossible. For you allege that there is nothing in the agent's character or circumstances to determine his act in one way or the other. But if any choice is motiveless, all choice is motiveless. Any one, therefore, may do anything. The Pope is as likely to advocate atheism in his next Encyclical and to make a Cardinal of Mr. Blatchford as to condemn 'modernism' and the writings of M. Loisy; the Tsar is as likely to declare for the Social Revolution as for further repression, and to become a Jew as to rebuild his navy. Thus all reasonable expectation is defeated; all continuity of character is destroyed, and with it all responsibility, which rests on the connexion between action and character. In short the inevitable conclusion is that a world, into which the least taint of Freedom enters, lapses into chaos.

Now though common sense might find it pretty hard to dissect this sort of argument and to refute its premises, it has little hesitation in declaring that its conclusions are

---

[1] Henry Sidgwick forms an honourable exception to whom these remarks do not apply. The discussion in his *Methods of Ethics* is scrupulously fair, and excellent so far as it goes.

absurd. Nobody has ever believed that in declaring in favour of 'free-will' he was committing himself to any such consequences. Nobody, therefore, could possibly be a Libertarian, if this were what Libertarianism meant. Probably, therefore, the Determinists have merely caricatured their opponents' position.

Investigation speedily raises this probability to a certainty. The grotesque cockshy which serves as the type of Libertarianism for the purpose of deterministic refutations is an absurd exaggeration of certain of its implications. But it is probably prompted, not so much by conscious unfairness as by an unconscious bias. It is derived ultimately from an unwillingness to take from experience our notions, either of the nature or of the range, of our Freedom. For if philosophers had only been willing to admit that alike what our freedom was, how much of it we had, how powerful it was, how far it baffled expectation, how far it loosened the joints of the universe, were all questions to be decided by empirical observation, they could hardly have helped seeing that their proof of the impossibility of Freedom was fallacious, and that Freedom, so far from being a puzzle leading to terrible consequences, was involved in every unbiassed description of the act of choice.

The central fallacy in the Determinist argument lies in the assumption that if a choice is real, it is necessarily motiveless. This assumption, however, rests on a confusion between three distinct conceptions—choice, absence of motive, and indetermination. Choice (in the Libertarian sense) implies indetermination, but *not* absence of motive. A choice is necessarily between alternatives, but these would not be such if they did not appeal to the chooser and influence his character. It is a choice, therefore, between alternative *goods*, and these goods are motives to action which cannot all be realized together. Choice, therefore, implies motives, but if it is a real choice, it is really 'free' to choose between them. Motiveless choice, therefore, is an implicit contradiction. Now all the terrible consequences of Libertarianism as depicted by the

Determinist, follow not from the choice, but from its assumed lack of motive. They are repudiated, therefore, in repudiating the latter.

Again, it is an error to conceive indetermination as absence of motive. Lack of decision is not the same as lack of motive. What is indeterminate in the act contemplated as 'free,' is precisely what is determined by the choice between the motives. The act, therefore, is indeterminate until we choose, and determine it. The indetermination is real, but it is determinable, and so terminable.

Now that such is the nature of the indetermination in acts of 'free' choice is precisely what introspection reveals. We never feel that we have to choose out of an infinite expanse of possibilities. The alternatives, which appeal to us and are real for us, are never numerous. Our character, our circumstances, our history, our habits, our ideals and notions of what is 'good,' do by far the greater part of the selection and immensely narrow down the field of abstract possibility. This is a simple fact of direct observation. But it is no less obvious that though all these forces determine by far the greater part, say nine-tenths, of our conduct, and form a fairly rigid framework which our 'freedom' presupposes and with which, and upon which, it operates, yet they nevertheless do *not* determine everything, but allow scope for apparently 'free' choices, which are accompanied by a heightened and peculiar sense of power and responsibility. Why, then, should we refuse to acknowledge this fact? Why should we not admit it as evidence that the choices, which seem real and feel real, are real?

Certainly the 'convenience' of conceiving events as determined affords no cogent reason for blinding ourselves to the facts. We have seen that there are limits to the convenience of methodological fictions. Nor does the difficulty lie in the conception of our nature which we have to entertain, if we would think it capable of Freedom.

For we have merely to think our nature as partly

plastic, and such that all its reactions have not yet grown rigid. We know that habits grow upon us, and that when they are firmly fixed, they irresistibly control our conduct. But while they are growing, may there not be a stage in which our response is still variable and really indeterminate, however determinate it may grow afterwards? And why regard this as 'irrational'? Is it not the essential function of 'reason' to keep habits plastic in their responses to the requirements of life? Do we not know that, if anything can raise us out of the rut of hampering habit, it is 'reason'? Is not 'reason' continually breaking up the habits which have grown too rigid for our good, restoring the plasticity of youth, and clearing the ground for fresh growth. This, if we look not to the abstract word, but to what it really does, is the true meaning of 'reason.'

This, moreover, is why the experience of Freedom is so closely bound up with the moral struggle. For at first the old habits and desires, which have become 'bad,' will frequently prevail over 'reason'; in the end they will be transformed into new habits which are 'good.' But while the process lasts, there will be a plastic stage in which action will be variable and indeterminate.

Clearly, therefore, Freedom is a concomitant of mental and moral growth, a consequence of an incomplete and therefore plastic nature. The alternatives, moreover, between which we 'freely' choose, will be the outcome of that nature. Both will always spring from that nature, and remain connected with it by psychological lines of descent which our logic can retrace. Our choices, therefore, will be real for our natures under our circumstances. Whichever alternative our act selects, will seem continuous with what we were and did before. It will not appear upon the scene as an unforeseen irruption from nowhere. It will seem to us a probable and reasonable thing to have done. It will astonish no one who knows, or thinks he knows, us. But we should not have judged otherwise the alternative which was rejected. Had it been enacted, our friends would still have said they quite expected it.

Before the event, therefore, either event seems equally probable. After the event, both still seem intelligible, though (according to the Determinist) only that which actually occurred was ever possible. But is it not absurd to say of such a doctrine that it destroys the continuity of character and the rationality of the universe? Has it not rather succeeded in satisfying the demand for a calculable order of events by representing Freedom as a choice between alternatives *all* of which are calculable, and in a manner rational?

It would seem, therefore, that the conception of Freedom, just as the plain man experiences and understands it, is quite rational and philosophic, and that it can be 'refuted' only by being travestied. But can we assume the offensive in our turn and refute Determinism?

The difficulty of this undertaking is due to a very simple cause. We have seen that the truth underlying metaphysical Determinism is its usefulness when conceived as a method of Science. It follows from this use that every fact presented by every science is capable of being conceived deterministically. Consequently we never seem to get at any facts which can be used against the deterministic view. Even our 'freely chosen' alternative may be represented as the only one which could have been chosen. Hence a *direct* disproof of Determinism seems impossible.

Our attack, therefore, must be more subtly planned. We may ask why does any one choose to be a Determinist? Now any one regarding Determinism merely as a postulate of Science has, of course, a cogent answer. If we desire to know and to predict and to prepare, we have no other choice. We must adopt the assumption which enables us to attain our end. So far from questioning this assumption the Libertarian must try to show that his own position is not incompatible with it.

He may, however, draw attention to the voluntary character of this fundamental postulate. Apparently, he may infer, the power of choice and the desire to attain ends are superior even to this great principle. For they select and constitute it. We can choose to adopt the

Determinist principle. We do choose to adopt it, because we prefer it to its alternative and it yields us what we want, viz. the power to control events. Now perhaps it may be denied that this refutes Determinism, because even though our choice seems free, it may really be determined. But still the fact shows that our human contribution to our conception of reality cannot be quite a negligible quantity and not worth mentioning. Is it not strange that the helpless victims of Fate should play such a leading part in the making of that Fate?

A still more curious fact for Determinism to consider is that though the whole world may be thought of as determined, it is just as easy and just as reasonable to think of it as pervaded by a streak of Freedom. The Libertarian view, as we have described it, is just as possible and as rational as the Determinist; *i.e.* it is just as capable of interpreting the facts. If one or the other is to be preferred, it must be by an act of choice. But this choice cannot be determined by logical considerations. For as a purely logical theory either will work. Our choice, therefore, must be a logically undetermined, *i.e.* a *free*, one between theories whose intellectual appeal seems equal, because both yield consistent interpretations which cover the whole field of nature.

Even, therefore, if a Determinist should never choose again, must he not exercise his freedom *at least once* in adopting his theory? Must he not prove its truth and make the interpretation which supplies his evidence, by a fiat of his will? But is not a Determinism which depends for its establishment on a free choice a self-contradiction of Determinism? We can be Determinists only because we are determined to deny our freedom. And *because we are free*, we are free to do even this!

In any case is it not a humiliation for Determinism to have to recognize a free choice underlying its whole fabric? For it has defined such choices as irrational. To a Libertarian on the other hand the situation seems quite reasonable. He has not defined choice as irrational as such, and has no prejudice against a 'free' one.

Nothing could be more natural to him than that the affirmation and the denial of Freedom should both be free choices. As William James aptly says, "Freedom ought to be freely espoused by men who can equally well turn their backs upon it."

Nor is the philosophic situation we have reached a paradox. It is quite in accord with the results of examining other fundamental questions. It is becoming clearer and clearer that ultimately our convictions everywhere rest upon acts of faith and of choice, which make demands upon the moral virtue of courage, and must precede what is called the 'proof' of their truth. The fact that we must believe that we are free to some extent and that our consciousness of choice is not delusive, and so must choose Freedom rather than Necessity, does not stand alone. We must, for example, have faith also and must choose to believe that the world is orderly rather than chaotic, in order to acquire the notion of the uniformity of nature; *i.e.* we must choose Science rather than impotence. We must choose to believe that our experience is real and no dream, and that its incidents are not the figments of a nightmare; *i.e.* we must choose a society rather than a solipsism. And lastly, we must choose to believe that the struggle of life is worth living and worth trying, and not worthless; *i.e.* we must choose a sort of optimism and not a pessimism.

In none of these cases, perhaps, can our position be established coercively against the contrary bias. For in all of them we have to make our venture and to choose our side, *before* we get the evidence which verifies and confirms our choice.

But what finer proof could there be of the fact that the functions of our intellect are intimately bound up with those of our will and our moral qualities, and that our 'reason' is designed to co-operate with our feelings and our instincts, and not to hold stupidly aloof and to criticize without understanding the dumb faiths of the living creeds which guide man's responses to the requirements of life?

XVII

THE DESIRE FOR IMMORTALITY[1]

ARGUMENT

Is man really distinguished above other animals by his preoccupation with death? If he is, he will show a concern about his future life of which there are few traces. Naturally, because hating to think of death, we avoid thinking of a future life. The practical inconvenience of the thought, and its relegation to the realm of 'faith.' Is Spiritism an exception? Yes, but that is why it fails to become popular. Other religious doctrines held in a peculiar manner, and called up or dismissed according to the sentiment of the moment. Why, then, has an entirely contrary impression prevailed? (1) the indifference of the mass *versus* the vocal few; (2) the memory of bygone interest. The possibility of testing the issue and discovering the facts by the *questionnaire* of the American Branch of the Psychical Research Society. Social taboos as bars to inquiry. The world not unknowable. The old fear of knowledge. Magic and Science. The need of social support in discovery.

IT is a venerable commonplace that among the melancholy prerogatives which distinguish man from the other

[1] This essay appeared in the *Fortnightly Review* for September 1901. It was intended to draw attention to the inquiry mentioned on pp. 328-330. Some 3000 answers were obtained, and, so far as they bear on the question which directly concerns the *Society for Psychical Research*, viz. to what extent is there a desire to know?—they have been discussed by me in a report in Part 49 of the *Proceedings* of the S.P.R. The whole material, however, is so extensive and psychologically so valuable as to need fuller treatment—when some one finds time to do it.

I may here avail myself of the occasion of expressing my conviction that there exist a number of questions concerning the psychological foundations of ethics, aesthetics, and logic which urgently need study by statistical methods. We have always to find out how men actually do feel and think before we can safely generalize or systematize as to what they *ought* to feel and think. Now at present the actual facts are very imperfectly known, even in the case which has received most attention,—that of the religious consciousness. As a rule writers have been content to go for their facts to their own preconceptions or to the analysis of their own individual consciousness. At most, they have noted, in a cursory and reluctant way, the more obvious varieties of sentiment whose existence was forced upon them by their notoriety. But there is no guarantee that all the relevant types of sentiment are even known to science; we have certainly no data for gauging their relative frequency. A question like this, *e.g.*

animals and bestow a deeper significance on human life is the fact that man alone is aware of the doom that terminates his earthly existence, and on this account lives a more spiritual life, in the ineffable consciousness of the 'sword of Damokles' which overshadows him and weights his lightest action with gigantic import. Nay, more; stimulated by the ineluctable necessity of facing death, and of living so as to face it with fortitude, man has not abandoned himself to nerveless inaction, to pusillanimous despair; he has conceived the thought, he has cherished the hope, he has embraced the belief, of a life beyond the grave, and opened his soul to the religions which baulk the king of terrors of his victims and defraud him of his victory. Thus, the fear of death has been redeemed and ennobled by the consoling belief in immortality, a belief from which none are base enough to withhold their moral homage, even though the debility of mortal knowledge may debar a few from a full acceptance of its promise. Such are the themes of endless dithyrambs, of inexhaustible eloquence on the part of our poets and preachers, such the constituents of a volume of uncontested literary tradition which the hardiest sceptic could scarcely dare to question.

And yet to one regarding human action in the merely inquisitive temper of psychologic science this mass of literary conventions is by no means above suspicion. If we look closely, is it so certain that it fully represents

---

What percentage of human beings use respectively aesthetical, emotional, prudential, and strictly ethical modes of valuation in their judgments concerning the actions commonly classed as 'moral'?—is at present simply unanswerable. But it *ought* to be capable of being answered, if not with mathematical exactness, yet with practically sufficient accuracy. And until we can answer it ethics will never be a science, and moralists will continue to beat the air and to tilt at windmills. I should propose, therefore, as a counsel of perfection, to be adopted on that happy day (now, I trust, approaching) when philosophers will no longer content themselves with idle speculation, but will speculate only to interpret and investigate the facts which form the final test of speculation, that societies be formed for the study of the psychological facts of actual human sentiment in these regions. Such societies would have to formulate their questions in a simple, interesting, and concrete way, to circulate them and to tabulate the answers. Such methods would, I believe, prove more fruitful than the laborious mimicry of physiology which at present passes for experimental psychology, though they need not conflict with the latter, and indeed might incidentally suggest to it some experiments really worth making.

the actual sentiments and accords with the *actions* of men? Is the assumption either of a universal consciousness of death or of a universal desire for immortality really so irrefragable? Certainly the evidence in its favour is far scantier and more ambiguous than we were inclined to suppose, and there are ugly facts which seem to put a different complexion on the matter. The ordinary conduct of men affords but little support for the notion that their life is a constant meditation upon death, tempered by the joyful anticipation of immortality. A visitor from Mars, dispassionately inquiring into human conduct and motive, might find it hard to detect more foreknowledge of death in men than in animals. From the palace to the hovel, from the laboratory to the oratory, he would find men everywhere pursuing ends of the earth, earthly, living for the present, or if circumstances forced them to take thought for the morrow, concerning themselves only with their immediate future in this world; while of the 'other-worldliness,' so often preached and preached against in the literature, he would hardly find a trace. To find it a dominating, or even an important, influence in human psychology he would have to seek it, not in the churches or the universities, and still less amid the bustle of active life, but in the asylums in which are secluded the unhappy victims of religious mania or melancholy, in whom an insane logic has overpowered the healthy indifference to death and its consequences, which characterizes the make-up of the normal mind. And this impression would be enhanced rather than erased if our Martian critic at last succeeded in observing the tremendous shock which the ordinary man receives when he for the first time truly realizes that *his* days are numbered. For such effects would seem to testify to the success with which the thought of death has until then been kept out of consciousness.

Of course the fact that men habitually live in the present, hating to think of the future, and detesting anything that reminds them of death, has not, in another connexion, escaped the sagacity of moralists and preachers. Many of their happiest efforts are concerned with castigating this particular form of human weakness and exhibiting its insensate folly. And in so doing our teachers have been no doubt abundantly justified. Only it appears to have escaped their notice that this count of their indictment against human nature accords none too well with their doctrine that death and immortality are absorbing objects of meditation. If it be true that we are culpably careless of the future, recklessly bent on suppressing all thought of death, it can hardly be that we live oppressed by the shadow of death, and consumed with desire for the consolations of a future life.

For if there is something wrong about the tradition as to the psychological importance of the thought of death, a similar error will probably be found to pervade also the traditional estimate of the importance of immortality. Unless men think constantly of death, they have no occasion to think of a future life. And as a matter of fact there seems to be the same dearth of tangible and indisputable evidence to attest the existence of a widespread preoccupation with the possibility of a future life.

Subjects which arouse wide and deep human interest will not down : from their deep-seated springs they bubble up through the crust of convention and inundate the arid surface of human life. They are constantly talked about, they fill the columns of the newspapers, they demand and obtain State support, they are lectured upon at the universities, they are cultivated by societies of enthusiasts, they are fostered by abundant supplies of the sinews of war. But of any symptom of the kind, to bear out the doctrine that men are keenly desirous of establishing their immortality, or even interested in the question at all, our Martian philosopher would detect little or nothing. It is a subject hardly ever mentioned in conversation, and indeed one which it would be bad form to allude to seriously. Ghost stories, usually of a palpably absurd and apocryphal kind, find admission into the newspapers only towards the end of the silly season, when the giant gooseberry has ceased to grow and the sea-serpent to agitate its cumbrous coils. No State has ever appointed a Royal Commission to inquire into the alarming allegation that its citizens are immortal, and cannot, if the worst comes to the worst, be finally disposed of by the hangman; no Legislature has ever contained a member 'faddy' enough to hold that the decision of this question had an important bearing on the greatest happiness of the greatest number, and to demand from the supreme official of a State Church a report on the prospective condition of the masses in the future life, and suggestions aiming at its amelioration. At no university are there any researches conducted with a view to a scientific solution of the problem; at most of the seats of learning, indeed, the attempt to do so would, in spite of our boasted freedom of research, be extremely hazardous, while a scientist who came forward with evidence tending to discredit and disprove the detested doctrine would be received with impunity and applause.

But, it will be objected, are you not overlooking the churches, and are they not conspicuous enough in advocating 'the hope of immortality' to the very verge of nausea? Precisely so, I would reply, the churches have their own peculiar methods of handling the subject, and men have their own peculiar methods of treating matters of religious faith. That is why the religious dogma of immortality cannot without reserve be adduced as evidence of a spontaneous human interest in the alleged fact. What the dogma means and what it proves may be considered later; at present it need only be urged that to be interested in immortality as a matter of religious faith, is not necessarily, nor usually, to be interested in it as a matter of scientific fact, or to think about it as a factor in ordinary life.

If you set aside the testimony of the churches, what of the Society for Psychical Research? Is it not a society, and learned, and devoted to the scientific elucidation of this very problem? And does not its existence dispose of the reproach that men do nothing to investigate the supreme mysteries of their existence?

Now it would ill become one who has been a patient

member of this much-enduring society for eighteen years (ever since it flashed across him that the subject had never been investigated) to depreciate its importance and its value; but when this eminently respectable body is expected to atone for the apathy of a whole world, and put forward as conclusive proof of the existence of universal interest in a future life and as the exemplar and high-water mark of scientific research into its possibility, it is hard to refrain from the exclamation *Parturiunt montes!* For what is the Psychical Research Society that for its sake judgment should not be passed upon the world? In the first place its officials would probably protest vehemently, and not without reason, against the assumption that its only, or even its chief, object was to conduct a scientific investigation into the question of a future life. In the second place its membership, after twenty years of strenuous and not unfruitful labour, remains stationary at less than 1500. In the third place its subscription is a guinea, and its gross income seems to be less than £2000. Can any one who reflects what these figures mean cling to the preposterous delusion that men are actively desirous of finding out about their future? In the whole wide world, it seems, there are almost 1500 persons taking an annual guinea's worth of scientific interest in finding out whether they have anything to look forward to after death, and if so what; nearly 1500 persons who are willing to pay for the possibility of this knowledge as much as for a box seat at a theatre! And observe that we are assuming what is very improbable, viz. that all the members are really interested and regular subscribers. Again, the total sum contributed to Psychical Research is well under £2000! It would be hard to mention a human fad or hobby, however trivial and despicable, which cannot make a better showing, to which there are not devoted more money, more time, more zeal, than to what is supposed to be the most important of all questions. If people really thought so, why don't they subscribe to have the matter properly investigated, and why should it be easier to raise the funds for a hospital for leprous cats than for a laboratory in which to test the *prima facie* evidence for human immortality?

Surely the paradox of such a state of affairs would be a sheer impossibility, if there really existed any desire for probing into the mystery of death. Is it not obvious on the face of it then, if there exists a desire for a future life in any sense, it is *not* a desire for scientific knowledge thereof, but a feeling of a very peculiar character which well merits further analysis? It is an attempt at such an analysis that I shall venture to contribute to the study of human psychology.

There is clearly some grave error in the plea embodied in the literary tradition we began by stating. But I am very far from thinking that it is mere cant and sheer humbug, or consciously deceptive. I hope to show rather that it springs in good faith from a natural illusion, and even that, in a manner, while distorting, it reflects a real truth about human feeling. And in explaining away this misleading tradition, I hope at the same time to divest of its paradoxical appearance the suggestion that the vast majority of men either do not desire a future life at all, or only do so in such a curious and limited way that this desire is a negligible quantity in the estimation of their actions.

I shall most fitly begin by suggesting an explanation of the phenomenon that *de facto* so little account is taken of the inevitableness of death. That this must be the case is a result which follows from the general principle that our attitude towards all the aspects of life, must be such as will enable us to act vigorously and efficiently. Applied to the prospect of death, this principle renders it certain that the thought of death cannot be allowed to paralyse action, that means must be discovered for carrying on the business of life in death's despite. Of such means two are most prominent, the suppression of the thought of death by a resolute and systematic determination not to entertain it, and a religious reinterpretation which so transfigures it that it no longer forms an impediment to action. Of these the latter is clearly the more truly logical and satisfactory, but as a matter of fact men mostly prefer (and probably always have preferred) the former alternative, and for ever strive to thrust the unwelcome thought into the background of consciousness. This is why all but the most inevitable mention of it is tabooed in polite society. The method on the whole is a social success, though it probably breaks down at least once in the final crisis of every one's life.

The next step in our investigation will be to consider how our attitude towards death affects the 'desire for a future life.' Now we know that most of the religions have insisted on the fact of immortality and made it man's great consolation in view of the prospect of death. Or, at least, that is what the religious doctrines appear to aim at. But it also seems probable that the great majority of men, instead of thinking of death tempered with immortality, prefer not to think of death at all. Hence it is natural that what is associated with the thought of something so distasteful should itself become distasteful. Need we look further for the reason why the prospect of a future life is, by the generality of men, regarded without enthusiasm and, as far as may be, ignored? Nor is it strictly accurate to say that this attitude has passed quite unobserved in the literature. Plato, who, in spite of efforts of modern commentators to prove the contrary, was of all thinkers perhaps the most seriously interested in the question of immortality and the most resolutely bent on moralizing the doctrine and rendering it effective, exactly hits off the great underlying mass of human feeling in the description he gives of the psychological history of Kephalos, the good old man who has learnt wisdom from the experience of a long life. In the *Republic* (331) he is represented as confessing that, throughout youth and manhood, he paid no heed to the legends about Hades, laughing them to scorn, but now that he had come to realize that his days were drawing to a close, he was *tormented by the fear* lest there should after all be some foundation for the belief in a future life.[1] Very much

---

[1] I find that Mr. Norman Pearson has taken much the same view as I have of man's actual feelings, in the *Nineteenth Century* for August 1883.

the same feeling peeps out through the conventional phraseology in the story of the old gentleman who, being a churchwarden of (in his own opinion) the most immaculate orthodoxy, was asked by Frederic Myers what he supposed would happen to him after death. After much hesitation he reluctantly admitted that he supposed he would enter into eternal bliss, but he *did* wish Mr. Myers would not bring up such depressing topics.

The old gentleman was quite right; a future life, no matter how gorgeously it is depicted, is, and must be, a depressing subject for people of his sort, comfortable, prosperous, and self-satisfied. For they feel that before they can make their triumphal entry into Heaven they have to make their exit from a world in which they are far more thoroughly at home than in any heaven they have ever heard of. Hence the difficulty about the rich man's entering the Kingdom of Heaven is not on the celestial side alone. The rich man, for his part, is not in a hurry to get there. And inasmuch as people of this kind set the tone in society, it is no wonder that scientific investigation of immortality is not encouraged. People do not want to hear about it, and above all they *do not want to know* about it.

For if once they knew, it would be most inconvenient. They would have to act on their knowledge, and that might upset the habits of a lifetime. And the older one gets the less one likes that. What the decision was would not so much matter; whether science decided for immortality or for annihilation, the blissful ignorance that enabled one to ignore the subject in ordinary life would be gone for ever. Hence an uncertainty to which we have grown adapted is instinctively or deliberately preferred to a knowledge that would involve the readjustment of ingrained habits.

It is curious to trace how the various religions, one after the other, effect their submission to this imperious demand of humanity. On the face of it, of course, they start pledged to uphold the entirely contrary thesis that life should include a proper meditation of death and immortality, and seem to constitute an imposing mass of testimony for the contention that the future life is one of our chief interests. But in practice their doctrines are satisfactorily accommodated to the temper of humanity. The religions renounce the attempt of maintaining immortality as a matter of fact, and of adducing tangible evidence in its favour. The doctrine becomes a dogma which has to be accepted by faith, and the obligation of raising it to positive knowledge is implicitly or expressly disavowed.

To illustrate: the Resurrection of Our Lord need not and *ought* not to have become a 'matter of faith' in any other sense than the death of Queen Anne, or any other event in history. The circumstances attending that event were *not originally* matters of faith at all: to the Apostles and other witnesses they were matters of direct experience. There was a time therefore when the exact course of events might have been ascertained, conceivably even to the satisfaction of persons like the critical experts of the Psychical Society. And so *they would never have become matters of faith*, if contemporaries in general had supported a Society for Psychical Research and been keenly observant and vigilantly interested in supernormal happenings: for they would then have done their duty by posterity and compiled records which would have left as little doubt about the facts and involved as little special strain upon our faculty of faith as any other of the events that fall without our direct experience. Thus it is the *negligence* of the past which imposes on us the burden of 'faith.' Now that such a very simple and obvious reflection should have an air of unfamiliarity is surely signal proof of how habitual has become our distortion of the original sense of religious propositions, of how far we have drifted from a treatment of them as plain statements of fact. But for this we should regard the evidential defects of our records as appropriate occasions, not for affirmations of a faith which glories in its heroism, but for expressions of regret similar to those which other gaps in our records of the past evoke.

The only exception to this peculiar way of transmuting the purport of the religious doctrine of immortality seems to be exhibited by Spiritism, which for this very reason is inexpressibly shocking to what one may call the religious sense of decency. For Spiritism is a religion whose sole essential dogma seems to be the assertion of the possibility of (in a manner) unifying this world with the next by communicating with the departed, and whose sole essential rite is the practice of such communication. This is what renders the psychology of Spiritism so interesting and worthy of analysis. In the first place it should be noted that it is not a scientific movement (in spite of a few notable exceptions), but a religion, nay, in all probability, the most ancient of all religions. And yet as a religion Spiritism has been and is a failure, and it may be suggested that the reason is just that *it does treat the future life as a hard* (and somewhat crude) *fact*. This is the source both of its strength and of its weakness. Of its strength, because no other doctrine can minister with such directness to the bereaved human heart, no other consolation can vie with its proffer of visible and tangible tokens that love outlasts death and that the separation death inflicts is not utter and insuperable. And so long as this craving for a sign possesses our souls, Spiritism will continue to win adherents, who embrace it, not in a calm temper of scientific research, but in an emotional convulsion, and, it may be, with a pathetic eagerness to deceive themselves.

But such agonies cannot be permanent. The wave of feeling subsides, and with it passes the attractiveness of Spiritism. Its weakness is that it appeals to emotions which cannot permanently occupy the mind, and it is a weakness far more fatal than the objections currently urged against it, its 'vulgarity,' its frauds, etc. Vulgarity, fraud, nay, sheer absurdity, have never been insuperable obstacles to the success of a religious movement which was in other respects congenial to human nature, and there was no reason *a priori* why Spiritism should have proved less successful than, *e.g.* 'Christian Science.'

A typical illustration of the psychology of Spiritism is

afforded by the history of a friend of mine, who, having lost his wife, long derived much consolation from the belief that he was, by 'automatic writing,' receiving communications from her spirit. His spiritist enthusiasm was, however, seriously checked when he discovered that his 'spirit guide' did not take at all kindly to his growing interest in a young lady 'in the flesh.' He has now married again, and is quite convinced that the automatic messages, which once seemed so expressive of his first wife's personality, were merely the productions of his own 'subconsciousness.' In time he will doubtless chime in with the current doctrine that there is something intrinsically 'degrading' in the notion that our departed dear ones can still communicate with us, continue to be interested in us, and *are watching us all the time.*

It is the notion of this *espionnage* which is intolerable and constitutes the unpardonable offence of Spiritism, in the self-centred eyes of those who have never stopped to reflect what intolerably dreary and irritating functions they would assign to the departed.

It seems pretty clear then that the anomalous case of Spiritism does not upset the results we have already arrived at: it forms a temporary anodyne for overwrought feelings; it cannot give permanent satisfaction, because it arouses the opposition of feelings which in the long run are more powerful. And in any case its interest in the future life is emotional and not scientific.

The other religions are more artful. They advocate the belief in immortality indeed, but with a significant distinction. The future life is a vision that floats before the eye of faith, not a brutal fact to be thrust upon a reluctant attention. The world can stomach a future life so discreetly formulated. Indeed, it rather likes the notion. There are times when we are out of sorts and the spectre of death will not down, and blank annihilation stares us in the face, and then it is a great comfort to turn to some religious tradition of another and a better life. We may even go so far as to consider heavens and hells agreeable topics for an occasional sermon, or like to use them, metaphorically, to strengthen our assertions. But all this in no wise implies that they are taken as facts and must be acted on as such. On the contrary, it is just because the religious doctrines of immortality are *not* taken as facts that they are accepted. For we are accustomed to accept matters of faith only at a large discount from their face value, and their acceptance scarcely affects the value of the hard-money facts of everyday life. Hence the religious doctrines with respect to the future life form a sort of paper currency, inconvertible with fact, which suits people and circulates the better because of its very badness. Their function is to conjure up pleasing and consoling visions whenever we are in a mood for them, to provide a brighter background for life than sheer extinction; but they are never allowed to grow insistent enough seriously to affect action. They are entertained in a complacent spirit of half belief, but no sensible man (and the mass of mankind are always appallingly sensible with respect to whatever does not tempt them!) allows himself to be distracted in his business and upset in his calculations by such shadowy possibilities. Consequently their practical effect is small and utterly out of proportion to their pretensions. The human spirit accepts them indeed in a religious—I had almost said a 'Pickwickian'—sense, and uses whatever elements in them minister to its needs: it rejects the indigestible remainder.

And here one cannot help thinking the churches make a grave mistake. They do not seem to realize that the cultivated minds of the present day have come to include in the indigestible remainder the greater part of what has hitherto been regarded as most distinctive dogma. Fortunately or unfortunately, neither Heaven nor Hell retains its efficacy, even for the purposes above described. Men no longer dream themselves in Heaven nor dread themselves in Hell. This puts the churches into the humiliating position of offering men the reward of a heaven which hardly any one desires, and of threatening them with the penalties of a hell which 'every one believes to be reserved for people a great deal worse than themselves.' Myers's churchwarden, who has already been quoted, may have reached an unsurpassable pinnacle of impeccable orthodoxy, but as an illustration of celestial attraction he is a failure. Similarly, when I expressed these opinions concerning the attractiveness of the notion of Heaven in the *Spectator*,[1] I elicited no contradiction, but only a number of anecdotes bearing out my contention. As for Hell, I never met but one man who professed to believe that *he himself* was destined to eternal damnation, but as he made this avowal with a smiling countenance, and without the least effort to alter his ways, his testimony must be received with caution. In view of this disappointing situation (for surely the fear of Hell, at least, was among the more effective, if also among the cruder, of the argumentative incentives to virtue), it might be well if the churches admitted somewhat greater latitude into their 'myths' of the future life (if 'myths' are all we are to be allowed to have); both the thought of spirit-communication and that of reincarnation appear to possess powers of consolation (in certain moods) that might advantageously be utilized.

It seems probable, therefore, that so far from modifying the impression produced by men's manifest indifference to and dislike for any scientific investigation of the question of their immortality, their attitude towards the religious doctrines only confirms our conclusions. The religious dogmas are accepted because they are what men desire, and so far as they are this: they yield a vague, remote guarantee against annihilation, which may be summoned up or dismissed at pleasure, and does not involve any immediate practical consequences. What is also very convenient, this policy enables men to avoid a scientific decision of the question and to give to every attempt thereat an air of religious impropriety: thus there is avoided all occasion for any practical readjustment, any rearrangement of life, which grows progressively more irksome and difficult as age advances. But inasmuch as influence increases with age, and our 'great authorities'

[1] November 24, 1900.

are all old, it is easily seen that the weight of all religious and scientific authority must be naturally opposed to any divergence from the established tradition. For the only sort of future life which would have any attraction for the old would be one in which they could go on very much as on earth. But I very much doubt whether, even then, they would care to pass through the ordeal of death in order to secure it.

It remains to account for the fact that the literary tradition has taken such a very different view of human psychology. Why has everybody always conspired to write as though the question of immortality were of the most tremendous importance and absorbing interest, if *de facto* the great majority of men have always avoided it as much as ever they could? I believe the answer to be exceedingly simple. The makers of the literary tradition have expressed what seemed true to them at the time of writing, what was true *for them*; and yet the mass of men were always indifferent or hostile.[1] Of course, however, the dumb, recalcitrant masses gave no sign of their dissent from a doctrine they were trying to dismiss from their minds, and hence the writers had it all their own way. In other words, the fallacy in the argument that all men naturally crave for immortality is identical with that in the proof of the efficacy of prayer by means of the votive offerings in the temple of Poseidon. Just as those who prayed and perished were not in a position to make offerings, so those who are not interested in a subject do not write books about it.

[1] I should very much doubt whether the 'ages of faith' were a real exception. No doubt it was, in those days, possible to get great and striking effects out of people by playing on their fears of Hell. But these effects were possible just because people were still more systematically averse from thinking on the subject, and still more contentedly ignorant and uncritical. Hence the crudest and most atrocious threats would be sufficient to drive men frantic *in extremis*, and the ruffianly baron, who had lived more brutally than any beast, would eagerly sign away the whole of the fruits of his lifelong rapine in order 'to make his peace with God.' I believe there is more real religion in the world at present than ever before, *i.e.* more lives conducted with a sense of constant communion with higher powers, as well as far more of the reasoned faith which only superficially resembles the unthinking acceptance of dogmas felt to be unintelligible, that so often usurps the name of faith. But just because we are more religious, we are less prone to an uncritical acceptance of whatever monstrosity comes to us in the disguise of faith.

Moreover in this case the illusion is greatly heightened by a very general psychological fact which at first sight seems to support the literary view. For it is probable that at one time or other (mostly in youth) nearly every one is in trouble about his soul and takes a keen interest in the question of a future life. But as a rule, the interest is short-lived and soon dies out, or rather, *is trampled out* by the social disapproval of the pretension to be more troubled about such matters than one's elders and betters. But the memory of this interest persists and wins from every one an easy, though nominal, assent to the assertions of those who expatiate on the importance of the question. The truth is that many *have felt* the importance of the subject, but that at any given moment only an infinitesimal fraction *actually feel* it, so that there is never any effective demand for its investigation. Even in the elect ranks of the Society for Psychical Research it is probable that the same law has been at work, and that the reason for the apathy of most of its members is that they have long lost the keenness of interest which originally nerved them to the prodigious effort of joining the Society.

It may be thought that the novel interpretation of human action and feeling which we have been considering is thus as fully established as it can be by argument. But in a matter of this sort one ought not to content oneself with argument while proof is attainable. And fortunately in this case the actual facts can be ascertained so soon as a sufficient number of persons desire to ascertain them.

The American Branch of the Society for Psychical Research has, under the auspices of Dr. Richard Hodgson, issued a circular, or *questionnaire*, designed to test and to bring out the feelings with which the prospect of a future life is actually regarded. It runs thus :—

There is a widespread literary tradition that men naturally desire a future life. From this assumed fact it has been variously argued that (1) such a universal desire cannot be destined to disappointment, and (2) it must vitiate convictions and engender illusory evidence in its own support.

But there is some reason to suppose, both from the ordinary

conduct of men and from sporadic declarations of individuals, that this tradition is very far from accurately representing the facts, and that these are actually more various and complicated. Moreover, it should not be forgotten that in India the literary tradition seems to be exactly reversed, and it is assumed that men naturally crave for extinction or absorption in the Absolute.

It becomes a question, therefore, what the actual sentiments of men are, and what, consequently, is the actual bias with which they are likely to receive the doctrines and the evidence that bear on the subject.

Both these questions are capable of being determined with sufficient precision by instituting a statistical inquiry over a sufficiently wide field—collecting answers until it becomes evident that the percentages of the various types of answer have become constant.

To determine the nature of men's actual sentiments and actual bias should be a matter of great interest, not only to the S.P.R. and psychologists generally, but also to every religious organization. For both the scientific labours of the former and the moral exhortations of the latter are likely to be in some degree, at least, ineffectual, so long as they are conducted in ignorance, and so in disregard, of what men really want. It is only when the facts have been ascertained that they can be argued from for the various purposes of the scientist, the philosopher and the theologian.

First of all, therefore, it is necessary to discover the nature of human sentiment; and to obtain it in its purity, it is desirable to exclude, as far as possible, all extraneous influences, whether of a religious or of a scientific kind. It is, of course, recognized that these may and often do influence sentiment, that they may engender or check it, and also that there may be a marked divergence between conviction or belief and *sentiment*. But as it is primarily the nature of the *sentiment* which has to be determined, these other considerations should be excluded as far as possible.

Hence the subjoined questions should be understood as directly referring only to the personal preferences, sentiments, or desires of those who answer them, quite irrespective of their religious faith or reasoned convictions, the influence of which, where it exists, may be recorded in answer to Question III.

N.B.—All names will be regarded as strictly confidential.

Questions

I. Would you prefer (*a*) to live after 'death' or (*b*) not?
II. (*a*) If I. (*a*), do you desire a future life whatever the conditions may be?
    (*b*) If not, what would have to be its character to make the prospect seem tolerable? Would you, *e.g.*, be content with a life more or less like your present life?

(c) Can you say what elements in life (if any) are felt by you to call for its perpetuity?
III. Can you state *why* you feel in this way, as regards Questions I. and II.?
IV. Do you NOW feel the question of a future life to be of urgent importance to your mental comfort?
V. Have your feelings on Questions I. II. and IV. undergone change? If so, when and in what ways?
VI. (a) Would you like to *know for certain* about the future life, or
(b) would you prefer to leave it a *matter of faith*?

It will be evident, I think, to any one who reads this *questionnaire* that if a sufficiently extensive collection of answers can be made to be representative of the sentiments of the educated classes in America and England, the views expressed in this article will be thoroughly tested, and the question of the actual nature of human sentiment can no longer remain obscure. And in addition a great mass of psychological material will have been accumulated, the critical sifting of which cannot fail to throw much light upon a number of most important questions of a religious, philosophical, and moral character. The results would be sure to be important and almost sure to be surprising. For unless the argument of this paper has been wholly mistaken, they would diverge very widely from the literary tradition.

Personally I shall be greatly surprised if the returns do not show that active and intense preoccupation with the question of a future life is an exceedingly rare state of mind. And yet if I should be wrong in this estimate, I should not be disappointed. For if it should turn out that real and extensive interest in the question actually exists, I should feel that the chief, and hitherto insuperable, obstacle in the way of actual scientific investigation of the question of fact was at length giving way.

I refer to the social taboo of any serious inquiry to which at present the scattered individuals who at any given time 'desire to know' are compelled to submit. This taboo seems to rest its appeal on the highest and most respectable motives, religious and scientific. It is enunciated with an air of the profoundest wisdom and couches its warnings in the solemn voice of immemorial experience. Yet I feel sure that the census of sentiments will not have to proceed far to make it clear that the traditional attitude of society rests neither upon reason nor upon religion, but really upon a blind feeling or instinct, against the domination of which all self-respecting persons will revolt as soon as they recognize its existence in themselves and in others.

It will consequently become possible for the few who desire to know the truth, and are prepared to take the steps ordinarily adopted in complicated scientific investigations, to treat the social taboo with the proper disrespect and to pursue their course without being thwarted by the many who do not desire to know and have hitherto held it to be their duty to prevent any one from finding out.

The present situation is indeed not far short of farcical, or rather would be entirely so, but for the pathos of the self-delusion which it implies, and the torture which it inflicts on its victims. We profess to believe that a knowledge of the fate which awaits each one of us in the comparatively near future would be, of all knowledge, the most precious. We lament, with many marks of sincerity, that the inscrutable wisdom of higher powers has inexorably precluded us from the attainment of this knowledge. We confess to have experienced, perhaps more than once, unspeakable agonies when we were forced to face death in our own persons or in those of our dear ones. Yet what do we do to extricate ourselves from this tragic situation?

We tell ghost stories! This we have done for at least ten thousand years, and the supply is as plentiful as ever. It is also, scientifically, as unsatisfactory as ever, for the social atmosphere still renders a serious testing of this material practically impossible. Is it not absurd therefore that we can neither stop retailing them, nor make a real effort to discover of what facts they are the adumbration?

The answer is simple. Ghost stories are what, on the whole, we desire them to be: they fulfil their function best by remaining as they are. They were never intended to be verified or investigated, and if they could be made scientifically valuable they would cease to be so emotionally, and would no longer serve to surround terrestrial existence with the foil which enhances its brilliancy. And instead of being the victims of an unkind fate which baffles our desire to know, we are ourselves the agency which keeps us ignorant.

It is as little true here as in any other matters of scientific inquiry that we are confronted with an inscrutable universe whose nature we ' were never intended to discover.' It is true, here as elsewhere, that society entertains a fierce fear of knowledge, a savage suspicion that to eat of the fruits of the tree of knowledge is a sin deserving of death, which thousands of years of contrary experience have done but little to eradicate. Social control of the scientific instinct, the 'desire to know,' is as real, and almost as stringent, as formerly,[1] even though in respect to a few favoured subjects of research, which are supposed to lead to materially useful results, it has been sufficiently relaxed to enable them to rise above the dense atmosphere of social intolerance which is continually being exhaled by our constitutional indolence and dislike of any readjustment of our habits and actions.

But in all other subjects the social atmosphere makes all the difference between success and failure, as the individual consciously or unconsciously breathes in its subtle influence. We fancy ourselves exceedingly enlightened and tolerant because we have (though only for a couple of hundred years) given up the sport of witch-baiting, and no longer regard all forms of scientific curiosity as 'black magic' to be checked by summary and premature cremation. But, even as there are many ways of killing a dog other than hanging him, so there are many subtler and more effective ways of producing conformity to social sentiment other than overt persecution, and the social factor in the discovery and recognition of truth remains of paramount importance. Truths which

[1] Cp. pp. 58-60.

lie in directions socially disapproved can either not be discovered at all, or when discovered remain a dead letter. As a rule indeed the absence of social hostility is not enough, but more or less active co-operation is necessary. The notion that a lonely thinker can spontaneously set to work upon some subject of inquiry which interests him, make discoveries of far-reaching import, and get them accepted and acclaimed by an admiring world is surely an illusion which the history of science should be sufficient to dispel. The lonely thinker has need of libraries, laboratories, and leisure, and without the consent of society he cannot get them. Single-handed and single-minded against the world he can do nothing: strive and labour as he may, he must sooner or later succumb to the overwhelming pressure of his environment.

And in no region of possible knowledge is the power of the social atmosphere more obvious, or the need for social co-operation greater, than in everything that concerns the 'mystery' of death. And nowhere else has individual curiosity been more brutally crushed out. Whoever conceives a desire to know the truth about the future life engages in a struggle with social forces which is almost sure to end in tragedy. To begin with he is deluged with assurances that what he desires to know cannot be known, and stuffed with pseudo-proofs, scientific, philosophic, and religious, to persuade him to drop the subject. If these do not satisfy him and he persists, he is next told that his desire is 'bad form,' that he must not appear odd, or make himself ridiculous by prying into matters which the wisdom of the ancients has from time immemorial decided to lie beyond mortal ken. 'My boy,' his parent or guardian will finally say to him, if he is unusually sympathetic and candid, 'I can well remember the time when I, too, felt about it just as you do now, and would have given worlds to know. So I read a number of books on the subject, and even went to a *séance* or two. But I got very little out of it, and when I found that I was thrown into the company of all sorts of queer persons and things, and heard that my friends were beginning to express serious concern for my sanity, and that I was endangering my professional reputation, I very wisely dropped the matter. Be sensible, therefore, and take my word for it, we are not meant to know about these things. Suppress your morbid craving for truth. You will soon get over it, and think as every one else does.'

As a piece of wordly wisdom this advice is unexceptionable, and not to be disregarded by any who would avoid the madhouse or the workhouse. But scientifically regarded, it is somewhat lacking in conclusiveness. A question which, on account of the resistance of social sentiment, it has never yet been possible to investigate with the dispassionate, and yet persistent, curiosity of science, can hardly be said to be settled. And if it should turn out as one of the results of the inquiry described above that on the one hand social sentiment has the character I have supposed, and on the other that a small (or even a considerable) number of persons are desirous of a real investigation, the latter would have a chance, slender perhaps, but at all events such as they have never had before, of combining to effect their object. The Society for Psychical Research, in particular, would, have to change its tactics. Instead of pouring out volume after volume of minutely and dully accurate reports of sittings with its Mrs. Pipers and Mrs. Thompsons, which the world ignores until the lapse of time, by removing the first-hand witnesses beyond the reach of cross-examination, has rendered its evidence as inconclusive as the testimony which in the past has failed to move the world, it would have to address itself, in the first instance, to modifying the existing sentiment of society. And whether it succeeded or not, it might at least induce us to be more honest with ourselves, and to cease from our insincere lamentings over the impossibility of a knowledge than which the gods could bestow no more embarrassing gift upon the generality of men.

XVIII

THE ETHICAL SIGNIFICANCE OF IMMORTALITY[1]

ARGUMENT

I. *Is Immortality an Ethical Postulate?* Yes, if it can be shown to be implied in the validity of our ethical valuation of the world. Objections: (a) *a pure morality needs no reference to another world.* But there is moral waste if goodness of character perishes, and ultimate moral failure when physical life becomes impossible on earth; (b) *it is immoral to relegate the sanctions of morality to another world.* Not if future happiness and misery are conceived as the intrinsic consequences of moral goodness and badness; (c) *we cannot live for two worlds at once.* Depends on how they are conceived. The thought of a future life morally bracing, and, like all forethought about the future, a mark of superior mental development.

II. *What is the value of an Ethical Postulate?* The postulate is not emotional but rational, and affirms the validity of our moral judgments. It is part of a system of postulates which all proceed similarly. Moreover, the ideals we postulate are coincident and bound up together. Ultimately Truth, Goodness, Happiness and Beauty must all be postulated or rejected together. The alleged superior validity of the ideal of Truth explained.

An ethical postulate, however, does not prescribe any special mode of its realization, for which we must look to scientific experience. There are also other questions which may modify, though they cannot subvert, our ethical demand.

WE are so accustomed in these days to hear the world-old traditions of the human race denied or ignored simply because they are old that the antique flavour inevitably attaching to any argument about Immortality almost suffices to secure its condemnation unheard. Yet such scornful treatment of authority is not justified by the present state of our knowledge. On the contrary, the antiquity and wide prevalence of an idea in themselves constitute a *prima facie* claim upon the attention of the

[1] First published in the *New World* for September 1897.

unprejudiced. Even on our most modern principles of evolutionist explanation, it means that the idea is somehow a response to a widely felt and persistent element in our experience. Its very antiquity, therefore, gives it an authority which may not be lightly set aside.

Still I do not wish to argue this question of Immortality on the basis of authority. There is another side also to the influence of authority, when that authority is old. It is probable in such cases that the idea supported by authority will be disfigured by the dust of ages, overgrown by all sorts of parasitic fungi of fancy, and rendered ridiculous by the incrustations of fossil formulas, until its best friends hardly know it and it becomes intellectually contemptible, morally outrageous and aesthetically repulsive to its foes. As something of this sort has probably happened to the idea of immortality, it will be the plan of this paper to argue the question on the sole ground of reason; its only stipulation being that the appeal be really made to the light of reason, shining without let or hindrance, and so far as possible, freed from all coloured spectacles of religious or scientific orthodoxy that might check its transmission.

The subject of Immortality is, however, too extensive for me to attempt to discuss it as a whole, and my efforts will be confined to a single aspect of it—the ethical. That is, I shall *not* try to determine whether there is immortality as a fact, but only whether the science of ethics needs this conception for its own perfection. Putting the question more technically, I propose to consider two things. First: Is Immortality an ethical postulate? Must a moral being, *i.e.* a being that can be judged good or evil, as such be deemed immortal? Secondly: If so, what does an ethical postulate prove? What is its general significance or logical status in the world of thought? The first of these questions is exclusively ethical. The second enters upon the realm of metaphysics, and may be expected to involve so much subtler and more difficult considerations that I would gladly evade it altogether if possible. But, unfortunately, to enforce the due respect for an ethical postulate, the case must be carried to the supreme court of metaphysics. Moreover, it is only the discussion of its metaphysical value that gives the ethical argument any direct bearing on the question, not here to be discussed as such, whether there is immortality as a matter of fact.

I

Let us take up, then, the first question, whether immortality is an ethical postulate. What can be urged in favour of this view? The argument for it is exceedingly simple: it consists in showing that without immortality it is not possible to think the world as a harmonious whole, as a moral cosmos. To show this, one has not to appeal to anything more recondite than the fact that in our present phase of existence the moral life cannot be lived out to its completion, that it is not permitted to display its full fruitage of consequences for good and for evil. Whenever Might triumphs over Right; whenever the evildoers succeed and the righteous perish; whenever goodness is trampled under foot and wickedness is exalted to high places; nay, whenever the moral development of character is cut short and rendered vain by death,—we are brought face to face with facts which constitute an indictment of cosmic justice, which are inconsistent with the conception of the world as a moral order. Unless, therefore, we can vindicate this order by explaining away the facts that would otherwise destroy it, we have to abandon the ethical judgment of the world of our experience as good or bad; we have to admit that the ideal of goodness is an illusion of which the scheme of things recks not at all.

But if we refuse to do this (and whether we are not bound to refuse to abandon our ideals at the first show of opposition will presently be considered), how shall the ethical harmony be restored if not by the supposition of a prolongation and perfection of the moral life in the future? Only so can character be made of real significance in the scheme of things; only so is it something worth possessing, an investment more permanent and more decisive of our weal and woe than all the outward goods men set their hearts upon, rather than a transitory bubble to whose splendour it matters not one whit whether it be pure translucence refracting the radiance of the sunlight, or the iridescent film that coats decay.

The ethical argument for immortality, then, is simply this, that, if death ends all, the moral life cannot be lived out, moral perfection is impossible, and the universe cannot be regarded as at heart ethical. But in spite of its simplicity this argument has been misunderstood in a variety of ways. Let us briefly consider the chief of these.

It is objected by well-meaning people, who rather pride themselves on their advocacy of a purer and higher morality, that the ethical sphere does not need supplementing by a future life. They grow indignant at the thought that 'the good men do is buried in their graves,' and does not survive to inspire and direct succeeding generations. They bid us therefore fight the good fight disinterestedly and without selfish reward, in order that our grandchildren, if we have any, may enjoy the fruits of our self-denial, and that the world may be the better for our efforts.

To this the reply is twofold. It is idle to say that Goodness is not wasted because the results of actions reverberate throughout the ages. The good men *do* may persist and work well or ill, but the good men *are* surely perishes. The human character itself passes away, and its effects are transmitted only through the characters of others. The character itself is an indefeasible and inalienable possession of the owner, and by no flight of the imagination can it be transferred to others. Whatever worth, therefore, we assign to character, that worth is lost to the world if immortality be denied. And, moreover, it is only in their effect upon his own character that a man's actions can be surely classified as good or bad. What the effect of actions will be on others, now or subsequently no one can foretell: the real objection to doing too much for posterity is, not that 'posterity has done nothing for us,' but the uncertainty as to what the effect on posterity will be. For that depends largely on the character of others, and *quisque suos patimur Manes*. Each can assume full responsibility for his own actions and his own character alone; the rest lies largely on the lap of the gods. If, then, you deny the persistence of character, you have denied the real basis of the moral order.

But, secondly, supposing even that humanity profited by our efforts, how far would this go towards re-establishing the moral order of the world? If the immortality of the individual be an illusion, surely that of the race is a transparent absurdity. If there is certainty about any prediction of science, it is surely, as I have elsewhere put it, this, that our racial destiny is "to shiver and to starve to death in ever-deepening gloom."[1] The prospective fortunes of the race, then, do not redeem the moral character of the universe. If the view of mechanical science be the whole truth about the universe, the race is of just as little account as the individual; suns and stars and the hosts of heaven will roll on in their orbits just as steadily and unfeelingly whether we prosper or perish, struggle on or resign ourselves to despair. Cosmically, the earth and all it bears on its surface is of infinitesimal importance: what does it matter then whether any one brood of mites that crawls upon it is better or worse than its successors, any more than whether it laboriously grubs up a few atoms of a shining yellow or of a shining white metal and fights about the ratio? No; the worthy people who think that George Eliot's 'choir invisible' can make a noise to compete with the whirl of worlds decidedly delude themselves, and 'an immortality of influence' is no adequate ethical substitute for personal immortality.

A second objection does not pretend to improve on the ethic of immortality, but criticizes it by descanting on the turpitude of basing morality on 'fears of Hell and

[1] *Riddles of the Sphinx*, p. 105, new ed. p. 104.

hopes of Paradise.' This objection also is urged by many worthy persons; and I have known some who have been sustained through life by the pride they took in showing that they could be just as moral without knowing why, as they were when they thought their eternal salvation depended on their conduct. But theoretically this objection surely rests on a misconception. The rewards and punishments for conduct are not to be looked upon as *motives* to conduct, but as the natural *results* of conduct, inevitable in a morally ordered universe. In an ethical universe, Goodness cannot be associated with persistent misery, because that would be an outrage upon the moral order; Badness must ultimately involve unhappiness, because only such retribution will reaffirm the outraged supremacy of the moral order. Rewards and punishments, then, are but incidents in that completion of the moral life for the sake of which immortality was postulated; they are not in themselves the sole motives for leading such a life. The very suggestion that they may be supposed to be, on whatever side it is urged, shows an imperfect appreciation of the nature of the moral life, indicative of a coarser moral fibre and of a lower stage of ethical development.

But we need not on this account entirely condemn this mode of regarding immortality. Fears and hopes of what may happen hereafter may not be the highest motives to morality; they may enforce as an external sanction what should be an intrinsic conviction; but they are not therefore valueless. For, if they are effective, they at least *accustom* men to right conduct,[1] and thus form the basis of sound habit, which is the actual foundation of all conduct in any case, and the necessary prerequisite for sound reflection upon conduct and the attainment of any higher view of morality. Our moral enthusiasm, therefore, need no more frown upon these lower motives than it need disband the police on the ground that a truly moral community should not need policing.

[1] Cp. pp. 33-5.

Still more radical than the objections we have considered is a third objection which denounces the essential immorality of looking to a future life at all in connexion with our conduct here. The habit of contemplating a future life, it is urged, engenders a pernicious 'other-worldliness' most detrimental to proper behaviour in this world. We cannot live for two worlds at once. The future life dwarfs the present; the supposed significance of the eternal life hereafter destroys the real significance of our life here and now.

Again, I think the objection labours under a misconception. It holds good only against a conception of immortality which, like the Buddhist Nirvâna, for example, conflicts and competes with the ethical view of this world: We cannot 'live for two worlds at once,' only if the principles of conduct required in them are fundamentally different. If extinction is the end to which we should aspire hereafter, then certainly it would be folly to prepare for it by a strenuous life on earth. The objection is irrelevant to an immortality which is postulated as the *completion* of mundane morality, which is not so much *other-worldliness* as *better-worldliness*, suggested by the ethical defects of our actual experience. In reality such a view indefinitely deepens the significance of the present life. Think what is involved in the assertion that character is permanent and indestructible, and passes not from us however the fashion of our outward life may change! Think of it, that we can never escape from ourselves, from the effect of our deeds on our character, and that every deed leaves its mark upon the soul, a mark which may be modified and counterbalanced, but can never be undone to all eternity! Will not the effect of such a belief be to make us realize the solemnity of life as we never did before, to nerve us to that unremitting self-improvement without which there is no approximating to the moral ideal? Instead of losing its significance, does not every act of life become fraught with infinite significance? Instead of becoming careless about ourselves, will it not, then, become worth our while to bestow upon our own character-building a care that would otherwise have been disproportionate? For, as most of them are thoroughly aware, ordinary people are quite good enough for ordinary purposes. Why, then, should they strive laboriously to change and remould themselves, and fall, perchance, into the exaggerated virtue of Jane Austen Beecher Stowe de Rouse, who was "good beyond all earthly need"? Is it not much more convenient to stay as one is, and to reply to the ambitions of an unquiet conscience as the General of the Jesuits replied to the Pope who wished to reform them, *Sint ut sunt aut non sint,*—'Let them be as they are or not be at all'? Is it not always inconvenient to think of the future, and is not the future life altogether too big a thing to think of? And is not this, and not any logical or scientific difficulties which the thought involves, the real reason why men seek to banish it from their consciousness,—why it is hardly ever more than a half belief in most men's minds? Human inertia, all that keeps us commonplace and sordid, unheroic and unaspiring is, and always has been, dead against it. And that is why moral reformers have always insisted on it. For their function is to overcome moral inertia.

It is, however, some consolation to think that the past course of Evolution seemingly sanctions the belief of those who would have us take account of a future which extends into another life. Certainly the expansion of the future, of which our action takes account, is one of the most marked characteristics of a progressive civilization. The animal looks into the future not at all, and the savage but little; but, as civilization grows, the future consequences of action become more and more important, and are prepared for more and more. When we have dared to forecast the future of the race when our coal supply shall be exhausted; when we have looked unflinchingly upon that unimaginably distant period when the sun's light shall fail,—shall we shrink from rising to the contemplation of a future that extends immeasurably further?

II

By thus replying to these three objections I hope to have sufficiently established the first part of my thesis,—that immortality is in truth an ethical postulate. But the second part still remains to be answered, namely, the question, What is an ethical postulate really worth? What is its value metaphysically? Is it more than an impulse of ethical emotion which shrinks into nothingness under the calm gaze of scientific truth? Does it amount to demonstration?

One often hears it said that immortality is an emotional postulate, unreasoning if not unreasonable; and that hackneyed phrase, 'the hope of immortality,' bears involuntary witness to the fact that the argument is not supposed to amount to demonstration. Now this is just the mental attitude towards the subject which I deprecate and wish to controvert. The people who cherish the *hope* of immortality I regard as people who, for the reasons given above, *sometimes hope there is no immortality*, or at least have not much faith in their own argument. It is more especially for the benefit of such weak-kneed brethren that I would maintain the following doctrine:—

The ethical postulate of immortality is not an emotional postulate, but as rational as any postulate, and has as good a claim for recognition in our ultimate metaphysic. Or, if they still prefer to regard it as emotional, and quote Von Hartmann's remark on the subject that metaphysical truths cannot be based on emotional postulates, I shall reply that, ultimately, truths will nowhere be found to rest on any other grounds.

(1) Hence immortality, as an ethical postulate, is of the same nature as certain other postulates without which we cannot harmonize our experience.

(2) It is bound up with those other postulates.

(3) Its assumption is justified in precisely the same way as that of the other postulates.

(4) If they cannot accept this as demonstration they will get no better anywhere in the world.

(1) Taking these points in order, let us ask what is the nature of an ethical postulate. It is nothing but the affirmation of the cosmic significance of the ideal of *Goodness*, of our *ethical valuation* of things. It claims that the universe is not merely a fact, but has a certain value which we call ethical. It is at bottom a moral universe, and potentially resolves itself into an ethical harmony. Now the logical method by which this argument proceeds is this: Given a part, to find the whole; given a few fragmentary data, to construct therefrom an ideal which may validly be used to interpret the data. It is the same method which is used by the palaeontologist when, from a tooth or a bone, he reconstructs some long-extinct form of life. The question, then, resolves itself into this: Have we the right to assume that our ethical data cohere and may be fitted together into an ethical ideal?

And (2), in sustaining this procedure the ethical consciousness does not stand alone. Its claim is supported by our procedure elsewhere. *All* the ideals of ultimate value are constituted in the same manner. How do we make good the claim that anything in the universe is beautiful? We assume that our judgments concerning beauty are not devoid of significance, but may be harmonized in an ideal of Beauty to which the nature of things is somehow akin. How do we make good the claim that happiness is possible? We believe in the prophetic significance of the pleasurable states of consciousness in our experience, and out of them frame the ideal of Happiness which we assume reality may realize.

Lastly, how do we make good the claim that the world is knowable? We assume that its facts somehow cohere, and may be arranged in an orderly system of Truth or Knowledge. In other words, we try to look upon reality as realizing our ideals of Knowledge, Beauty, Goodness and Happiness, and thereby constitute it a cosmos, knowable, beautiful, ethical and delightful. But in each case we are checked by the same obstacles. The ideals certainly do not float on the surface of life. They are not congruous with the raw facts of experience.

They have to be sought with infinite pains, and ere we have dragged them forth and proved them valid, lo, death comes and, ruthlessly impartial, cuts short the careers of the man of science and of the man of pleasure. Life is imperfect and fragmentary all round,—not only in the eyes of ethics. Emotionally, intellectually and aesthetically, life as it stands is no less inadequate than ethically. The ideals of Happiness, Knowledge and Beauty postulate realization no less and in no other way than Goodness; the murky atmosphere of earth, poisoned by the breath of death, no less derides their possibility. What we ask, then, for one we ask for all, and we ask it in obedience to the same law of our being,—that life *must* show itself congruous with the ideals from which it draws its value.

And (3), these ideals are not only cognate, but coincident; we cannot in the last resort affirm one while denying the rest; nothing short of a complete harmony can wholly satisfy us. Truth, Goodness, Happiness and Beauty are all indispensable factors in Perfection, the varying facets which the one ideal reveals to our various modes of striving.[1]

This is generally denied only by the votaries of the ideal of Truth, and so it will perhaps suffice if I content myself with pointing out to them how untenable is their position. We have all heard some postulate of human feeling met with the cold sneer of a short-sighted science and the query, Why should the universe take account of goodness and its completion? Well, I contend that if this sneer is worth anything it must be extended so as to include all human activity, that we might with equal cogency go on to ask, Why, then, should the universe take account of Knowledge and its establishment, or of Happiness and its attainment? We have, I claim, no logical ground for supposing the world to be knowable, and yet utterly disregardful of Happiness and Goodness. For a world supposed to be wholly knowable, *i.e.* wholly harmonious with our intellectual demands, while remaining wholly discordant with our emotional nature, would *ipso*

---

[1] See *Riddles of the Sphinx*, ch. xii. § 9.

facto include an intellectually insoluble puzzle which would render it fundamentally *unknowable*. Nay, more, is not the supposition directly self-contradictory? Does not a knowable world satisfy at least one of our emotional demands,—the desire for Knowledge? It cannot be then, as alleged, *utterly* out of relation to our emotional nature. But if it can satisfy one such postulate, why not the rest?

The ideals, then, stand and fall together. They are rooted in the unity of the human soul, in the final solidarity of life's endeavours. And when the supreme need arises, the outcry of the soul can summon to its aid all the powers that minister unto its being; it wields a spell that reaches from the iciest altitudes of scientific abstraction to the warmest pulsations of concrete emotion, and from the most ethereal fancy of the purest intellect to the blindest impulse of agonizing passion; it can extort from every element of our nature the confession of its solidarity with the rest of life, and set it in array on that dread battlefield whereon the Gods contend against the Giants —of Doubt, Disorder, and Despair.

For it is because of this solidarity of the ideals that the denial of them confronts us with the gravest issues. They all assert, in varying form but with unvarying intent, the same great principle—the conformity of the world with the capacity of our nature. And unfamiliar as some of the applications of this principle may be to our ordinary habits of thinking, we have to remember that the principle itself can hardly be impugned. For inasmuch as in the end our 'world' is human experience, and a world which we neither did nor could experience would not be one we need argue or trouble about, this principle really amounts to an assertion of the intrinsic coherence and potential harmony of the whole of experience. Without it where should we be? What would our attitude have to be towards a world in which the ultimate significance of our ideals was denied, that is, a world which was no world, a world in which nothing really meant anything, nothing was really good or beautiful or true, and in which the hope of happiness was nothing but illusion? To say that the prospect of such a world would reduce us to the most despairing depths of the most abject Pessimism hardly depicts the full horror of the situation: it would be a world of which the hopelessness would disarm even the suicide's hand. For, in a world which had really renounced its allegiance to the ideal, all action would be paralysed by the conviction that nothing we desired could ever be attained, because the existent was irreconcilably alienated from the desirable. The foundations of the cosmos would be shattered, and we should have to realize that nothing is worth doing because nothing has any worth, because human valuations have no significance in establishing the nature of things. We should be plunged, in other words, in that unfathomable abyss where Scepticism fraternizes with Pessimism, and they hug their miseries in chaos undisguised.

(4) We can reject, then, the principle on which the ethical postulate of immortality rests only at the cost of entire Scepticism and utter Pessimism. By those not prepared to pay that price the principle must be accepted, like the other assumptions that render the world a fit sphere for the satisfaction of other human activities. Take, for instance, the assumption that the world is a knowable cosmos. Is this proved? Certainly not; nor can it be until everything is known: until then it always remains possible that the world may not turn out really knowable at the last. Can we avoid assuming it? Certainly not; without it we could not take a single step towards any science or practice. We simply *must* assume that the world is an intelligible world, if we are to live in it. As a matter of fact we do assume it, all except a few who bury their dissent in the seclusion of the madhouse. Is the assumption confirmed? Yes, in the only way in which such fundamental assumptions ever are confirmed: the further we trust it the more we know, the more confident in it we grow.

The assumption of a moral cosmos is made and confirmed in the same way. We cannot prove it to be correct so long as the world is not morally perfect; we cannot wholly exorcize the recurrent dread that, after all, the moral order may of a sudden lapse into chaos before our eyes: but we cannot organize our moral experience without this assumption, and in the course of moral development our confidence in it grows.

But, it may be said, if there is no essential difference between the assumption of a moral and that of an intellectual order in our experience, how is it that the former appears so much less certain than the latter? Why are we so much more confident that the world is subject to natural than to moral law? Why are *moral* so much more commoner and more successful than *intellectual* sceptics? These facts are not to be disputed, but perhaps they can be explained. Undoubtedly the moral order is not so strong as the scientific, and its principles have not such a hold on human nature. The rebels against the moral order are not all in prison; our rascals largely run about unhanged. 'Moral insanity' is pleaded in mitigation of the punishment which it should render inexorable. But the difference is due simply to the different amounts of experience behind the two assumptions. Historically man was a knowing being long before he was an ethical being. He had lived long, as Aristotle said, before he had lived well; both in time and in urgency, perceptual adaptation to the physical order took precedence over ethical adaptation to the social order. Man had to assume, therefore, the principles that constituted the world a knowable cosmos long before he needed to assume a moral order. Hence the beliefs in the uniformity and calculability of Nature and the like have a much greater and more unequivocal mass of racial experience and hereditary instinct behind them than any moral instinct we have yet acquired. But this does not show that the nature of the several assumptions is not essentially the same.

If the argument of this paper has commended itself so far, there will probably be little difficulty in granting the last point, that the demonstration of Immortality proffered by the ethical argument is as complete as any that can be devised. But, to enforce the point, allusion may be made to the fact that demonstration is in its very nature what the logicians call *hypothetical*. It proceeds in the form, If A is, then B must be. But how are we to know that A is? The premiss has to be assumed or conceded in every demonstration. The utmost we can do is to rest our demonstration on an assumption so fundamental that none will dare to question it; and this we here seem to have accomplished. For what could be more fundamental than the assumption on which the ethical argument rests —that the elements of our experience admit of being harmonized, that the world is truly a *cosmos*? If this be not absolute certainty, it is at least certainty such that, while no assertion of any special science is *less* hypothetical, none rests upon an *equally* indispensable assumption.

On the whole, then, the ethical argument for immortality seems logically as sound and metaphysically as legitimate as any argument can well be; but it will not be amiss to allude in closing to two points about which nothing has so far been said. The first is the fact that, when immortality has been shown to be an ethical postulate, nothing has been decided as to the *content* of that idea. All we know is that immortality must be of such a sort as to be capable of being an ethical postulate. And it is quite possible that the science of ethics would on this ground find much to protest against in many of the traditional forms of the belief in immortality, while it would find little to object to in others which are less familiar. It is difficult, for instance, to see how eternal damnation could be regarded as an ethical postulate, while some appropriate modification of the Hindu notion of *karma* might seem ethically welcome. But though ethics could thus *prohibit* certain ethically outrageous beliefs in immortality, it cannot aspire *positively to determine* the way in which its postulate is to be realized. That problem lies beyond its scope, and has to be determined, if at all, by considerations of a scientific and metaphysical character. Hence the moral argument for immortality is in a manner incomplete: first, because a moral postulate cannot as such inform us as to the method of its realization; and secondly, because, disguise it as we may, our faith in a cosmic order which includes the moral remains still capable of further confirmation. For, however firm our trust in the rationality of life, few would contend that the discovery of scientific facts consonant with our ethical demands would add nothing to the assurance of their faith.

And so, lastly, a word must be said on the subject of these scientific and metaphysical arguments about immortality which were excluded as irrelevant to the ethical aspect of the question, in order to bring out the important fact that, however they may be supposed to result, the ethical argument maintains its independent validity. So far as I can see, these further arguments may result in three different ways. They may confirm the ethical argument—in which case our confidence in immortality will be strengthened. They may balance each other—in which case they will leave the field open for the ethical argument. Or, in the worst event, they may preponderatingly conflict with it. But, even so, it would not follow that they were right and the ethical argument was wrong, at least until the plea for the essential solidarity of the ultimate postulates had been invalidated. A world in which the ethical ideal is abrogated and annulled cannot be a harmonious world; and if it be not harmonious throughout, we can feel no confidence that it is harmonious in any part. In other words, so long as we trust in the ultimate presupposition of all knowledge and all action, we could never quite trust the non-ethical arguments that are supposed to plunge us in perplexity.

XIX

PHILOSOPHY AND THE SCIENTIFIC INVESTIGATION OF A FUTURE LIFE[1]

ARGUMENT

The use of Philosophy in scientific inquiry—the general logical criticism of fundamental postulates and working methods. This is most necessary and helpful in a new science, and safest in one which, like 'Psychical Research,' has not yet obtained professional endowment. Special interest of a discussion of the assumptions made in a scientific inquiry into the possibility of a future life. (1) The general scientific assumption of 'law,' *i.e.* knowableness. (2) The axiom of proceeding from the known to the unknown. This life must give the clue to our interpretation of an 'other' life, which could not be wholly 'other' without paralysing thought. Misconceptions on this score explain (*a*) the practical weakness of the 'belief' in a future life; (*b*) the prejudice against an anthropomorphic future life; and (*c*) against the spiritist hypothesis. Assuming, therefore, that as a working theory personal survival is conceivable, how can it be verified? The future life must be conceived (1) as natural; (2) as psychically continuous with the present, in spite of the difficulty of obtaining proofs of identity; (3) as only dissociated from our world by secondary processes traceable in our normal psychology. Result that a future life scientifically provable would necessarily *seem* humdrum and unsensational.

II. *The philosophic basis of the conception of a future life.* Philosophies which reject it *a priori* are gratuitous. For an idealistic experientialism the conception has no difficulty. How we pass into another world. How, why, and to what extent, are dream worlds 'unreal'? 'Death' as 'awakening' to a more real world. Philosophers on death. Four paradoxes about death. Their explanation by idealism. The construction and dissolution of the common world of waking life. The ambiguity of death. Does it leave the chances equal? Impossibility of disproving a future life wholly severed from the present. Possibility of empirical evidence that the severance is *not* complete. Philosophy clears away prejudices that obstruct investigation, but leaves discovery to science.

THE philosopher, as the genius of Plato long ago perceived,[2] is a very strange being. He is in the world, but not of

[1] An expanded form of a paper originally read before the Society for Psychical Research, and published in its *Proceedings*, Part 36, February 1900.
[2] *Republic*, 490.

it, residing mainly in a 'Cloud-cuckoodom' of his own invention, which seems to have no relation to the actual facts of life, and makes no difference to anything or anybody but the philosopher himself. Its sole function seems to be to make the philosopher himself feel happy and superior to everybody who does not understand his philosophy enough to enter into it, that is, to everybody else in the world.

But even so the philosopher is not happy in his paradise—of sages. He is terribly worried by all the other philosophers, each of whom is quite as cantankerous and cranky as himself, and wants to carry him off into his own private Nephelococcygia. And as he will not, and indeed cannot, enter into it, they all get very angry. They get so angry that they cannot even laugh at each other. But when they get a little calmer (not that there is really such a thing as calm among philosophers any more than among *cirrus* clouds—only they live so far aloof and aloft that people cannot see how they behave) they fall to criticizing. And so when one of them has built himself a nice new Nephelococcygia high up in the clouds, the rest all try to pull to pieces the abode of his soul, and bombard him with buzzing chimeras bottled in vacuum tubes and riddle him with sesquipedalian technicalities. In this they are usually successful, for, though so perverse, they are immensely clever, and their critical acumen is as wonderful as their unconsciousness of their own absurdity. And so, one after the other, each loses his scalp, and is buried in the ruins of his system.

Or rather he is *not*; for the burial customs of philosophers are as strange as the rest of their behaviour, and unlike those of any other tribe of men. Among the Scientists, for instance, there are also savage wars, and they practise vivisection. But the Scientists are not head-hunters. They forget the errors of their vanquished warriors and bury their remains, preserving only the memory of the work they did for Science. And thus do they keep clean the face of Science, and every morning wash away every bloodstain and every speck of error in the waters of Lethe, so that the many may believe that Science is infallible and its history is one unbroken progress; which is both more Christian and more worldly-wise.

But not so the philosophers. They still believe in the discipline of dirt, and keep the face of the fair goddess they profess to worship like unto the face of Glaucus the sea-god,[1] and the thicker grow the incrustations of historic error the better they are pleased. For they are simply devoted to the memory of ancient errors. They venerate them and collect them and dry them (in their histories of philosophy), and label them and exhibit them in glass cases with the scalps of their authors. They compile whole museums of such antiquities, and get themselves appointed the curators thereof. One of our universities is popularly believed to have appointed about two dozen such curators of the relics of the great fight between Aristocles, the son of Ariston, and Aristoteles, the son of Nicomachus. And the cause thereof was not Argive Helen, if you please, but the transcendence of the universal! Verily philosophic immortality is as terrible a thing and as hard to bear as that of Tithonus!

Such, I cannot help suspecting, are the real sentiments of intelligent men of the world concerning philosophers, though only a philosopher could be rude enough to set them down in black and white. But calumny, like murder, will out, and only so can it be met. And so those who, like Plato, have had the deepest faith in the value of philosophy have ever also been the readiest to admit and to confront the allegations of detractors.

And yet, at bottom, this was never quite an easy thing to do. The weaknesses of philosophy are manifest; its obscurity, its flimsiness, its intense individuality,[2] its remoteness and uselessness for the ordinary purposes of life, cannot but catch the public eye. Its virtues (if any) are hidden out of sight. It seems safer, therefore, on the whole, for the sage to flaunt his shame and to assume its

---

[1] Cp. Plato, *Republic*, 611 D
[2] For the explanation of which see *Personal Idealism*, pp. 50-51.

burden; boldly to disavow all purpose to better or instruct the world, cynically to confess that whether or not his astounding feats of conceptual prestidigitation can entertain the gaping crowd, they do at least amuse himself, honestly to disclaim the search for some more subtle service springing from his exercises. It may have happened here and there that the prescience of some wild and philosophic guess outstripped the plodding march of science. It may have happened now and then that in some reflective soul the conduct of life has been improved by study of its theory. But over most men habit bears such sway that this would be a marvel, and such precarious incidents are not enough to prove the useful nature of philosophy.

And yet if it were permitted to appeal to the philosophic heresy which just now is stirring up in all the bottled chimeras a buzzing fit to burst their vacuum tubes, if we might argue as pragmatists, it would seem obvious that even philosophy must have some use. For if it had not, society would scarce continue the endowment of philosophy, whose professors might thereupon find themselves reduced to breaking stones instead of systems. It is quite true that there is always a flavour of impertinence about the intervention of a philosopher in a subject of scientific research. For he cannot, as such, be trusted to make original contributions to the facts, and when he makes an attempt to criticize the contributions of others, it is quite true that he is terribly prone to do so from the *a priori* basis of some far-fetched cosmic theory which nobody else in the world besides himself believes in or even understands, and so achieves a comic rather than a cosmic interest. If, again, he contents himself with ponderously pondering on the accepted facts of a science he becomes a bore, consuming time and getting in the way of more practical workers.

It must be admitted, therefore, that the usefulness of a philosopher is very limited. It is undeniable only in cases where he is needed to clear out of the way other philosophers who have become obstreperous and obstructive; but such occasions do not occur frequently, and no really vigorous movement pays much heed to what philosophers are saying.

Nevertheless philosophy seems to me to have also a more important function, which may enable it to be scientifically suggestive and serviceable, at all events at a certain stage in the development of a science.

The function in question is that of discussing the working methods of a science, of exhibiting their full scope and logical implications and connexions, and considering the merits of the alternative ways of treating the subject. Such a critical *methodology* of a science is necessarily dull, but, perhaps, on that account, all the better adapted for philosophic discourse. And in view of the intellectual myopia which scientific specialism engenders, there are, perhaps, few things more salutary, as an unpleasant medicine is salutary, than for a science to become conscious of the working assumptions, or methodological postulates, on which it proceeds.

In the case of Psychical Research, in particular, the discussion of such methodological assumptions seems to be more novel, easier and more useful than in disciplines which have already reached a more assured position among the sciences. It is likely to be more novel, because of the novelty of the whole subject. It is likely to be easier to dissect out and contemplate in abstraction the methodological assumptions of an inchoate and infant science, because its organism is not so strongly knit and the flesh of fact does not so closely shroud the bone of method by which it is supported; it is still in a low stage of organization in which the whole may be taken to pieces and put together without much injury to the vitality of its parts. An advanced science, on the other hand, is far more difficult to handle: it imposes on the philosophic critic by its very mass of coherent and consistent interpretation; it appeals to him by its noble record of service to the human race; it crushes him by the sheer weight of immemorial authority. In it facts and theories have long been welded together into so indissoluble a union that the former can no longer be questioned, while the latter have for the most part risen to the dignity of indispensable 'necessary truths' implied in the very nature of the human mind and underlying the whole structure of human knowledge.[1] We gain little help therefore from the assumptions of sciences like mathematics and mechanics in considering what assumptions should be made in a new subject like Psychical Research; we learn little about the making of a science from sciences which can neither be unmade nor remade, and in whose case it requires a considerable effort of philosophic thought to realize the methodological character of their fundamental postulates. More might perhaps be learnt from the assumptions of *parvenu* sciences which have but recently obtained full recognition, but for the fact that a critical dissection of their methods is decidedly dangerous. For the '*arbor scientiae*' seems in their case to have developed a symbiotic arrangement greatly resembling that whereby certain trees protect themselves; just as any attack on the latter is ferociously resented by a host of ants which the tree provides with food and shelter, so any interference with such a science is sure to draw down upon the mildest critic the onslaught of an infuriated professor who lives upon the science. In Psychical Research, on the other hand, no such danger is to be apprehended; we have not yet developed any professionals whose mission it is, as William James has wittily remarked,[2] to kill out the layman's general interest in the subject, and hence the philosopher may proceed at his leisure to observe how the science is made and to try instructive experiments with its working methods, without fear of offending vested interests.

Again, a philosophic discussion of possible methods is likely to be more useful in Psychical Research because such methods are still plastic cartilage, as it were, which has not yet grown into rigid bone, and may be moulded into a variety of forms. Hence by reflecting betimes upon the advantages of alternative methods, the philosopher may flatter himself that he can be of real service

---

[1] See *Axioms as Postulates*.   [2] *Human Immortality, init.*

in guiding the course of investigation, or at least in helping it to avoid certain pitfalls. Not, of course, that even here he would be wise to presume to lay down the law *a priori* as to the actual working and merits of the various methods; he should content himself with expounding the logical characteristics which sound methods in Psychical Research must possess, and explaining why exactly they must possess them.

I do not propose, however, on this occasion to discuss the methodological value of the assumptions made in Psychical Research generally, but only in so far as they affect the question of a future life. The reasons for this are obvious. The possibility of a future life provides much of the motive force in such inquiries. Most of the active members of the Society are probably interested in this question, and whether they desire or fear a future life, they agree in wanting to know what chance or danger there is of it. It is true that the S.P.R. is unique in aiming to solve this problem in a scientific way, but though we are scientific, we may yet be honest—in avowing the existence of a practical motive. If attacked on this score, let us meet our critics with the doctrine that in this respect at least we are *not* unique, inasmuch as in the end all true science is inspired by practical motives, and that it is the fear, no less than the hope, of a future life that renders its possibility so urgent a subject for scientific consideration. Moreover, just now the evidence in connexion with Mrs. Piper's trances seems to have brought this possibility well above the horizon of the S.P.R., while at the same time much confusion and prejudice still seem to prevail about it which philosophic criticism may help to dissipate. For a comprehensive statement of the new evidence and new interpretations of old evidence which render it the bounden duty of the philosopher to readjust himself and his formulas to the growth of knowledge, I can now (1903) point to Frederic Myers' valuable work on *Human Personality and its Survival of Bodily Death*.

I may begin by passing over with a merely formal

mention the assumptions which are required for every scientific investigation. As a matter of course we must assume that the phenomena under investigation are knowable and rational in the sense of being amenable to determinable laws. The need for this assumption is so plain that *a priori* attacks on Psychical Research on the score of undermining the fundamental principle of all scientific research can hardly be put down to anything but voluntary or involuntary ignorance of the grossest kind.

Next we must enunciate a methodological axiom with which at first sight few will be disposed to quarrel, viz. that we must proceed to the unknown from what is known to us. The remark is Aristotle's,[1] and I may be suspected of quoting it merely because Oxonians can but rarely resist a temptation of quoting Aristotle. But in reality it is not such a truism as it appears, at least in the meaning I propose to put upon it. It means in this connexion that, both psychologically and logically, we must interpret any supposed future life by the knowledge we have acquired of our present life. It is a methodological necessity, in other words, that we must project this world into the next, if ever we purpose scientifically to know it. Our assumption may be wrong in the sense that it may be wrecked on barrier reefs of impenetrable fact—possibly it will be—but, right or wrong, we can work with no other at the outset. As we go on we shall no doubt detect the initial crudities of our assumptions, and correct them as our knowledge grows. But whatever differences we may discover between the two worlds must rest upon the postulate of a fundamental identity, in default of which our reason would be merely paralysed. From a complete otherness of the other world nothing would follow; a future life in which everything was utterly different would mean nothing to us, and in proportion as the difference grows the practical efficacy and theoretical knowableness of the conception diminish.

Now this, I venture to think, is a philosophic result of no small practical importance.

[1] *Eth. Nic.* i. 3. 5.

(1) It goes a long way towards explaining the anomaly of the feebleness of most people's religious beliefs about the future life. For the heavens and hells of the various religions, in spite of their pretensions to evoke forces which should utterly dwarf the threescore years and ten of our mortal life, are found in practice to constitute motives so weak that they are continually routed and set aside by the trivial temptations of the moment. The reason is that they have ordinarily been conceived as differing too radically from the known conditions of life to excite the same serious belief, to require the same matter-of-fact forethought as, *e.g.*, next year's crops or to-morrow's money market. And so the belief in a future life, even where it has not been degraded into a merely verbal assent to a traditional formula, has commonly lacked that intimacy of association with the ordinary concerns of life which is needed to render it psychologically efficacious as a stimulus to action.

(2) Again, it turns out that the spiritists were by no means wrong in principle when they proceeded to construe the future life, of which they believed themselves to possess cogent evidence, very much on the lines of our earthly life. Their constructions may in detail be as crude and absurd as their adversaries allege—I am neither familiar enough with the literature to discuss this point nor convinced that they are—but it is a mistaken prejudice to reject such accounts *a priori* as too trivial or undignified to be ascribed to the inhabitants of another world. Owing, no doubt, to the unduly tragic view we have come to take of death, the prejudice that the decease of Brown, Jones, and Robinson must instantly transmute them into beings of superhuman powers and tastes, and transport them into regions where they are initiated into the uttermost ecstasies and agonies of the scheme of things, has become inveterate. Indeed, I have often been amused to see how strongly this notion influences people who are really entire disbelievers in the possibility of any future life; while scorning everything 'supernatural,'

they reject the spiritist's version thereof as *not supernatural enough*, because they are quite sure that if there were a future life at all, it would have to be as full of angels and demons as what they would call 'the traditional mythologies.' In a more respectable form the same feeling shows itself in the large number of persons who refuse to accept the evidence, *e.g.* in the Piper case, because they think they would not like the sort of life to which it seems to point. This may seem a somewhat naïve *ignoratio elenchi*, but the psychical researcher can hardly afford to smile at it, for he is continually having it impressed upon him how very serious are the obstacles which prejudices of this sort form to the discovery and recognition of the facts, and how manifestly the 'will to believe' is the *ratio cognoscendi* of truth. Hence a systematic challenge of the whole assumption that another world must be as different as is conceivable (or rather inconceivable) from this, is needed to clear the atmosphere.

And inasmuch as the groundlessness of a false assumption is never revealed more clearly than by a request for the reasons on which it rests, I should like, for my own part, to add to the general challenge a particular request, asking philosophers to show cause why a hypothetical 'other' world must necessarily be conceived as out of time and out of space. The conviction that this must be so underlies, I am sure, much of the high philosophic scorn of empirical spiritism and popular theology, but I do not think it would be easy to support it by a valid and cogent philosophic argument. For so long as temporality and spatiality form indispensable characteristics of the only real world we experience, the presumption surely is that they will pervade also any other, until at least a definite method has been suggested whereby they may be transcended.[1]

(3) Thirdly, it must be recognized that the methodological principle of interpreting the unknown by the known tells strongly in favour of the simpler, and *prima*

---

[1] So far as time is concerned the conception of ἐνέργεια ἀκινησίας would seem to involve this. Cp. p. 212.

facie easier, theory of the agency of personal spirits as against the more complex and unfamiliar notions of an impersonal clairvoyance, or subliminal consciousness, or non-human modes of cognition by gods, devils, or cosmic principles of a more or less unknowable kind. I am very far from thinking that we should in such matters hastily commit ourselves to the interpretation which *prima facie* seems the most plausible, or, indeed, to any definitive theory whatsoever, and I should be sorry to see the ingenious attempts to provide a non-spiritistic explanation of the phenomena in question prematurely abandoned—if only on account of their excellence as mental gymnastics—but I cannot admit that such attempts are one whit less anthropomorphic in principle than the 'spiritist' hypothesis (they only stray further from their human model), while I cannot help admitting that methodologically they are more cumbrous and so considerably inferior. The spirit hypothesis has the same kind of initial advantage over its rivals as the 'solid' atom has in physics over the 'vortex ring' or the 'ether stress.' And while our knowledge remains in its rudiments this advantage is considerable, though, as the parallel shows, it may easily become problematical.

Admitting, therefore, that as a working theory the hypothesis of the persistence after death of what we call the human personality possesses considerable advantages over rival theories, let us inquire further by what methods, resting on what postulates, that theory may be verified.

(1) We may rule out once more the notion that such a future life is essentially supernatural in character. This notion has been a favourite with believers, but it is easily turned into a terrible weapon in the hands of their adversaries. For the supernatural is, as such, conceived to be insusceptible of investigation, and belief in it must be mere faith, exposed to every doubt and jeer, if, indeed, it can be even that, seeing that a real faith must be nourished by at least partial and prospective verification in fact. Hence the answer to this notion is simply this: that if the future life be really 'supernatural' in the sense of

having no connexion of any sort with nature, there could not possibly be any evidence of it, and it would have to be for us non-existent; while if there be evidence of it, this would *ipso facto* include it in the widest conception of nature, and render the nature of the connexion between this world and the next a legitimate subject for scientific research. If, therefore, the connexion be rare and precarious, the reason cannot possibly be that from time to time some audacious spirit has impiously achieved the impossible by breaking through the natural order; it must lie in the peculiarities of the natural order itself. Or, to sum up in a single phrase a discussion which would long have become needless but for the persistence of attempts to dispose of an inconvenient investigation into facts by logical quibbles about words, if 'supernature' is to be retained, it must not be in the sense of something alien and hostile to 'nature,' but strictly as meaning a higher department or aspect of nature itself.

(2) We must suppose a certain continuity of psychological constitution in the human spirit throughout every phase of its existence. Without this we should not know ourselves again after death. This does not imply that death may not be a great event, involving a great gain (or loss) in the intensity and extent of consciousness and memory; it asserts only that if we are to have knowledge of a future life at all, we must assume that the general characteristics of mental life will persist. Without this, too, there could be no proof of 'spirit-identity' to others: without 'spirit-identity' there could be no proof of a future life. Unfortunately, however, this assumption of ours would lead us to expect that the proof of 'spirit-identity' would be difficult. For it is psychologically far more probable that the moral character and the feelings would traverse the shock and change of death unshaken, than that little bits of knowledge about terrestrial affairs would persist in equal measure. Yet it is these latter that afford the best tests of 'spirit-identity,' and it is suggestive that whereas at

first Mrs. Piper's 'G.P.' communications abounded in such tests, they have gradually grown rare.

(3) As we must try to explain all the facts by principles already known to be valid, we must account for the remarkable dissociation between this world and the next by the principle of psychological continuity. That such dissociation must exist will hardly be denied by any one who has realized how very rare an experience a 'ghost' is, even with the most expert of ghost seers and in its most favoured haunts. But it would seem that if the departed still retained their personality and psychical continuity, 'ghosts' ought to be more plentiful than blackberries, and unhedged by that divinity which makes people so reluctant to make a clean breast of their ghost stories. *Prima facie*, therefore, it requires explanation that in spite of psychic continuity so much dissociation should prevail.

Nevertheless it may, I think, be shown that the assumption of psychical continuity would be quite compatible with the prevalence of an almost complete dissociation between this world and the next. For any great event tends to dissociate us from our past, and this would apply *a fortiori* to an event like death, which *ex hypothesi* launches us into a new world. A new world, moreover, would engross us not only by its novelty, but also by the practical need of accommodating ourselves to new conditions of existence. Hence the psychological conditions for great concern about the world we had left behind us would hardly be present. This argument, moreover, could be considerably strengthened by psychological observations with regard to the interest which is taken in the affairs of our world by the aged. For it would be unlikely that an interest which had already grown faint should effectively maintain itself amid the distractions of a new life.

And even if the desire to communicate were felt, it could hardly be assumed that the knowledge and power to do so would at once be at the disposal of the new-comer, who, for aught we know, might find that, as upon his entry upon this scene, a period of helplessness and dependence analogous to infancy had to be passed through.

It would seem probable, therefore, that to render communication effective, quite as systematic and sustained an effort would be needed on the other side as is being made by the S.P.R. on this, while the self-regarding motives for making it would be indefinitely less potent. For while each of us *ought to have*[1] the strongest personal interest in determining what his prospects may be after death, no such case could be made out for a retrospective interest of the departed in our world. And in their world the prevalent social sentiment might esteem it better to leave us in our present doubt and discourage attempts to pry into the possibilities of communication with another world. That would only be to suppose that their social sentiment is the same as ours. Only it would in their case be more reasonable. For why should they incommode themselves to impart to us a knowledge which each one of us is bound to gather for himself within a few years more? And this suggestion will appear the more probable when we remember that, according to the principle of psychic continuity, the *same* people will be making the same sentiment in both cases. Nevertheless, it is conceivable that some day a fortunate coincidence of the efforts of an infinitesimal minority on both sides should succeed in establishing spirit-identity and forcing upon the reluctant masses of men the scientific fact of a future life which they did not in the least desire to have so established. Even then, however, we should still be very far from any definite and detailed knowledge of the nature of the future life in itself, the difficulties of transmitting which would increase enormously in proportion as the dissociation between the two spheres of existence became greater.

Thus the general upshot of our discussion so far would be that a future life which was accessible to scientific

---

[1] I emphasize the 'ought,' for, as a matter of empirical fact, the present number of those who are *scientifically* interested in the question to the extent of a guinea per annum appears to be about 1400!

methods of proof would necessarily appear to be of a somewhat homely and humdrum character, displeasing to spiritual sensationalists. Broadly speaking, our conceptions of it would rest on the assumption of social and psychic continuity, and they would tend to suppose that the reward and punishment of the soul consisted mainly in its continuing to be itself, with the intrinsic consequences of its true nature revealed more and more clearly to itself and others. Hence there would be but little scope for epic flights of a lurid imagination, and those who hanker after the ecstasies of the blessed and the torments of the damned would have to go, as before, to the preachers and the poets. We may, however, trust these latter to work up a more copious material into pictures quite as edifying and thrilling as those of Homer, Dante, and Milton.

II

I have assumed hitherto, without a hint of doubt, the general possibility of the conception of a future life. But, after all, this also is an assumption, of a very vital character, and one which has been strongly impugned on *a priori* grounds. I shall devote, therefore, my concluding remarks to disposing of such philosophic attempts at an *a priori* suppression of the question and to stating some of the philosophic considerations which lead me to think the conception of a future life a valid and non-contradictory one, whether or not we are able or anxious to find empirical evidence of its actual existence. On the first point I may be brief: I should not deny that it is possible to devise metaphysical systems which will render the persistence of the individual consciousness improbable and even impossible, and which consequently close the question to all who conscientiously adopt them. Personally, I believe those systems to be demonstrably wrong, but it is enough for our purpose that they should be gratuitous, and that we may, at least equally well, adopt metaphysical views which leave the question open, or even lead us to regard a future life as *a priori* probable enough, and needing only verification *a posteriori*.

Hence, speaking for myself—and in so personal a matter it is best to speak for oneself if one wants to speak to the point—I cannot at all appreciate the enormous antecedent difficulty which so many philosophers profess to feel about the conception of a future life. Even its most difficult implications, like, *e.g.* the transition from one world to another, seem to become quite easy, if we start from the proper philosophic basis. Let us, for instance, assume—as I think we must do in any case—the philosophic position of an idealistic experientialism. I use this clumsy phrase to designate the view that 'the world' is primarily 'my experience,' *plus* (secondarily) the supplementings of that experience which its nature renders it necessary to assume, such as, *e.g.*, other persons and a 'real' material world. In that case the world, in which we suppose ourselves to be, is, and always remains, relative to the experience which we seek to interpret by it, and if that experience were to change, so necessarily would our 'real' world. Its reality was guaranteed to it, so long as it did its work and explained our experience; it is abrogated so soon as it ceases to do so.[1] Hence we may conceive ourselves as passing through any number of worlds, separated from each other by (partial) discontinuities in our experience, each of which would be perfectly real while it lasted, and yet would have to be declared unreal from a higher and clearer point of view.

Nor would this conception remain an empty form, which we could not find anything in our experience to illustrate. I venture to affirm that we are all of us perfectly familiar with what it feels like to pass from one world into another. When we fall asleep and *dream*, we pass into a new world, with space, time, persons, and laws (uniformities) like our own. But though these fundamental features *persist in principle*, they are *not the same* space, etc.,[2] and have no very obvious connexion with the corresponding characteristics of our waking life.

---

[1] Cp. p 193. [2] Cp. 32.

It is true that the reality of each dream-world is very precarious: it is dissolved by every clumsy interruption from a more 'real' world, in the *ex post facto* judgment of which the dream-world is fleeting, chaotic, and unmanageable.[1] But the philosophic critic cannot thus presume the theoretical correctness of our ordinary judgment. To him all modes of experience are, in the first instance, real.[2] He can find no standing ground outside experience whence to judge it.

All our distinctions, then, between the 'real' and 'unreal' are *intrinsic*: it is the dream-world's character itself that leads us to condemn it.[3] And if in our dreams we found ourselves transported into worlds more coherent, more intelligible, more beautiful and more delightful than that of daily life, should we not gladly attribute to them a superior reality, and, like Mohammed, hold that in our sleep our souls had been snatched up to heaven and privileged to commune with the gods?[4] The fact, indeed, that such experiences have played a signal part in the lives of nearly all the world's greatest heroes, and thereby left an indelible mark upon its history, should make us chary of dogmatic denials of the value of such 'dream-worlds.' But as a rule we do deny without a scruple, and, reasoning as pragmatists, do ruthlessly reject them for yielding nothing that sense can use and sanity can tolerate. Hence the consensus of common sense declares dream experiences to be unreal—though, it may be noted, it has taken men a long time to arrive at this conclusion and to disabuse themselves of the notion that after all there must be a literally veridical and inspired meaning in all their experiences. What has not been realized with equal clearness—probably because the observation seemed to have no direct practical bearing—is that the existence of unreal worlds of dream-experience casts an indelible slur on the claim of our present waking life to absolute reality.[5] What has happened once may happen again, and when we wake to

[1] Cp. p. 113 note. [2] Cp. p. 192. [3] Cp. p. 195.
[4] Cp. pp. 22, 32. [5] Cp. p. 198.

another world our terrestrial life may appear as grotesque a parody, as misleading a distortion, of true reality as the most preposterous of dreams.

Nay more ; even in this life we cannot call it an illicit and unthinkable ambition to discover modes of rising from our waking world to one of a higher order, whose superior reality would demand acknowledgment from all so soon as either its experience had become communicable to an appreciable fraction of society, or it had proved to be of use for the purposes of 'waking' life.[1] Philosophy could not indeed provide the Columbus of such idealist discovery. But it might sanction his assumption of such risks. Just as an enlightened physics might have contended, long before Magellan, that the earth was circumnavigable if it could find the daring soul to sail right round it, so philosophy may declare that if the whole world be experience, *new worlds* may be found by psychical transformation as probably and validly as by physical transportation. And it must decline to treat the fact that the other worlds we know are apparently less real than that of waking life [2] as being a conclusive proof that more real worlds are nowhere to be found.

Thus the passage from world to world is familiar enough to our experience. But, as experienced by us in sleep, it is not *irrevocable*. We *return*, that is, to the same waking world. And that makes a difference between sleep and its twin brother death. For from death we are bidden to believe that there is no return. Still we must not exaggerate the difference ; for *to* our dream-worlds also we do not (usually) return.

Hence this return, which is regarded as an *awakening* of the soul from the point of view of the subject of the experience, is at the same time the *dissolution* of his dream-world and life. The severance of his relations with the world of his former experience, therefore, has a double

---

[1] Cp. p. 41.
[2] A remark subject always to certain reservations on the score of the subjective worlds of the mystics and founders of religions. Common sense hardly realizes how its principles here cut away the foundations of all the religions which, nevertheless, it imagines itself to value and believe. Cp. p. 114 note.

aspect. On the one hand, his 'dream' passes away as he passes into a region of higher reality ; on the other, *he passes away* out of the dream-world that imposed itself upon him into his 'waking' life.[1] For we have seen that even dreams are not entirely unreal. Even at their lowest, the features they present refer to the truth, and foreshadow the reality, of a superior world : they are to some extent *veridical.* Hence we must contemplate the situation also from the point of view of the beings who interacted with the 'dreamer' in the 'dream' life and world. For them, his awakening means his *withdrawal* from their world. When *Alice* awakes, she of course declares *Looking-Glass Land* to have been a dream, and its inhabitants to have been the creatures of her fancy. But while she was with them they were vividly real. And Alice, after all, herself was not *quite* satisfied with this vulgar explanation. It will be remembered that she suspected the black kitten of having transformed herself into the Red Queen of Looking-Glass Land. And this would raise an interesting question : if we should chance to survive death, should we merely declare earth-life to have been unreal, or should we not rather trace in its happenings some subtle presage of a fuller truth ?

It seems quite worth while, therefore, to look at the situation from the point of view of Looking-Glass Land, to whose denizens it would appear quite different. Tweedledee, no very cogent reasoner, perhaps, but a thoroughgoing idealistic monist in his argument, asseverated that the dream was not Alice's at all, but the Red King's, and that if and when he left off dreaming her, the phenomenon called Alice would simply disappear. His notion as to the manner of her disappearance was that she would "go out bang!—just like a candle," but herein he may have been mistaken. Still he has at least suggested to us that when one of us withdraws from a world, the world may misinterpret his action as his *death*.

Now *death* is a topic on which philosophers have been astonishingly commonplace. The reason of this cannot have been that it was not a splendid topic for reflection,

[1] Cp. p. 39.

nor yet that their doctrines were not capable of throwing light upon its nature. Perhaps they have lived in as great terror of it as more ordinary mortals, and so lacked the courage to think about it at all. At all events I can readily believe, from a study of their doctrines, that Spinoza was quite right in maintaining that there is no subject concerning which the sage *thinks less* than about death.[1] Which, nevertheless, is a great pity. For the sage is surely wrong. There is no subject concerning which he, *if he is an idealist and has the courage of his opinions*, OUGHT to think more, and OUGHT to have more interesting things to say.

In partial proof of which let me attempt to arouse him to reflection by propounding some old [2] *paradoxes about death* which will, I think, be germane to our subject.

(1) *No man ever yet perished without annihilating also the world in which he lived.*

(2) *No man ever yet saw another die; but if he had, he would have witnessed his own annihilation.*

(3) *The world is the greatest of all conventions; but all are unconventional enough to leave it.*

(4) *To die is to cut off our connexion with our friends; but do they cut us, or we them, or both, or neither?*

Now these paradoxes contain nothing but necessary inferences from the idealistic view of the world, if it is applied practically to the phenomenon of 'death,' and no philosopher who really and seriously accepts that view should have the slightest difficulty with them. But for the sake of the others I feel that it may be better to add a short commentary. "No man ever yet perished without annihilating also the world in which he lived," *i.e.* the world of *his* experience, or as we may perhaps say with still more accuracy, the objective world, in so far as it was assumed to explain *his* experience. Moreover, "no man ever yet saw another die, but if he had he would have witnessed his own annihilation": inasmuch as he could never see the other's self and so *a fortiori* could not observe its de-

---

[1] *Eth.* iv. Prop. 67.
[2] Cp. S.P.R. *Journal* for March 1898, vol. viii. p. 204.

struction ; what he saw was the 'death' of a 'body' which was merely a phenomenon in his own world of experience. But if, *per impossible*, he could have witnessed the destruction of the subject of a world of experience, his own destruction, as a phenomenon in such a world, would have been included in the catastrophe. Thus both these paradoxes are designed to bring out the essential and incurable philosophic ambiguity of 'death.'[1] Death is not the same thing for him who experiences and for him who witnesses it. It forms the limiting case which involves the breakdown of the great social convention, whereby we postulate (for practical purposes) a common world which is experienced by us all. (No. 3.) Even during life that convention is maintained only at the cost of excluding from 'reality' all such experiences as are personal, or divergent, or incapable of forming a basis for common action. At death it breaks down altogether, and the long-suppressed divergence between the world of 'my' experience and the 'objective' world, which is nobody's experience but is supposed to account for everybody's, dominates the situation.[2]

When a man dies his relation to the common world

---

[1] Cp. also *Riddles of the Sphinx*, ch. xi. § 8.

[2] This is the simplest description of the actual situation and begs the fewest questions. The monistic metaphysicians who arrogate to themselves exclusive rights to an idealism which they cannot use, and which dies away in their hands either into naturalism or into platitude, prefer to distort it by postulating as its explanation a 'divine' consciousness which somehow embraces or contains all the subject-consciousnesses of our fellows, and thereby (*sic*) guarantees the absolute commonness of the 'common' world which is really the 'object' of the divine consciousness. But the expedient proves utterly futile. For (1) the conception of one consciousness (divine or diabolical) including another has never yet been shown to be capable of anything like intelligible statement (cp. Dr. Rashdall in *Personal Idealism*, pp. 382-4). The only clue in experience to anything of the sort is to be found in the highly suggestive, but quite inadequately studied, facts of 'multiplex personality,' and it seems extremely doubtful whether even these would lead to the desired conclusion. The metaphysicians in question, moreover, are about the last people in the world to concern themselves with empirical phenomena of this sort. (2) The divine world-image, so far from explaining the plurality of our individual world-images, only adds one to their number. It remains involved in the old Platonic difficulty of the transcendent universal. Or, if it is taken as really immanent, it becomes merely a hypocritical description of the 'harmony' of the individual images, and lapses into atheism. And (3) in many cases the 'harmony' is very imperfect, and there is not, strictly, a 'common' world at all. That is, the communion is neither pre-existent nor absolute. It is an *achievement*, reached by infinite labours and unending struggles, to a limited degree, for a limited period. We do not, as a matter of fact, experience our common 'objects'

apparently ceases, and so " to die is to cut off our connexion with our friends; but do they cut us, or we them, or both, or neither?" But for what reason we cannot say. It may be that the deceased has ceased to be; it may also be that he has ceased to interact with us—until we also have followed his example. Similarly, when we witness a death, all that we can safely and scientifically say is that a peculiar feature in our experience which impelled us to assume a self-conscious spirit, analogous to our own, in order to account for the behaviour of the complex of phenomena we called the body of our fellow-man, has undergone a change such that the behaviour of his 'body' no longer warrants the inference of the presence of his 'spirit.' Again, the reason may be either that the spirit is destroyed, or that it has ceased to animate the 'body.' Thus it would seem as though all that could be affirmed for certain about death was that it was a disruption of the common world in which spirits acted together; what else or what more it was would remain in doubt—the spirit may have perished or it may just have 'passed away.'

---

alike. Hence the infinite diversity of individual judgments and valuations. But if this were all, there would be no possibility of what Professor Ward has well called 'intersubjective intercourse.' So we have managed to some extent to act concordantly with regard to the 'objects' of our most pressing practical concerns. You and I, *e.g.*, are said to perceive a 'common' *red*, when we classify colours alike. But whether your experience in perceiving 'red' is the same as mine, it is meaningless to ask (p. 31). For the 'common red' means merely such practical agreement. And when we go on to ask what is 'beautiful,' and 'good,' and 'right,' and 'pleasant,' we soon discover how narrow are the limits of such practical agreement, and are forced to realize that to a large extent we still literally live in different worlds. And, as noted above, 'death' seems to terminate the common world in time as completely as individuality limits its extent. (4) The Absolute or 'universal consciousness' on scrutiny turns out to be neither divine nor conscious. Or rather the connotation both of 'God' and of 'consciousness' has to be radically changed to accommodate it. An all-containing consciousness cannot be a moral being. It is the Devil just as much as God, and indeed the 'Absolute' must be defined in Hegelian terms as the synthesis of God and the Devil. And however much it may 'contain' consciousness it is hard to see how it can be itself conscious. Indeed in the end it seems describable in negatives alone, and by contrast with the contents of our experience; it 'has' all things, but *is* not any of the things it 'has.' For the whole cannot *be* anything that we predicate of its parts.

In short it seems impossible really to think out the conception of a single subject of all experience except upon solipsistic lines. If one consents to solipsism it is easy enough, but not a bit more satisfactory. For solipsism is just the view we are driven out of by the considerations which induce us to construct a common world.

Thus, so far as philosophy can determine, it would seem as if the chances of destruction and survival were exactly equal, and that we were doomed to doubt for ever. Nevertheless, considerations may be adduced which must add decisively to the weight of the latter alternative. For it should be noted that the two alternatives are not equally well situated with respect to empirical evidence. No conceivable empirical evidence can suffice to establish the destruction of the soul at death, because none can even be relevant to the real issue as it presents itself from our philosophic point of view. For it can only concern appearances in the common world of the *survivors*, it can only prove that the rupture of connexion with it at death is utter and entire. But that is not enough. Even if a ghost returned to announce to us the complete extinction of the soul at death, we could not credit so Hibernian an assertion. A scientific proof therefore, of the annihilation of the soul is rigorously impossible. On the other hand, there is no such intrinsic impossibility about a scientific proof of the persistence of consciousness through death; there is, in fact, no particular difficulty about conceiving empirical evidence sufficient to establish this doctrine with as high a degree of certainty as we have for any of our beliefs as to matters of fact. The whole difficulty consists in getting the evidence. If we had succeeded, the theoretic readjustment of our opinions would be easy; all we should need to do would be to modify our original assumption that death meant an *absolute* rupture of relations, an utter dissolution of the common world. We should have to say instead, that death altered the mode of communication of spirit with spirit, rendering it different and difficult, without interrupting it altogether. But, properly interpreted and manipulated, the common world would persist through death. What exactly would be the nature of the common world, thus extended to include a life after death, philosophy could not, of course, forecast; that would remain a question for positive research to determine.

Here then we reach the limits of philosophic speculation. When the philosopher has shown that no *a priori* impossibilities block the pathway of discovery, and no authentic fact can be too anomalous for explanation, when he has cleared men's eyes of the prejudices which obstruct a clear prevision of the goal and has aroused a sufficient will to know, a sufficient conviction that it is well to look before we plunge, and to try to see whither we go before we go, he must modestly stand aside, and leave the empirical explorer into the puzzling mazes of psychical science to cut down the barbed-wire entanglements of hostile human prejudice, and step by step to fight his way through the thickets of complex and perplexing fact. And so the glory of discovery will not be his, but will reward the scientist who has borne the labour and danger of the day of battle. And yet the discoverer will owe perhaps the faith which sustained his courage and endurance in no small measure to the apparently unmoved spectator who watched the struggle from afar, and this faith may justify the thinker also when he is called upon to render an account of the use to which he has put his powers.

INDEX

Absolute, an abstraction, xxii; no starting-point, xxiii; the death of morals, 2; its transcendence of distinctions, 3; triviality of its contemplation, 4; its monotony, 14, and irredeemable perfection, 14; as unknowable and a useless theory, 41, and hence to be called false, 59; as explaining objectivity, 60, 371-2; Lotze's theory of, 62-84; suppresses difficulties *ex officio*, 108; an interpretation of reality, 119-20; a misconception, 126; unites God and the devil, 167, 263, 372; Bradley's, 187-191; as *asylum ignorantiae*, 188; transmutes appearances, 189, 199; unknowable, 191; inaccessible, 192; solipsistic, 252; neither divine nor conscious, 372

Absolute Idea, 96, 102-3
Absolutism, xxviii
Abstraction, the kingdom of, xxii; from time and individuality, 98-9; its value, 100-102; its teleological subordination, 104; as instrument, 120; mathematical, why judged real, 120; as method of simplification, 145-8; produces timelessness, 212
Accidents not distinct from 'essence,' 222
Activity, purposive, condition of knowledge, 12, 234, 238; speculative, 25-6; of intelligence, 130; of Mephisto, 180, and substance, 204-27; transcending change, 205; of divine life, 212; motion as, 214; is substance, 225; Hume's criticism of, *235-48*
Actuality, 67, 208, 224, 226
Adaptation, argument from, to an adapter, 131; its imperfection, 131; shown by Darwin to be conceivable without adapter, 132; origin of, 142; growth of, 142; novelty of, 143; not due to natural selection, 154; instantaneous in perfect life, 215-16
Alexander, S., 261

Alice, 369
Analysis, of cause, 238; of 'complex' and 'simple,' 56
Anaximander, 156
Animism, 239
Annihilation of soul incapable of proof, 373
Anthropomorphism, xxi, 13, 240, 361
Antinomies, 108-9
Appearance and Reality, 3, 101, 226; antithesis of, 183-203
Apriorism, 231-3
Aristotle, 19-40, 67, 203, 205-27 *passim*, 253, 257, 285, 353, 358
Arnold, Matthew, 2
Ascham, R., 34
Associationism, 240
Astrology, 298, 300
Attention, why volatile, 217
Authority, 273; argument from, 335, and old age, 326
Automata, 133-4
Axioms as Postulates, ix, xi; notes 33, 44, 50, 92, 94, 95, 129, 183, 227, 355

Balfour, Arthur, xii, 6
Barbarism, and Humanism, xxvi
Bateson, W., 135
Beatific Vision, 203, 212
Beauty, ideal of, 344-5
Becoming, 107, 118, 207, 208, 210, 216-17
Being, and nothing, xxii; Aristotle's ideal of, 205, 226; unchanging, 207, 216-17; as perfect harmony, 225
Belief, and action, 251
Berkeley, 126, 223
Bias, 298, 301, 307, 312
Blatchford, R., *283-312 passim*
Bradley, F. H., 3, 38, 96, 101, 108, *183-201 passim*, 244, 272 n.
Buddha, 158, 168
Burnet, J., 212

Calculus of probabilities, 126, 150

Calinon, 86, 89
Carroll, Lewis, 53, 216
Causation, 64; as analysis, 238; Hume's criticism of, 232-3, 235-6; immanent—not more intelligible than transient, 68-9; volitional theory of, 235-48
Cave-dwellers, 21, 23, 41, 43
Chance, as originating world, 72; as excluding intelligence, 150
Change, and identity, 69; problem of, 73, 101; endangers adaptation, 143; as fact, 188; as defect, 211
Choice, as real, 303; not motiveless, 306-11
Coexistence and interaction, 65
Cognition as moral act, 15; not intellection, 233-4; not passive, 236
Coherence a psychological fact, 52-3; feelings of, 52; not always logical, 53; due to interest, 53; use as test of reality, 119
Colour-blindness, 116
Commensurability, Lotze's argument from, 70
Common sense, xxi, xxiii, xxv, 6, 190, 232, 235, 257, 272, 305-6
Common world, result of effort, 31, 371
Comte, 201
Conduct, controls theory, 4; thought a mode of, 4; survival value of, 133; rewards and punishments as results of, 340
Consciousness, as accident, 130; economy of, 241-2; perfection of, 216-218; one, as subject of world, 371-2
Contradiction, principle of, 185-6, 188
Cope, E. D., 135
Correspondence, of subject and object, 256
Criteria of reality, 114-8, 121; absolute, 185, 189
Crypto-solipsism, 254, 262

Damnation, of Faust impossible, 177; eternal, not an ethical postulate, 349
Dante, 365
Darwin, C., 128-56 *passim*
Darwinism, 71; its implicit atheism, 72, and design, 128-56
Death, foreknowledge of, 314; not thought about, 315-21; as withdrawal from common world of waking life, 369-74; idealist paradoxes about, 370; ambiguity of, 371
Degeneration, 139, 140
Delbœuf, 86, 90
Demonstration, hypothetical, 349
Descartes, 253, 257
Design, 128-56; argument from, its theological value, 130; its weaknesses, 131; attacked by Darwin, 132; ultimately strengthened by evolutionism, 154-6
Desire to know, 234, 330-4
Determinism, as postulate, 15, 301, and Monism, 49, and responsibility, 283-312
Dewey, J., ix, xiii
Dialectic, Hegel's, 95, 97, 103
Dogma, 278-82
Dogmatism, 229
Dreams and superior reality, 22, 32, 282; as individual truths, 60; their alleged incoherence and unreality, 114 *n.*, 119; private worlds of, 196; of metaphysics, 226, and the transition to other worlds, 366, 369; in relation to solipsism, 285-6, 312; inferior reality of dream worlds, 367-8

Economic man, 146-8
Eleaticism, 206-7
Elimination of unfitter, 132
Eliot, George, 339
Empiricism, 229, 231-2; radical, 237, *q.v.*
End, affair of finite individuals, 105; or good, 160
Energeia, Aristotelian conception of substance, 204-27; as life and perfection of activity, 221, and energy, 223
Energy, 246, dissipation of, 214, and 'energeia,' 223
Epistemological question, prior to ontological, 9; but conditioned by ethical, 10, and ontological, 114
Equilibration, as 'death,' 219-20; as life, 220-21
Equilibrium, 188, 214-21
Error, 251, 257, 259, 261, 275, 292, 299
Ethical theory dependent on practice, 33-5
Ethics and Pragmatism, xvii, and psychological facts of conduct, 313
Eugenics, 288
Evil, 78-80
Evolution, its essence, 108; factors of organic, 134, 136; not explained by Darwinism, 138-43; facts of, do not exclude intelligence, 149-50; mechanical views of, 155
Evolutionism, 108, 129, 144; its antiquity, 155
Experience, ambiguous, 231 *f.*
Experientialism, idealistic, 366

Fact, as value, 10, 55; its recognition provisional, 12, and truth, 46; valued as 'true,' 57; cannot decide

INDEX

between teleological and antiteleological interpretation, 153; judgments of, 161; are values, 163
Faith and reason, xvii, 7; its venture, 16, 79-80; Dr. McTaggart's, in the unknown synthesis, 96; extralogical, 97; ultimate appeal to, 99; needed for ultimate assumptions, 153, 312; need for, due to past negligence, 322; 'ages of faith' not really religious, 327; in 'supernatural,' 361-2
Falsehood, and uselessness, 37, 40; practically untenable, 38
Feeling, 233
Fichte, 254
Fiction, 10, 11 *n.*, 146, 147, 308
Formal Logic, ix, x; *notes*, 2, 125, 185, 238, 268
Freedom, 15, 77, 176, 182, *283-312*; and habit, 303; and indetermination, 306; inconvenience of, 302-3
Future life, why a 'matter of faith,' 324; scientific investigation of, *351-74*; too much to think of, 342; interest in, 357; cannot be wholly different, 358; unduly tragic view of, 359; *a priori* objections to, 365; possibility of empirical proof, 373

Galton, Sir F., 288
Geometry, Euclidean and non-Euclidean, 85-94; its certainty, 91; real validity, 91; necessity and universality, and 'a-priority,' 92
Ghost, of Banquo, 116; rarity of, 363
God, not the Unity of Things, 76; not the Absolute, 77; nor author of evil, 80-81; vagueness of the current conception, 81; *a priori* proofs of, worthless because too wide, 82; must be given an *a posteriori* reference, 83-4; thought of, does not constitute human reality, 121; as author of adaptation, 131; united with the devil in the Absolute, 167, 372; Aristotle's, 203, 211, 253; perfection of, 226; not the one subject, 371
Goethe, 166, 180
Good, conditions true and real, 9; supreme power of, 12; idea of, 41, 207; of organism determines racial conduct, 133; the, 208; must be attainable, 217
Goodness, ultimately harmonious with truth, 24, 28, and truth, 62; as ideal, 162; its apparent waste, 338; a matter of character, 339, and happiness, 340
Gorgias, 186

Green, T. H., 112, 212, 235 *n.*, 236 *n.*
Gymnosophistic, 35

Hallucination, individual, 115; collective, 116; how distinguished from reality, 119
Hamilton, Sir W., 237
Happiness, as ideal, 159; its validity, 162, 344, 345
Harmony, and individuality, xxvi, includes system, 50; the real as, 119; includes non-contradiction, 187; a postulate, 189; result of growing knowledge, 200; perfect, 203; ethical, postulates a future life, 337, 344; of experience potential, 346; must be universal, 349
Hartmann, E. von, 158
Heaven, conception of, 177, 212-3, 336-7, 365; its inefficacy, 325, 359
Hedonism, and pessimism, 158-9
Hegel, xxvii, 54, 97, 186, 218
Hegelism, 99
Helmholtz, 131
Herakleitos, 39, 42, 207, 284
Herbart, 85, 186, 187
Historical method, 107
Hobbes, 216
Hodgson, R., 328
Homer, 365
Howison, G. H., xiii
Humanism, xx-xxix; its naming, ix, xx; relation to anthropomorphism, xxi; to Protagoras's dictum, x, xxi; to common sense, xxi, xxv; as a method, xxii-xxvi; relation to radical empiricism and pluralism, xxiv; to Humism, *225-48*; to personal idealism and pragmatism, xxv; to scepticism, 230; to solipsism, 251, 263-7; antithesis to barbarism, xxvi, and scholasticism, xxvii, and naturalism and absolutism, xxviii, 13, 197
Hume, 197, 205, 209, 223, *228-48 passim*, 253
Hyperaesthesia, 115-6

'Idea,' 256-7
'Idealism' and reality, 110-26; 'absolute,' 252; epistemological and metaphysical, 112; a paradox because not acted on, 197-8; false, 198, 262; subjective, 252
Idealistic, art of passing into superior worlds, 18; experientialism, 366
Ideals, denial of, leads to pessimism, 159; freedom to realize, 182; of knowledge, 203; not to be abandoned, 342; their claims, 343-4; of activity and rest, 218

Immediacy of experience, 101
Immediate experience, xxii, real, 192; not sufficient, 193; of cause, 239-240; superior reality of, 195; return to, 202
Immortality, desire for, *313-34*; ethical significance of the idea, *335-50*; hope of, 317, 343, and fear of death, 314; not taken as fact, 325; scientific investigation of disliked, 326
Imperfection, 102, 109; of life, 345
Indetermination of Real, xxiv, 12, 307 *f.*; implied in Pragmatism, 15
Individual, is real, 122, 123; not compounded of universals, 123, 126
Individuality, of philosophy, xxvi, 265, 353; of experience, 31; abstracted from, 98; real, 102; extralogical,123; degrees of, 124; in process, 124; inexhaustible, 126; limits extent of common world, 372
Infallibility, 268-82
Infinity, as metaphysical ideal, 214
Intellection, not knowing, 234
Intellectual insight, dependent on action, 34
Intellectualism, xvii, 6, 230, 248; of Hume, 233-4; of Mephisto, 173, 181; kinds of, 233-4
Intelligence, divine, human or animal in evolution, 129; as otiose, 130; animal, as source of adaptation, 131; divine, in conflict with benevolence and superfluous, 132; not necessary for natural selection, 133; question of its efficacy, 134-5; non-suited, 150-51
Intolerance, 274, 276, 282
Interaction, develops both subject and object, 113; necessary to coexistence implied in existence of world and primary fact, 65-6
Interest, xvi, 51, 53; in future life, 328, 330; in ' future ' life greater than in past, 364
Intuition, 285
Irrationalism, 5

James, W., vii, xii, xiii, xx, xxi, xxiv, 5, 7, 15, 27, 52, 117, 119, 152, 246 *n.*, 312, 356

Kant, xxvi, 7, 9, 29, 85, 92, 94, 205 *n.*, 233, 238, 243 *n.*, 247, 257, 258
Karma, 349
Kidd, B., 6
Knowledge, its unity, 23; its usefulness, 23; useless, relatively so or indirectly useful or apparently so, 40; about, *vs.* ' acquaintance with,'

189, why power, 200; as opposed to opinion, 259-60; as ideal, 344; as postulate, 348
Knox, H. V., 189

Lamarckian factors in evolution, 136
Law, 300-302
Lechalas, 86
Leroy, E., 278
Lie, 47
Life, as equilibrium, 214-6
Locke, 253
Logic, reform of, ix, x, xiv, xvii; abstract, xvi; relation to psychology, x, xvii; should not abstract from interest, 52; nor exclude psychology, x, 53; of Darwinism, 144
Loisy, 306
Lotze, 7, 10, *62-84 passim*, 224, 254

MacTaggart, J. E., xiii, *95-109 passim*
Magic, 298-9
Mainländer, 219
Man, as the measure, xxi; maker of science, xxiv; starting-point, xxi-xxii
Measure, man as the, xxi, xxiv
Mechanism, its value, 242
Metageometry, 86, 89, 93
Metaphysics, an immoralist, 4; its foundations in ethics, 10; quasi-ethical, 13; abstract, 99, 105, 107; subordinate to concrete fact, 102; ultimately ethical, 105, 107, and epistemology, 112; critical denial of, 161
Methodological assumption, of Darwin, 146; of Law, 104, 297-312; in psychical research, 355-65
Methodology, 355
Mill, J. S., 223 *n.*, 225, 238
Milton, 365
Mimicry, 48, 152
Mind! 116 *n.*, 156 *n.*
' Modernism,' 268-84
Mohammed, 367
Monads, 124
Monism, Lotze's proof of, 63; not implied in mere existence of a world, 66; the One not substantial, 67; its besetting sin, 75; religiously worthless, 77; Eleatic, 206; idealistic, 369, 371
Moore, A. W., 7, 56
Moore, G. E., 256
Moral Order, 181, 254-63
Motion, 246; as imperfect energeia, 210, and time, 212; equilibration of, 213-4
Multiple Personality, 266
Myers, F. W. H., 321, 325, 357

INDEX 379

Natural Selection, 8; sifts mechanically, 133-46, 149, 153-4; as universal condition of life, 135-44; does not exclude special creation, 141; not a moral guide, 143
Naturalism, xxv, xxviii, 235, 243-5
Nature, not indifferent, 13, and supernature, 362; its 'uniformity' why assumed, 300-302, 348
Necessary matter, 37
Necessity, and need, 36, 37; feeling of, 52; of controlling phenomena, 119, 300-301
Nephelococcygia, 352
Nirvâna, 219, 341
Nordau, M., 139
Normative sciences, rest on fact of valuation, 55
Novelty, 228, 280, 301

Objectivity of perceptions useful and teleological, 31; of truth, 55, 57, 60, 258; of world, 371
Omnipotence, of natural selection, 134, 136; its limitation, 181; cannot overcome Mephisto, 182
Omniscience, 118, 121, 126
Ontological question, conditioned by epistemological, 9
'Opinion,' 259-60
Optimism, 161, 164, 312
Ostwald, W., xvii, 223
Other-worldliness, 315, 341

Parmenides, 218
Pearson, N., 320
Peirce, C. S., 27
Perfection, must be universal, 181; its metaphysical character, 226-7; moral, requires future life, 338
Persecution, 269, 281-2
Personal Idealism, xxv
'Personal Idealism,' xi, xii, xxi, 52 *n.*, 353 *n.*
Pessimism, why not judged true, 50; of divorcing truth from goodness, 62, and scepticism, 74, 163-4, 347; its difficulty, 79-80, 157-65; its definition and philosophic importance, 172-3; Mephisto's, 168-70; Faust's, 170-72, and distaste for life, 180; as denial of the validity of ideal postulates, 312, 347
Philosophers, eccentricity of, 350-3; use of, 353-5, 374
Piper, Mrs., 334, 357, 360, 363
Pius X., 280, 282
Plato, ix, xxi, 12, 19-43 *passim*, 85, 97, 203, 207-10, 217, 230, 233, 235, 248, 250, 259, 285, 320, 351, 353

Plato or Protagoras? ix
Pluralism, relation to Humanism, xxiv, xxv; to solipsism, 251; in logic, 49; admits unity of universe, how, 66
Plutarch, 267
Poincaré, H., 86, 90, 260 *n.*
Postulates, in logic, xv-xvi, 15, 33, 50; as *a priori*, 231; Darwin's, 132; of law, 300-302, 310; of universal salvation, 181; harmony, a, 188-9; of higher realities, 195; of religion, 197; once dreams, 226; immortality an ethical, *334-50*; emotional and rational, 342; origin of, 264-5; solidarity of ultimate, 350; methodological, 355; of continuity of 'other' world with this, 358; of survival of personality, 361-4
Potentiality, 67, 208, 224-6
Power, Hume's criticism of, 235 *f.*
Practical value, a determinant of truth, 4; reason has, 7; a test of superior reality, 23; of criteria of reality, 117
Pragmatism, logic of, ix, xi, 294, central thought of, xiii; effect on logic, ix, xiii-xvii; in science, xvii; in ethics, xviii, and religion, xviii-xix, and Humanism, xxv; as logical method, xxv; to be reached how, 5-8; definitions of, 8; a travesty of, 11; a tonic, 13, and perfection, 15, and indetermination, 15, and moral responsibility, 15; and the Pope, 269 *f.*; as a theory of the relation of knowledge and action, 27-43; as a principle of selection, 58; anticipated, 105; and methodological assumptions, 147; and logical valuation, 163; asserts value of philosophy, 354; denies value of dreams, 367
Prince, M., 266
Pringle-Pattison, A. S., 77, 112
Progression, problem of, 140, 142, 144, 153, 154
Protagoras, ix, x, xxi, 31
Psychic continuity, 362-3; dissociation, 363
Psychical Research, 355-8, 360; Society for, 41, 313, 317-8, 322, 328, 334, 351, 356-7, 364; prejudice against, 201
Psychology, relation to logic, x, xvii, 50; to philosophy, 231; teleological, its influence on logic, 8; of Hume, 247; of truth, 51-61; physiological, 314; of spiritism, 323
Punishment, 289-90
Pure Reason, xvi, xvii, 235, 279; a figment, 6; impossible, 7; logica fiction, 10
Pythagoras, 85

Radical Empiricism, how related to Humanism, xxiv-xxv, 237; to Humism, 238
Rashdall, H., 254, 371
Rationalism, 232-3, 247, 274
Rationality, of real, 117; as test of reality, 118
Real, depends on good, 9; its alleged rigidity, 11; its nature determinable not determinate, 12; indeterminate before trial, 12; relative to purpose, 12; not to be abstracted from good, 12; relation to Becoming, 107; primarily everything, 113; individual, 122, 125
Realism, 11, 197, 253; new, 254-61
Reality, must be knowable, 9; 'as it is in itself' unknowable, 10; varying accounts of, relative to purpose, 11; objective, 32; not separable from thought, 46; variously constructed by human efforts, 49; its time-aspect abstracted from, 98; more than rationality, 106; may change in time, 109, and 'idealism,' 110-26; truth valid of, 162, and appearance, 183-203; higher, continuous with lower, 192; to start with immediate experience, 192; higher, secondary, 193, 195; of primary experience, 113, 195; altered by thought, 195, 199; what perfects experience, 225; meaning of, for idealistic experientialism, 366; absolute, of waking world doubted, 367
Reason, antithesis to faith, xviii; how related to faith, 7; to habit, 309; a weapon in the struggle for existence, 7
Referendum, 115
Reid, T., 237
Reincarnation, 241
Religion, xviii-xix, 196, 278, 321, 324, 327, 368
Renouvier, C., 86
Rest, ideal of, 218-9
Riddles of the Sphinx, notes xxi, 2, 54, 67, 159, 163, 212, 214, 217, 219, 225, 339, 345, 371
Risk, of novelty, 279, of Pragmatism, 14, of selection, 238
Ritchie, D. G., 110-27 *passim*

Scepticism, of Bradley, 189, 191, of Hume, 229-30, 232; and Pessimism, 74, 163, 164, 347; moral and intellectual, 348
Scholasticism, and Humanism, xxvii
Schopenhauer, 158, 168
Schurman, J. G., 135

Science, method of, compared with that of religion, xix; of magic, 299; depends on abstraction, 100, 102; its use of abstraction, 103; subordinate to practical ends, 105; of ends, the highest, 165; mocked by the unique, 153; not interested in historic errors, 353; infant, parvenu, and advanced, 356
Selection, 255, 306; its danger, 14; by attention, 53; of subjective valuations, 58
Self-evidence, 36; aesthetic, 50; of world's existence, 67
Sensationalism, 233, 248
Sidgwick, A., xiv, 185
Sidgwick, H., 306 *n.*
Sigwart, C., xiv
Social control, of truth, 58, 98, 333-4; of interest in immortality, 328-30; of desire to know, 201, 332
Socrates, 285
Solidarity, demands universal salvation, 181; of ideals, 346; of ultimate postulates, 350
Solipsism, 112, *249-67*, 312, 373
Space, 33, 85-94; four-dimensional, spherical, pseudo-spherical, 87; its homogeneity, 89; perceptual and conceptual, 89-90; its ambiguity, 93; real, 120; in an 'other' world, 32, 360; persistence of, in dream worlds, 366
Spencer, H., 155, 191, 215, 219-21
Spinoza, 97, 370
Spirit identity, 362-4
Spiritism, 323-4, 359-61
Spiritual beings detached from the Absolute by Lotze, 75
Stewart, J. A., 212
Struggle for existence, Darwin's postulate, 132; for bare life, 142
Studies in Humanism, ix; notes 8, 12, 240, 252, 260, 265
Sturt, H., 233
Subject, dependent on object, 260-1
'Subjectivism,' 230, 256
Substance, Lotze's theory of, 67; rests on individual real, 123; Aristotelian theory of, 204-27; soul-substance useless, 223; as individual law, 224
Substratum, view of substance, 205, 222-3; permanent possibility of activity, 225
Supernatural, 361-2
Survival-value of conduct, 133; of intelligence, 134
System, as definition of truth, 47, 51, 277; refusal to call true what does not fit into, 162

INDEX 381

Taylor, A. E., 4
Teleology, 71, 129, 133, 137, 143, 148, 149, 152-5
Theages, 27
Theodicy, 167, 181, 182
Thompson, Mrs., 334
Thomson, J., 158
Thomson, Sir J. J., 281
Thought, pure, does not account for actual thinking, xvi; as acts, 15, 52; purposive, 8, 52, 53, selective, 255; not to be separated from reality, 46; no pure, xiv, 51, 52; movement of, due to psychological interest, 51; transcended by reality, 114, 120, 121, 122-3; and its 'other,' 125, and sensation, 203
Time, and succession, 94; process, reality and value of, 95-109; its alleged unreality, 189; its passage into eternity, 212; in 'other' worlds, 360; persists in dream worlds, 366
True, what works in practice, 7, 36; depends on good, 9; true for our needs, 30-1; is useful, 37; as what fits into a system, 46; not useless, 58
Truth, *44-61*; eternal, xvi; not infallible, xxi; 'absolute,' 271-8; does not exist apart from human agency, 10, 275, 282; for the sake of, 24; its claims, 26, and goodness, 28; and history, 278; of sense-perception relative to us, 33; eternal, of mathematics, 33; apart from use remains potential, 36; definition of, as agreement of thought with reality, 46; as systematic coherence, 46; consistency a mark of, 47; variously to be constructed by human effort, 49; psychological terms in its definition, 51; immediate apprehension of, 52; a form of value, 54, 162; a means of prediction, 297-8; as individual valuation, 55, 58; as valuation of fact, 57, 162; formal and material, 57, 98; plural, 273, 276; relative to purpose, 296; a social product, 58, and goodness, 62; of abstraction, 98, 100; a claim, 98; eternity due to abstraction, 99; methodological, 104; as ideal, 162; cannot be noxious, 201
Tweedledee, 369

Ultimate question for philosophy, 10
Ultimate reality, worlds of, 32; realizes ideals, 120; non-contradictory, 185; harmonious, 187, 199; continuous with immediate experience, 192, 195; conception of, how reached, 194; must be satisfactory, 200; must establish harmony, 202; must become immediate experience, 203
Ultra-Darwinians, 134, 137
Unity of the universe, not to be hypostasized, 67; not proved by Lotze, 72; neither personal nor moral, 79
Universal laws, shorthand for habitual interactions, 125
Usefulness of knowledge, 23, 28, 42; determines social recognition, 59
Useless persons allowed to pursue useless knowledge, 60; useless is false, 37-8, 40

Validity, if unrealizable not valid, xvii; timeless, 98; as practical working, 98
Valuation, pervades experience, 8, 10; truth, 8, 61; knowledge a form of, 10; of indetermination, 15; of truth, 50; as 'true' and 'false,' 55; difficulty of sustaining it in society, 58; systematized in ideals, 159; nature of ethical, not accurately known, 313; ethical, affirms ideal of goodness, 344; doubt of significance of human, 347
Value, source of validity, xvii; essential to 'truth' of a 'system,' 50; truth as, 55; no fact without, 55; of practically important, 117; of life denied, 160; judgments of, and of fact, 160; truth as, 162; are facts, 163; failure of scheme of, 164; inferior value of dream worlds, 367
Variability, Darwin's postulate, 132, 139
Variation, 132, 134, 145; accidental, 132, 135, 146; causes of, 137; discontinuity of, 136; indefinite, 135, 146, 148, 151, 153; origin of, 135, 142; purposive direction of, 137; facts of, 148-9
Verification in science and religion, xix
Virtue, as knowledge, 285
Vischer, F. T., 177 *n.*
Voluntarism, 8, 231, 233

Wallace, A. R., 144
Ward, J., xii, 372
Will to believe, xii, xx, 5, 153; to know, 11, 16, 312, 321
Wisdom, speculative and practical, 24-6, 28; opposition between them, 29-30
Worlds, of higher reality, 18, 32, 193-8, 368; of relative reality, 366; of inferior reality, 367-8
Wundt, xiv

Zeno, 22, 186, 206
Zöllner, 118

Printed by R. & R. CLARK, LIMITED, *Edinburgh*.

The following pages contain advertisements of books by Dr. F. C. S. SCHILLER, and a selection of other Works on Philosophy published by

MACMILLAN AND CO., LIMITED.

By Dr. F. C. S. SCHILLER

Third Edition. 8vo. 10s. net.

RIDDLES OF THE SPHINX

A STUDY IN THE PHILOSOPHY OF HUMANISM

Second Edition. 8vo. 10s. net.

STUDIES IN HUMANISM

Second Edition. 8vo. 10s. net.

HUMANISM

PHILOSOPHICAL ESSAYS

8vo. 10s. net.

FORMAL LOGIC

A SCIENTIFIC AND SOCIAL PROBLEM

8vo. 10s. net.

'AXIOMS AS POSTULATES'

IN

PERSONAL IDEALISM

PHILOSOPHICAL ESSAYS

Edited by HENRY STURT.

MACMILLAN AND CO., LTD., LONDON.

By Professor HENRI BERGSON

CREATIVE EVOLUTION. Translated by ARTHUR MITCHELL, Ph.D. 8vo. 10s. net.

LAUGHTER: An Essay on the Meaning of the Comic. Authorised Translation from the Sixth Edition by CLOUDESLEY BRERETON, L. ès L. (Paris), M.A. (Cantab.); and FRED ROTHWELL, B.A. (London). Extra Crown 8vo. 3s. 6d. net.

A CRITICAL EXPOSITION OF BERGSON'S PHILOSOPHY. By J. M'KELLAR STEWART, B.A., D.Phil. 8vo. 5s. net.

By Professor HENRY SIDGWICK

THE METHODS OF ETHICS. 8vo. 8s. 6d. net.

OUTLINES OF THE HISTORY OF ETHICS FOR ENGLISH READERS. Crown 8vo. 3s. 6d.

PHILOSOPHY: Its Scope and Relations. 8vo. 6s. 6d. net.

LECTURES ON THE ETHICS OF T. H. GREEN, MR. HERBERT SPENCER, AND J. MARTINEAU. 8vo. 8s. 6d. net.

LECTURES ON THE PHILOSOPHY OF KANT, AND OTHER PHILOSOPHICAL LECTURES AND ESSAYS. 8vo. 10s. net.

By Professor HARALD HÖFFDING

A HISTORY OF MODERN PHILOSOPHY: a Sketch of the History of Philosophy from the Close of the Renaissance to our own Day. Translated by B. E. MEYER. Two vols. 8vo. 15s. net each.

THE PROBLEMS OF PHILOSOPHY. Translated by GALEN M. FISHER, and a Preface by WILLIAM JAMES. Globe 8vo. 4s. 6d. net.

THE PHILOSOPHY OF RELIGION. Translated by B. E. MEYER. 8vo. 12s. net.

OUTLINES OF PSYCHOLOGY. Translated by M. E. LOWNDES. Crown 8vo. 6s.

MACMILLAN AND CO., LTD., LONDON.

THE SCHOOLS OF PHILOSOPHY

A HISTORY OF THE EVOLUTION OF
PHILOSOPHICAL THOUGHT
BY VARIOUS WRITERS

EDITED BY

Sir HENRY JONES

PROFESSOR OF MORAL PHILOSOPHY IN THE UNIVERSITY OF GLASGOW

Ready.

THE EVOLUTION OF EDUCATIONAL THEORY. By Professor JOHN ADAMS, M.A., B.Sc., LL.D. 8vo. 10s. net.

In Preparation.

THE HISTORY OF GREEK PHILOSOPHY FROM THALES TO ARISTOTLE. By Professor JOHN BURNET, LL.D.

THE HISTORY OF MODERN PHILOSOPHY FROM HOBBES TO REID. By Professor G. F. STOUT.

Other volumes to follow.

HISTORICAL STUDIES IN PHILOSOPHY. By Professor EMILE BOUTROUX. Authorised Translation by FRED ROTHWELL, B.A. 8vo. 8s. 6d. net.

THE PRINCIPLE OF INDIVIDUALITY AND VALUE. Being the Gifford Lectures for 1911. By BERNARD BOSANQUET, LL.D., D.C.L. 8vo. 10s. net.

ÆSTHETIC AS SCIENCE OF EXPRESSION AND GENERAL LINGUISTIC. Translated from the Italian of Benedetto Croce by DOUGLAS AINSLIE, B.A. 8vo. 10s. net.

In the Press.

ETHIC. By BENEDETTO CROCE. Translated by DOUGLAS AINSLIE, B.A. 8vo.

THE VALUE AND DESTINY OF THE INDIVIDUAL. Being the Gifford Lectures for 1912. Second Series. By BERNARD BOSANQUET, LL.D., D.C.L. 8vo.

ON THE CONSCIOUSNESS OF THE UNIVERSAL AND THE INDIVIDUAL. A Contribution to the Phenomenology of the Thought Processes. By FRANCIS AVELING, Ph.D., D.D. Crown 8vo.

THE CROWNING PHASE IN THE CRITICAL PHILOSOPHY. A Study in Kant's Critique of Judgment. By Rev. R. A. C. MACMILLAN, M.A., D.Phil. 8vo.

MACMILLAN AND CO., LTD., LONDON.